Kenneth Cragg

THE CALL OF THE
MINARET

Second Edition, Revised and Enlarged

COLLINS

Collins Liturgical Publications
8 Grafton Street, London W1X 3LA

Distributed in Ireland by
Educational Company of Ireland
21 Talbot Street, Dublin 1

Collins Liturgical Australia
PO Box 3023, Sydney 2001

ISBN 0 00 599918 3

First edition published in 1956, copyright © 1956 by Oxford
University Press, Inc., Reprinted as a Galaxy Book, with
corrections, Oxford University Press, Inc., 1964. Second
edition, revised and enlarged, first published by Orbis Books,
Maryknoll, N.Y. 10545, © 1985 by Kenneth Cragg. This
edition published by Wm Collins Sons & Co 1986.

Made and printed in Great Britain by
William Collins Sons & Co Ltd.

TO

HENRY HILL

AND

GEORGE FRANCIS GRAHAM-BROWN

IN GRATITUDE

CONTENTS

iv

PART THREE
Minaret and Christian
157

PREFACE

Almost thirty years have elapsed since *The Call of the Minaret* was written and several years since it went out of print. Now that a new edition has been called for, how should it explain itself? Part 1, on the contemporary setting, plainly needed complete rewriting to come abreast of the myriad changes of the intervening years. Chapter 8 also, "The Call to Service," required radical overhaul. So many aspects and occasions of what could earlier be service have been overtaken by developments, both political and technological. "The Call to Participation" now seems a more apt description of what the active practice of relationship might mean.

For the rest, with minor points of detail revised or updated, the broad themes of Islamic exposition and of Christian obligation, theologically and spiritually stated, remain constant. Short of rewriting the whole burden of intention in the book, which would not meet the interest in its reissue, there was no other option. No authorship, least of all in an evolving situation, can well keep all its instincts intact over so long an interval. Yet these can still identify critically with their first venture. Later publications, which I have immodestly listed in the Book List, may indicate how further ventures have shaped meantime.

Certainly the *Adhān,* or summons to prayer from the minaret, has persisted steadily every dawning and fading day of all the passing years. As then, so now, it is "an imperative invitation" to Muslim faith and practice, confronting Muslims with their own vocation and alerting the attentive outsider to what shapes and makes Islam. The call of the minaret is the epitome of Muslim belief and action. To seek in it the clue to Islam, and from that clue to learn the form and dimension of a Christian relationship to what it tells, is the purpose of this book.

These chapters are one man's effort at an interpretive study of what the muezzin says. It is inspired by the obligations belonging to Christian conviction. Some will say that these preclude objectivity—a point faced in chapter 6. No study can either begin or end *in vacuo*. It may be that Christian commitment, with its concern for the significance of God and humankind, is a surer context for the study of Islam than the academicism that knows only how to analyze and not how to worship. Whether this will prove so, only a reader's verdict, not a writer's preface, can say. All that can be recorded here is the ambition for understanding.

The minaret, of course, is aligned by the mosque on the *Qiblah* ("direction of prayer") toward Mecca and the central *Ka'bah* of its Great Mosque, to which all responsive *Salāt,* or ritual worship, turns. When, in the early days of Muhammad's establishment in Medina, this Meccan axis replaced the first *Qiblah* toward Jerusalem, the turn away from the monotheist symbolism toward the still pagan shrine held by the obdurate Quraish was a deep puzzle to the Prophet's anxious entourage. The Qur'ān had a reassuring word for them: "God," says Surah 2.143, "is not rendering your faith vain." Or, as translation might run: "God will not let your faith go to waste, or prove futile."

That change of *Qiblah* may be taken to enshrine much that continues to be exacting and stressful in the relations between Muslim and Christian. For it signaled the decisive identity of Islam in counter terms to the other faiths of Jerusalem. When, as it is said in tradition, Muhammad worshiped at the *south* wall of the *Haram* in Mecca, he could face *both* the *Ka'bah and* Jerusalem in his northward stance. But from Medina the *Ka'bah* direction is southward, away from Gethsemane and the Mount of Olives. The vindication promised in Surah 2.143 could, then, belong only unilaterally to Islam and, as such, generate the human efforts—familiar to all religious establishments when persuaded of divine approval—to make it self-fulfilling.

Subsequent developments institutionalized what vindicated

faith should mean—and did so, as Muslims saw it, exclusively in
Islam. It was no longer possible to wonder, as far as Muslims were
concerned, whether the authentication of faith might be a shared
experience. The proof of a true faith and worship was henceforward to belong with the patterns of the physical recovery of
Mecca and with the resultant dimensions of the realized Islam as
its only proper and final institution.

So much is, and has long been, history. But, beyond the asser-
tions, the estrangements, and the polemics it has bequeathed,
what should the "vindication" of a faith mean in our world
now—a world of pluralism in a vortex of crisis? Can the "vindica-
tions" of diverse faiths be somehow mutual? How do their meanings not "run to waste" in the postures of their coexistence and in
the drain of secular indifference? How should we cope with the
belligerence or the fanaticism which develop when "futility" appears to threaten and establishments forget that the pledge of
their continuing relevance is from God alone? How should religious convictions affirm themselves as "not going by default"
(another translation of Surah 2.143) in the stresses of contemporary bewilderment?

Such perplexity, in the pluriform world, is more unnerving
than that of the first Muslims in the "interreligious" implications
of their disturbing reorientation. Given the historic *Qiblah,* then
fixed in fact and symbol, what are our souls "toward" in the
vocations of today?

These are still underlying echoes of the call of the minaret. The
adjective in *Hādhihi-l-Da'wat-al-Tammah,* "this perfect summons," has to do with present achieving as well as given status.
Muslims are challenged, so to speak, to become what they are. It
is also a sense of something to be achieved that strikes the Christian hearer of the call of the minaret. To give shape and definition
to this sense is the hope of the third part of this book.

To be aware of the full measure of Islam and to be committed
to all the meanings of Christ is to be summoned to a large duty. It
is first to learn and then by God's grace to attain an authentically
Christian relationship to the mosque and its world. As the muezzin says of the summons to his own, it is an inclusive business,
which, for the Christian neighbor, requires all the resources of the
Holy Spirit. There are times when Islam almost compels a lover of

the faith of Christ to borrow the words of the guards in Shakespeare's *Hamlet:*

> Sit down awhile
> And let us once again assail your ears,
> Which are so fortified against our story.

In this area of its purpose this book invites the reader not merely to an exposition, but to an adventure. Only in such terms could it do justice to "this inclusive call."

The deep personal debts that I acknowledged in the Preface to the first edition, in 1956, have continued through all the intervening time. These pages owe everything to the stimulus of Muslim friendships and associations extending more than four decades and involving several academic centers in the Middle East, in Africa, and in the West. A book aspiring to be as inclusive as this one leaves many duties unfulfilled and associated themes excluded. Subsequent ventures in publication have aimed to satisfy some of these, without displacing a first venture and a first love. Its reissue can only be a new and grateful confession of innumerable helps.

I have followed now general patterns in the transliteration of Arabic words. *'Ain,* final or medial *hamzah,* and long syllables, have been indicated. Where no *waslah* was involved, I have indicated a *ta marbutah* with an English *h.* But where, as in *Zakāt* and *Salāt,* it is preceded by a long syllable, I have preferred a *t.*

The spelling of names and terms almost inevitably involves an arbitrary decision here and there. One has to decide whether a word is finally anglicized like "Mecca" or can still be held to an Arabic form like *Al-Tā'if.* Opinions are bound to differ on such points. To me *Makkah,* however correct, seems tediously pedantic. On the other hand, outside geography, I have tried to be exact, renouncing those unhappy spellings, "Mahomet," "Koran," "Moslem," which have too long distorted Arabic, confused outsiders, and offended Muslims. It is surely part of courtesy to denote treasured names as their possessors do, apart from the pressing reasons of sound scholarship.

Nonitalicized words of Arabic origin—"shaikh," " 'ulamā', " "Sunnī," "Shī'ah," "Sufism"—I have considered suf-

ficiently English to warrant this rendering. Italics are used where
terms may still be considered technical, as such *ijmā'*. It is hoped
that the context makes the sense of such terms clear without a
glossary. Where the adjective "Muhammadan" occurs, it refers
strictly to what concerns the person of the Prophet, as in "Muhammadan qualities of leadership." The word has no proper
meaning as a synonym for "Muslim." The abstract from it ought
not to exist. "Islam" is the sole, sufficient substantive for the
faith it denotes.

On grounds of economy, diacritical points indicating heavy
consonants in transliteration have not been used. A certain option
has been taken with the Arabic letter *yā*, whether *y* as in *Wahȳ* or *i*
as in *Jāhilī*.

Where "Tradition" is capitalized it refers to the total corpus as
a source of law, as distinguished from an individual "tradition."

All here is meant as a gentle invitation to a great invitation. The
title tells what it would constitute, as well as what it would
describe. And the one because of the other. Can we become so
aware of Islam as to enter into all its implications for the Christian? Inasmuch as that ambition, and the pages that here serve it,
must always turn upon the wide compassion of God, they must be
prefaced with that most inclusive and cherished of all Muslim
invocations: "In the Name of the merciful Lord of mercy."

KENNETH CRAGG

PART I

ISLAM AT THE NEW CENTURY

The clock is an important item in the mosque. The muezzin must be punctual in announcing the call to prayer. His timepiece marks the points for Salāt, "prayer," between dawn and sunset. A calendar is also needed, to note the arrival of Ramadān, the month of fasting, or to alert would-be pilgrims to the month of pilgrimage to Mecca. Daily clocks and annual calendars have their place in the order of Islam.

What is the instrument of measure to report the centuries? Muslims have a tradition of finding the turn of the centuries impressive. How do historians interpret them, surveying in long retrospect what has been lived through by the clock? The significance they aim to find is to be had only from the flux of the ordinary. Crude graffiti on sidewalks, political scrawlings of the moment, may be like "the writing on the wall" that Daniel saw in his vision of Belshazzar's feast. So, indeed, it proved in the Iran of Shah Muhammad Reza. But how is the historian to know?

Whether the clock, or the calendar, or the century, time is only one dimension. There is also location. Continents, as well as centuries, come into the story. The geography of Islam is as panoramic as its history. Its origins belong with the bridge of continents in what we call the Middle East. It has a long occupancy in Asia, as far as the China Sea. It is a vigorous element in the manifold of Africa, south as well as north of the Sahara. In Europe it now has a minority population with a growing profile. Its natal language, Arabic, does not have the ecumenical reach of English, or the mother-tongue diffusion of Chinese. But in the Islamic liturgy it has the most frequently and sacredly repeated sentences in human speech. Both in space and time, Islam presents the student with a fascinating wealth of meaning and narrative, the clues to which abound in bewildering supply. Witnesses from within, exponents from without, are many.

There may well, then, be merit in letting the incidence of a new century serve the imagination in the effort to comprehend Islam.

i

CHANGE AND CONTINUITY

I

It was in November 1979 that the fifteenth Islamic century began. For Muslims, that was the month of Muharram ("January") of the year 1400 A.H. *(anno Hegirae)*. Fourteen hundred years had elapsed since the *Hijrah* (commonly "Hegira" in English dictionaries)—the "emigration"—of Muhammad from Mecca to Medina in 622 A.D. Islamic years, composed of twelve lunar months, are eleven days shorter than Western years of twelve solar months. Islamic centuries, hence, are shorter by some three years.

November 1979 (Muharram 1400) was celebrated throughout the Muslim world by statesmen, scholars, propagandists—reformers and conservers—of every kind. There was a chorus of salutation and review, retrospect and prospect, as Muslims took counsel with themselves in honor of the landmark in their history.

They pondered a very different scene in 1300 A.H., which coincided with 1882 A.D., the year when Britain occupied Egypt and Charles Doughty was writing, in tense prose, the chronicle of his epic journey in *Arabia Deserta* made in 1295–96 A.H. Riyadh,

3

now the capital of the richest monarchy on earth, was then a walled fortress town, remote among the Bedouin and sought only by explorers. "Here is a dead land," he wrote, "whence, if he die not, a man shall bring nothing but a perpetual weariness in his bones."¹ Today Cadillacs and videos, computers and universities, hospitals and a wealth of consumer goods, abound in Saudi Arabia. Purists suspect and fear a softness in the bones.

In 1300 A.H. Jerusalem was a shabby provincial town of some twenty-five thousand inhabitants, with an Ottoman governor and a languishing economy. Theodor Herzl was a student in Vienna. The political Zionism which was to turn Jerusalem into a metropolis of some six hundred thousand inhabitants was still unborn. Abū Dhabī and Dubai were negligible shaikhdoms on the Trucial Coast, scarcely changed from the time of Muhammad. Now they house concentrations of sophisticated technology and they control important oil levers of international finance.

It was in 1299 A.H. that Muhammad Ahmad in the Sudan announced himself to be the promised Mahdi, "guide," with a destiny to purge away the corruption of the Ottoman regime in a *jihād* against Islamic "infidels." The event was symbolic both in its dramatic fervor and its rapid political collapse. Beyond the doom of General Gordon lay the Anglo-Egyptian Condominium which was to retain the Sudan for sixty years. It was not the revivalists who put an end to imperialism, but factors in world history, hidden from sight in 1880, of which the Mahdists could neither have dreamed nor approved. In their time the Middle East was in the long shadow of the Anglo-French rivalry that was to spell bitter frustration for Arab nationalism many decades more.

Indian Islam in 1300 A.H. (1882 A.D.) was of divided mind. Sayyid Ahmad Khān had lately founded his Aligarh College in an attempt to chart an Anglophile future for the Muslim community and to provide a leadership which would galvanize it from the torpor and dismay that had followed the collapse in 1857 of the first war of Indian independence. But an opposing school of traditionalists whose predecessors had given the Wahhābī heritage to Arabia stood for the rigorous purity, as they saw it, of original Islam. In the same 1880s, Mirzā Ghulām Ahmad, claiming to be the "renewer" at new century, launched what became the Ahmadiyyah Movement around his own role as the promised Messiah.

France greeted the new Muslim century by taking over in Tunisia, at which point one of the first pioneers of modern political thought in the Arab world, Khair al-Dīn, migrated from Tunis to Istanbul, where his ideas on how Islam should react to European "superiority" had attracted the attention of Sultān 'Abdul Hamīd II. His views on how Muslims should understand themselves and renew themselves, under the pressures and disconcerting puzzles of their encounter with Europe, were a perceptive agenda for the century ahead.

These and other random coincidences of the calendar serve to remind us of the great range of movement and its quickening pace. But they are only part of the story. There are all those cumulative changes better symbolized by the muezzin's clock, the ceaseless incidence of birth and death, the flux of attitudes between the generations, the steady, inexorable metamorphosis of cities and landscapes. The Cairo and the Jakarta of 1300 are scarcely discernible today in the vast conurbations with populations doubled and then quadrupled.

Ahmad Amīn, the Cairo man of letters, belonging to the middle generation of the three in the century, noted wryly the subtle disparities between his father's and his children's attitudes of mind.[2] Hazards of continuity are not only in the externals of politics and wars and programs but also in the inner flux of consciousness which novelists strain to capture and able diarists record. Among the latter a moving example is that of a former Prime Minister of Iraq, Muhammad Fādil Jamālī, writing letters to his son while imprisoned and under sentence of death. Yearning, in daily personal peril, for his son's future and that of Islam, he wrote:

> I grew up in a religious environment, for my father was a scholar of divinity, and my late mother was a mullah, and I grew up to study religion, then natural sciences, then philosophy, psychology, and education. Moreover, I experienced life in a stereotyped, fanatic, and superstitious environment before moving to one which contained the most up-to-date views and scientific, philosophical, social, and spiritual theories. I served in various societies and organizations which worked to bring closer to each other varying points of

view and to broaden the intellectual and spiritual horizon of man. I experienced, during the last fifty years, the course of human history and the life of man with all the happiness and misery which it contains. I believe that a person with these qualifications is entitled to express a modest opinion in which he may be right or wrong.[3]

This passage, with its wistfulness, range, insight, and open-ended quality, could well be read as an epitome of the human scene within Islam and of its claim upon the sensitivity of any fair observer. Though in suffering and given to deep reflection, the writer was nevertheless a politician and it is certainly with politics we must begin.

II

For reasons built into its origins, Islam has always been a confidently political religion. The salient fact of its fourteenth century was an exhilarating, complete, uneven, and, for some, disenchanting, recovery of political self-responsibility. Statues of Queen Victoria in Lahore, or of Lord Kitchener in Khartoum, have gone into museums or into college precincts far away. The Egypt of Gamal Abdal Nasser and Anwar Sadat is worlds removed from that of Lord Cromer, the British Resident. What Islam has experienced, at different intervals in the period after World War II, and in some cases earlier, is not only the withdrawal of Western empire but, therefore, a positive return of power to Muslim hands where it properly belonged. The long period of domination by non-Muslim rulers—as in India under the British, the East Indies under the Dutch, North Africa under the French—could be seen in perspective only as a sad aberration in history, the end of which would be like a return from exile.

Muslims, by definition, were never meant to be alien-ruled. Their state was an inseparable part of their religion—witness Muhammad's career, witness the very structure of the Qur'ān, witness the *Hijrah* as the establishment of the Prophet's preaching by the Prophet's power structure. To have forfeited that ruling status was the sting, the disquiet, the misery, of nineteenth-century history across the Islamic world. By the same token, to have reversed that distressful pattern and ousted the alien empires was like coming home into authenticity.

It is small wonder that this sense of liberation released a surge of self-confidence and hope. The times were marked by a wealth of pamphleteering setting out the relationship of Islam to peace, justice, equality, economic welfare, the family, capitalism, communism, banking—to a score of issues, on which Islamic ideology could now both speak and expect to operate, whereas, through many long decades the effective decisions had been taken by Europeans.

For the moment the strenuous tasks of this recovery were only glimpsed. The immediate mood was confidence and glad surprise. The most telling example of this will to be self-responsible was the creation of Pakistan by the partition of the subcontinent of India in 1947. Despite all the reasons that could be urged for all-India unity, the Muslims of the areas where they were the numerical majority opted passionately for separate statehood. Logically, Pakistan could be said to be absurd. For it enclosed at the start a larger proportionate minority of non-Muslims within its borders than Muslims themselves constituted in the whole of India. Thus it violated its own principle of minority separatism more than did the India from which it demanded to secede. It also violated the Islamic principle of Muslim unity by making alien citizens of thirty-five million Muslims outside its borders in Nehru's India. It occasioned massive human suffering and tragedy. But illogicality and human cost could be seen as the necessary price for a vital decision in line with Islamic destiny.

Pakistan is thus the most eloquent single index to the self-understanding of Muslims—namely, that, wherever feasible, they are not to be seen as a "religious" community but as a religio-political nation-state. It follows, of course, that Muslims inside secular India—a very large segment indeed—have necessarily to live by other lights. This makes them a very significant index of another kind.

Elsewhere across the household of Islam, if less traumatic, the same pattern of Pakistan is evident. In Indonesia, most populous of all, in Malaysia, in Africa north and south of the Sahara, emergent nationhood has displaced colonial rule. Grimly and bloodily as in Algeria, transitionally as in Khartoum or Lagos, the pattern holds. There remains the large representation of Muslim peoples within the Soviet Union exempted from this category, as well as Muslim minority groups within South Africa and in western Europe and America. These, and India and the Philippines, apart, the recovered amalgam of faith and power within Islamic societies is almost everywhere complete. This renewed and effective politicization of Islam is the most important single fact of the new century.

The remembrance of a transcended past under aliens still triggers powerful emotions. Just as Qur'ān readers continue to recite an abrogated verse of the book to remind themselves of the ways and mercy of God in the change, so the new present keeps in mind the recent past, in gratitude for the resumption of the proper self-sufficiency of Islam.

III

History is full of ironies. Islamic political recovery has been beset by proliferating problems—social, economic, and moral. The first is the issue of Islamic unity, given the new and insistent nationhoods by which "independence" was expressed. That unity had been symbolized, until 1924, by the Ottoman Caliphate, itself the successor to the caliphal order of Islam dating from the year of Muhammad's death, 632. But the new Turkey of the 1920s had given it the coup de grace in terminating the empire to which it was attached. Though understood as crucial to Islam through thirteen centuries, the Caliphate seems now to be permanently extinct. The nation-states of Islam have come to stay, fragmenting the orthodox concept of the single *Ummah,* "people," of Islam. How is that solidarity to belong with the separatisms that flout it, many of them, especially in the Middle East, drawn along frontiers decided by those very Western powers whom new nationhood was to erase from history and whose presence was said to be the very fount of division? If they "divided in order to rule," ceasing to rule is not ceasing to divide.

Some, like the renowned philosopher-poet, Muhammad Iqbāl, credited with the initial concept of Pakistan, argued that nationalism, albeit compromising Islamic oneness, was a necessary factor in the expulsion of empire and so might be expected to pass once its work was done.[4] This was his romanticism. Others, more pragmatic, borrowed the parallel he drew between Western nationhoods generated at the end of the Middle Ages as the solution to the needs of Europe in the aftermath of the medieval Empire and Papacy, and simply assumed that Muslim nations were inevitable when Islam was making a comparable exit from a dying past.

An Islamic "bloc" in the United Nations, conferences of Muslim heads of state, a permanent Islamic secretariat, and the like, can mitigate what is inimical to common interest and partially reconcile the idealism of one *Ummah* with the realism of nations that are there to stay. Even the purists and the fanatics who, like the Muslim Brotherhood, dispute the nationhoods and deplore their policies as states, have nevertheless to pursue their ideals and their politics—and in some cases their intrigues—within structures which they deny. But the irony of their position at least demonstrates the tensions of diversity within the claim of unity.

IV

More immediate are the strains within state structures. In face of them, the exhilaration natural to the coming of statehood has given way to a sober awareness of intractable difficulties. Islam has come again into its own history precisely at the point where world history has become steadily more exacting and bewildering.

The first of the problems, on which many of the others turn, is the shape of the state itself. When the political is seen as the clue to all else, how could it be otherwise? "Seek first the political kingdom and all other things will be added to you,"[5] is both a rallying cry and a *non sequitur*. What form is the state to take? Constitution-making was a central concern, for example, after the creation of Pakistan. A state deliberately created by costly partition in the name of a religion could hardly avoid being a proving ground of how such statehood should define and fulfill itself. Sharp questions arose in the early establishment of a Basic Principles Committee to define what Islamic statehood meant and to plan the requirements to ensure it in the concrete.

To be sure, conformity to the Qur'ān and the Sharī'ah, "holy law," would be paramount. But might this perhaps be more easily expressed in the negative form of nonrepugnancy? Should there be a committee of, say, twenty-five learned 'ulamā' to whom all legislation should be referred to ensure its Islamicity? If so, how were they to be chosen? Being nonelected, how could they be reconciled with the democratic ideal? They might enjoy a whip hand over governmental policies. If, however, one argued that Muslim electorates, voting on candidates who were all Muslims, could be relied upon to produce legislatures reliably Islamic, was such democracy the Islamic way and was it dependable? Perhaps power was not meant to be vested in the—partially untutored—people?

As a result, and given the inevitable factiousness in questions so close to the springs of power, Pakistan lost its way in the art of constitution writing. When one was finally and laboriously achieved, it was immediately abrogated by a military regime. Muhammad Ali Jinnah, the astute founder of Pakistan, had always argued that the state must be secured first, and defined later. This may have been a necessary tactic in securing it. But it meant that a great number of disparate intentions were hidden in an artificial unity and they came home to roost. Through an alternation of military dictatorships and political party regimes, Pakistan has found Islamic statehood elusive of definition and frustrating in practice. The military regimes have differed widely in their view of Islamicity, their attitude to political parties and the role of party government, and their interpretation of what, Islamically, "democracy" should be said to be and to require. Meanwhile, through long decades of trial and error, population multiplies, strains persist, and aspirations stagnate. There is honor in the debate. But what if it never concludes?

Turkey is its own case in point, too, as to Islamicity. It began its emancipation from Ottoman domination in a downright and vigorous spate of secularism, forcibly led by Mustafa Kemal Atatürk, the national savior from the ignominy of 1922. His insistent secularization of everything Turkish—government, law, education, culture, society—meant a generation-long abeyance of active Muslim expression, imposed by a dictator. In the aftermath of that remarkable experiment, under the Democratic Party of the 1950s, came a gradual return of Muslim religion, and with it a reopening of the issues as to what its character should be.

Ziya Gökalp, the ideologist of the Atatürk revolution, had subordinated Islam to the role of a cultural item in the Turkism to which he gave pride of place in his sociology. When Muslim liturgy and practice reentered Turkish life, via the return of Islamic education, the renewal of Turkish Sufism, and a political opportunism that utilized religious feeling, ultimate questions of definition, as in Pakistan, conduced to political instability, followed by military intervention. Turkish history in the last half century provides an object lesson, different from that of Pakistan but no less fascinating, in the problematics of defining and achieving the politics of Islam.

Established regimes in several countries, such as Egypt, Syria, Jordan, Morocco, and even Saudi Arabia, have been taken to task by conservative theorists of the Islamic state for their compromise of a true Islam. Whether monarchies or military regimes, their Islam represents, in varying degrees, an accommodation to elements—legal, social, economic, and cultural—that purists, such as Maulānā Abū-l-'Alā al-Maudūdī in Pakistan, or Sayyid Qutb in Egypt, reject as wholly un-Islamic. When Nasser expounded his Arab socialism in *The Philosophy of the Revolution* in 1952, he listed Egypt's spheres of action as the Arab world, Africa, and Islam—in that order. Underlying all the issues of these and other Muslim nation-states, in their internal structures, their international policies, and their popular fortunes, is the perennial question of what it means and what it takes to be duly Islamic in the concept and the exercise of power.

Islamic revolution in Iran has lately given this theme dramatic prominence on the world stage. The Ayatollah Khomeini's interpretation of the Islamic state draws its intensity from the Shī'ah tradition, which differs sharply from the Sunni philosophy of power. The Shī'ah, from their very origins, have a long history of political revolt, though their will to it was often muted by the doctrine of *taqiyyah*, "simulated submission," when regimes were too strongly entrenched for effective repudiation. Under cover of docility, the Shī'ah would cherish the hope of overthrow when circumstances were ripe. The rule of the Pahlavis, with its foreign-born "Satanism," its grave compromises of Islamic ethics, and its flaunted wealth, was such a regime. The thrust of Ayatollah Khomeini's appeal was his insistence, in the 1960s, that the Shah's regime no longer qualified for discreet *taqiyyah*-style "tolerance," but was at all costs to be denied allegiance.

This was a main source of his stature from his place of exile and a main element in his outflanking more moderate 'ulamā' who still stood for a *taqiyyah* attitude. His greatest asset was his ability to recruit the masses. It was in the streets and bazaars that his victory was won. Various factions joined in the bandwagon of his success, but the primary secret was a leadership totally disavowing the existing order in a *jihād* for a pure Islam. That leadership drew its force from the Shī'ah doctrine of the Hidden Imām, whose reading of Islam—the only authoritative one—is entrusted during his *Ghaibah,* "concealment," to the *mujtahids*, "experts in the law," who speak on his behalf. This "power by divine right," hinging on "the divine wisdom," may mobilize popular support, but the role of the "clergy" alone guides and manipulates the masses.

In this, Khomeini is at odds with the thinking of 'Alī Shari'ātī, often regarded as the chief philosopher of the Islamic revolution. His death in 1977 stilled one of the ablest minds in recent Iranian history.[6] He set great store by Surah 114.3, which describes *Allāh* as *Ilāh al-Nās,* "the God of the people," and other passages which, he claimed, located Islamic authenticity squarely in the custody of "the people." To Khomeini the people were simply a factor to be enlisted for successful overthrow of illegitimacy. The new Iranian constitution enshrines this sovereignty of the Ayatollah as the authoritative guarantor of Shī'ah Islamic legitimacy in state and society.

V

When observers turn to Indonesia, the most populous Muslim state of all, they find a very different story. Here we must say "Muslim," rather than "Islamic," state. Although Islam is the major religion, its interpreters within Indonesia, in both the Sukarno and the Suharto periods since 1957, have reacted in various ways within a strongly nationalist order, busy with secular development and comprising sizeable non-Muslim plural elements. Some have withdrawn in uncharacteristic disillusionment from political action. Others have gone into armed resistance and have been nullified. Others again have sought to accommodate Islam to government policies in return for partial successes in maintaining Islamic norms of ritual and behavior.

From the point of view of these norms, Suharto in 1966 was a poor exchange for Sukarno who, despite his policies, kept faith with Islamic practice, made the pilgrimage to Mecca, and was even rewarded with the title "Hero of Islam." In the present situation, it would seem that the 130 million Muslims of Indonesia will have to be content, reluctantly or otherwise, with a statehood falling short of their hopes, and will be left with the option, so uncongenial in Muslim tradition, of concentrating on culture and piety alone.

That, of course, is a role which has been the vocation of Indian Islam since partition in 1947. The Indian state is secular. Hindus predominate. Secularity has meant the forfeiture of communal precedence formerly enjoyed by Muslims—for example, at Aligarh and Osmania Universities. It has also meant a long redrawing of the map of the Muslim psyche. Although the secular system has allowed very high national eminence for Muslims, including the Presidency itself, it has also required radical, and still continuing, reappraisal of what it means to be Muslim in a plural world.

VI

The varied forms of constitutional order in Islamic states and of political expression in Muslim societies, though complex in their incidence and taxing in their demands, are not the only aspect of the Muslim recovery of independence in the last half century. Solutions, to be sure, have to be political. But political solutions do not solve. They disenchant the losers. They tempt the gainers. They may well debase religious coinage by making faith serve party politics.[7] Politics everywhere is beset in these ways. The further irony is that independence, so difficult to express constitutionally, coincided with vast changes and accentuated social problems.

The most awesome of these is undoubtedly that of population. Numbers grow apace in every state. In Egypt, Pakistan, Bangladesh, Nigeria, and Turkey, populational pressures on crop acreage intensify. No Muslim country has tackled this burden of its growth statistics with anything like the stringent measures taken by China and India. Sporadic efforts for birth control have been made—for example, in Egypt under Nasser and in Pakistan in the time of Ayyūb Khān, but little is heard of them now. The Jamā'at-i-Islāmī pressure group in Pakistan made opposition to family planning a central point in its political program. The argument that children are not the sole concern of parent begetters, but of society and the future, is not accepted. The fear of infant mortality among the masses as an urge to large families has not been dispelled by clear evidence of its falling rate. Means of birth control are seen as a route to permissiveness and an interference with God's will expressed in the natural order. They could also be repudiated on the grounds of their Western origin. The argument from Islam as enjoining due care for the quality of life and for a responsible *khilāfah*, "stewardship," in nature makes slow headway against the fears and the bias of the popular mind.

Sadly, the greatest incidence of population growth does not coincide with areas of new wealth. The skeptic might say that geology sets a major problem for theology, in that oil resources do not coincide with human need. The social and religious issues arising from development, of which oil is the most striking example, create sharp tensions. The Saudi regime in Arabia has thus far been able to contain them, thanks to its long tradition of partnership between the Saudi ruling family and the Wahhābī shaikhs and to their success in managing the crises they have experienced. In 1964 they checked a drift under King Saud by the substitution of his brother, King Faisal, a much more effective conserver of Islamic values and an architect of discreet change. They have shrewdly allied the benefits of development—education, hospitals, settlement of Bedouin, industrial complexes, pilgrimage facilities, and the like—to a careful Islamic ethos by presenting these benefits as within the Sharī'ah, as it obtained for an original community long antedating them. Radio, for example, could marry with the mosque sermon. Girls' education could multiply the family virtues exemplified by the Prophet's wives. Throughout, the authority of the 'ulamā' has been enlisted to preclude divisive opposition from that source and maintain concerted action. The main, but thus far containable, exception to this pattern has been in the Shī'ah areas of Hasa, the eastern province.

Effective Saudi/Wahhābī-style management of developmental conservatism, striving to contain the influence of the influx of foreign personnel, has not been so ready a possibility elsewhere. Everywhere, too, there are hardly containable problems, having to do with banking, interest, usury, and technology. There have been a variety of responses by Muslim theorists to the problem of usury, first of interpreting and then of applying the Quranic "prohibition" of usury to conditions of modern development, where the role of interest is very different from that of *ribā'*, "usury," in the time of the Qur'ān. These responses have revolved around, for example, the legitimacy of pensions—dependent as they are on investment funds; in what ways borrowing and lending in Muhammad's own Mecca were non-usurious; and whether the veto on usury extends to all forms of production—agricultural and commercial. Further there is the question whether there are valid legal devices to which appeal may be made within a general prohibition.[8]

Other legal issues in matters of social and criminal areas of the Sharī'ah have been engaging both controversy and action within Muslim nations in the wake of independence. Almost all the countries of the Middle East have made far-reaching changes in their civil and criminal codes, even within the field of personal status law, which has always been the most sacrosanct of Islamic securities. French, Swiss, Italian, and English codes were sources for Turkish radical changes in the 1920s. There the new was not merely adapted, it was applauded, at least by the innovators. It was not merely the change in the substance of the law that mattered, it was the philosophy. Whereas the Sharī'ah, properly understood, was to be obeyed because it was divinely given, law was now to be grounded in human wisdom. In the eyes of the old conservatism, to elevate human constructs to the level of Sharī'ah, binding because it was divine, was to commit *shirk*, "idolatry," the supreme sin. It exalted the human to the status of the divine, in that the sanction of law was no longer the decree of God but the will of the state. To secularize Sharī'ah was actual—not merely conceptual—atheism.

In the case of Turkey such scruples were of no weight. Atatürk intended to be brusque with the past. When the Preamble to the Swiss Code he borrowed referred to "approved doctrines and traditions" as a valid area of appeal where a judge found the code or customary law silent, he feared the phrase might leave a loophole for reactionaries. He, therefore, substituted "scholarly investigations and judicial decisions."

Elsewhere, secularization of law has been tacit rather than explicit. And well it may, for it can be argued that Islam is essentially progressive—responsive to history as an active liability under God—and is, therefore, no slavish perpetuation of what must never yield to change. Whether or not that claim is pressed, whether it is decried or discouraged, significant legal changes have been achieved across the Muslim world. They have meant tentative—and in some areas, radical—revision of many norms relating to the family, the role of women, and the nature of marriage.

VII

It was as early as the first quarter of the fourteenth Islamic century that Qāsim Amīn, in Cairo, published his *Tahrīr al-Mar'ah* ["Women's Liberation"] and *Al-Misriyyah* ["The Egyptian Woman"] (1899), championing women's rights. We should not foreshorten our perspectives to exclude such pioneers. Nevertheless, when, forty and more years later, Doria Shafīq, with a thousand feminist followers, besieged the Egyptian parliament complaining that its representation ignored half the nation, they were voicing a notion which would have seemed to their parents and grandparents of both sexes preposterous and absurd. Today Qāsim Amīn's ideas are widely admired and adopted. Support for them has been confidently adduced from the Qur'ān, where the crucial passage in Surah 4.3 can be read as a *virtual* prohibition of all plural marriage and so, in effect, a requiring of monogamy.

Changing ideas of marriage are reflected in many new developments both in the home and in society. The always illiterate, often very young, brides of former generations, whose orbit was within domesticity, make way for the more educated, career-conscious wives and mothers of today. What a popular Egyptian writer called "the unused lung"[9] is coming more and more into action for the benefit of the body communal and social. Enlarging the dimensions of her own world, the modern Muslim woman widens the potential of her whole society.

Inevitably, rearguard action against such changes are fought strongly wherever forces such as those of the Khomeini revolution or of the Muslim Brotherhood find occasion. For they read the Sharī'ah in immutable terms of its letter and see the true bastions of decency, well-being, and sanity as consisting only in the rigors of the unyielding tradition. For these there is no option between chronic permissiveness and the strictest literalism. Nor is this simply a male verdict or an authoritarian tyranny. Secreted in the home and behind the veil, Muslim womanhood finds no immolation or feminist restlessness, but devoted fulfillment of authentic Islam in a role positively undertaken. Sociologists may explain the phenomenon as they will. Religion has as great a capacity to resist modernity as to survive it. Only the opinionated would identify which is the truer Islam.

VIII

Constitutions, population pressures, economic ideals, law in society are all issues of the politics of Islamic self-responsibility in the new century. They are all affected by the global alternates of capitalism and communism and the socialism that aims to mediate between the two. All three claim to be prescriptions for that well-being which the muezzin calls *falāh*.

The world expansion of the communist system was one of the salient facts of history during the last half century, and especially after World War II. A glance at the map indicates that the Soviet and the Muslim worlds are contiguous, from the Balkans to Afghanistan, and where they are not, Islam is a large factor in Marxist calculation. Astride the common frontier are Muslim minority groups, such as the Kurds and the Azerbaijanis. The U.S.S.R. encloses a numerous variety of Islamic peoples.

Beyond these facts of physical and racial adjacence, Muslim/Marxist interaction opens up a bewildering array of fascinating issues. The communist pattern of totalitarian, one-party regimes fits better the experience of Muslim states than does the Western-style democratic pluralism that presupposes traditions, levels of personal independence, and propertied citizens hard of attainment generally in Islam. Communist philosophy has a direct appeal to activists in its picture of an opiate religion in which such activists can recognize the Islam they reject. It has also an element arguably akin to something important in Islam—namely, an apocalyptic, a sense of destiny, requiring and justifying total loyalty.

On the other hand, the capitalist system, properly sobered and restrained—as Islam will restrain it by inheritance laws and the ideal of *Zakāt*—allows of the legitimacy of private property, indeed demands it. Otherwise no almsgiving could happen. And there is, of course, the steady theism of Islam militating, at least theoretically, against any truck with Marxist atheism. But this has to be deepened—as it could be by a wise attention to communism —into a care for why it is that the religion which affirms the sovereignty of the "God of justice" has, by the reproach of its own purists, quite failed to actualize the good society throughout its historical existence as the revealed law of God. In that sense, communism compels us all, in religious commitment, to attend honestly to the mystery of human perversity and not to shelter behind evasions like: "All would be well if only we lived up to our faith." For communism, in its radical way, is calling, in matters economic, for something more than charity, and in matters religious, for something more than penitence. This is the more urgent in Islam, because of its often quite sanguine notion that *Dīn* and *Daulah,* "religion" and "government," are one.

In practical terms, state socialism, as in Egypt, has taken some notice of the tide of rising expectations, by land distribution, food subsidies, and the like. But a socialism of the mixed economy tends, as everywhere, to remain victim, often to a deep degree, to the market forces of the capitalist order, so that developmental investment operates in what serves the well-to-do and the foreigner, rather than lifting the local standard of living. This has been the undoing of the Shah's regime in Iran and of the Sadat years in Egypt.

The West, to be sure, bears a heavy responsibility in this context, for its dismal failure to put capital to work overseas as an intelligent conscience would dictate. In appreciating the strong politicization of all issues in Islam, we must not miss the bondage to economic factors in our own. There is too much vulgarity in Western assessments of Islam, of communism or socialism in the Muslim world, a vulgarity occupied with markets and profits, with bases and alliances.

Perceptive Muslims, as we shall see in chapter 8, bitterly resent the degree to which Western "interest" in Islam, and scholarship to interpret it, are suborned to, or funded for, intelligence to governments and entrepreneurs, whose concerns are pacts and returns on loans. This means more than guessing at communist party membership above or below ground, more than labeling every restless striving "communist intrigue." Selfishness, especially when it is afraid, is a poor hand at diagnosis. Our need is to realize that the communist, capitalist, and socialist complex of contention means that never since the rise of their faith have Muslims had to reckon on so many fronts with so vigorous a challenge to both creed and will.

IX

The foregoing by no means exhausts the tests and crises of being Islamic as they confront the political order in Muslim societies and nations. It is time to turn to the intellectual burdens they impose. How are the problems of leadership in thought, of authority in religion, of authenticity through change—in a word, of a dynamic Islam vis-à-vis modernity—being handled and resolved across its wide dispersion?

Two broad generalizations have been current among observers. The one is the familiar contrast between "the Herodian and the Zealot," as Arnold Toynbee phrased it,[10] between the acceptors and the rejectors of change, between the "liberals" and the rigorists. The other is to note how that distinction is mirrored in, and fostered by, the deep division in Muslim education. On the one hand there is the modern stream, future-oriented, scientific and rational, and related to modern skills. On the other hand are the traditional disciplines, past-oriented, concerned to transmit orthodox faith, and based on its given absolutes of Scripture and the Sharī'ah. Each equips for its own orbit and all too few of the mosque-centered theologians and believers are ready or able to move freely within the others' world, whose habitués, in their turn, live uneasily, or passively, with the traditional faith.

This broad characterization of the situation has certainly held through recent decades and is largely still the case. However, such diagnosis needs to remember how the doctrinaire temper can overtake minds accustomed to modern attitudes. Sayyid Qutb, for example, executed in 1966 for his passionate conservatism within the Muslim Brotherhood, had been a literary critic with a research fellowship in the U.S.A. Rashīd Ridā, of the *Al-Manār* journal, is an example from an earlier generation. Scholarship and objectivity can seem a feeble, even escapist, luxury in the presence of urgent tasks religiously undertaken, just as abstractions such as academic freedom may seem pointless to revolutionary spirits.

Contrariwise, there are many examples of the modern mentality espousing its own version of religious commitment. The most famous example must be Muhammad Iqbāl, the poet-philosopher (1876–1938) who took it as his mission to revitalize Islam in terms drawn from Western philosophies of creative evolution. His "reconstruction of religious thought in Islam," as he called it,[11] was too erudite to reach more than an isolated intelligentsia and his effective fame is far more in the field of politics and literature. But there is a symbolism in the status his memory enjoys, especially in Pakistan. For it may be read as a token of a perceptible shift in the leadership of Islam, a kind of laicization, whereby eminent figures in science make inroads into the old monopoly of the 'ulamā', the religious experts, over the determination of what Islam must be and Muslims must do and think. Rebounds can happen, as in Iran of late, in the other direction. But if there is any parallel in Western experience, religion, where secularism threatens, must necessarily moderate its reliance upon enclosed authorities and concede that it may both need and find allies from outside its own orthodoxy or widen the ways in which that orthodoxy relates to past and present.

These themes of contemporary Muslim society in its intellectual and educational expression are simply the present form of the care for consensus, through competence to shape it, which Muslim history knows as *ijmā'*, "consensus," and *ijtihād*, "competence to implement *ijmā'*." Because political, and now—more than ever—economic, factors are decisive areas for such thinking and action, it is natural that the effective voices are those of practitioners in those fields. Ancient institutions, such as Al-Azhar in Cairo, Al-Zaitūnah in Tunis, the Qairawiyyah in Fez, Deoband in India, or the traditional core within them when modern studies have been added, have, in measure, yielded their primacy in the definition of Islam to the modern campuses of great state universities, throughout Islam.

As secular realities multiply, of which the High Dam at Aswan is a superb, though quickly accommodated, instance, so do new attitudes of mind. The "religious" graduate, the *'ālim,* is liable to find himself a less esteemed, less significant, member of the community; the "scientific" graduate enjoys a more lucrative and estimable role. It is, in part, this recession in social status that underlies the assertive temper aiming to arrest it, though aggressive conservatism of mind can also be found among students in scientific disciplines determined to resist their secular temptations.

The sensitive observer will recognize the human emotions these tensions entail, for—in human terms—there is nothing about them unique to Islam. Indifference, apprehension, bewilderment, drift, or just preoccupation characterize societies everywhere caught in the stresses of life and religion, and the crosscurrents of faith and the world. Mosque personnel and their "lay" critics, preachers and their hearers, pundits and rebels, interact like their counterparts elsewhere. Islam is not static. For many the old allegiance loses its sacrosanct authority. Religion may then be a cultural expression, rather than a sure conviction. There is a leaven of new attitudes, with the result that the quality of the Islam of this generation differs subtly from that of its predecessors, at least in its situation if not in its temper.

X

Conceding that the mental energies of Muslim communities have been busy with the urgent claims of politics, scientific skills, technology, and economic ideology, what, it may be asked, of their duty to scholarship relating to the faith itself and its document, the Qur'ān? Have they been solely occupied in traditional exegesis within basic dogmas not open to scrutiny? To what degree are the absolutes of the faith susceptible of genuine doubt so that they prevail, not by authoritarian insistence but by sensitive authority? Answers vary with place and time. By and large it has to be acknowledged that religious thought in Islam gives little evidence of a capacity for existential doubt. The divine source, character, and content of the Qur'ān, its literary quality as miracle, and the utter exemplariness of Muhammad, are not to be interrogated. It is the field of law and practice, rather than that of dogma, which admits of creative adaptation and loyal revision.

Some thinkers outside formal theology have wrestled with the ultimate problem of theism, notable among them the prominent Egyptian novelist Najīb Mahfūz, whose novel *Awlād Hāratinā* ["Children of Our Quarter"][12] and short stories reflect the radical skepticism of such Western writers as Franz Kafka, Albert Camus, and Samuel Beckett, as to the credibility of any "lord of the worlds." It is, however, fair to say that such existential despair has not registered among the custodians in the mosques and *madrasah*s, or at least not in articulate form.

Scholarly freedom of inquiry was effectively asserted as long ago as mid-century (A.H.) by Tāhā Husain, despite a near crisis in the Cairo Cabinet of the day with respect to Islamic tradition and to history beyond the Prophet's day.[13] But the text of the Qur'ān itself remains sacrosanct as, on its own assertion in 2.2, "a book in which there is nothing to be doubted." The main questions at stake here—a penetrating exploration of which need in no way diminish the essential authority of the Scripture—have to do with how to understand the role of Muhammad as a Prophet, how to relate the "occasions of revelation," as they are called, to the content, and how to assess the formation of the text of the Qur'ān. There are Muslim scholars, many of them securely established in Western centers of learning, who reject the minutiae of traditional Quranic commentary, plead for the "major themes" of the book, and aim to invoke them by intelligent translation of their meaning in the seventh century A.D. to their relevance today.[14]

The great potential gain here would be a liberation of Muhammad himself from a mechanical view of how inspiration occurred. To see him deeply involved in mind and heart, and not as a neutralized channel of celestial dictation, would release Quranic reading into a new dimension of realism and integrity. Conservative minds fear this situational approach, lest the plea that the Qur'ān has its time and place should lead to the notion that it cannot, therefore, speak to present time and place. This fear is groundless and, far from spelling a loyalty to the written word, sadly inhibits its active authority today. Traditionalists, by and large, remain quite unreassured at this point and some among them even seek to make the nonchronological shape of the Qur'ān a plea—impossible in all good conscience—for its utter timelessness.

In the general area of faith and reason, doctrine and the sciences, the pattern since Muhammad 'Abduh (d. 1905) has been to affirm the entire harmony of the one with the other, provided that each is rightly understood. Where there appears to be a conflict, either the Qur'ān and Tradition have not been wisely read and must be understood to tally in their intention, or rational sciences will adjust themselves to what is harmonious when further studied and researched. In some quarters this sanguine confidence has generated a variety of ingenious explanations of Quranic passages aligning them with scientific inventions or theories. In other quarters, however, this practice has been deplored as ingenuous, superficial, and disloyal to the real purpose of the Qur'ān as sacred Scripture.[15] It is wiser to seek the teaching of the Qur'ān about nature, humankind in nature, and the order of the universe, not in the details of the natural sciences, but within the sacramental principle of the Qur'ān, in the āyāt, "signs," with their wonder, beauty, mystery, and amenability to both engineer and poet.

XI

It would be foolish to assume to comprehend Islam and Muslims, or the falāh to which the muezzin calls, only by reference to states and governments, to politicians and publicists, to scholars and scientists. We need to keep close to peasantry and private lives, to measure less by the century and more by the immediacies of the clock and the calendar, the question of the next meal among the myriad poor, of health and sanitation and disease, of mortality and the average life span.

There is a deep folk Islam of ordinary people among whom illiteracy, despite all efforts to surmount it, remains high. They are not immune, of course, from creeping awareness of the seeming omnicompetence of human nature, the intrusion of human processes—medical, surgical, technical, managerial—into the dailiness of life. Nor are they imperceptive of the recession, in their thoughts, of the instincts to fear and pray, to relate their emergencies urgently to God, when the resources of the clinic, the technician, the official, seem so much more present and more efficacious.

Yet, even with these amenities, tentative as their distribution may still be, the old associations persist. The shadow of the saint's tomb may bring the wanted pregnancy. The votive ribbon on the grille of the mosque may do good to the sick child. The blue bead may still avert the evil eye. If only in terms of double insurance, the *barakah* of the holy may corroborate and prosper the skill of the technique. Or the man in the white coat with the stethoscope may be the high priest of the divine inscrutable will.

In any event, miseries of human provenance abide and deepen. In them human capacities shadow and shatter the everyday world and, making all things bitterly precarious, call back the superstitions and the anxieties that modern techniques may have subdued in the workings of nature. No reading of the contemporary Muslim scene can be complete without measuring, for example, the long tragedy of Palestinian dispersion and exile. It has involved thousands of ordinary Muslims in the sharpest of personal distresses. As such it has evoked a deep literature of despair and defiance. It now spans three generations and holds within itself the most fundamental human issues of identity, justice, and redemption with which any religion can be required to cope. How does the muezzin understand himself in the camps of Sabra and Chatila? How may the prisoners heed him in their internment in Ansar?[16]

Apart from that desperate measure of major travail of Islam today, there is the slow drama of the peasantry, captured, for example, in Richard Critchfield's vivid narrative, *Shahhat: An Egyptian:*

To Shahhat, the Nile was *al-Bahr,* the sea, the giver of life. This was the month, August, when the river always rose to flood its banks. Now, just since his fifteenth year the High Dam at Aswan had held back its waters. The Nile would never flood again. Shahhat wondered what his life would have been like if the river had not been tamed. Poorer, but

lived in the old natural rhythms and certainties. For the dam
had brought the incessant field work, even in hottest summer.
It had brought the diesel pumps, the fights to load sugar cane,
the feuds and frustrations. . . . It had fed his mother's extrav-
agance and fierce expectations. To Shahhat, order and reason
were limited and no scientific or technical progress could
enlarge them: rather they made life more difficult. For did
not hidden demons, blind fate, the solicitations of Satan, the
hot fury of one's own blood, await every man in ambush at
the crossroads? Why, then, change? He heard distant sounds
of life and listened, straining his ears. He could make out the
doleful braying of a donkey; a vendor's familiar cry, "Onions
sweet as honey"; a bagpipe played a wedding tune; the faint
wail of mourning women. Someone had married, someone
had died. . . . Life seemed unrelenting and absurd. But
things were what they were, predestined and part of Allah's
plan. That was what human life meant. "Everything is from
Allāh," he said aloud. "I cannot decide anything. Everything
we are is from Him."[17]

XII

From dawn to after sunset the clock in the mosque, measuring
the sun's own cycle, punctuates the life of Islam with the consciousness of God and disciplines the response it demands.
Lengthening, tediously or otherwise, into a century, those dawns
and twilights bring innumerable, often barely perceptible, sequences of change, and the last completed century more than all
its predecessors. All of them, whether in studious retrospect or
present personal experience, are the material of faith-definition
and faith-fulfillment. Change is the content, and continuity the
theme, of the story. What is Islam? Who and how is the Muslim?

As a term and as an entity "Islam" is capable of receiving new
meanings. In the diversity of the contemporary scene "Muslim"
may describe a variety of attitudes. One revered Muslim expounds Islam without a single reference to the Prophet.[18] Pakistan in 1974 declared non-Islamic a sect that describes itself as
"Ahmadiyyah, the True Islam." An esteemed Muslim scholar,

whose "major themes of the Qur'ān" is keenly approved by many in his faith, resigns the directorship of the Central Institute of Islamic Studies after a press campaign in which he was branded an "infidel."[19]

President Sadat associated his peace mission to Israel with Islamic inspiration and likewise his offer of sanctuary to Shah Muhammad Pahlavi. Both acts were vehemently disallowed by the Ayatollah Khomeini and by the Muslim Brotherhood, in the name of Islam. Examples need not be multiplied. There is, of course, nothing unique to Islam in this kind of situation. If the history of such examples is long, all traditions know it.

There are those who cannot find the ancient reality in the new thoughts, others who cannot identify the ancient reality without them. In the strange but indispensable interaction of the faith and the faithful, the structure of belief and the participant believer, Islam and the Muslim, change is absorbed and continuity attained. That it is so is the genius of the partnership.

Let us follow a typical muezzin, noting the clock and making anew the age-old summons. Imagination had better follow his ascent of the minaret to the parapet where, hands cupped, he cries across the rooftops. In these days of electronic devices he no longer has need to climb or to utter his voice. Yet the vividness we need to savor is in the old tradition of the visible figure and the vocal summons. But, either way, to what is he calling the faithful, as with others across five continents he repeats through five prayer hours of every day the call to prayer and to prosperity? In the words he uses, or replays, there is unbroken continuity since first the pattern was formed. With slight variations in the number of the repetitions, the familiar sentences are:

God is most great, God is most great. I bear witness that
there is no god except God: I bear witness that Muhammad
is the Apostle of God.
Come ye unto prayer.
Come ye unto good.
Prayer is a better thing than sleep.
Come ye to the best deed.[20]
God is most great. God is most great.
There is no god except God.

PART II

MINARET AND MUSLIM

The use of the phrases of the call to prayer as a basis for a presentation of Islam has much to commend it. For prayer, in whatever sense the term may be used, is the recognition and expression of a relationship, and such a relationship between God and humankind Islam emphatically is. The Adhān, *as Muslims name the Call—from the same verbal root that gives us our anglicized "muezzin"—contains the basic creed of Islam. "There is no god except God and Muhammad is the Apostle of God." It uses the all-important Arabic word for "I bear witness" upon which the issue—Muslim or non-Muslim—turns for every human being. To confess this confession, with intention, is to be a Muslim. And further, in the inclusive word* Falāh *to which, in and through the prayer, the Muslim is invited lies an epitome of the essence of Islam as a communal allegiance, a social order, and a religious experience. Variously translated as "salvation," "well-being," "good," "welfare," and "cult," it stands, not for an experience of redemption from sin, but for a state of spiritual and social "prosperity" brought about by pardon and obedience to God's revealed law in the state of* islām *"submission." It, therefore, serves as a comprehensive concept within which we may describe the Islamic order for human society. In this way all the central doctrinal and practical aspects of Muslim religion can be suitably considered under the muezzin's guidance.*

There are other considerations also. The Adhān *supplies a welcome principle of inclusion and exclusion. In so rich and com-*

plex a theme as Islam, would-be expositors may easily be bewildered by the quantity of material and be tempted to perhaps unsound criteria of what they should treat and omit. Moreover, the subject is beset with prejudices and can easily generate unproductive controversy. It may perhaps be possible to demonstrate at least the will to positive relationships with Muslims if a Christian writer keeps close to the pattern set by the mosque itself. There is also the fact that this path of exposition has not frequently been followed in the many manuals, small and great, that have been published about Islam. The most useful of them listed here in the notes and bibliography must be consulted by the reader who intends a more comprehensive history or analysis than these pages can offer.

But the final reason is what Pascal might have called "a reason of the heart" and is calculated to appeal to the imagination—that source and spring of the active understanding. We do not merely aim at a resumé of Muslim belief and practice. We take it in its own most intimate and inward imperative because we seek to know it, as far as may be, from within. We wish to hear at the minaret what it is that greets every rising sun and salutes every declining day for millions of our contemporaries and thus to enter with them across the threshold of the mosque into their world of meaning. For it is a world that deserves to be penetrated with understanding and for which, as we believe, there is endless significance in another world of faith, whose trustees we are and whose interpreters we would become.

What, then, does the minaret say to the Muslim?

ii

GOD: THERE IS NONE SAVE HE

I

In the Muslim confession of God there are seven syllables and six occurrences of the *l* consonant: LĀ-ILĀHA-ILLĀ-ALLĀH. The first three of the *l*s are what phonetics writers call "clear" dentals. The second three are "dark" alveolars for which "the tip of the tongue comes back and touches the teethridge, and at the same time the back of the tongue is raised toward the back of the soft palate or velum." A heavy sound is then produced; if not unique to the divine name, it occurs there most notably.

If readers are alarmed at this linguistic beginning, they need only recall that the muezzin is our theme. There is a quality about the authentic pronunciation of the first clause of the Muslim creed that impresses itself upon every sensitive hearer. The "clear" consonants run into the emphatic final syllables of the word *Allāh*: these syllables cast their force forward into the consonant of the particle "but," "except" (*illā*), and the result is a kind of powerful climax which matches the emphasis of the sense. It is true, of course, that the diction of many muezzins is raucous and strained, and that the divine name often loses its forcefulness

in certain grammatical or other circumstances. But there can be
no mistaking the insistent and incontrovertible character of the
affirmation within the utterance. No English rendering quite cap-
tures the Arabic enunciation of the Muslim witness to God. *Lā
ilāha illā Allāh*.

It is for this very reason that in all that follows the use of
the anglicized "Allah" is avoided. It is so far from its Arabic
original, when pronounced with a thin English consonant and
feeble vowels, that many an Arab Muslim would find it unrecognizable. But more important, there have grown up associations with the English usage of Allah that are sentimental, having
to do more with melodrama than theology. They should be
shunned. There may also be the idea in users' minds that in referring to God in Islam as Allah they are distinguishing that deity
from the God whom normal English usage denotes. When the
word "Allah" is intentionally used in this way it raises a serious
implication that is here rejected.

Inasmuch as both Christian and Muslim faiths believe in one
supreme sovereign Creator-God, they are obviously referring,
when they speak of God under whatever terms, to the same Being.
To suppose otherwise would be confusing. It is important to keep
in mind that though apprehensions differ, their theme is the same.
The differences, undoubtedly real, between the Muslim and the
Christian understanding of God, are far-reaching and must be
patiently studied. But it would be fatal to all our mutual tasks to
doubt that one and the same God over all was the reality in both.
Those who say that *Allāh* is not "the God and Father of our Lord
Jesus Christ" are right if they mean that God is not so described
by Muslims. They are wrong if they mean that *Allāh* is other than
the God of the Christian faith.

The source of the confusion of thought encountered here is that
to say *who* God is necessarily goes beyond saying *that* God is. If
we agree on the second, what we say relates to the same theme or
subject, even though we may differ markedly as to the first. No
faith or believer, of course, can say *that* God is without being
involved to some degree in *what* God is. But unless there is radical
inconsistency within the very concept of existence itself as applied
to God—the sort of difference that does not obtain between
Muslim and Christian—we are speaking of the same subject.

Perhaps the matter is well put if we say that predicates about God may differ widely but God as the subject of differing predicates is the same subject.

Before, however, leaving the Arabic term *Allāh* in order to keep to the English equivalent, God, we must investigate its precise literal meaning. The Arabic form *ilāhun*, meaning "a god," is similar to the Hebrew and Aramaic words for deity. When used with the definite article, *Al-ilāhu*, meaning "The God," the *l* consonant of the article coalesces with the same letter in the first syllable of *ilāhu(n)*, eliding the *i* sound to compose *Al-lāh*. If we take the word to be of genuine Arabic form, this is the obvious origin. If, as some scholars believe, the word does not have this origin but is historically derived from a sister language, its significance is the same. *Allāh* means "God" with the connotation English achieves by dismissing even the definite article and using the capital letter—a device that Arabic lacks.

It is clear from the negative form of the Muslim creed, "There is no god except God," that the existence and lordship of *Allāh* were known and recognized in pre-Islamic Arabia. The Prophet's mission was not to proclaim God's existence but to deny the existence of all lesser deities. The fact that Muhammad's own father bore the name 'Abdallāh ('Abd-Allāh), "slave of God," demonstrates that God was known by that name prior to Islam. The Qur'ān in many passages refers to Muhammad's adversaries in Mecca, swearing by God, invoking God, and recognizing God's sovereignty as Creator. The name *Allāh* is also evident in archeological and literary remains of pre-Islamic Arabic. But the Meccans did not understand or allow that God alone should be worshiped. Indeed they contended against Muhammad that if God had willed it, they would have refrained from believing in other deities (Surah 6.148), clearly implying that God approved of their concurrent idolatry. When Muhammad conveyed to them the divine claim to exclusive worship, they discredited the messenger.

There can be no doubt, then, that the Prophet's contemporaries knew of a Supreme Being, but not as one who dominated their minds. Rather they thought more directly and frequently of the lesser gods, the daughters, perhaps even the sons, of *Allāh*, who were far more intimately related to their daily lives, their

wars, their harvests, and their fertility. They were also much concerned with a multiplicity of demons and jinns who inhabited
natural phenomena, especially winds, hills, and wells. The fascinating theme of Muhammad's inner revolt against these notions
and the pattern of his crusading controversy with the Meccans in
the name of the divine unity must concern us in the chapter to
follow, on the second clause of the muezzin's witness.

Here in the context of God and the divine oneness we are faced
with the supreme sin in the Muslim reckoning, itself the corollary
of its negation of polytheism. This is the sin of associating with
God. The Arabic term is *shirk*. Its significance must be clearly
understood if we are to enter validly into the meaning of the confession. Associating is the belief that God has coexistents or
partners. There must be no alienation of the Godhead, or God-
ness. It is not merely that God has no coequals. There are no
associates of any kind or rank. This was the gist of the Prophet's
contention against the Meccans. God and idolatry were incompatible. It was not enough to confess that God was; He must be
recognized as God alone. All the partners whom the pagan Arabs
associated with God were truly nonentities. They did not exist and
they had no right to recognition. Muhammad, it is true, continued to believe in the existence of angels and jinns, but he repudiated any notion that these were deities.

This tremendous breaking of the idols, dramatized by the physical cleansing of the central sanctuary in Mecca after its conquest
by Muhammad, was the supreme achievement of Islam. It was an
iconoclasm that came tragically to include in its great negation
also the Christian faith about Christ. In abolishing the daughters
and sons of the Meccan *Allāh*, Muhammad failed to distinguish
the wholly different meaning of the sonship of Christ. To this day
the Muslim principle of unity stubbornly refuses to accept any
understanding of unity which it thinks at error by the criteria
needed to purge Mecca of multiplied divinities. It has not distinguished between pagans alienating God's prerogatives and God in
undivided glory working according to them. But the Christian
problem of Muslim attitudes in this realm is to be faced below.

So it came that Muhammad, son of 'Abdallāh, Messenger of
God, proclaimed the divine unity and disqualified all other wor-
ships, annihilating in word and in action the partners whom the

pagan Arabs associated with God. The word "*Allāh*" itself is grammatically incapable of a plural. It is a proper name. Repeatedly the Qur'ān refers to God as *Al-Wāhid*—the One. The Surah of Unity (Surah 112) declares:

> He is God alone, God the Eternal [undivided]
> He does not beget and He is not begotten
> There is none co-equal with Him.

It may be that this brief Surah is a reply to a question from Jewish or Christian doctors as to the Muslim doctrine of God, though tradition regards it as a very early utterance before such questions could have been formulated. It is held to be worth a third of the whole Qur'ān. The seven heavens and the seven earths are founded upon it. To confess this verse, a tradition affirms, is to shed one's sins as one might in autumn strip a tree of its leaves.

This doctrine of the divine unity, of the inalienable quality of God's divinity, was a tremendous passion in Muhammad's heart. By virtue of remoteness beyond all intermediaries, God was half unreal to the pagans. To Muhammad *Allāh* was the only real God, whom the Meccans might acknowledge and yet ignore, saving their intimate worship for familiar substitutes. Did not God say (Surah 50.16): "We know what man's soul whispers and are nearer than his neck artery"? The messenger was dominated by the divine reality and spoke of God and for God in the burning language of conviction.

The strictly theological problems were all postponed, to be taken up in the centuries after Islam's expansion by thinkers other than Arab with more inquiring minds and less intensity of purpose. Indeed "postponed" is perhaps an inexact term. The problems were not consciously deferred. They were not even felt. They had no place to develop in a mind that was fully possessed with its single mission. There is no valid understanding of Muslim theology that does not first strive to enter into this vivid awareness where it had its genesis.

II

"There is no god except God." Except God. The negation was the form in which Mecca could most arrestingly be given the affir-

mation. Muhammad proclaimed God to them in a sequence of
descriptives that have been called, on Quranic ground, the
"Beautiful Names," *Al-Asmā' al-Husnā*. They number ninety-
nine, though the collections are not always quite identical. Most
of them are found in the Qur'ān itself, the remainder being traditional. Their variety is explained in part by the poetic style of the
Qur'ān, which tended to the use of rhyming endings, derived
from a much smaller number of original roots with nuances or
shades of adjectival meaning. The Names have been variously
classified and interpreted by theologians. Edwin Arnold's *Pearls
of Faith* is one familiar English rendering. The well-known
Muslim "rosary" (*subhah*) or chain of beads, in thrice thirty-
three arrangement, is a means of recollecting serially the Ninety-
nine Names of God. They may also be seen in the Arabic numerals
81 and 18, adding up to 99, which can easily be read in the left-
and right-hand palms of one's hands.

The most important of the Divine Names in Islam are the twin
titles *Al-Rahmān al-Rahīm*, usually rendered into English "the
Compassionate, the Merciful." They derive from the same verbal root, meaning "mercy" or "compassion," but the first
should probably be regarded rather as a noun than an adjective,
with the second qualifying it: "the Merciful Mercier" or "the
Compassionate Compassionator." The sequence is not mere
repetition. The *Rahmān* is the one who is merciful in character.
The *Rahīm* is that same one in merciful action. He who is merciful behaves mercifully. Mercy is of the divine essence, and also
of the divine deed. This double title is used as an invocation at
the head of all the 114 Surahs of the Qur'ān, with the exception
of Surah 9. The *Basmalah*, "In the Name of God, the Compassionate, the Merciful," is, after the *Shahādah*, the most familiar
epitome of Muslim devotion. It is used in the recognition of God
in all the ventures and vicissitudes of life even more widely than
the confession itself.

Before pondering further the quality of the divine mercy, it is
necessary to study the more significant of the Beautiful Names.
The next most familiar are the contrasted pairs: "The First and the
Last: the Outward and the Inward"—sometimes called "the mothers of the attributes" because they comprehend all else. They
suggest God's eternity, omniscience, and self-sufficiency. The

same attributes are affirmed in: "the Living," "the Compre-hending," "the Self-sufficing," "the Abiding," "the High," "the Mighty," "the all-Powerful," "the Exalted," "the Great," "the Praiseworthy," "the All-Compelling," "the Guardian," "the Victorious." Another title used only twice in the Qur'ān, *Al-Qayyūm*, may be translated as "the Self-subsisting," though Al-Baidāwī, the most famous Muslim exegete, suggests the physi-cal sense of "the Always Erect"—"the Standing." The term graphically conveys the idea of God in alert relationship to the world.

This eternal and all-encompassing God is described as "the Creator," "the Fashioner," "the Life-Giver," "the Provider," "the Opener," "the Bestower," "the Prevailer." God brings to life and brings to death, is "the Reckoner" and "the Recorder," "the King of Kingship" and "the Lord of the Worlds." It is re-peatedly declared in the Qur'ān that there is no strength and no power save in God, who "is over all things supreme." God's knowledge is the final knowledge. For the Muslim who has en-tered into this understanding, all problems end in, or are lost in, the phrase: "God is the Knowing One." God is the one who is always "aware." God hears, sees, and discerns. Nothing escapes the divine watchfulness or eludes the divine gaze.

The actions appropriate to these names, most of which are par-ticipial or adjectival forms, are frequently noted in the events and situations of the Quranic story. The relation of God to the Prophet, to the believing community, and to adversaries is de-picted in the active sense of these attributes. The Names are far, then, from being mere attributes to be listed in a theology: they are awesome realities of daily life. For God is *Al-Haqq*—"the Real," the supreme reality of all existence, whose nearness, judg-ment, and will are the great facts of human life.

The relative frequency with which the different names occur is a matter of deep interest. Terms, or their corresponding verbs, that have to do with strength, majesty, and greatness are most promi-nent. There are also certain nouns used occasionally, such as "Peace" (Surah 59.23), with the sense, probably, of self-perfection, "Justice" (in the tradition only), and "Light." The last occurs in the oft-quoted passage from the Surah (24.35) that bears the title "Light":

> God is the Light of the heavens and the earth. The likeness
> of His Light is a niche wherein is a lamp. The lamp is in a
> glass. The glass is like a brilliant star lit from a blessed tree,
> an olive neither of the East nor of the West, whose oil would
> almost give light though no fire touched it. Light upon light.

The Prophet, it is said, was once asked about seeing God. "Can
one see light?" was his reply.

There are a few passages, apart from the very frequent usage of
Al-Rahmān al-Rahīm, that refer to God's mercy. The word *Qud-
dūs*, "Holy," is used in the Qur'ān of God on two occasions. It is
also applied to the Spirit, to Gabriel the archangel, to the angels,
and to places of revelation. Its precise connotation is not readily
apprehended. God is described as "the Forgiver" in several passages using three different derivatives from the same verbal root.
He is also described as the "One who repents and relents," "the
Kindly," and "the Clement." Two passages only use the word
Wadūd, "Loving," the second adding: "The Lord of the Throne,
the Glorious, the Doer of what He intends" (Surah 85.14–16).
That final phrase is indeed the perpetual condition of all the attributes. They are to be understood finally as characteristics of
the divine will rather than laws of the divine nature. Action, that
is, arising from such descriptives may be expected, but not as a
matter of necessity. What gives unity to all God's dealings is that
God wills them all. He as Willer may be recognized from time to
time by means of the descriptions given. But God does not essentially conform to any of them. The act of the divine will may be
identified in this or that quality; the will itself is inscrutable. One
may not, therefore, say that God is necessarily loving, holy, righteous, clement, or relenting, in every and all relationships.

It is this fact that explains the antithesis in certain of the Names.
Such antithesis would not be theologically predicable if either element within it were essential to God's nature. Because they are
not, God's action may demonstrate each element in differing relations. The antithesis is dogmatically resolved in the realm of will,
in that God wills both—in every other sense and realm, antithesis
remains. But the problem has no anguish and is, indeed, inscrutable, given the conviction of the divine will as an ultimate beyond
which neither reason nor revelation go. So God is "the One who

leads astray," as well as "the One who guides." God is "the One who brings damage," as also does Satan. God is described also by terms such as "the Bringer-down," "the Compeller" or "Tyrant," "the Haughty"—all of which, when humanly used, have an evil sense. In the unity of the single will, however, these descriptions coexist with those that relate to mercy, compassion, and glory.

Because we are concerned with Muhammad's own awareness of God, we must leave aside pressing intellectual questions as to the relationship of this unity of divine will to the ultimate unity of divine Being that Islam confesses. It is the first unity that is perhaps most fully expressed in the single expression *Al-Rabb*, "the Lord," by which Muhammad proclaimed God, especially in the period of his greatest preaching.

One final observation on the Beautiful Names will introduce another important aspect of the Muslim understanding of God. There are other adjectives among the *Asmā' al-Husnā* that are also used of humans; they stand for both the divine and human sides of the same transaction. *Shakūr* for example, means normally "the grateful"; when applied to God it means "the Cognizant of gratitude." God acknowledges human thankfulness. One epithet suggests both postures. Similarly, *Al-Mu'min* used of God means "the Trustworthy"; normally it means "the trusting." God is the object and humankind the locus of faith.

Perhaps most interesting of all, because nearest to the Christian teaching on the Comforter, is the word *Al-Walī*, sometimes translated "the Friend" or "Patron." The root is very widely diversified. It means in its simplest sense "one who is near." Surah 10.62 refers to "the *walīs* of God"—a phrase on which much mystical devotion to the saints of Islam has been built. Humans may stand in nearness to God, even as Abraham was the *khalīl*, or friend of God. But God is also *Al-Walī*—"the One alongside" —in whose protection and succor humankind may find strength. So we have in the same term the idea of the human dependent on God and the divine patron of the human. It may be added here that the Qur'ān does not contain any articulated conception of God as Holy Spirit, though the terms "spirit" and "holy spirit" are variously used in connection with the mediation of revelation.

III

Mention of these dual terms leads into the large and crucial theme of divine-human relationships. For insofar as any doctrine of God is meaningful, it is an account of such relationships. No theology could exist on the assumption that its theme meant nothing and mattered nothing. Certainly a monotheism so tremendous as that of Muhammad and Islam is through and through a divine-human encounter. As such we must strive to know it. Whenever we study or confess doctrines of God we proceed upon parallel affirmations about humanity. So inseparable are the two realms that every theology is inevitably also a view of the human. By what he means when he says "I bear witness that there is no god save God," the muezzin is involved in an equally compelling faith about those who walk the streets and come to worship in the court beneath him.

God's relation to humankind begins in and with creation. The created universe takes its rise from God's fiat. God says, "Be," and it is. The initiative in creation is itself inscrutable. We need not relate the motive to the *nature* of God. God *wills* it. And all the sequences and generations of life are likewise willed. Nothing exists save by divine providence, and there is nothing except God and creation. All arises directly from and through God.

As far as the Qur'ān is concerned there is an unresolved duality about the divine and human wills, though reconciliation is not recognized as necessary. Many passages refer to the will of God as the immediate source of all events. God has created both men and women, and their actions. There is no other Originator. God's is the *qadar*, "determination," of all things and his *taqdīr*, "subjection," covers all humankind and all history. Nature, whether animate or inanimate, is subject to his command. All that comes into existence—a summer flower or a murderer's deed, a newborn child or a sinner's disbelief—is from him and of him. Had God so willed, there need have been no creation, there need have been no idolatry, there need have been no hell, there need have been no escape from hell.

This complete and stringent sovereignty of the divine will is, however, counterbalanced by corresponding truths. The Qur'ān proceeds upon them and leaves the tension of duality to subsequent theologians. Clearly neither life nor religion can subsist on the inclusive hypothesis that God is *immediately* involved— involved, that is, without any human intervention—in all that is and all that happens. The Holy Book assumes that human beings are responsible creatures. Muhammad repeatedly exhorted his hearers to repent and believe. He treated them as capable of response and as responsible for their states of mind. He harangued them as creatures of will.

Creation itself, though in origin inscrutable, results nevertheless in a universe whose signs may be read for those who will to understand. The world is a witness to God's goodness and a means to divine worship. Surah 4.79 remarks: "Whatever of good happens to thee is from God: whatever evil happens to thee is from thyself." And there is the familiar passage, frequently cited in modern discussions of this theme: "God does not change what has to do with a people until they change what has to do with their own souls," arguing clearly that there are necessary human conditions upon which what God will, or will not, do is made to turn. The passage adds, however, that if God has willed evil to a people, then none can turn it away (Surah 13.11).

That quotation epitomizes the Quranic situation. God is the direct source of all existence and all occurrence, but men and women are treated as responsible and, therefore, in some sense also free, creatures. The most characteristic descriptive of the human status before God is *'abd*, "servant" or "slave," a term that is so frequent an element in Muslim names. The human creature stands under the divine authority in all realms, as one who masters the natural world, insofar as one is allowed to, only by stooping to obey the conditions it imposes. The span and course of days are ordered by God. Humanity is the creature of the divine purpose and responds to it in worship and in submission. We are creatures also in that, when we fall short of that law, the offense is seen as lapse rather than defiance. In its discussion of Adam as the archetypal man, the Qur'ān does not see him as rebellious. That would be to enlarge his stature over against God. It sees him rather as weak and forgetful, or lacking in firmness and resolve.

Though still his responsibility and sternly requited if God so wills, his sins are nevertheless more weakness than revolt.

Quranic man in other words is neither Promethean nor Shakespearean. When the stubborn recalcitrance of unbelievers appears to be a calculated defiance of God, it is understood rather as a delusion possible only by divine permission and as the prelude to their condemnation. They are not able spontaneously to flout the divine revelation. If they appear to do so, it is because God has ordained this way to their destruction. For the rest, the sins of believers, the delinquencies of the faithful, are lapses, over which there is hope that God may be lenient and merciful.

The status of *'abd* makes the meaning of *islām*, "submission," the only appropriate relationship with God. But to enter it consciously, to accept it for what it is, is itself by God's permission. The belief, or unbelief, by which human beings are distinguished into Muslims and non-Muslims is itself the determination here of God. Within the relationship of surrender, the Muslim recognizes the entire sovereignty of God in worship and behavior, in the two great concepts of the Call to Prayer—*Salāt* and *Falāh*—which will be studied in later chapters. The postures of Muslims in the one and the dispositions of their conduct and possessions in the other are alike expressive of the single state of submission.

In its finest form as exemplified by the Prophet himself, and by such successors as 'Umar, this relationship of the *'abd* to the Lord means a constant quality of consciousness and will unique to Islam. It produces a sense of totality in religion evident in the familiar refusal of the classical Muslim mind to differentiate between sacred and secular. Though many of the attitudes of Muslims within religion may seem to outsiders to be in tension with their *'abd* relationship, those attitudes are, as the Muslim sees it, nevertheless controlled and tempered by it. It is so because God is inescapable, to whom relationship in everything is inescapable:

> There is not a private conference of three, but He is their fourth, nor of five but He is their sixth, nor of a lower or a higher number but he is with them wherever they may be. Then on the day of resurrection He will tell them what they have done. God knoweth all [Surah 58.7].

It was this realization that gave to Muhammad's Islam its overwhelming sense of "the face of God" everywhere constraining the due submission of servants.

IV

Surrender implies the revelation of the will to which obedience is rendered. The Quranic account of the relation between God and humankind hinges upon the fact of revelation. The Holy Book is the climax of a long sequence of volumes of revelation with which it is continuous, granted to a long succession of prophets of whom Adam was the first and Muhammad the last. Belief in God, therefore, for the Muslim involves also belief in God's prophets, angels, and books. For these are the agencies of God's making known the divine law to humankind. Revelation is conceived of, not as a communication of the divine Being, but only of the divine will. It is a revelation, that is, of law, not of personality. God the Revealer remains unrevealed. The Qur'ān is a guide for the world. It brings that which humans need to know in order to relate themselves to God as servants.

Revelation is not a personal self-disclosure of the divine. It is for this reason, apart from its fear also of compromising unity, that the Qur'ān does not use the term "Father" in relation to God, or children in relation to believers. It allows only *Rabb* and *'abd*. In either case, the terms require each other. If God is not addressed as Father, neither is it as children that Muslims come to God. There remains beyond the revelation the impenetrable mystery of the divine.

Revelation tells how God wills that humanity should live. It has a practical intent. It is true that intellectual curiosity has apprehended the Qur'ān in many more senses than the practical. Revelation, too, whatever its intent, is necessarily involved in implications beyond law. The Qur'ān has itself been understood as proclaiming this larger relevance. A crucial verse in Surah 3.7 distinguishes between the unambiguous and the ambiguous, the clear and the allegorical. A succession of mystics found endless scope for their reverent minds in the manifoldness of the Qur'ān. Nonetheless it remains broadly true that the substance of what God reveals is the divine will rather than the divine nature, and that the end of revelation is obedience rather than perfect knowledge. God sends rather than comes. The God who makes plain remains above. Revelation is by *tanzīl*, as the phrase goes, by "causing to come down"; God is withdrawn in *tanzīh*, "transcendence."

Though there has been a vigorous, if intermittent, Muslim theological expression in history, the crux of Islam was law, not metaphysics. Muhammad certainly was concerned only with what God demanded. His conviction was that God, in proclaiming the divine oneness, proclaimed an all-inclusive sovereignty. In revealing the divine Names God revealed the divine relationship. In sending the prophets and books, God communicated the divine intention for the world. Response and submission were the sole necessities. These beliefs were their own justification.

The Qur'ān was the speech of God, breathed instrumentally into the ear of the unread Prophet and transmitted to human ears by preaching and to the human mind by the written record. Problems implicit in the precise relation of that speech to God were left to develop in later ages. God was simply uttering through Muhammad the words that would proclaim the divine unity, warn "the associators" or idolaters, and guide the faithful. It was auricular revelation in that it came to the Prophet's ear, as he understood it, in independence of conscious mental processes. It was oracular, also, in the sense that Muhammad uttered it without other argument than its own content, claiming implicit acceptance on the sole ground of its status as revealed, and his status as its messenger. The revelation did not envisage or establish the kind of situation in which human beings may speak to God as to each other, and yet in the expression of those thoughts become truly instruments of a divine revelation to all generations of the world. That pattern, exemplified in the Hebrew psalms, is uncongenial to the Qur'ān. We cannot fully appreciate the Quranic doctrine of God apart from an understanding of its concept of revelation as something in which God uses agents but teaches them by word rather than by travail, by ear rather than by thought, by audition rather than by anguish.

A counterpart of the Quranic truth of God as revealer is the reality of God as judge. Indeed the imminence of the divine judgment was a most compelling note in the original Muhammadan preaching. The day of judgment was not some distant event, but terrible and close at hand. It is proclaimed in some of the most eloquent passages of the Qur'ān. It was the day of the encircling wall closing inexorably upon the wicked; the day of reckoning; the day of separation. Surah 101 on this theme is almost untranslatable. "The *Qāri'ah*, who shall teach you what is the *Qāri'ah*?" it begins. The word has been rendered "the Clatterer" (Arberry); "the Calamity" (Pickthall and Muhammad 'Alī); "the Striking" (Bell); "the Smiting" (Palmer); "the Blow" (Rodwell). All of them fail. It might almost be called "the Knocking" if one keeps in mind the hell's gate of the porter in *Macbeth*. It is a fearful summons striking terror into the hearts of all and ushering in the dread assize, the day of the retribution of God upon humankind. Those whose deeds weigh heavy in the balance will lead a pleasant life. But those whose deeds are light in the balance will be thrown into the mother pit. "And who shall teach thee what is the pit?—a raging fire."

That day is in the absolute disposal of God alone. It is a day, as Surah 82.19 declares, on which "no soul hath any power at all for any other soul." The terrors of punishment and the blessings of paradise are graphically portrayed, with vivid detail. The judgment turns mainly on belief or unbelief, with the idolaters and "associators" or polytheists in certain and condign damnation. There is some ambiguity on the point as to whether confessed Muslims will enter the fire. Though there are passages, and many more traditions, to suggest they will not, there is no ground for presumptive assurance. Only at the end will the end be known.

There are many aspects of the doctrine of divine judgment into which we cannot enter in this context. The doctrine itself completes for present purposes the understanding of God—One, Sovereign, Omniscient, Revealing, and Judging—that Muhammad proclaimed. Wherever the Qur'ān is read, pondered, and experienced, this is the sense of God it conveys. When the muezzin in his witness links together God and the Apostle, he bears witness to the identity, for multitudes, of the God they worship and the God Muhammad preached.

V

The fullness of the *Shahādah*, however, is not appreciated by limiting ourselves only to the Prophet's word and time. A preacher's silences, in retrospect, are sometimes as meaningful as his words. It might be possible to expound the Muslim doctrine of God, in a further stage, not so much for what it says, but for what it forbears to say. It will be well, however, to attempt to hearken to the silences by means of subsequent Muslim thinking which did something to explore them. By these means also we shall be listening, as Emerson once said, to the centuries over against the hours. The fourteen centuries of Islamic existence, or some of them, must be consulted, if we mean to penetrate into the meaning of God in Islam.

It should not be supposed that the "silences" of Muhammad were culpable. His purpose, as we have insisted, was not theological debate. He was a preacher, not a systematizer; a prophet, not a theologian. His vocation was to confront others with the living God, the law, the claim, and the judgment of God. But, precisely for this reason, the doctrine needed to be related by philosophic minds to its own assumptions and to other creeds. Islam in expansion through the first two centuries after the Prophet's death came into contact beyond Arabia with Christian, Persian, and other influences that contributed considerably to its classic form. The entire Umayyad (Damascus) Caliphate (A.D. 661–750) was occupied with physical expansion and the arabization and islamization of the territories absorbed. Then there began to develop under the 'Abbasids (from A.D. 750) the articulation of Muslim theological problems in the minds, for the most part, of non-Arabs. There is no intention here to attempt even the outlines of that story. The desire is to sketch the main themes of intellectual concern, without losing sight of the fact that our purpose is not a history of theology but the Muslim apprehension of God. We must confine ourselves to those questions that serve to illuminate further what Muslims understand God to be and to will.

VI

All the questions were in some way aspects of the meaning of divine unity. *Tauhīd* was the term used to describe that theological principle by which there was only God and God was one. And all the points were somehow involved in the silences of the Prophet, the issues he had not recognized or raised.

The earliest questions were, characteristically, practical. In the time of the Umayyads, Muslims, even exalted ones, became careless and worldly. Many were content to confess the faith, but unwilling to live austerely in its obedience. Were they then true Muslims? And if rulers, had they the right to be obeyed by Muslims who were true? A group known as the Khārijites thought they had no such right and refused allegiance on the ground that the Islam of such rulers was invalid. Here was the problem of faith and works. Did confession alone make a Muslim, or was performance indispensable?

This problem merged into larger ones. Who should decide? The community, the "puritan" groups, the worldlings, or God? How was God's will to be known in this matter? For indubitably God had a will and, moreover, nothing but this will could be done. How, then, explain the quarrel? If the will of God was being done in fact, the complaints were baseless, if not blasphemous. If it was not being done, as the Khārijites insisted, then in this respect the will of God was being overborne. How came it that persons could behave with such recalcitrance?

These questions, fed by other perplexities, shaped themselves into the most characteristic of Muslim theological inquiries: the relation between the human and the divine will. The reader may be assured, or warned—as mood requires—that we intend no exhaustive investigation of predestination, Muslim or Western. The question was simply an aspect of *tauhīd*. Was God all in all? Was there no other god than *Allāh*? If not, why was not God's will necessarily done? Could there be any successful alternative to the divine will? If not, why were human beings ever involved in disobedience? The course of thought oscillated for two centuries over this question. But despite some "liberal" tendencies, perhaps overesteemed in Western orientalism, the Muslim mind was rarely ready to accept any view that left a real freedom, even unto lawlessness, within the permissive sovereignty of God.

In the early tenth century the discussion reached its term in the classic solution associated with Al-Ash'arī. It was a solution that gave the questions back in the form of an answer. The Muslim mind was not prepared to compromise its belief that God was the sole Creator. Therefore God was the final source of every event and every deed. But it was necessary to recognize the role that

human doing played in life and the reality of moral choice. To
hold the two together, the concept of "acquisition" (*kasb*) was
developed. Human beings "acquired" the action that was created
in them by God. God willed evil in the act of the sinner and good
in the behavior of the righteous. God remained the sole source of
creativity; the human being remained responsible. The power and
choice by which individuals perform actions are God's; they "acquire" the action that is consequently theirs. Though this theory
may serve to explain the illusion of freedom, if such it be, it hardly
succeeds in reconciling moral responsibility with divine sovereignty. But it pointedly illustrates one facet of what orthodox
Islam means by the confession "There is none other than He."

Belief in the divine unity led into an even more searching question. Was God morally accountable? How were the different aspects of God, his Beautiful Names, reconciled where they were
morally antithetical? Could God be both "loving" and "the best
of deceivers"? If we answer yes, because God is one will and both
attributes describe that one will at different points, then what of
the moral sense that inclines some to say, even of God, "This
ought not to be"? Can we in other words forbid attitudes to God
which, when found in humans, are morally reprehensible? The
instinct was always to answer no, because no limits could be
placed on God's action and no criteria placed upon God's
choices. God's will was God's law.

There were, however, sensitive thinkers in the ninth century
who felt that if there were to be valid moral distinctions applicable
to human beings, they must have their ground in the divine
character. God, too, must be motivated by them. Otherwise they
would also lose their human authority. These thinkers, therefore,
preferred to think of "justice," rather than "will," as the ultimate term of reference to God, so that what God willed was always just and God could not be conceived as willing something
unjust.

The majority of thinkers, however, feared that this meant
somehow a limitation of God. It left them also with the problem
of how to account for evil, if the thesis of only a good will in God
were accepted. Moreover, they were reluctant to believe that God
was under any necessities, even moral ones. So they fell back
upon the belief that God was open to good and evil as God pleased

and that the divine will was finally inscrutable. This was the measure both of the price they were ready to pay for the concept of divine unity, and of the way they understood it.

VII

There are other clues to this understanding of God's unity that must be considered in order to estimate it further. "There is no god save God" says the witness. How were human minds to understand the relationship to God of the realities that issued from God? These were chiefly two: the created world and the revealed law. Clearly God was in relationship to the world, and to humanity as "slaves" of God. From God other existences took their rise. But were they necessary to God? Orthodox Islam has always inclined to deny they were. God is self-subsistent. Had God willed otherwise, no worlds would have been. Yet to believe that the world is not necessary to God is a poor basis for religion, because it threatens the belief that humankind has meaning for God. If prayer and worship are to be meaningful, we need to believe that they are meaningful to God.

Much mysticism in Islam has solved this problem devotionally by bringing God and the world closer together and explaining divine unity in pantheistic terms. But, though built upon possible Quranic exegesis, this attitude has remained suspect among orthodox theologians. Yet if God is one in a religiously meaningful sense, the oneness must leave room for the world as somehow within its range and yet maintain the self-sufficiency of God. This was the problem of creation.

It had ramifications in other areas of life, notably in relation to physical causality. When leaves fall and the seasons change, when fire burns and wounds fester, are these physical events to be accounted for by causal connections in the chemical or physical environment? If so, are they an area distinguishable from the divine will? Are they independent of God? In what sense are they attributable to God? In more recent times this question has been sharpened by our increasing ability to manipulate natural causality for our own ends. The modern Muslim tends to understand this as an aspect of the authority given to the human race in the Qur'ān. But many in an earlier time were required, by their understanding of the principle of divine unity, to believe that all these multifarious events issued directly from the action of God.

The problem involved in revelation, however, is even more controversial in Muslim intellectual history. The Qur'ān was God's word, God's speech. It was what God had said. When, however, you use an apostrophe after the word "God," and refer to "God's speech," or even "God's will," or "God's face," you may appear to speak of a second thing besides God. What is spoken is clearly not the speaker. Yet it cannot be a second God. Nonetheless, if it is truly God's speech, it must be as eternal as God.

From musings of this kind rose the bitter controversy, which reached its climax in the ninth century, on the status of the Qur'ān. Was it created or eternal? The final orthodox view was that it was uncreated. For to think otherwise surely would be to render dubious its divine origin. More adventurous thinkers, who were finally overcome, were impressed with the problem of regarding as eternal that which was involved in temporal issues, in the fortunes of specific battles and the domestic relationships of particular families. If these occasions in time were themes or points of revelation, were they somehow eternal also?

This question merged into an equally puzzling issue where the Muslim mind found decision difficult. It related to the sense in which the divine Names or attributes should be understood. When adjectives such as "kind," "gracious," and "wise" were used of God, did the same meanings hold that the terms carried in normal usage? To answer with an unqualified yes seemed to bring God and the human too close together and so compromise transcendence and otherness. This might amount to a violation of *tauhīd* and be an indirect form of *shirk*, because human descriptives were "associated" with God. But to answer with an unqualified "No" threatened all theology with meaninglessness. In any event such terms were used in the Holy Qur'ān and in the Tradition. Their use must, accordingly, be valid.

Classical Muslim theology developed a form of compromise solution in effect inclining to the negative answer. There developed the idea of *Al-Mukhālafah*, "the difference." Terms taken from human meanings—and there are of course no others—were said to be used of God with a difference. They did not convey the human connotation but were used in those senses feasible of God. When the further question was pressed: What, then, do they convey as applied to God? no precise answer could be formulated. Islam here falls back upon a final agnosticism. Terms must be used if there is to be religion at all. But only God knows what they signify. Muslim theology coined the related phrases *Bilā kaif* and *Bilā Tashbīh*. We use these names "without knowing how" they apply and without implying any human similarity.

In a real sense the Muslim awareness of God is an awareness of the unknown. Revelation communicated God's law. It does not reveal God, who remains inscrutable and inaccessible to knowledge. Sometimes described as the negative theology, this conviction that only God knows the sense of the terms in which we speak of God has characterized Muslim attitudes far beyond the range of those who can understand its intellectual grounds. If some readers find the point under discussion abstruse, they can be assured that it attaches to the Muslim sense of God in everyday life. Only God knows. The problem of meaning in language belongs with all religions and is not unique to Islam. It can be solved only within the conviction that the divine and the human are truly meaningful to each other, only in the confidence that the relationships God has with us are really indicative of the divine nature. Christians only put these convictions more shortly—and sublimely—when they say: "God is Love." Islam has never felt able to say that. The pressure of these problems is the measure of its reluctance.

VIII

This brief attempt to convey something of the historical travail of Islam over its belief in the one God must face one other issue—and seek forgiveness for the torturing brevity into which it is compelled. This formal problem, like all the foregoing, arises out of the doctrine of unity. As a religion of revelation Islam believes that God has communicated the divine will and has taught the faithful to use, if not fully to apprehend, the Names. This realm of revelation, however, is not the sole source of human knowledge. There is natural human reason operating from sense experience to study and know the external world. In the Qur'ān there are fervent appeals to recognize the splendor of God in nature and the sureness of his ways.

A ready example can be found in Surah 55, with its repeated refrain: "Which of the favors of your Lord will ye deny?" and its eloquent celebration of the punctual sun and moon, the pearls of the sea, and the fruitful oases. "Lord of the daybreak" is one of the titles of God, who has set in the heavens the lamps of the stars and bounded the everlasting hills. "Praise the Name of Thy Lord most High Who creates and makes complete. He determines the ends [of things], then guides them. He brings forth pasture and turns it into tawny stubble" (Surah 87.1–5). "Wilt thou not regard . . . the heaven, how it was raised . . . and the earth how it was spread forth?" (Surah 88.18–20). These passages are also understood as injunctions to the scientific spirit. From this natural scientific area of human knowledge, certain ideas of God and the world, of duty and meaning, may be constructed by rational processes. There comes, then, the problem of reason and revelation in their interrelationship—again a large issue, not unique to Islam.

The Muslim doctrine of the unity of God includes the unity of truth. Truth is not inconsistent with itself. Though it may be known by different methods, it is one essential truth. Accordingly, traditional Muslim thought has tended to explain the difference between reason and revelation primarily as a difference in method or means. It has two words, 'aql and naql, to describe reason and revelation: what intelligence investigates and what God delivers.[1] There is a tendency evident in some Muslim thinking to leave aside the task of reconciling what reason thinks and revelation says, on the ground that they are simply different methods. This may generate an insensitivity in some theologians to the full impact of scientific criticism. It tends to immunize dogma from critical exposure and to leave science mistrustful of faith.

Some of the greatest Muslim thinkers, however, have erred in the other direction. Writers of great eminence have inclined to the view that religion and faith were the form in which the vulgar throng in the mosque could grasp spiritual truth. They needed the help of symbol. Philosophers, however, with their educated minds, could dispense with external forms and hold loosely to established dogma. Such thinking was hard to detect under outward conformity. Founded on an aristocracy of reason, these attitudes were by no means common. But they represent another form of the tension in the Muslim mind between *'aql* and *naql*, and an original account of their relationship.[2]

There are some in contemporary Islam who accept religious dogmas as a political or communal necessity without giving their minds to them. Moreover, the obligation to concerted theological thinking is not stimulated by the underlying feeling that only God knows. Conviction about the oneness of truth sometimes excuses the mind from the task of understanding its unity.

It is for these reasons that the Islamic faith that God is God alone is not always adequately articulated in the intellectual sense. As Professor Gibb remarks, the genius of Islam is finally law, not theology.[3] In the last analysis the sense of God is a sense of divine command. In the will of God there is none of the mystery that surrounds the divine Being. God's demands are known and the believer's task is not so much exploratory, still less fellowship, but rather obedience and allegiance.

The foregoing venture into some of the characteristic issues of Muslim thought on God is in no sense an adequate analysis. It does scant justice to its vast theme. It is intended only as illustrating what faith in God has meant to Muslims, insofar as that meaning can be gauged in external debate. We can perhaps understand more fully the all-embracing principle of unity if we take note of what it has meant to some who have essayed its exposition. We turn now to some of the significance of the confession of the one God for the moral life of the believer.

IX

The first duty of the Muslim is belief; belief in God, God's unity, revelation, prophets, books, angels, and the Last Day. This *īmān*, "faith," must issue in *Dīn*, "religion." The latter has its five pillars: Confession, Prayer, Almsgiving, Fasting, and Pilgrimage. These will be discussed in later chapters on religious and social life in Islam. They are the particular focus of the inclusive sovereignty of God that is held to pervade the whole of life. Islam does not accept the interpretation of religion that allows it to be understood as a branch of human life, a piece of personal privacy, or the area of existence that relates to God. All things relate to God and the God-relationship of humankind involves all its affairs. This inclusive interpretation is under some criticism from within in view of factors demanding the separation of politics from religion. But it remains the classic Muslim concept—a God-relatedness in all things.

The ideal does not, in its Muslim form, take note of the human capacity for insubordination. It knows, of course, that in all realms—political, social, and personal—there is failure fully to do the divine will. But it does not take that knowledge seriously into account in its doctrinal estimate of the situation. It believes that human life is a realm in which the divine will can be done simply by its being known—as known it is in the Muslim law. All is, therefore, in the classic view, an aspect of 'ibādah, "worship." 'Ibādah is the abstract noun defining the attitude of the 'abd, "servant."

This does not mean, however, an extravagant saintliness or abstraction. On the contrary, the law, when the demands that might in some contexts be called "religious" are fulfilled, leaves individuals and society a wide freedom. The customary division of ethical categories in Islam is fivefold. There are those actions the performance of which is obligatory and their omission forbidden. Conversely there are actions that must be shunned absolutely and whose commission is forbidden. In the center are a great number of actions that are matters of indifference, where there is an entire option. On either side of these, but not as far as the two absolute extremes of "must" and "must not," are actions not commended but tolerated, and not forbidden but disapproved. Among the worst of the latter, incidentally, is divorce.

Inasmuch as our purpose is to understand the sense of God, there is no occasion to pursue this analysis further as an ethical study. Though the demands of God are thought of as paramount everywhere, there are many areas where they neither enjoin nor prohibit. These areas of complete human option are evidence of the largess of God. But even where no specific injunction controls an act, the sovereignty of God is to be recognized in the attitude that enjoys the freedom.

These issues implicit in the Muslim understanding of God occupied the minds of successive generations of Muslim theologians and philosophers especially from the ninth to the eleventh Christian centuries. A close study of the course of their debate would be a most effective commentary on the theme of this chapter. It would then, however, cease to be a chapter and become a tome. Some scant justice may be done to its history by means of three representatives. The first two belong to the "classical" age, the third is possibly the most adventurous of Muslim philosophers in the twentieth century. There will remain one vital task when these three authorities have been heard.

X

Inasmuch as three out of many scores is drastic selection, it may be well to explain why Al-Nasafī is first chosen. Of no great distinction in his own right, he was the author of a creed in the second quarter of the twelfth century. It had prolonged currency as a textbook and manual. It became the basis of later commentaries. Al-Nasafī himself was a disciple of Al-Māturīdī, whose school of teaching, along with that of Al-Ash'arī, formed the main orthodoxy of Islam after the controversies of the earlier centuries. With little to choose between them, the two schools fashioned and dominated the mind of Sunnī Islam. To quote the main paragraphs of Al-Nasafī's creed in relation to God is to have in convenient form a concise statement of how orthodoxy understood its own confession. The translation is by Duncan Black Macdonald:

> The Originator of the world is God Most High, the One, the Eternal, the Decreeing, the Knowing, the Hearing, the Seeing, the Willing. He is not an attribute, not a body, nor an essence, not a thing formed, nor a thing bounded, nor a thing numbered, nor a thing divided, nor a thing compounded, nor a thing limited: He is not described by quiddity, *Māhiyah*, nor by modality, *Kaifiyyah*, and He does not exist in place or time. There is nothing that resembles Him and nothing that is beyond His Knowledge and Power.
> He has qualities from all eternity existing in His essence. They are not He, nor are they any other than He. They are Knowledge and Power, and Life and Strength and Hearing

and Seeing and Doing and Creating and Sustaining and
Speech.

And He Whose Majesty is majestic speaks with a Word.
This Word is a quality from all eternity, not belonging to the
genus of letters and sounds, a quality that is incompatible
with coming to silence and that has a weakness.

God Most High speaks with this Word, commanding and
prohibiting and narrating. And the Quran is the uncreated Word of God, repeated by our tongues, heard by our
ears, written in our copies, memorized in our hearts, yet not
simply a transient state in these. And creating is a quality
of God Most High from all eternity. . . . and Willing is a
quality of God Most High from all eternity, existing in His
essence. . . .

And God Most High is the Creator of all actions of His
creatures whether of unbelief or belief, of obedience or of
rebellion: all of them are by the Will of God and His sentence
and His conclusion and His decreeing.[4]

After discussing the human ability to do actions of choice
within this decreeing, the creed adds: "God leadeth astray whom
He wills and guideth aright whom He wills, and it is not incumbent upon God Most High to do that which may be best for His
creatures."

XI

An older contemporary of Al-Nasafī and a far more significant
figure was Al-Ghazālī (A.D. 1059–1111). A formal creed is one
thing but a deep personal travail of conviction is another. There is
no more eloquent document of religious experience in Islam, outside the Qur'ān itself, than the autobiography of Al-Ghazālī, *The
Deliverer from Error*. Though responsible in part for an unhappy
anti-intellectualism in subsequent Muslim theology, Al-Ghazālī
illuminates, as no other writer does, the meaning of faith. Beginning as a successful teacher in the Asharite tradition, he experienced in his late thirties an intense crisis in which rational
confidence forsook him. He was overcome by a deep religious
skepticism and a sense of self-reproach from which he was finally

delivered by reliance on the path of moral discipline and intuitive insight. Herein he was greatly influenced by Al-Muḥāsibī, and others of the Sufi, or mystical, school, who taught that the knowledge of God turned upon purity of soul, to be sought by sustained asceticism and spiritual renunciation.

Al-Ghazālī himself renounced his role as an academician and became for some years a pilgrim and a wanderer. Out of the fullness of his inner experience he found certainty of a different quality from that which he had known within scholastic theology. Something of his legacy might loosely be expressed in the idea that he altered the "person" in the Muslim confession from: "There is no god save He" to "There is no god save Thou." The use of "He," only, conveys a sense of inadequacy in the formal relationships of orthodoxy in the soul of Al-Ghazālī. He saw the importance, as he said, of experiences rather than definitions, and recognized his lack, not of instruction, but of ecstasy and initiation. In *The Deliverer from Error* he examined the theological limitations of reason and defended *kashf*, "discovery through illumination," as the sure way to the knowledge of God. Yet he was careful to recognize creedal theology and he saw in the Qur'ān and the Prophet the supreme example of revelation through and to the pure in heart.[5]

In this understanding he was aided by a remarkable sense of the psychological in worship and religious practice. His greatest work, known as *The Revival of the Religious Sciences*, discusses such themes as the psychology of temptation, the relationship between ritual and belief, the disciplines of the soul and its intricacies. It contains forty books divided into two parts: (a) external acts of religious devotion and (b) the heart and its workings, including both the destructive and the redeeming elements in human life. The whole is an eloquent compendium of living religion, more deeply self-aware, more alert to its duties and dangers, more vibrant and intense, than anything in the history of Islam after Muhammad. Here many of the earlier "silences" are treated with a painstaking devotion.

A prolific author, Al-Ghazālī reproduced many of the arguments of his *magnum opus* in short manuals for believers. He also expounded his view of the theological limitations of reason in a famous work, *The Disintegration of the Philosophers*. Elsewhere

he expounded the stages of the mystic's way through the degrees
of the divine unveiling.

No summary can do him justice. There were many commentators on his works. But thanks, in part, to the suspicion of reason
he helped to generate, Muslim theological activity became more
and more a matter of Quranic exegesis and traditional commentary. The celebrated names after him are those of Quranic commentators and historians of past theology.

Nevertheless, no attempt to understand the meaning of *Lā ilāha illā Allāh* is complete without a deep reckoning with Al-
Ghazālī. He lived to express that conviction on its inward side as
an experience and a way of life. He sought a psychology that
would subdue every subtle challenge in the recesses of the will and
spirit to the sole mastery of God. He practiced a loving submission that went far beyond the bare requirements of the pillars as
traditionally understood. He taught others to realize that the
Beautiful Names of God were not for description merely, but for
imitation. Muslims were to strive after a divine likeness, even
when they confessed God's creedal unlikeness. The emphasis was
not on the ways in which God could be meaningfully defined but
on the attitudes in which God was to be devoutly obeyed. If God
was called "the Repenter," the Muslim must know the meaning
of repentance. Something of the starkness of transcendence was
corrected and human knowledge of God became a ground of
communion with God. For: "If it assuredly be that God is beautiful, He must certainly be beloved by him to whom His beauty is
revealed." The creature might remain the *'abd* yet be also a lover,
and this was the clue to the meaning of the health of *ibādah*.

It is not without significance that the subtitle of *The Deliverer
from Error* is Al-Muwāsil, "the bringer unto" the Lord of might
and majesty. For Al-Ghazālī was concerned not only to escape
falsehood but to enter into truth and peace. Perhaps we may say
that, for him, the Muslim confession "There is no god save God"
had come near to meaning: "Whom have I in heaven but Thee?
there is none upon earth that I desire beside Thee" (Psalm 73:25).

XII

There is a pregnant Islamic phrase that may serve as a bridge
from Al-Ghazālī to Muhammad Iqbāl, from a great medieval fig-

ure in Islam to a twentieth-century thinker. It is the command
"Be fashioned after the fashion of God," or "Seek the character
which God has." For this conception, which summarizes much of
the message of Al-Ghazālī, is also often cited by Iqbāl. Born in
1876 in the Punjab, Iqbāl became famous as a philosopher and
poet. He has been remembered, since his death in 1938, with great
fervor and admiration. It would not be improper to regard him as
the patron saint of Pakistan, where Iqbāl Day is a national festival. In his poems, and in a series entitled *Lectures on the Reconstruction of Religious Thought in Islam*, he set forth a dynamic
theism that, though not everywhere accepted or even understood
in Islam, represents an attempt to express anew the fundamentals
of Islamic faith in terms of modern thought.

For this reason, though without analysis and only the scantiest
exposition, he may be taken here as expressing the meaning the
Shahādah has come to hold for some modern Muslims. Iqbāl had
studied Nietzsche, Bergson, and Bernard Shaw, among others,
and sought in part to interpret the God of the Qur'ān along the
same lines. Crusading against apathy and decadence, he proclaimed the cultivation of the self, or ego. The universe was itself
growing and maturing in dynamic creation, ever moving toward
an unrealized perfection. Iqbāl tended to see in the Quranic deity
this continuous flow of creative energy, and in the prophets the
special agents of creative life in which a dynamism was at work, to
overcome inertia in the on-going surge of the life-force.

As a poet he availed himself of the privilege of suggestiveness,
allusion, and even inconsistency. He was more concerned to
galvanize believers than to define belief. He summoned Muslims
to exalt their egos so high that God would consult them before
determining their destiny. He did not explain how so daring a
sentiment was to be reconciled with the traditional Muslim understanding of the sovereignty of God. His *Lectures* were of necessity
more integrated than his poems. Nevertheless they left unfaced
many questions involved in the "reconstruction."

For himself, and for numbers of his subsequent expositors,
Iqbāl found the secret of Islam in creative dynamism. "God is
most great" meant that God is the inclusive Ego. Muslim history
became for him a unique example of dynamism at work. The worship of "the Lord of the worlds" was the ego affirming itself.
Iqbāl addressed God in the words: "How farest Thou without

me, O my whole?'' The God whom Islam proclaimed was also
''the not-yet,'' the still to be realized unfolding of infinite possibilities. Creation was not a deed that made the world something
''other'' than God. It was, and is, the self-revelation of the great
''I Am.'' The Islamic doctrine of the divine oneness meant that
there is no reality outside God. Nature is to the divine Self as
character is to the human self.[6]

A critical evaluation of the form Iqbāl gives to classic Islamic
meanings cannot be undertaken here. This brief reference does
justice neither to the daring range of his intellectual flights nor to
their often tenuous connection with what is historically Islamic.
But their boldness and the reputation of their author are sufficient indication that, for all its authoritative simplicity, the
Muslim creed is capable of widely diverse interpretations.

Without searching for the meaning of Quranic passages to Muhammad himself and his immediate hearers, modern interpreters
proceed to borrow and claim them for beliefs that may well owe
more to current philosophy than to traditional faith. Such spirits
are, no doubt, part of the valid fullness of any wide religious system, however disconcerting they may be to the orthodox. Even
the most emphatic dogma stands finally in the meaning believers
give to it. The faith that ''there is no god save God'' is terse
enough, inclusive enough, vast enough, to mean tremendous, and
not always recognizably compatible, things to different Muslims.

XIII

If we have concentrated on the classic historic meanings in this
chapter, that is no more than a duty to the consensus of the
Muslim centuries. But it is with the fifteenth in the series that we
are also concerned. Iqbāl, who, for all his provocative quality,
deserves fuller study, is here no more than a witness to the inex-
haustible meanings that Muslims may yet find and proclaim
within their ancient creed of the oneness of God. Though the
muezzin and his colleagues in the mosque are among the last to
yield to the possibility of these modern interpretations of their
familiar words, the sense of God is evidently more fluid, less
clearly definable, among many of their listeners.

It is into this realm of the awareness of God in the Muslim

community that we finally attempt to pass. Leaving behind the traditional issues of theology and representative leaders of interpretation, there is need to face the question: What does the fact of God mean in the life of the individual? Theology always issues in doxology when it is true to its theme. It is the worshiper, in the fullest Muslim sense of the word, who really demonstrates what faith in the divine unity means. The temper it fashions in those who hold it is the final clue to the nature of a religious faith.

Yet how formidable a task rightly to identify and to describe the elemental truths about this Muslim sense of God! Multitudes of humble believers have given no tongue to their experience. The sultans and viziers do not always speak for them. There are competing voices and discordant sounds. Shall we take Hārūn al-Rashīd and his splendid autocracy in Baghdad as an index to the faith, or its gilded tapestry? The stories of *The Thousand and One Nights*, though, for all their diversity of origin and content, unmistakably Islamic, give the lie to as many Muslim virtues as they depict. That unpredictable tyranny, the cheapness of life, the successful villainy, the unabashed casuistry—are these to be taken as the consequence, in some sense, of the enthronement of celestial will? The *Assemblies of Al-Harīrī*, among the most famous of Arabic literary works, breathe a dubious piety and make a hero of a charlatan. Should their moral, then, be the ethical discredit of excessive transcendence in popular theology? And that old familiar charge of fatalism, perpetually dogging Muslim believers, with their apathetic conclusion that what is, had to be, and what will be, will be—should these be the text of a critic's sermon on the *Lā ilāha illā Allāh*?

Hardly. These are elements in the total picture. But they, and much more from all the centuries, could as well be attributed to the enervation of faith as to its vitality. Though the kind of compromise that happens to a faith is sometimes a clue to its nature, it is not in compromise that faiths should be finally judged. Students must acquaint themselves with all that Muslim literature and history have to tell about what God came to mean to Muslims. But it will be soundest in the end if they assess the lights more than the shadows.

They will find a consciousness of God that has produced a recognizably Muslim character, sometimes even of face, always of

conduct. Pressures of secularity may have gone far to transform it
in this century. But in history it is there. It is a temper that is grave,
perhaps even a little joyless, but marked by probity and discipline.
The sense of God's oneness, at its purest, has emancipated believers
from all other fears and so fostered imperturbability and strength
of soul. Legality and communal consciousness may have their
demerits, but they generate a dignity and loyalty that are characteristic Muslim virtues.

Islamic faith in God has taught the oneness of believers. Class
consciousness, though it may be economically real, is religiously
repudiated. The relative ranks of society diminish alongside
the sole sovereignty of the divine. Then there is hospitality, that
identifying quality of Muslim society. There are attitudes of
responsibility—to family, to community, to God—that mark the
believing Muslim, as a moral consequence of the recognition of
God.

But the task of assessing fully the bearing of the *Shahādah* on the
making of the characteristically Muslim temper and attitude is in
the end too large and intangible. Nor are the necessary criteria all
agreed. Our duty is rather to incite students to keep always in view
the reciprocity between the idea of God and the idea of life as it
abides through the Muslim story, and to trace its workings as best
they can.

No doubt their surest clue will be the Prophet himself. For the
meaning of God to Islam is told and retold in the biography of the
Prophet in its inward compulsion and its outward success. We
come back in the end to that eloquent link between the unity of God
and the apostleship of Muhammad in the muezzin's witness. It is in
what Islam came to believe about the Prophet of God that the
community found and learned its awareness of God's nature and
relation to humanity. As Muhammad was the final instrument of
revelation, so his story in all its aspects provides the framework in
which we may understand the God revealed.

iii

MUHAMMAD,
THE APOSTLE OF GOD

I

"I bear witness that Muhammad is the Apostle of God." So says the muezzin and so every Muslim, in the indispensable second clause of the *Shahādah,* with its inseparable relationship to the first. Though there is no doctrine of divinity as to Muhammad in Islam, but rather sustained insistence to the contrary, the Prophet of Arabia's is the human name most closely associated with that of God. In many a mosque, great and small, the name *Allāh* appears on the right, that of Muhammad on the left, above the *mihrāb* or above where the dome springs from its supporting arches.

The two names are the double motif of calligraphic design and are uttered in close succession on the lips of multitudes of the faithful. "I bear witness that there is no god save God and that Muhammad is his Apostle." Small conjunctions often carry profound significance. There is none more tremendous than that which links the one God with the human instrument of God's revelation and will, in the creed and the devotion of Islam.

61

A few sentences from a familiar manual of adoration in one of the orders of Muslim mystics, or Sufis, will serve to illustrate and introduce this theme. After the proper acknowledgment of God, there follows the traditional petition:

> Let blessing and peace, O God, be upon the noblest of all creatures, among men and jinns, the master of glorious illumination. O God, let blessing and peace be upon him, his people, his children, his wives, his seed, the members of his household, his brethren among the prophets and faithful ones and also upon whoever believes in him and follows him, from the first to the last—our master and guardian, Muhammad. O God, make him unto us a spirit, and to our worship a secret [of well pleasing]. O God, cause his love to be our nourishment, whereof I seek help in magnifying him. O God, make the celebration of him life in our hearts. I perform it seeking help from it for his remembrance, and the remembrance of his Lord.

There, in the same intimate association, is the recollection of God and of the Prophet. This mystical ardor may, in degree and expression, but not essentially in kind, go beyond the perception of Muhammad that pervades Islam. The more strictly orthodox disqualify some of the terms of Sufi fervor. Yet these only give a warmth of personal intensity to the general attitudes toward Muhammad in the community that confesses his apostleship and lives by the confession.

In the spate of new publications in Islam there have been more Muslim biographies of the Prophet in recent decades than in the same number of centuries past. Most of them dwell enthusiastically on the same features of excellence and uniqueness. That by 'Abbās Mahmūd al-'Aqqād, a noted Egyptian author, may be taken as typical. Entitled '*Abqariyyat Muhammad* ["The Genius or Excellence of Muhammad"], it proclaims that his greatness is evident in all fields.[1] He entered a world that had lost faith, and with it the secret of inward peace and outward order, a world that, accordingly, was waiting for the liberating voice of Islam. Muhammad was the paragon of both the preacher's and the soldier's virtues. He had the eloquence, conviction, and intensity of the one; the courage, chivalry, and success of the other. Superb in his gifts and character, he dominated his time as he dominates all succeeding history. No event that has since happened, writes the biographer (the date is 1942), has been what it would have been had Muhammad never appeared. Before him history is one thing; after him another.

In similar vein writes another biographer, Muhammad Husain Haykal, former president of the Egyptian Senate and author of the longest and most scholarly of Muslim studies of the Prophet in Arabic.[2] At the close of an intimate discussion of the pilgrimage in *Fī Manzil al-Wahÿ* ["In the Home of Revelation"], Haykal writes of Muhammad:

> His is a power that can lift humankind to the heights of the spirit where life will be brotherhood and love and care for the knowledge of all that is in the world of existence, so that knowledge may illumine neighborly concord and love, and that both may grow in human worth and excellence and bring us by their protection into the fullest peace.[3]

Comparable expressions of the surpassing merit and influence of Muhammad could readily be quoted from scores of Muslim pens in this generation. Our duty is to study how Muhammad is for these multitudes the supremely significant figure in history and what their conviction means in their experience.

What is this Muslim meaning of Muhammad? The attempt to answer will be the aim of what follows, not an analytical biography. Biographies can be found in several competent studies in English. Our purpose may be served by adopting a division used in a popular account published in 1954 by Fathÿ Radwān, Minister of State in the first revolutionary cabinet in Egypt following the 1952 changes, entitled *Muhammad: the Greatest Revolutionary*. On the title page are the celebrated words of Abū Bakr, the close friend, father-in-law, and first successor of the Prophet, who, summoned to his daughter's apartment after Muhammad's death, turned back the coverlet and addressed the departed leader: "Thou art my father and my mother, O Apostle of God, most sweet in life, most sweet in death"—Muhammad in life, then, and Muhammad in death, or rather, in history.

II

There is a passage in the Qur'ān (Surah 58.12) enjoining an alms on all who seek an interview with the Prophet, though it is added that this is not to deter them if they lack the means. The Prophet was always accessible, though in later years, because of greater pressures or wider veneration, almsgiving became an appropriate prelude. To come into spiritual colloquy with the life of Muhammad is an aspiration that exacts a claim on imagination and is painstaking. The student must be ready to pay in diligence the price of understanding. The Qur'ān, although its biographical data are limited, is our prior source. The traditions are very numerous. Both sources are demanding in their character—the former with its almost untranslatable "feeling," as well as its discouraging repetitions, its lack of order, and its intricacy; the latter with their strange meticulousness, bewildering variety, and tedious fullness. Then there are the difficulties deriving from times and places contrasting so completely with our own, not to mention the formidable relationships between dogma and history in this field. All conspire to make a challenging task for any who would seriously face the question: "What manner of man is this?"

It is not that the general outline of Muhammad's biography is not clear. The hard part is understanding the full import of the facts. The latter can be readily set down. The historical fulcrum of Islam is the *Hijrah,* "emigration," of Muhammad and his small community of believers from Mecca to Medina. This event, marking the beginning of Muslim chronology in A.D. 622, makes the story of Islam a tale of two cities. The transition also marks an evident development in the function of the Prophet, implicit in the transition of the preacher into the ruler, the "warner" into the warrior. Dates in the earlier life of the Prophet have to be reckoned backward from the *Hijrah* at which time he had been teaching and preaching for some twelve or thirteen years. This sets the original call to prophecy at A.D. 609–610, when he was about the age of forty, the date of Muhammad's birth being A.D. 569 or 570. Few figures of comparable significance in history have begun their active careers at so late an age as did the Prophet of Islam.

Mecca was the first of the two towns in the story of primitive Islam. Though often surpassed in later history by imperial centers—Damascus, Baghdad, Córdoba, Istanbul—it has always remained the focal religious point in Islam, its name a synonym for a magnet of the faithful. Such was Mecca at the time of Muhammad's birth. The pilgrims who then came to it from widely scattered areas in the Arabian peninsula were pagans. The *Ka'bah,* or shrine, in the heart of Mecca, contained the famous Black Stone, an object of immense veneration, as well as numerous idols, the most familiar among them being *Al-'Izzat,* goddess of power, *Manāt,* goddess of fate, and *Allāt,* goddess of fertility. These deities were far from being the only objects of worship. Arabian paganism at that time is best described as polydaemonism, the worship of a multiplicity of divine powers or agencies associated with particular natural phenomena or events or places.

There is overwhelming evidence, from inscriptions and from pre-Islamic poetry and nomenclature (as mentioned earlier, Muhammad's own father was named 'Abdallāh), that there was knowledge of a supreme deity called *Allāh*—the God. The essence of Muhammad's message was not the enunciation of the existence, but of the *sole* existence, of *Allāh* and of the criminal folly of all other worship.

Another notable feature of contemporary Arabian society was belief in jinn possession, often evidenced in ejaculation, divination, and the utterance of rhyming prose. One of the first and most persistent accusations against Muhammad was that he was demon-possessed. It seems likely that he feared this himself before he grew into a firm conviction as to the heavenly origin of his revelations. There were dark features about this pre-Islamic Arabian society, this *Jāhiliyyah,* "time of ignorance," prior to the coming of Islam. The pressures of poverty led to the practice of infanticide among the Bedouin tribes. Outside the months of truce there was widespread feuding and intertribal warfare. Attempts had been made earlier, in the sixth century, to bring about some political order and unity, but they had failed for lack of a compelling moral and religious force, such as Islam was shortly to supply.

The picture, however, is not wholly dark, even on the religious side. The Qur'ān speaks of the *Hanīf*s, whose anti-idolatrous sentiment was an important factor in the background of Muhammad's experience. The extent and precise form of the *Hanīf* attitude are somewhat obscure, though the subject has great fascination. But Islam is later described as fulfilling the religion of the *Hanīf*s, whose great ancestral prototype was Abraham, the hero of ancient iconoclasm in the name of the single sovereign Lord. It seems reasonably certain that Muhammad was, in some sense, the spiritual kinsman of these disclaimers of idolatry and that they planted in his searching spirit the seeds of ardor against idol worship, which blossomed into the experience that made him the prophet of the divine unity.

III

The other, and apparently greater, factor in the formation of Muhammad's mission was the presence of "the peoples of the Book"—the Quranic phrase for Jews and Christians—greater because they symbolized the germinal idea of prophecy and of peoples unified around a scriptural center. Scholars have differed widely both as to the details of Arabian Jewry and Arabian Christianity in the sixth century, and as to the circumstances and quality of Muhammad's personal contact with these sources. Traditions about his acquaintance with Christian monks and priests on caravan journeys have to be treated with reserve. If we take the contents of the Qur'ān as the decisive area for discussion of this problem, it would seem conclusive that Muhammad had no personal contact with the written Scriptures of either antecedent faith. The biblical narratives reproduced in the Qur'ān differ considerably and suggest oral, not direct, acquaintance. There is an almost complete absence of what could be claimed as direct quotation from the Bible.[4]

The matter hinges in part on the vexed question of Muhammad's literacy. The well-known phrase *al-nabī al-ummī,* "the unlettered prophet," could signify "the prophet to the people without a book," to those who are as yet scriptureless. Certainly a great part of Muhammad's vocation lay in the conviction that his fellow Arabs should also have their divine book, an Arabic Qur'ān, a purpose that awaited an Arab prophet in the same tradition as Moses, David, and Jesus. Because non-Jews are referred to in the Qur'ān as *ummī,* the word is sometimes taken as meaning "without scriptures of their own," rather than "illiterate," though this argument is weakened by the fact that Jews also are occasionally referred to as *ummī*. In their case it can only mean "illiterate." When the Qur'ān states explicitly that Muhammad did not write the Qur'ān, it may mean that he did not compose it—as orthodox Islam firmly insists he did not—rather than that he could not actually pen any word.

Be the historical verdict on this question what it may, two facts are clear. Traditional Islam believes Muhammad to have been actually illiterate, so that the Qur'ān is indubitably and entirely God's Word. Muhammad can hardly in fact have been a *reader* of any older Scriptures. What then of his oral sources of knowledge? Here, too, there is a tantalizing divergence of opinion. Some hold that the predominant influence was Jewish, others that it was Christian. The most confident theory on the Jewish side is that which actually gives Muhammad a Jewish rabbi for tutor in Mecca, assuming that he sought out such a person when his religious yearning was first aroused.[5]

All that can be said with certainty is that Muhammad knew of Jews and Christians and something of their history; that the former were numerous around Medina and present in Mecca; that the latter were strong across the Red Sea in Ethiopia and had a checkered declining role in southern Arabia and in the border areas of such princedoms as the Ghassanids in the north, where Byzantium merged into the peninsula. It was not, by and large, a Christianity calculated to present Muhammad with a fully authentic picture of Christ and the Church. Some of the urgent issues of early Church history—docetism and monophysitism— are mirrored in the Quranic account of Jesus as noncrucified Prophet-Messiah. But it gave to Muhammad, under what precise circumstances may never be known, the most fundamental concepts in his vocation and in subsequent Islam: a sure monotheism and a prophetic mission in which a divine relationship of revelation, through scriptures, created a community of faith. It was a tremendous step when Muhammad became assured of himself as a new and final term in prophetic continuity, making a new book, and thence a new faith.

IV

If this be the creative background of Muhammad the Prophet, what of the circumstantial setting of Muhammad the man? Mecca was "no mean city," with its pilgrim prestige and its wide-ranging caravan commerce. For Islam was not of desert origin, despite the persisting illusion that calls its rigid monotheism a reflection of desert vastness and the majestic sun. In its genesis it was an urban entity. Its founder was not one of the *badū,* but a citizen and reputedly a merchant. He was a posthumous child and became in early boyhood a complete orphan, protected first by his grandfather 'Abd al-Muttalib and later by his uncle Abū Tālib. His parents were 'Abdallāh, grandson of Hāshim, and Āminah. The young child thus knew the privations of poverty and yet also the dignity of a family line. For his parents belonged to a branch of the powerful Quraish, custodians of the sacred *Ka'bah* and the leading tribe of Mecca.

History has little to record, though tradition is fertile, about those early years. Muhammad rose to manhood with a reputation for reliability and at twenty-five was married to Khadījah, a widow his senior in years, in whose service he is said to have been employed. The marriage gave Muhammad security and domestic happiness though not—unhappily—any male issue surviving. Four daughters of the union grew to adult life. Two sons died in early infancy. Muhammad remained in sole wedlock to Khadījah until her death, which occurred at a very low ebb in his fortunes, just before the scene moves to Medina. His plural marriages belong entirely to the period following Khadījah's death. She played an important role in the formative years of Muhammad's vocation and he was steadfastly devoted to her memory. Her death is probably reflected in some of the changes that later supervened.

Little is known about the Prophet's personal and commercial life in the decade and a half between his marriage and his prophetic call. But undoubtedly two formative ideas were working deeply in his soul—the oppressive folly of idolatry and the role of prophethood, through scriptures, in the life of great religious communities, both corroborated by the strong, if rare, example of the *Hanīf*s, with their repudiation of idols and their wistfulness for larger truth.

Brooding in the gaunt foothills of Mount Hirā' in the region of his native Mecca, Muhammad came to the strong conviction that idolatry was criminal folly and that the one God commanded utterance against it. "Let the word be spoken." "Cry in the name of the Lord." God who taught man the use of the pen and from whom flowed all the scholar's wisdom was about to teach a more urgent and more potent truth, a word of mouth, an oral affirmation. Steadily the mission to be the mouthpiece apprehended Muhammad until it drove him into preaching and transformed the Meccan citizen into the "warner" from the Lord.

Such was the ground and meaning of Muhammad's call, in a brooding wilderness experience, where facts of conscious observation in the contemporary scene became articulate in a personal calling to utterance and warning in the city. Though Muslims in general hold that Muhammad's call did not derive from the conscious processes of his mind, but came wholly from without, so that what he felt and said was entirely God's and not the product of genius, or travail, or even of intelligence that were the Prophet's own, it seems impossible to do justice to his stature without reference to the personal context.

Let us, then, accompany Muhammad on the decisive journey to Mount Hirā' when the first revelation came. It was the forerunner of many and the climax of a deepening experience. The earliest accounts vary in lesser details but describe Muhammad as within, and then without, a cave. He became aware of a voice and of a figure that stood compellingly on every line of vision wherever he turned or walked. The figure was the angel Gabriel bearing the message of God. Gabriel's command, if the traditional identification of the first revelation is correct, was to recite, cry, speak, in the name of the Lord:

> Recite in the name of thy Lord Who created
> Created man from a clot.
> Recite! For thy Lord is most gracious
> Who taught with the pen
> Taught man what he knows not [Surah 96.1–4].

The commanding voice assured the wondering listener that he was the Apostle of God. Referring later to the same experience, Muhammad is made to say:

It is none other than a revelation revealed. One mighty in power taught it to him, One endued with strength and he stood erect on the highest horizon. He drew near and came nearer still, until he was within two bows' length or nearer and He revealed unto his servant that which he revealed [Surah 53.4–10].

The injunction was to "read," or "recite." The word means the making vocal of that which is already written. The revelation, here in its initiation and throughout, is understood as the coming down of a preexistent book, a transaction that extended over some twenty-three years during which the contents of the original book ("The Mother of the Book") preserved in heaven with God were uttered, recorded, and then perpetually recited in devotion, on earth. The instrumentality of this process known as *tanzīl,* "sending down," is usually that of Gabriel or of a divine spirit. The recipience on the earthly side is Muhammad's alone, standing as the last in the long series of prophets each of whom had received earlier books.

It was in the nature of Muhammad's initial experience that it should be successively repeated, from that first occasion in the month of Ramadān until death terminated the then perfect book and took away the point of its earthly impact. It was well that the experience renewed itself, for Muhammad's first reaction was dubiety and apprehension. He feared lest he had been beset with malicious jinns or was the victim of a destructive illusion sent to mock him. Reassurance, however, slowly displaced misgiving, thanks in part to the tenacious confidence and discerning kindness of Khadījah, who solaced and supported her husband. He had great need of her faith and friendship.

The revelations were accompanied by intense emotional stress, physical limpness, perspiration, and a state of trance. Though the onset of the experiences subsequently came to occur without the same intensity of these phenomena, they seem always to have been present in some form as the qualifying accompaniment of the "Quranic" state, as distinct from the other, personal deliverances of the Prophet incorporated into the later traditions. In some accounts the state of Quranic revelation had further physical symptoms, so that a camel, for example, sank down under the sudden weight when the Prophet was riding. It would appear that the coming of the experiences was unpredictable. In the Medinan years they bear more the appearance of conscious relationship to particular, legal, or administrative situations for which directives were necessary. This is not the time or place to seek to penetrate into the deep inward mystery of Muhammad's revelatory experience. It is perhaps too distant and too charged an area of historical significance for any purely scientific analysis to be either feasible or sound. What is of vastly greater importance is how these experiences shaped Muhammad's life story and what they came to mean for him in terms of character and destiny and for his followers as a God-given reality.

V

As his assurance of the validity of his call increased, Muhammad began slowly to fulfill the preacher's commission and the revelations came in greater frequency. The style and form of his message is reflected in the earliest Meccan Surahs of the Qur'ān, with their ecstatic quality—short, staccato sentences, proclaiming the majesty of nature, the evil folly of idol worship, and the impending judgment. Though the style later became more argumentative and hortatory, with lengthy passages developing the themes of patriarchal history, the earliest deliverances are fervid and trumpet-like.

Muhammad's reception in Mecca was at first dubious. His hearers were uncertain how to take him. Was he unbalanced, jinn-possessed, or eccentric? As he persisted, however, and became more defiantly assertive, within his small, mainly domestic, circle of early adherents, bemused interest passed into scorn and contumely. These, in turn, grew into active hostility as the Meccans came increasingly to sense in Muhammad's doctrines a threat to their dearest vested interests. They could not have known that their *Ka'bah,* purified of its idols, would remain as the integral center of Muhammad's monotheism, its pilgrimage prestige unimpaired. Had they known this in advance, their championing of idolatry might have been less insistent. But in prospect a threat to idols looked unmistakably like a threat to the *Ka'bah* and thus a threat to the hegemony and income of the Quraish.

Despite this intensifying antagonism, Muhammad was per-

sonally secure in the constancy of his powerful uncle Abū Tālib,
who without accepting Islam refused to bow to intimidation or
subterfuge and surrender his nephew. Others in the small group
of believers, being more exposed, suffered considerably. In the
sixth year of the revelations Muhammad encouraged a party to
seek refuge in Ethiopia, whither a second emigration followed
shortly afterward. The earliest of Muhammad's prominent disciples after Khadījah was Abū Bakr, *Al-Siddīq,* "the trustworthy," two years Muhammad's junior and a staunch comrade.
'Umar, another close associate often thought of as the Saul of
Islam, by reason of his dramatic conversion, acceded after the
Ethiopian emigration. Both were to become fathers-in-law to
Muhammad.

The fewness of these converts and the resistant quality of Meccan heathenism perplexed and tried the Prophet.[6] Was the new
movement to remain perpetually in jeopardy, a despised minority
with no Arabian foothold, compelled to seek sanctuary across the
Red Sea and denied victory in the central citadel of the idolatry
against which it was set? Muhammad slowly ripened into a decision that shaped the whole future of Islam. The faith must find
expression in a community that would assure it external force and
the opportunity to prevail against the opposition. The Qur'ān, in
this middle Meccan period, lays increasing stress on the historical
parallels of earlier prophets, all of whom are pictured as manifestly victorious over their foes. Noah's detractors are drowned
in the flood; those of Moses in the Red Sea. Abraham and Joseph,
teachers of the divine unity, come into their own. Just as it has
been with those generations, so it would be with the scornful fellow citizens of the Meccan Prophet.

Little is clearly known about the internal organization and worship of the Muslim group inside Mecca during these early years.
Institutional Islam is more readily studied in the second city of its
genesis—Medina. Meanwhile, however, that city had not come
within the conscious hopes of Muhammad. But the decision was
shaping within him that if Mecca did not respond, the faith of
Islam must root itself elsewhere and find some civic cradle where
it might one day grow into a purging conqueror of Mecca. The
eleventh and twelfth years after Muhammad's call moved imper-
ceptibly in the direction of such thoughts, with the future center

beginning to present itself. The developments came only just in time to save Islam from the possible Meccan consequences of the deaths, in 619, of both Khadījah and Abū Tālib, the devoted wife and the loyal protector.

Though their passing exposed and saddened the Prophet, it also sharpened the decision facing the Meccans. Should they slay Muhammad, their own kin? Putting him under a ban had been tried without success. There seemed no hope of silencing him. Nor was he to be cajoled into retreat. On the other hand, since 'Umar, he had won no conspicuous allegiance. Even while they were debating, he had returned from a preaching mission to Al Tā'if, southeast of Mecca, chastened, scorned, and upbraided, with nothing save scars and defeat. There seemed little likelihood that any other center would receive him. Though Abū Tālib no longer remained to deter their threats, they perhaps need not take the irrevocable step. Islam might peter out in the frustrations of an odd enthusiast.

If they did reason thus, the Meccans reckoned without Yathrib, the important city to the north, soon to be renamed *Madīnat-al-Nabī*, "the city of the Prophet." A few of its pilgrim people encountered Muhammad in Mecca after his return from Al-Tā'if. They showed a welcome interest in his message and took back in their hearts the seeds of potential discipleship. Jewish influence in Medina was greater than in the Meccan region and may have disposed its citizens toward Muhammad's message. There were also family ties. Muhammad's great-grandfather Hāshim had married a Medinan. Internally, the situation in Medina awaited a master hand that might curb dissension and unite the factions. In 621 the Medinan group returned on pilgrimage and to Muhammad's great joy demonstrated its continued affinity with his teaching. In the First Pledge of Al-'Aqabah, they bound themselves to abandon idolatry, theft, adultery, fornication, and infanticide, and to obey the Prophet in all that was right. They returned to their city and subsequently called for a teacher who had marked success in widening the Muslim allegiance.

Muhammad's hopes grew. "Northward, look!" he might have said, "the land is bright." He bided his time, concealing from the Meccans his Medinan links. He knew they could be relied on to appreciate that Muhammad at large would be far more serious a danger than a restive and frustrated Muhammad in Mecca. In 622, the Medinan Muslims returned, reporting a larger adherence to Islam, and entered into the Second Pledge of Al-'Aqabah, this time binding themselves to defend the Prophet.

This undertaking was all that Muhammad needed. It was an implicit invitation to seek a new base of activities in the northern city. He ordered his disciples to emigrate to Medina where the Medinan Muslims were ready to receive them. The famous *Hijrah* happened with most timely expedition. The suspicions of the Quraish had been aroused and they had been anxious at all costs to forestall such a departure. But they were the victims, in part, of their own indecision and had not reckoned that the whole Muslim band would forsake all their immovable property. When at length they did take action, Muhammad and Abū Bakr, following in the wake of the main emigration, succeeded in eluding pursuit and made good their escape.

VI

The emigrating party was probably less than seven score strong but it made one of the most successful voluntary exiles in human history. The step brought clearly into the open the logic of Muhammad's inner decision. The faith was built into a community. The city of the lawgiver and ruler made possible the ultimate reconquest of the city of the preacher. The tale of the two towns passed into its second period and both Muhammad the man and the Qur'ān the book reflect the inclusive meaning of the transition. Muhammad had spent more than twelve years proclaiming the message in which his mission was generated. The following ten years were to see him establishing the empire in which his mission was embodied and enforced.

Henceforward, the biographer finds an increasing amalgam of faith and rule, of creed and organization, in the Prophet's story. Those parts of the Qur'ān belonging to the Medinan years are predominately legal and political. Their concern is with campaigns, confiscations, customs, and behavior, rather than with patriarchs and preaching. There are corresponding changes in the role and quality of the central leader himself. Those unmistakable elements of greatness in the suffering preacher-prophet, bearing obloquy and calumny with tenacious fidelity to the truth he had been given to see, loom greater in retrospect than the qualities demonstrated in the mingled magnanimity and opportunism that mark the post-*Hijrah* leader.

When Muhammad arrived in Medina the position was fraught with peril. The allegiance in which he had read an invitation to immigration was far from unanimous. The non-Muslim Medinans, at worst resentful, at best uncommitted, needed to be brought into unequivocal allegiance. Even the Muslim Medinans were committed only to a defensive pledge. Islam now had two component groups, in a situation potential of much strife and misunderstanding unless a sagacious mind controlled them. For the Meccan fugitives were without homes and possessions, helpless guests of their Medinan co-religionists. Yet they had been longer in the Prophet's obedience and had suffered more. Tact and statesmanship were manifestly required. That Muhammad lacked neither was symbolized when he rode into the city and, throwing the reins on the neck of his camel, vowed that the camel should decide where his headquarters and the first mosque should be located—thus saving himself from the invidious consequences of any personal choice.

Though he succeeded resoundingly in riding out these initial difficulties, there was one area of his expectation where Muhammad suffered acute disappointment. Throughout his preaching he had looked confidently toward the Jews and Christians, as "people of the Book," to welcome and accept his prophetic claims. In Medina this hope had occasion to be tested, at least in respect of the Jews, far more extensively than was possible in Mecca. The result bitterly contrasted with the Prophet's hopes. Closer proximity to larger numbers of Jews soon revealed to Muhammad that, far from acknowledgment, Jewry treated him with amused disdain. His claims they flatly rejected as pretentious. The inevitable consequence was that Muhammad became increasingly hostile to the Jews and interpreted their nonacceptance as disloyalty to their own inheritance.

Islam became, from this point, much more distinctive and consciously self-sufficient. The Quranic passages exhorting to friendly relations with the "people of the Book" and confirmatory study of their scriptures give way to flat disavowal and explicit condemnation. "God fight them, what liars they are" (Surah 9.30). Most significantly of all, the *qiblah*, "direction" of Muslim prayer, was changed at this time from Jerusalem to Mecca, evidently to the initial consternation of some of the Prophet's own followers.[7] At this time Mecca, though associated with traditions of Abraham, was still idolatrous. The change of *qiblah* surely implied the intention to repossess it. The monotheism of Jerusalem was a perennial symbol, which was nonetheless abandoned in the name of Islamic independence and distinctiveness.

Apparently in the same context is the greater emphasis concerning Abraham at this time. In the early preaching he had been cited as a preacher of God's unity and as a champion against idols. Ishmael now comes into great prominence in association with Abraham and both are linked with Mecca and the building of the *Ka'bah*. Islam is proclaimed as the faith of Abraham, going back beyond the Mosaic law, whose Jewish legatees had been unfaithful. Similarly we find in the years after the *Hijrah* a growth of distinctive Muslim rituals and practices, some of which will be our concern in the chapter that follows.

Meanwhile the Jews, having failed to fulfill Muhammad's expectations, came increasingly into the line of Muslim hostility. But they were not alone in this experience. A kind of triangular situation developed in which the "corners" are Muhammad, the Meccans, and the Jews—excluding the non-Jewish, non-Muslim elements in Medina itself, whose steady approximation to Muhammad's cause was brought about largely by their involvement with him in other struggles. It proved difficult to live in the same city as Muhammad and not become physically implicated in his purpose. War, deliberate if intermittent, is what followed.

VII

To set forth this period in the Prophet's career objectively and without offending modern Muslim susceptibilities is difficult in the extreme. His departure from Mecca and Meccan hostility to the prosecutor of its idols certainly made for a situation of potential conflict. It should be noted that some in Muhammad's allegiance and circle, remaining in Mecca after his departure, were unmolested. The Muslim thesis, however, is that the campaigns that followed were essentially defensive. They were necessary to the survival of Islam. The position of the Qur'ān itself is that war, not least in the month of truce, is essentially an evil, but the threatened extinction of Islam is a far greater evil (Surah 2.217). Peace, therefore, is not to be preferred to war, until Islam is inviolable and secure. Muhammad is to be the judge of the extent and persistence of the danger that justifies fighting.

Some observers interpret this necessity to fight as arising from the need to provide, through booty, for the unhoused *Muhājirūn,* "immigrants," to consolidate all Medina by implication in Muhammad's cause, and to accumulate the means of warfare for the final conquest of Mecca. But taking the basic thesis of Muslim apology that the wars were defensive, another basic decision is evidently involved—namely, that religious survival should be served and guaranteed by force. Muhammad's policy, as recognized by the highest Muslim evaluation of the events now to be summarized, was to answer the situation as the soldier does.

Medina under the Prophet's rulership thus found itself increasingly implicated in hostilities with the Meccans. They began over the Meccan caravans whose route to the north passed precariously within Medinan range. The Muslims participating in these activities became steadily more bold and more numerous until the Battle of Badr closed the first chapter of the Medinan period with a clear victory to which the Qur'ān refers as "the day of the *furqān,*" "criterion"—a day of putting to the test and of the emergence of Islam as the signally favored, and so distinctive, cause (Surah 8.41). The battle might better be described as an encounter: by later standards the numbers involved were slight. But even skirmishes can be historically decisive.

Having tidings of a Muslim venture, a returning Meccan caravan from the north sent for protective reinforcements from the city and it was with these that the Muslim band engaged. Under the Prophet's own skillful military leadership, some three hundred Muslims dispersed a thousand Meccans, losing only fourteen slain to some fifty of the Meccans, not to mention a large number of captives. Muslim history regards the Battle of Badr as crucial. Certainly the sword was unleashed and the scabbard cast away. The *jihād,* "appeal to battle," had been irrevocably invoked.

Before the Muslims faced the inevitable Meccan reaction to this reverse, the opportunity was taken to bring increasing pressure upon the Jews, several of whom were put to death or dispossessed. Within a month after the return from Badr there were individual acts of intimidation, culminating in the expulsion of the Banū Qainuqā'a. Almost a year after Badr came the Meccan advance to revenge. This time the issue was more in their favor. Apparently in overconfidence the Muslims lost discipline and were in danger of being routed. They were rallied only in a desperate effort by the Prophet himself. The Quranic passage relating to the battle (Surah 3.120ff.) rebukes the Muslim presumption and interprets the reverse as a test of faith and a deserved chastisement. Over seventy Muslims were slain to some twenty of the Quraish. Muhammad had need of all his resourcefulness to survive the serious loss of prestige, though the Meccans on their side do not seem to have realized or utilized the full extent of their victory. They withdrew after mutilating the dead and Muhammad, after a delayed show of pursuit, returned to Medina.

Perhaps enheartened by this setback, perhaps fearful of further Muslim acts of hostility, the Jews of the Medinan region began to make closer cause with the Quraish. Their economically superior position exposed them to dangers of expulsion such as had already been indicated. The increasing menace from the Muslims suggested common action with Mecca, with which, however, there were few other ties. It was the familiar story of the common enemy bringing together unwilling allies.

Although it seems clear that Jewish elements were implicated in Meccan enmity to Muhammad, it is also clear that both elements in the uneasy alliance were blundering and vacillating. Any situation like that confronting them, and relating to an adversary of Muhammad's resolve and resource, calls for comparable resolution and tenacity. These the Jews and Meccans lacked—as is only too evident from the ill-starred and inept "siege" of Medina known in Muslim history as "the Battle of the Ditch." Acting inadvisably out of fear and bewilderment, they succeeded only in fulfilling their worst dread.

The siege was raised after the besiegers found the weather too cold for them and the irresolute Quraish, lacking energetic leadership, withdrew, leaving their Jewish partners to face the accumulated wrath of Muhammad. There followed the massacre of the Banū Quraizah, which marks the darkest depth of Muslim policy, a depth that the palliatives suggested by some modern Muslim historians quite fail to measure. The whole tribe was dispossessed and, after suing for clemency, the women and children were enslaved; the men, traditionally numbered at seven hundred, were executed beside long trench graves in a day of signal terror. The dreadful fate of the Banū Quraizah far outweighed their deserts and contrasted darkly with the magnanimity of Muhammad when subsequently he faced their Meccan allies in the "siege" after his reconquest of the holy city.

But the circumstances were different. Muhammad, by canons of soldierly wisdom, could hardly yet afford to be magnanimous. Not all the *Muhājirūn* Muslims were yet repropertied, nor was the situation at all secure in the region. In approving, and later eulogizing in a funeral speech, the judge who had decreed the sentence on the Banū Quraizah, Muhammad was no doubt following the behests of a stern policy. Certainly the step succeeded. Disaffection, both religious and political, was cowed into paralysis, if not submission, throughout Medina.

The next major confiscatory enterprise took the Muslims some hundred miles north to the Jews of rich Khaibar, who could have been only remotely related to Medinan affairs but who nonetheless were made to forfeit all their possessions. This immense plunder greatly consolidated and enlarged Muhammad's potential.

Muhammad's decision to revisit Mecca in A.D. 628, six years after the *Hijrah,* revealed the direction in which his policy was moving and for which the potential was required. The Meccans, having word of his coming, refused to admit him as a pilgrim, fearing the consequences, but entered into an agreement whereby he would be free to make the pilgrimage peacefully the following year, when the Meccans themselves would evacuate the city for three days. As part of this compact, known as the Treaty of Al-Hudaibiyyah, Muhammad agreed to a ten-year truce between the Muslims and the Quraish, during which either side would be free to federate with other tribes. He also allowed a Meccan right to extradite all fugitive Meccans coming over to Islam, and conceding that any fugitive Muslims returning to Mecca should not be handed back by the Meccans. This seemed to some of Muhammad's followers a concession of weakness. He was criticized also for deferring to a Meccan demand that he should not sign the treaty document as Apostle of God, but as Muhammad, son of 'Abdallāh.

But the Prophet was playing his hand shrewdly and overrode the querulous Muslims. He had established a kind of equality with the Meccans, by having negotiated with them. The pilgrimage permission was important. He calculated that there would be few, if any, Muslim fugitives to Mecca, and would-be converts sent back to Mecca would be rescued by Islam in the final conquest. The truce would give valuable time for preparations and tribal accessions. When Muhammad returned to Medina, the logic of events leading to their consummation in Mecca's reconquest unfolded itself steadily. Within two years the Prophet returned not to debate with the Quraish but to accept their capitulation. The story of the two cities was moving to a dramatic climax in which they would both become Islam's.

There was first, however, the intervening pilgrimage duly performed in 629, under the terms of the treaty, which the Meccans strictly observed, evacuating their city while Muhammad and the Muslims performed the rites, but refusing, when requested, to prolong their absence more than three days. The visit brought Muhammad a few notable converts, including the custodian of the *Ka'bah* and a future leader, Khālid, destined for great military exploits.[8] The star of Islam was moving into the ascendant; that of the Quraish was waning.

Muhammad's plans for the final settlement with his Meccan adversaries were carefully laid and boldly carried through. Despite clearly growing aspirations for the expansion of the faith into northern regions, indicated in letters summoning several potentates in the Christian world to islamize, and in expeditions into Ghassanid territory, he concentrated on the prior Meccan objective. When a tribe bound in treaty with the Quraish attacked another tribe in alliance with Medina, he denounced the truce and refused to heed the pleas of Abū Safyān, personally made in Medina, for its restoration. The head of the Quraish returned to Mecca with no assurances and much misgiving. But even with this premonition, the Meccans were completely surprised by the speed and thoroughness of the Prophet's moves.

Muhammad gathered a formidable force and set out early in the ninth year after the *Hijrah,* not revealing his destination until secrecy had become unnecessary. As he drew near to Mecca, Al-'Abbās, his uncle, came out and joined him and was followed later by Abū Safyān. The Quraish resistance evaporated before it could be mobilized. Four Muslim columns entered the city and occupied it in the name of Islam. The Prophet's triumph was complete. The tale of the struggle of the two cities had ended; the tale of their new empire was about to begin.

VIII

Muhammad, conqueror of Mecca, proved a magnanimous victor. The Meccans were required to abandon and destroy their idols and seem to have done so with far less compunction than later characterized the heathen of Al-Tā'if. There was almost no bloodshed. The Meccans were assured that their city was the dearest place on earth to the Prophet's heart. Its citizens as Muslims underwent no confiscations—the returning *Muhājirūn* did not even re-claim their former properties. Muhammad was anxious to pacify Mecca as rapidly as possible and to incorporate the purged *Ka'bah* into Islamic pilgrimage, thus preserving for the new faith the cohesive power of Meccan prestige.

The subsequent year was spent in extending the sway of Islam over an increasing number of tribes beyond Mecca until, at the pilgrimage of the tenth year after the *Hijrah,* Muhammad, who was not present, caused the "Immunity," or "Release," to be read as an edict by 'Alī. This document, preserved in Surah 9, served notice on all pagans that they could no longer participate in any pilgrimage to Mecca. It gave the tribes four months in which to return to their homes and, thereafter, declared them lawfully immune from protection and exposed to any Muslim attack as long as they failed to islamize—saving only those having treaty arrangements with the Prophet. When these had run their course, such groups might also be attacked.

In the same Surah, though not in the "release" itself, is the command to fight Jews and Christians until they also become subject peoples. Thus was enunciated the basic principle of *jihād,* "martial endeavor," on behalf of Islam, going beyond the earlier provision that enjoined fighting only after the enemy had first attacked. It thus became a ruling precept in Islam that all areas of non-Islam were areas whose conquest the true Muslim was enjoined to seek until the inhabitants either submitted or were reduced to subject status, the second alternative obtaining only in respect of the tolerated minorities, "the people of the Book." It will be seen that this principle was the extension in permanent, legal form of the plan of action developed by Muhammad in the early years of the *Hijrah.* The pattern that had been brought to conspicuous success in the case of Mecca was to become the precedent for all other victories, far and wide, over territories yet to be brought under the political suzerainty of Medina and into religious allegiance to Mecca, now cleansed of idolatry.

The Prophet himself survived to see only the beginnings of the *jihād* that, within a decade of his death, was to add Egypt, the Levant, the valley of the twin rivers, and western Persia to Islam in one of the swiftest conquests of history. Symbolically, at the onset of his last illness, an expedition was ready to set out into the borderlands of Arabia and Byzantium. He completed the farewell pilgrimage to Mecca, one year after the "release." In a moving address he proclaimed the perfecting of the religion, *Al-Islām,* as the culmination of the divine mercy to humankind.

Muhammad was sixty-three years of age. Worn by two and a half decades of intense emotional and spiritual stress—as recipient of the Qur'ān, as leader, ruler, legislator and nerve-center of a new and vibrant politico-religious entity—he seems to have sensed the approaching end. The climax of his last illness was dramatic. When death took him, it seemed to some of his stunned and grief-stricken disciples that it could not be. It was A.D. 632. When finally Abū Bakr, his longtime companion and immediate successor in authority, prevailed upon the distracted assembly gathered in the mosque to realize the truth of the incredible, it was with the reminder that the Prophet, who had now breathed his last, was no more than the servant of the ever living God. Abū Bakr's speech beside the death precincts linked together, as the call to prayer has never ceased to do, the one God and the Apostle, the first faith of Islam that belongs with the second: "There is no god save God and Muhammad is his Messenger."

To the numbed and distraught faithful in Medina and beyond, to the new and sometimes dubious adherents throughout the peninsula, some of whom were ready to withdraw in pagan reassertion, it was as if some giant oak that filled the landscape had been felled, making a great void that left the very scheme of things shorn and unfamiliar. How Abū Bakr, and 'Umar after him, succeeded in rallying the whole cause and launching it upon the vast career for which the Prophet had shaped and destined it is part of Islamic history. What faith, devotion, and religious awe have done with the vacuum left by the Prophet's death, filling it with the possessive instincts of communal memory, will concern us shortly in this chapter. It remains to try to take, in some inclusive assessment, the measure of the historical Muhammad.

IX

Of the broad sweep and import of the facts as now summarized there can be little doubt, though specialists will be always delving afresh to reconsider some particular aspect. In the final analysis, it is not so much the facts but the criteria that constitute the problem for the biographers of Muhammad. Should they look backward into Arabian paganism and find the Prophet great and reforming? Should they look forward into the first Muslim century and beyond to see in this biography one of the rarest potentialities of human history? Or should they look backward into the great Old Testament prophetic tradition, to Amos, Hosea, and Jeremiah, to find in Muhammad a strange, and yet unmistakable, shift in the whole concept and expression of prophethood? Or backward, less far, to the hills of Galilee and Judea where there are criteria of almost insupportable contrast? Should the criteria be only local and contemporary, when Muslim faith and practice give to the facts of that place and time a significance of universal range? Perhaps here, as not seldom in human relationships, the task of outsiders is only to formulate the right questions. They can never give the answer from within, though they may well be in a better position than the adherent to see what it should include.

Two crucial points are all that can be made. It should be understood, in the first place, that to account for Muhammad in terms of personal genius, though an increasing number of Muslims tend to do so, is to part company with orthodoxy. When Sayyid Amīr 'Alī, for example, in his well-known and often reprinted *The Spirit of Islam,* spoke of "the wisdom of the inspired lawgiver" and referred to Quranic institutions as Muhammad's provision, he was adapting the older belief that the revelation came wholly from God, without involving Muhammad's conscious will or reason. The traditional view insists throughout on the instrumentality of the Prophet, not his initiative; on his being the agent, not the originator. Nevertheless, it is impossible to resist the conclusion that historical Islam is decisively shaped by the manner of man Muhammad was.

In the second place, there is need to beware of missing the ultimate in the circumstantial details. The latter have been the theme of much unhappy controversy that has tended to end in confusion. Too much and too little is then made of him. Too much, it may be, of plural marriages and too little of their political, and other, significance and of Muhammad's devotion to Khadījah; too much of the opportunist tactics, too little of the unswerving singleness of mind; too much of the tribal confiscations and repressive measures, too little of the solicitude for orphans and magnanimity to certain foes; too much of his ruthlessness, too little of the hypocrites and false dealers with whom the Qur'ān affirms he was often surrounded. Or it may be that, conversely, too much is made of Muhammad's circumstances and too little of his obligation to the absolutes of every age. If much of the criticism is too naive, it shares that quality with much of the vindication. Muhammad has been condemned, and justified, in terms that have not taken the measure of their theme. He has proved, both for good and ill, profounder than much criticism and eulogy.

Where, then, shall we seek this ultimate decision? Surely in the supreme crisis of the biography where the faith has located and dated its genesis. As the tale of two towns, the Prophet's biography is finally the story of a crucial choice, no less crucial than that implicit in the contrasted Gospel saying: "The cup that my Father has given me, shall I not drink it?" It is the decision arising from the question: "How should prophethood succeed?" What is the final relationship of the messenger of God to those to whom he is sent when they refuse to hear? The Muhammadan decision here is formative of all else in Islam. It was a decision for community, for resistance, for external victory, for pacification and rule. The decision for the Cross—no less conscious, no less formative, no less inclusive—was the contrary decision.

It is impossible to say precisely when the choice became final in Muhammad's career. We have suggested that he determined on a new center because he sought a means of prophetic victory. But it may be that, finding himself in a new center, he resolved to make it an instrument for the submission of the old. Some have argued a marked deterioration in the character of Muhammad in the Medinan years. That is probably too simple, mistaking a symptom for its source. The deeper truth is that at some point Muhammad elected for a religious authority armed with sinews of war and means of government, and that the decision worked itself out in character, conduct, and destiny. Externally it succeeded. It has become fashionable in vindicating the decision to insist that it was reluctant and uncharacteristic:

> He who never in his life had wielded a weapon, to whom the sight of human suffering caused intense pain and pity, and who against all the canons of Arab manliness, wept bitterly at the loss of his children or disciples . . . this man was now compelled from the necessities of the situation, and against his own inclinations, to repel the attacks of the enemy by force of arms, to organize his followers for self-defense, and often to send out expeditions to anticipate treacherous and sudden onslaughts.[9]

The earliest Muslim historians do not bear out this idealistic view. But the more out of character the choice, if so it be, the more evidently chosen. The more fully the modern Muslim interpretation of the choice be accepted, the more decisive its quality as the way Muhammad took to answer the fundamental question confronting all religious mission: "How shall, how should, the truth prevail?" Opposition there was, in Mecca; vested interest, bigotry, sin, and evil. Bearing the brunt of that opposition in single-minded devotion, Muhammad the preacher is a person whose nobility still reaches us through the intervening years. Is the returning conqueror a greater figure?

X

The meaning of the muezzin's witness to the Apostle of Islam is not, of course, limited to his biography. The Prophet's passing, as we saw, left a tremendous vacancy in the lives and emotions of his followers. But death itself in certain ways closed up the gap it had created and Muhammad in death became the universal possession of Muslim history, so soon and so far to spread in the world. It did so in that the vacuum, for all practical purposes, demanded to be filled.

The institution of the Caliphate was the answer. Abū Bakr immediately stepped into the administrative authority of Muhammad and with 'Umar, his next successor, provided the leadership for which the new day of Muslim expansion called. Whether we regard this as a divinely willed succession or an empirical solution to an obvious need (the latter view being very recent), the fact is the same. Muhammad had been so towering a figure that wherever his mantle fell it necessarily conferred immense prestige and authority. Its first two bearers were equal to their destiny, and what they inaugurated continued through all vicissitudes until 1924.

This succession, however, was civil and administrative only. Muhammad as the Prophet was unique, final, irrepeatable. Thus death closed as well as occasioned the prophetic break. It was true that Muhammad would no longer be there to receive Quranic revelation. But by the same token that volume was now entire and complete. The loss of the Apostle was the final fulfillment of the Book. Those twenty-three or so years had sufficed for its coming down and the point of its earthly impact was in that sense no longer necessary. Muhammad passed into history, in the legacy his death had made final and his apostleship had made complete. Any consideration of Muhammad in history takes us at once to the holy Book of Islam, of which he was the human instrument and which epitomizes so much of his story.

Some brief attempt will be made below, in chapter 7, to appreciate the Muslim significance of the Qur'ān. This book, among the shortest of Holy Books if allowance is made for much repeated material, shows a marked development of style from the sharp poetic language of the earliest Surahs, to the long, prosaic, legal form of the latest. The substance also reflects a similar evolution. Muhammad is first the "warner" and prophet proclaiming judgment on idolatry. He passes into exhortation and preaching, drawing at length on the example of patriarchs and former prophets to enforce his appeal against recalcitrants. Later this historical material gives way to the themes of the legislator and the leader, directing his community in peace and war, amid the gathering issues of its life and struggle. The whole Book is a repository of the Muslim story, though it never sets out to be biographical or historical. References to historical events outside Arabia and Islam are rare. But the very stuff of the development, arising from the original call to recite and culminating in the perfecting of the religion, is here in all its inward quality and drama. The Book perpetuates, as it were, the preaching and the leading by which the Prophet both summoned and shaped his people.

The Qur'ān is the ultimate miracle of Islam. It is the final evidence of the divine origin of the Prophet's mission. Its Arabic eloquence is indicative of its source in God: its bearer was illiterate. Its literary form, in the orthodox view, is inextricably part of its nature. Its contents alone do not constitute it as the Qur'ān. Inasmuch as translation inevitably destroys the form, however successfully it renders the contents, translation has been regarded until the second quarter of this century as generally inadvisable and impossible. The initiative for translation has mainly come, until lately, from non-Islamic sources. Although orthodoxy has come now to admit the desirability of making it available for non-Muslims, such non-Arabic renderings are technically not the Qur'ān, but only its meaning.[10]

The Qur'ān has a culminating relationship to all other scriptures which it confirms insofar as they are valid and corrects where they have been corrupted. Muhammad is thus the "seal of the prophets" with whom divine revelation reached its climax. This conviction of continuity with previous scriptures is an important reason why the Muslim is satisfied that Islam is final and that all valid religion tends toward it.

The Qur'ān is the determinative source of all dogma and law. Through it the overriding sense of God through the Prophet, of the Prophet on behalf of God, that makes Islam, is continually

renewed to the devout soul. The Qur'ān brings Mecca and Medina, as the Prophet addressed them, into the ken of every generation. In these pages, "he being dead yet speaketh." If attention
to doctrine compels us to correct ourselves and say "God
speaketh," there is perhaps no great point in the distinction. For the
whole Muslim status of the Qur'ān is that God here speaking has
Muhammad for a voice. Forever wedded together and heard by the
pious soul in mosque and wilderness, in home and street, is the cry
of the seventh-century Apostle as the speech of the eternal God.
Every memorizer of the Qur'ān, every reciting muezzin or *khatīb,*
"preacher," renews in this living perpetuity the words that made
Islam. Muhammad in the Qur'ān becomes, so to speak, the great
contemporary of them all.

Nor need there be serious doubt that the voice in the Book is
authentically the voice of the Prophet. That there are critical
problems connected with the Qur'ān no intelligent student will
deny—not least among them the chronology and the vocabulary
sources. But there is no place for serious misgiving that what is here
was substantially what the Prophet said or that what he said under
conditions of Quranic inspiration is not here. Though at first
recorded on diverse scraps that lay to hand, animal bones, leaves,
skins, and the like, the growing revelations were carefully treasured
and devoutly memorized. When the contents were collected in
Zaid's recension, later made the basis of 'Uthmān's authoritative
version, or canon, of the sacred scriptures, it was believed that the
Prophet's own will in the matter had been fulfilled. It can hardly
have been that the Prophet himself made any final decision on the
order and arrangement of the holy Book. Had he done so, it would
seem impossible for anyone else to have undertaken the task.
Perhaps it was that death overtook him before this could be taken
up.

'Uthmān, it is true, ordered the destruction of all alternative versions such as had been gathered in different centers—
Kūfā, Basrah, Damascus—thus making almost impossible any
comparative study. Nonetheless the consensus view—Shī'ahs
excepted—is that the Qur'ān as it stood in 'Uthmān's recension
omits no significant and includes no extraneous material. The
Prophet's death had decisively closed the Book. Twenty-three years
and sole authorship allowed no time or opportunity for con-

fusion and the canonization was complete before the original Arabian generation of readers had finally passed away. All these factors, coupled with the retentive memory and reverent literalness of the faithful, seem to have ensured an authoritative text, whose puzzles are not of authorship.

XI

Despite the authority and sanctity of the volume of revelation, it does not exhaust the historical legacy it enshrines. Muhammad has a place in history beyond that implicit in his being the spokesman of the Qur'ān. Given its brevity and its context of events, the Qur'ān proved an incomplete source of communal guidance as the community spread into new lands and discovered new cultures. The Qur'ān, for example, contains no single comprehensive code of personal or commercial or social conduct, though there are several passages that suggest codes in embryo.[11] It is full and detailed on certain matters, especially those of personal status. But in other realms it is either completely silent or strangely brief. Orphans find more legal space than do caliphs, and private heirs find more than do public courts. Although exegesis and interpretation have greatly widened the scope of Quranic brevity, the very existence of alternative, though subordinate, sources of law demonstrates that the Qur'ān alone awaits and requires enlargement consistent with itself.

Where, then, should Islam better turn than to the person, the behavior, the *obiter dicta* of the spokesman of God's directives and of the holy Book? This explains the rise of Tradition, *Hadīth,* on a vast scale, giving to the biography of the Prophet a kind of implicit, legislative quality and turning the indicative of description into the imperative of law. "Muhammad did this," it runs, "the Muslim ought to do the same."

It should be clear that Muhammad as the source of Tradition stands in a different category from Muhammad as the recipient of the Qur'ān. The latter status is that of *wahȳ,* "revelation," accompanied by external signs, in limpness of body, swoon, ecstasy of spirit, which have remained a perpetual and puzzling theme to his biographers. Quranicity is more than Tradition. It is God's speech, which the Prophet hears and relays. But this recipience

gave Muhammad such status in the community, such uniqueness
in the divine economy, that everything about him, even outside this Quranic sphere, came to be considered in some sense
revelatory. This further role met, and largely satisfied, the extra-
Quranic needs of the community, though requiring to be supple-
mented further by analogy and communal consensus. Tradition
thus became the second major source of Islamic law. A term less
weighty than *wahȳ* and indicating non-Quranic inspiration is used
to designate this exemplary quality attaching to Muhammad's deed
and word. Tradition as a matter of record is called *Hadīth;* as a
matter of obligation, it is called *Sunnah.*

Undoubtedly, large areas of customary law in the conquered
lands came into Islam in the form of traditions about the Prophet,
Muhammad being credited with behavior or preferences or attitudes that reflected newly absorbed practices compatible with
Islam. Similarly the main political and local factions and divisions that developed in Muslim history during the decades after
his death inevitably expressed themselves in terms of competing
traditions about him, each party being anxious to give its position
the sanction of his anticipatory favor. The development of Tradition thus became a prerequisite of the development of law in
Islam and Muhammad became, so to speak, the posthumous arbiter of his people's destinies and daily lives. His mind and his
example were endlessly, and inconsistently, invoked, until a host
of traditions related the Prophet, positively or negatively, ap-
provingly or disapprovingly, with almost every conceivable issue
of life and society.

The great mass of traditions later required rigorous pruning.
The name of the most famous of the outstanding traditionalists,
Al-Bukhārī, has a tremendous sanctity in Islam. Al-Bukhārī is
said to have been aroused to his life task as editor of traditions by
a vision in which he saw the sleeping Prophet's face pestered with
innumerable flies, which a merciful fan kept at bay. It certainly
was a life task he and his fellow traditionalists undertook. For the
verification of a tradition depended not primarily on the substance or *matn* but on the *isnād* or chain of attestation. The question was not so much: Could the Prophet have said this? Is it
reasonable and in character? but rather: Who said that he said
this? Was that reporter an eyewitness? Was that reporter honest?

And who tells us now that they heard or saw the Prophet do or say it? Is the chain of attestors unbroken? Did they all know personally the man before them in the sequence going back to the first source?

All these technical questions, though they had their importance, almost excluded internal concern for substance. Biographical lore about attestors and companions became voluminous. Traditionalists traveled across the continents in search of authentication or in order to add their own name as the last in the chain, through face-to-face contact with the immediately preceding reporter. To eliminate the indirect and the secondhand became more important than to identify the conjectural.

This fascinating subject might be pursued much further but we must strive, as the best traditionalists did, to keep close to the Prophet. Despite the prolixity of invented or unverifiable traditions, there remains a substratum—variously estimated by scholars, Muslim and Western—of biographically valid data. But if we cannot always be sure that we are receiving authentic material about the Prophet, the question of criticism is perhaps unimportant. It is not so much whether this or that is validly Muhammad's, but that numbers of Muslims thought so. It is the principle rather than the detail that here matters, the fact of belief rather than the bare fact. Muhammad became the universal exemplar. The assumption, theologically unexamined, was that in *this* particular—Muhammad in Arabia A.D. 570–632—the universal made itself manifest. The good, worthy to be the timeless, example was available for recognition and imitation *in this life at that time.*

This meeting of the universal and the particular, the plural and the singular, the eternal and the temporal, is the ultimate mystery of all existence. There is, therefore, nothing unfamiliar in thus conceiving of the universal as having become an inclusive particular, a singular that embodies, in a revelatory way, the eternal. Christianity sees just this fulfilled and realized in the Incarnation of "the Word made flesh," in "God with us." It acknowledges this situation with joy as an act of God in grace and assurance.

The instinctive Muslim acceptance, however, of a universal significance for the person of Muhammad not only lacks, but specifically repudiates, this metaphysical confidence in God made human. Nevertheless, the view of Muhammad implicit in the traditions amounts to some form of the belief that a human particular has become a universal, that all humanity may know God's will. But this attitude to Muhammad has never been expressed in a recognized metaphysical doctrine of his person that would undergird its tremendous ethical and legal role.[12] As often elsewhere, Islam has been content with the practical result. Some effort to think out the implications in the relationship of this exemplary Muhammad to God is long overdue.

These considerations, though theological, are inseparable from any adequate discussion of Muhammad in history. For Tradition implies a cosmic relevance in his historical character. It proceeds upon it with great thoroughness and close detail. Even the smallest points about the Prophet become significant. Al-Ghazālī writes on the *Sunnah:*

> Know that the key of happiness is following the *Sunna* and imitating God's Apostle in all his goings out and comings in, in his movements and times of quiescence, even in the manner of his eating, his deportment, his sleep, and his speech. I do not say that concerning his manners in matters of religious observances alone, because there is no reason to neglect the traditions which have come down concerning them: nay, that has to do with all matters of use and wont, for in that way unrestricted following arises. God said: "Say: 'If you love God, follow me and God will love you'" (Surah 3.29). And He said: "What the Apostle has brought you, receive; and what he has forbidden you, refrain from" (Surah 54.7). So you must sit while putting on trousers and stand while putting on a turban. You must begin with the right foot when putting on your sandals, and eat with your right hand. When cutting your nails you must begin with the forefinger of the right hand and finish with its thumb; in the foot you must begin with the little toe of the right foot and finish with the little toe of the left. It is the same in all your movements and times of quiescence. Muhammad b. Aslam used not to eat a melon because the manner in which God's Apostle ate it had not been transmitted to him.[13]

To this meticulous degree Muhammad became the norm of true Muslim behavior and the unconscious source of the manners and total conduct of the community as far as a pattern could be ascertained. The whole phenomenon, whose detailed illustration might be—as it often was—a life study, is one of the most remarkable of the Prophet's legacies. There are some traditions that indicate it was an unintended legacy, though many more sustain the contrary. But however precisely this outcome is associated with the conscious will of Muhammad, there could be no clearer evidence of his stature and uniqueness in his day and beyond. Only a very few so effectively determine the shape of the world after they have left it, and maintain their authority by their example so far, so deep, and so wide. The Muhammad of Tradition belongs to all ages of Islam, inasmuch as each of them returns in some measure to him as its criterion of all that it approves.

It can hardly be doubted, however, that the process is in some sense reciprocal. It is not simply that the historical Muhammad fashions the values and standards of the centuries, but that the centuries in their turn make and define the traditional Muhammad. Almost from the beginning, forms of customary law, or policies of special groups, were read back into prophetic conduct or table talk and in that form found Islamic expression. Down the centuries there has been, in differing degrees, the same tendency to draw the image of the Prophet in harmony with prevailing needs. The tendency is conspicuous in our own day. Muhammad is taken out of the seventh century and emerges in some biographies as the protagonist of the welfare state, as the first practical socialist, the prototype of Lincoln or Garibaldi, the spiritual ancestor of John Stuart Mill and Henri Bergson.

It may be argued that all great personalities who belong to the ages come to be reinterpreted in new lights and their "legend" is not always strictly tested by their historical role. But it can also be argued that these posthumous achievements are part of the historical role itself, seen in large perspective. Historians are obliged to take note of what the communal memory affirms to have been, as well as what the chronology contains. There are few personalities where this double duty is more important than in respect of the human founder of Islam. This is true perhaps most of all for those who would be Christian ministrants to his heirs.

There are yet other aspects of Muhammad in history that will become apparent in the two succeeding chapters—the Sufi re-possession of the mystical Muhammad; the social reformer's invocation of the iconoclast and the rebel; the contemporary philosopher's appeal to the dynamic Muhammad. There can be no hope here of completeness. Nor is the story itself finished. The process, so to say, is proceeding. But perhaps we have succeeded in doing some justice to the muezzin's total meaning when he reiterates his conviction that Muhammad is the Apostle of God. It is those Arabian years, now fourteen centuries away; it is how the Muslims of those centuries have understood those years and what the sacred Book has made of them as believers and followers.

iv

PRAYER AND RELIGIOUS LIFE IN ISLAM

I

From the twofold witness we have now considered, the muezzin passes to a twofold summons to response, with an interesting imperative or evocative verb that might well be translated "Look alive," or, more usually, "Come." It calls the hearer to prayer, *Salāt*, and to good, *Falāh*. These are inclusive concepts whose significance is the theme of this and the following chapter. The form used as an imperative is in the singular. For though the response involves community, it is made by the individual. Moreover, the word does not differentiate, as other imperatives do, between masculine and feminine. It is a kind of common singular, including all who harken and respond.

Even those who know least about Islam are somewhat familiar with the place of prayer in its life. If they have traveled, they may have seen Muslim seamen on shipboard, or stevedores on a quayside, observe the hours of prayer, with a naturalness, an absence of self-consciousness, surprising to the Westerner. Or they have seen photographs of serried ranks of prostrate forms behind a leader—*imām*—filling the wide mosque spaces, or pictures of a solitary cameleer spreading his prayer mat on the desert sands.

Islam and prayer are in truth inseparable. Just as Muhammad's career revolved around Mecca, the city of his first prophetic warnings and his final victory, so his community acknowledges the religious centrality of the Meccan *qiblah*, "direction of prayer," toward which all praying Muslims turn their face in a gesture that makes them part of one history and one solidarity. "Come unto the prayer," says the muezzin. For generations Muslims have actualized their Islam in their response. The ground, meaning, and pattern of the resulting religious life deserve patient and discerning study. For, however true it may be to speak of Islam in our time as a cultural or a political expression, it is such only because it is primarily a religious allegiance. As such it must first be known.

The institution of Muslim prayer rests upon the precept of the Qur'ān and the example of the Prophet. The word itself is perhaps better translated "worship"[1]: it means "to supplicate with adoration." The same word is used of God in the familiar invocation upon Muhammad: "May God magnify (or exalt) Muhammad and preserve him in peace." It should be distinguished from spontaneous and intercessory prayer, known as *Du'ā'*, where individuals may use ejaculatory phrases of their own choice, Quranic or otherwise, without following any necessary pattern or ritual. *Salāt*, however, is strictly ordered. The form must be followed if the prayer is to be valid. "Establish" or "perform" the worship is the usual formula by which the Qur'ān enjoins the practice, often in the context of conversion. There is no doubt that Muslim prayer is meant to be a distinctive rite, the fulfillment of which is a witness to the new allegiance.

Apart from the enjoining of the *qiblah*, the main details of the *Salāt*, including its fivefold daily iteration, rest on extra-Quranic injunctions. In one passage (Surah 11.114) the Qur'ān directs: "Establish worship at the two ends of the day and in the parts of the night close to them" (see also Surah 24.58). Tradition, however, has understood the directive to include the five prayers as follows:

Salāt al-Fajr—the dawn prayer, said when the dawn has broken and before the actual sunrise.

Salāt al-Zuhr—the noon prayer when the sun passes the meridian.

Salāt al-'Asr—the late afternoon prayer.

Salāt al-Maghrib—prayer immediately after the sun sets.

Salāt al-'Ishā'—prayer after sunset before retiring to sleep and not later than midnight.

Each occasion of *Salāt* has its stipulated number of ritual movements or *raka'āt* and never less than two. In addition to the five obligatory prayers there are two optional ones: *Salāt al-Lail*, said in the night after sleep but before dawn and *Salāt al-Duhā*, which would fall between the dawn and the noon prayer and perhaps coincide with breakfast. It can be seen at once that these daily prayers make a considerable demand upon the faithful. Though their performance takes a brief time, their frequency requires a readiness to combine prayer with other affairs. Many exponents have seen this as one of their chief lessons—the obligation of the believer to recognize God in the midst of, rather than in escape from, distractions and duties. For a similar reason Islam does not recognize a Sabbath. The daily hours replace the holy day.

The ritual of each *raka'h* (plural: *raka'āt*) is carefully prescribed and rigorously followed. It consists of seven movements, each having certain accompanying recitations:

1. The two hands are raised to the ears, while those at prayer stand, facing the *qiblah*. They say the *takbīr*: "God is most great."

2. The right hand is then placed over the left upon the chest or bosom with ascriptions of glory to God and the confession of submission, ending with the phrase : "I seek refuge with God from the accursed devil." Then the opening Surah—*Al-Fātihah*—is recited. This position is called "The Standing."

3. With a new *takbīr*, worshipers lower the head with the palms of the hands on the knees—a position called "The Bending." They repeat ascriptions of praise to God.

4. A standing position is resumed, followed by the prostration

proper. The forehead, both hands, both knees, and the toes of both feet touch the ground or floor, while ascriptions are repeated.

5. With a *takbīr*, worshipers raise the upper part of their body to the sitting posture with two hands on the knees. A prayer for mercy and protection is offered.

6. A second prostration, repeating the praises of the first.

7. Worshipers return to a standing position, saying a *takbīr*, and the *raka'h* is at an end.

There are certain slight divergencies according to whether or not the series of positions known as a *raka'h* is the last in the sequence of the whole prayer. The final one ends with a salutation on all fellow Muslims and the angels, with the face turned right and left as in greeting. The prescribed phrases must be used in Arabic if that language is known. Worshipers may add praises of their own only when the ritual is complete.

The whole ordinance is intended as indicative of the relationship to God implicit in the Muslim understanding. Though Islam prides itself upon its freedom from sacramentalism and priesthood, in that all worshipers worship for themselves, it is evident that the *Salāt* postures are profoundly sacramental in a general sense. Prostration, in particular, proclaims and serves to actualize a totality of surrender. The face, the proudest thing in human personality, comes into contact with the dust, the lowest thing in nature. The physical thus embodies and expresses the spiritual.

The same may be said of the careful washing, *wudu'*, that precedes every *Salāt*, typifying a cleansing of the soul accomplished therein. "Prayer," according to Surah 29.45, "preserves from impurity and evil." To remember God in this way is to be restrained from evil. The washing, therefore, both fits worshipers for prayer and demonstrates what their worship is meant to do for them.

The washing is done to those parts of the body that are most exposed—the hands and arms to the elbow, the mouth and nostrils, the face and the head, and finally the feet to the ankles, beginning with the right foot. Running water is always preferred for Muslim ablution and it is used from, not in, receptacles. Hence the fountains in mosque courts. If water is not available, a less desirable cleansing can be had with the use of sand or clean earth. The familiar prayer mat is linked in the same realm. It protects the worshiper from possible contamination and makes clean the immediate area of prostration. To pray in a dirty state would be improper and nugatory. The Quranic passage (Surah 5.6) that stipulates the washing explains that God does not wish to be tedious with worshipers, but seeks to purify them and fit them for the divine goodness.

All times of prayer must be prefaced by the *niyyah*, "intention," just as is the case with the other four pillars of religion or obligatory ordinances of Islam. The "intention" is the declaration of purpose. It would be possible to go through all the motions and phrases of the ritual without in fact performing the prayer, just as the syllables of the confession recited, for example, in a grammar lesson, would not constitute a personal witness. The need for the "intention" makes evident that true prayer cannot be perfunctory or mechanical. It is a means of defense against inattentive and external performance. The movements no doubt become habitual, but habituation should not lead to forgetfulness.

The place and pattern of the mosque in Muslim religious life is a vital topic to which we shall return. But discussion of prayer would not be complete without reference to its public, but in no sense exclusive, place. The English word "mosque" is a corruption of the Arabic *masjid*, "place of prostration." If a mosque is accessible and convenient, it is always desirable to use it. Water for washing is available there, if anywhere, and there is the stimulus of association and fellowship. But everyone's prayer mat is a portable mosque and wherever they choose to spread it they can find their *qiblah* and worship God. They need no priest or mouthpiece: the prayers are known by all. Because prayer has to intermingle with journeys, trading, and conversing, worshipers cannot always repair to certain precincts. The physical mosque is dispensable.

Nevertheless the noon prayer on Fridays is to be said as far as possible in the place of corporate prayer. When so said its four *raka'āt* are reduced to two. Occasion is taken for a discourse from the mosque pulpit and the worshiper shares the unison prostrations as led by the *imām* standing toward the niche, *mihrāb*, that indicates the direction of Mecca. The Friday, however, in contradistinction to the Jewish Sabbath and the Christian Sunday, is not a day of rest. Business precedes and follows the noon prayer (see Surah 62.9 and 10). For the *Adhān*, "call to prayer," the mosque is, of course, indispensable. But the duty to which it calls may be answered without as well as within.

II

Prayer in Islam is by no means confined to ritual forms. There is the whole realm of petition and adoration in which the Muslim soul relates itself to God in the various crises of existence and in the lesser occasions of daily life. Even here, however, the worshiper tends to rely on familiar phrases or forms of an ejaculatory kind, many of them derived from the Qur'ān or Tradition. A newborn infant is greeted with the phrases of the muezzin's call recited in the ear. At death there are prayers over the dead body in the mosque or dwelling or at the graveside, after the corpse has first been thoroughly washed, beginning with those parts that are customarily cleansed in the *wudu'* before prayer. The *imām* and those present recite the *takbīr* and the *dhikr* of the Prophet with variant forms of intercession in which there will be phrases such as the following:

> Forgive, O God, our dead and our living. Cause him who is alive among us to live in Islam, and he whom Thou takest to Thyself let him die in the faith. Do not forbid him his reward; make gracious his reception and spacious his coming in. Cleanse him with water, with snow and with ice, and purge him of sins as Thou cleanest a white cloth of its stain.

At marriage there are exhortations setting forth the duties of the parties and recitation of the *Shahādah*, as well as various optional prayers for the welfare of the couple and the prosperity of all families. Many of the routine events of daily life are occasions of ejaculatory petition—entering and leaving the house, entering and leaving a lavatory, retiring and rising, or visiting the sick, passing a graveyard, embarking and disembarking, before and after meals, in front of a mirror, after a bath, on first partaking of any item in the yearly harvest, in distress, and in trial. In many cases the words have come down from traditional practices or phrases of the Prophet himself. The purpose of such devotional recognition of God in the minutiae of the everyday is to make one's *islām* ("submission") comprehensive and alert, and to evoke the spirit of gratitude and humility. Bodily functions, which may so easily go awry and which in their wholeness are so wonderful, should be the occasion of ejaculatory worship.

The characteristic phrases of these acts of devotion deserve study. The keynote is surrender and trust. "O God, I have given my soul, my journey, my objective, into Thy charge." The idea of submission is usually linked to that of refuge and the reiterated phrase is "I seek refuge with Thee," from the accursed one, from wandering and error, from danger and mischief, from fear and calamity. This seeking argues reliance, expressed in the words *'Alaika Tawakkaltu*: "In Thee have I trusted," often to be seen inscribed on trucks and buses and elsewhere. These attitudes are no doubt comprehended in the most familiar of all phrases, *'Bismillāh*, "In God's Name," which when used with attentive sincerity confesses the God-relatedness of all things. Other petitions make the occasion a parable of larger need: a bath may denote spiritual purity, entering a house may serve to recollect the entering of heaven, and a mirror's reflection may remind one of the call to be virtuous as well as comely.

The Muslim principle of *tauhīd,* "unity," runs through all these prayers. God is alone a sure protector, or right guide. There is no other arbiter, no other enricher, no other Lord. Hence the blessing of God is indispensable. Its enjoyment or its denial makes all the difference. May we, then, as the opening Surah has it, be among those upon whom God shows favor, not among those who stand under divine wrath. The awesome distinction felt and feared here is an everpresent element in the form and quality of these prayers.

A glance at a selection of other prayers used in the Qur'ān shows that the devout Muslim in incidental petitions is close to the temper of the holy Book. Many of these Quranic phrases are recited voluntarily after the *Fātihah* on any occasion when the latter is used. They express a strong sense of the precarious nature of life and the decisive role of faith. "O our Lord, grant us good in this world and in the world to come, and save us from the pain of the fire." "O our Lord, do not let our hearts stray after Thou hast guided us, and grant us mercy." "O our Lord, forgive us our transgressions and our excesses." "Let us die with the righteous and bring unto us what Thou hast promised by the apostles and let us not be confounded on the day of resurrection." Throughout, there is this sense of the confrontation of the believing and the unbelieving, and the confidence that the former are the gainers and the latter are the losers. Yet there is no presumptuous assurance. The categories are clear and fixed, but membership is not. "If Thou forgive us not and dost not have mercy upon us, then are we verily among the losers." "O Lord, indeed I am a poor man in need of all the good Thou bringest down unto me."

All these prayers are associated, in some sense, with the character and attributes of God. The ninety-nine Names are used, with varying frequency, as the ground of the petition or the point of the aspiration, as well as in adoration. The Christian notices at once the entire absence of anything resembling the traditional Christian phrases of commendation: "for the sake of . . ." or "in the name of. . . ." For the offering of prayer depends altogether for its acceptability upon the divine will and all that can rightly be said is to associate some known descriptive of God with the relevant petition. In one respect the pattern is the same. For the Christian use of the Name of Christ is the invocation of that inclusive sense of God, upon which all prayer depends, as it is made plain and sure in Jesus Christ. The Christian's standing in Christ is not external to God, as if it were a persuasion from without. It is rather a recognition of the place where God has made grace actual and accessibility indubitable. Muslim prayer links itself to the attributes of God without believing that they are anywhere finally pledged or necessarily operative.

As for the question of the intercession, *shafā'ah*, of prophets and saints in Islam, there is some uncertainty as to how the Qur'ān should be understood. There are several passages like Surah 74.48, which affirms: "The intercession of those who make *shafā'ah* will not avail them." Surah 2.48 depicts the day of judgment as a day on which no intercession will be allowed. These verses, however, can be understood, in a less than absolute sense, as disqualifying certain groups from intercessory power or efficacy. Such an interpretation is confirmed by other verses that attribute intercession to the angels or speak of it as occurring by

God's permission. Surah 2.25, it is true, asks: "Who should intercede with Him [God] even by His permission?" But Tradition has given an affirmative answer and has expressed itself fully as to those capable of intercession by divine consent. There are prophets, martyrs, saints, and apostles, as well as angels. But traditional belief is insistent that Muhammad is the truest intercessor, where he is not also the sole one. A repeated tradition describes the day of judgment when all the prophets from Adam to Jesus transfer, each to the next, the role of intercessor, all disclaiming the privilege. Finally Muhammad takes it up and intercedes with God, by God's permission, until there are left in hell only those for whom no intercessor can avail.

Intercession is much more widely believed in Shī'ah Islam, and belief in the saintly efficacy of holy founders is one of the main factors in the cohesion of Sufi orders. There are also strong traditions of Muhammad's own practice during life in visiting cemeteries, often by night, to seek from God the forgiveness and the welfare of the dead.

III

The ordinance of *Saum*, "fasting," in the month of Ramadān, in which the Qur'ān began to be revealed, is at once a product of, and a reaction against, Jewish-Christian practices. Though Ramadān seems to have been a holy month among the Arabs prior to Islam, its designation as a month of fasting derives from the example of ascetic discipline among the "people of the Book," and the fast of the Day of Atonement. In the Meccan days the early community appears to have followed something of this pattern and Surah 2.183 declares: "Fasting is enjoined for you even as it was enjoined for those before you." But in the sequel to this passage is the record of the duty prescribed for and by Muhammad when his experience with the Jews in Medina provoked him into studied disconnection. The Day of Atonement fast in Muharram was abandoned, except as a voluntary act, for one of a month-long duration in Ramadān. Moreover, a still later revelation transferred the fast from the period between sunset and sunrise to that between sunrise and sunset. "Eat and drink until it appears that a white thread may be distinguished from a black, then keep the fast strictly until nightfall'' (Surah 2.187). The same passage indicates that abstention from sexual intercourse by night is not incumbent as part of the fast.

The observance of Ramadān is binding upon all adult Muslims of both sexes, save for the aged, the sick, pregnant women, nursing mothers, and travelers. When the exempting circumstances no longer prevail, the equivalent period of consecutive fast is to be observed. The month of fasting is a rigorous exercise and is probably more widely practiced than the daily prayers. Muslims who may sometimes omit the latter keep the former. No food or drink is to pass down the throat, from the break of dawn to sunset. Food is partaken during the hours of darkness.

The fast closes with the *'Īd al-Fitr,* the feast of the breaking of the fast, which is the Little Festival of the Muslim year. It is begun when the new moon appears and is celebrated with even greater éclat than the Great Festival, or *'Īd al-Adhā,* which coincides with the offering of pilgrimage sacrifice at Minā, near Mecca. *Bairām,* an alternative name generally but not solely used for the feast that ends Ramadān, is derived from the practice of giving and receiving gifts of sugar sweets. Greeting cards also are exchanged.

Indeed there are some aspects of the *'Īd al-Fitr* that resemble certain features of the Western Christmas season. It is a time of general desire after better things. Presents symbolize mutual affection and there is a surge of satisfaction and aspiration that, for Muslims, terminates an exacting discipline. Evil is somehow temporarily allayed. Shakespeare, in *Hamlet*, found the nights of the Christmas season joyously wholesome:

> The bird of dawning singeth all night long
> > . . . no planets strike
> No fairy takes, nor witch hath power to charm,
> So hallowed and so gracious is the time.

The Qur'ān observes that on the night in Ramadān of the first descent of the Book: "Angels and the Spirit descend to earth. . . . and it is peace until the rising of the dawn" (Surah 97.4 and 5).

Through the fast there is also an emphasis on deepened devotion and more frequent mosque attendance. "Be at your devotions in the mosque'' says the passage enjoining Ramadān (Surah 2.187). The need for the ''intention,'' daily repeated, emphasizes the conscious discipline the soul requires, and into which it enters intelligently. The traditions and Muslim theologians concur in this understanding of the fast. Though, doubtless, multitudes in Muslim history observed it as a fiat of their own faith, as an ordinance that required no justification, the perceptive modern exponents recognize that in itself the transference of eating and drinking to hours of darkness has nothing intrinsically to commend it. What is significant is the assertion that human nature has larger needs than bread, that the body is to be the servant, not the master, and that ordered voluntary privation is a fine school of patience and endurance. There is no doubt of the value of the fast as a witness to these truths, though, when the revolving Muslim calendar brings Ramadān into the trying summer heat, it may be questioned whether exasperation and strain are not also a consequence. These, it will be said, are part of the price of a necessary institution.

There is no general tendency to permit symbolic interpretation of the fast to weaken the actual observance. Ramadān may stand for spiritual discipline but those who so interpret it cannot claim their own freedom to override it. Islam, by and large, is as tenacious of its times and seasons as any other faith, including those more commonly described as sacramental. Fasting is good. But to fast in Ramadān is traditionally thirty times better than at any other time.

Such other fasts are possible as a means of expiating manslaughter, or a broken oath, or the killing of game while on pilgrimage. Though traditions emphasize the meritoriousness of fasting in general, there is a strong insistence, throughout the Qur'ān and in Muslim practice, upon the errors of asceticism. Ramadān sufficiently demonstrates the priority of the soul. This truth must always be kept in mind. But the stipulated fast suffices. The good things of nature and of appetite are to be taken in moderation and not refused. It is unwise and unbecoming to reject the gifts of God. Whatever may be said of Muhammad's debt to hermits and monks as examples of solitary devotion, the Qur'ān in the Medinan period repeatedly urges that the reasonable desires and needs of bodily life—food, drink, sex, and sleep—be properly and thankfully satisfied. Islam disavows "monkery." There is nevertheless a strong, though limited, temper that seeks the ascetic way, thus dissociating itself from the general teaching.

Al-Ghazālī insists that a fast that means only a consequent hunger and thirst is not a finally meaningful fast. For if only hunger results, the fast is only physically felt. It should be an occasion of that remembrance of God which is not a temporary, negative abstinence, but a positive preoccupation with God. So understood, there are fasts for the eyes, from impure seeing; for the ears, from unsavory listening; for the mouth, from scandal and gossip. Such purposeful asceticism as a pathway to the divine knowledge is admittedly a special vocation. As a deep and important area of Muslim religious life, we shall take note of it later. Its existence only serves to throw into contrast the more general attitude to natural satisfactions and to the Ramadān fast as a yearly reminder that the gracious God, who gives for enjoyment, also requires that Muslims observe a month of special endurance as an education in submission. Christianity is often reproached by Muslim writers for its alleged renunciation of this world. It errs in asking too much of human nature and so remains either an unsound, or an unfulfilled, ideal.

IV

By reason of the *qiblah*, Islam made Mecca the center of day-to-day devotion. Pilgrimage, *Hajj*, the fifth pillar of religion, makes it the focal point of a yearly homage that often represents the aspiration of a lifetime. The pilgrimage is, so to speak, the annual expression of the constant centrality of the *Ka'bah* and its environs in the practice and faith of Islam.

The Qur'ān, in Surah 3.97, lays upon loyal Muslims, who are capable of travel to Mecca, the obligation of pilgrimage once during their lifetime. "Whoever is able to make his way thither" should visit the holy city, the navel of the earth, and the haunts of Abraham and Ishmael where the holy Prophet was born. 'Arafāt and Minā in the Meccan vicinity are included in the pilgrim rites but Medina, city of the Prophet's death and burial, is not, though many pilgrims include Medina in their travels before leaving the

Hijāz—the western coastland of Arabia, north of Asir.

What constitutes ability to be a pilgrim has been much discussed within the schools of law and by individual Muslims deciding whether and when to make the journey. Lack of means, slavery, feebleness of mind, lack of escort (in the case of women) are traditionally recognized as legitimate incapacity. The first has often been extended to excuse neglect on the ground of preoccupation with necessary affairs, insecurity on the road, hazards to health, and the like. With others strength of will has made up for arguable deficiency of means. In the long history of Islam there have been many, Caliphs and shaikhs, the mighty and the erudite, as well as the lowly, who never sought the sacred precincts. There have been others, such as Hārūn al-Rashīd and his predecessor Al-Mansūr, who made repeated pilgrimages to the Holy City.

It would be impossible, as well as idle, to attempt a statistical assessment of the incidence of pilgrimage in any single generation. Some inveterate travelers in the heyday of Muslim tradition-building and of science wandered almost incessantly over the wide areas of the Muslim world, taking in Mecca at pilgrimage time as they went. There have been communities that, over long decades, by reason of circumstances, local or Meccan, through schism or indifference, sent scarcely a trickle of visitors to the sanctuaries. Into these vicissitudes we cannot enter. A full and detailed history of the pilgrimage in Islam is yet to be written. It should be remembered also that the glory of Mecca has been borrowed or usurped by other centers, for pilgrimage is a powerful factor in the cohesion of empires. Thus *Shī'ah* Islam has its Karbala and Najaf, and Persian Muslims have Meshhed and Qum.[2] These rivals apart, the holiest city in Islam has been at times besieged by rebel Muslims. Nevertheless the agelong sanctity remains and the pilgrimage today is a powerful unifying factor in the life of Islam.

In recent years official returns place the annual number of pilgrims at one and a half million. A major proportion are now airborne. The airline agent is more and more replacing the old *muqawwim* into whose care a caravan would entrust itself when setting out from Cairo or Damascus. Pilgrim ships to Jiddah are also more commodious than of yore. There have also been great improvements in the facilities for the health and security of pilgrims on Arabian soil. Several leading Muslim states have opened national hostels in Mecca for their citizens. The deterrents that formerly intimidated the intellectual or the cultured have now been greatly mitigated. Currency control is more the stumbling block now to some would-be pilgrims than the lack of health control that daunted earlier generations.[3]

There are many intriguing issues connected with the contemporary pilgrimage but the temptation to discuss them must be resisted. Our purpose here is with an understanding of its general role in Muslim life. No discussions of numbers and conditions, however, would be complete without the observation that the pilgrimage in Islam involves and affects more persons than physically perform it. It becomes in a sense a vicarious experience. The village, the small mosque community, or the city quarter greets returning pilgrims with possessive pride. It relives in their tales the emotions they have known. Their impact provides, so to speak, a participation by proxy. In this way real defaulters, if not stimulated into action, at least know what they have neglected. Believers who are genuinely incapable of pilgrimage enter in part into an awareness of Mecca that compensates for their inability to go there. Attendance thus mediates the meaning of Mecca to all the local levels of Muslim society. How many there are who are impervious to this secondary influence it is impossible to say. More important to discover is what the pilgrimage experience constitutes for those who directly or vicariously partake of it.

It should be clear that pilgrimage, like any other pillar of Islam, can be physically performed without being spiritually fulfilled. It is possible and desirable to visit Mecca at any time but the proper pilgrimage is that which takes place, with intention, in the stipulated month of Dhū-al-Hijjah. This, like all Muslim months, rotates round the seasons. The summer pilgrimages are the most exacting. There is a lesser pilgrimage, known as the 'Umrah, which is not fixed to any particular month. The rites are restricted to Muslims. No non-Muslim has in fact entered Mecca except in disguise or by subterfuge.[4]

The confession of the pilgrimage is symbolized by the ceremonial state of consecration, ihrām, into which pilgrims must enter at some point between their departure and their arrival in the Hijāz. This state is symbolized by the wearing of a white, unsewn robe thrown across the body leaving the right arm and shoulder bare. The robes should be simple, silk being forbidden. While in the state of *ihrām* the pilgrim neither shaves nor washes, apart from the ceremonial ablutions at the various stations of the pilgrimage. Women are traditionally clad in a long robe reaching from head to foot. The veil is held off from the face in some way, so that the skin is technically uncovered. Sexual relations and other infringements of the *ihrām* render the pilgrimage null and void.

The stages of the pilgrimage, in brief, are as follows. After arrival in Mecca pilgrims make seven circuits of the *Ka'bah* in the Great Mosque, during which they touch, or if possible kiss, the sacred Black Stone in the wall of the shrine. The circuits are performed barefoot. Leaving the mosque by another door from that used for entry, pilgrims make the ceremonial running between two points in a wide Meccan street. This procession may be a recollection of Hagar's search hither and thither for water for Ishmael and is also connected with Abraham's eluding Satan. On the eighth day of the pilgrim month, these ceremonies being completed, the pilgrimage proper begins.

After a mosque discourse the pilgrims set out for Minā and 'Arafāt some five and thirteen miles, respectively, from Mecca. The former is a narrow defile and the latter an open area, below the Mount of Mercy. Here the pilgrims stand from noon to sunset and sermons are delivered. This is the ninth day of the month and the climax of pilgrimage. The night is spent in the open at Muzdalīfah, on the route back to Minā. The following day comes "the stoning" in which each pilgrim casts seven small stones upon a large stone heap. Abraham is believed to have dismissed Satan by this means.

The stoning brings to an end the pilgrimage proper and pilgrims prepare to withdraw from the state of consecration. They sacrifice a sheep, a goat, and a camel and have their head shaved. They return to Mecca where again they do a *Ka'bah* circuit and bathe in the water of the holy well of Zamzam, or sprinkle themselves with it. There follows on the eleventh, twelfth, and thirteenth days of the month the so-called *tashrīq,* "relaxation and pleasure." The consecrated state is terminated though stone-throwing ceremonies continue. Before leaving Mecca pilgrims briefly resume the *ihrām* for a farewell visit to the Great Mosque.

Precise details of the ceremonies differ from time to time and from school to school. The lesser pilgrimage makes circumambulation the central ceremony and desacralizing follows at once. Simultaneously with the sacrifice at Minā and the *tashrīq,* of the pilgrims at Mecca, the whole Muslim world celebrates its Great Festival, the *'Īd al-Adhā,* when besides exchanging presents the devout Muslim may offer sacrifice. This association of the Great Festival with the pilgrim rites serves to bind into one celebrating community the whole household of Islam within and beyond its religious center. After the completion of their farewell, pilgrims, in the state of *ihlāl,* "secularity," make their way home, visiting en route as they wish.

Some aspects of pilgrimage have passed into Islam from pagan Arabian practice. Other elements of that origin, such as circuits at 'Arafāt and the state of nakedness during the *Ka'bah* circuits, were eliminated by Muhammad. The "standing" at 'Arafāt is probably a pre-Islamic survival, as is also the sacrifice at Minā. But Islam gave new meaning to the surviving practices and baptized them into its strict monotheism. The incorporation of the pagan pilgrimage into Muslim ritual may be seen as the ceremonial counterpart of the political importance of Mecca.

No discussion is possible here of the topography of Mecca and the historical affinities of the pilgrimage. The writings of Burton, Rutter, and Hurgrönje abound in descriptions of the Meccan terrain and the pilgrimage rites as they appeared to these observers.[5] More significant here is the *Labbaika* cry with which pilgrims punctuate their devotion from their first entry into the consecrated state to the completion of the stoning at Minā. The cry of the *takbīr,* "God is most great," is, of course, characteristic also of all the pilgrim stages.

But *Labbaika* takes us even more expressively into the heart of this experience at its best. "Doubly at Thy service, O God" is perhaps the best English rendering of the cry. It is twice repeated, each time in the dual form to indicate emphasis. Arabic grammar describes it as an absolute complement of its original verb. It thus means that pilgrims present themselves wholeheartedly before God with no other thought than this divine encounter. Their physical coming to Mecca is a kind of parable of their spiritual response to the revelation and law of God that they believe were historically communicated at this focal point. Their cry of recognition of God and of what God has sent down pledges them to a sustained and ever renewed devotion. They are gathering the rest of their life in the protestation of unfailing allegiance: "Thee it is before Whom I stand."

A description of the pilgrim rites and the observations of travelers, Muslim and Western, suggest to some outsiders a feeling of strangeness, if not revulsion. What can be the significance of thousands of flying pebbles and of animal carcasses strewn on the ground after a devotional "massacre," or of seething multitudes of humanity in the hot discomfort of unwashed garments and unshaven faces? Abuses, too, of pilgrim devotion there have sometimes been, and other unhappy features incidental to the whole. These are diminishing in face of a stricter system and more developed organization. But in any event it is well for outside observers to look with understanding, even where they quite fail to penetrate the secret.

Diverse and sincere participants have expressed in Muslim literature, old and new, their sense of elevation and insight during the pilgrim days. The pilgrimage, known from within, appears as a potent sacrament of Muslim unity and conveys a sense of inspiring solidarity. It is a yearly renewal of Meccan, or rather of Muhammad's, history in the Muslim soul. It is a geographical expression of religious heritage.

Perhaps the surest way to enter into this experience is to study the pilgrim prayers. Various manuals of pilgrim devotion, known as *Manāsik al-Hajj*, are supplied to Muslims bound for Mecca. A few extracts follow from one of them. On first beholding the buildings at Mecca, the pilgrim prays:

In the name of God, the compassionate, the merciful, O God, let this become to me an abode and grant me herein a valid profit.

On entering the precincts of the sacred *Ka'bah* the pilgrim cries:

O God, this sanctuary is yours, the country is yours, the safekeeping is yours and the worshiper is yours. I have come to you from a distant country with many transgressions and evil deeds. I beg you, as one who has deep need of you, seeking the merciful remission of your punishment, to receive me in your pure pardon and to bring me into your spacious paradise, that gracious abode. O God, this is your sanctuary and the sanctuary of your apostle. So keep me, flesh and blood and bone, inviolate from the fire. O God, preserve me from your condemnation on the day when you raise up your servants. I beseech you, for you are God, there is none other than you, the beneficent, the merciful. Blessing and peace be upon our Lord Muhammad, upon his household and his companions. Let it be a great, eternal peace.

The prayer at the seventh circuit of the *Ka'bah* reads:

O God, I ask of you a perfect faith, a sincere assurance, a reverent heart, a remembering tongue, a good conduct of commendation, and a true repentance, repentance before death, rest at death, and forgiveness and mercy after death, clemency at the reckoning, victory in paradise, and escape from the fire, by your mercy, O mighty One, Forgiver. Lord, increase me in knowledge and join me to the good.

At the "standing" of Abraham, the pilgrim prays:

O God, you know my doings, public and secret. Receive my plea. You know my need; grant me my petition. You know what is in my spirit. Forgive me my trespasses. O God, I ask you for a faith that will occupy my heart and a sincere assurance so that I may know that nothing will befall me except what you have written for me. You are my guardian in this world and that to come. Let me die a Muslim and join me to the good. O God, do not let there be in this standing any guilt, save what you have forgiven; no grief, save what you have assuaged; no need, save what you have satisfied and made easy. Render our affairs prosperous, enlarge and illumine our hearts, and seal our deeds with good things. O God, let us die Muslims and raise us to life as Muslims, and join us to the good, not as those who are ashamed or as those who are seduced.[6]

V

The prayers of the pilgrim at Mecca bring us back to the Meccan direction of all prayer, and so to the mosque, the local focus of Muslim devotion. Imaginative and observant study in the mosque may more truly apprehend the nature of the Muslim's religion than many a treatise in Islamics. Each mosque is in some sense an epitome of Muslim life and the Muslim story. Some of them are former churches recognizable still, yet unmistakably transformed. Others are vast, original monuments of Muslim architecture and vitality. Not least appealing are the unpretentious and modest ones that in their very ordinariness seem to embody more intimately the life of believing generations. Nor are they all out of the far past and laden with years. The traveler in Algeria, for example, will come upon many new mosque structures, gleaming in their whiteness, an index to the vigor of the Society of the 'Ulamā' responsible for their erection.

Whether old or new, majestic or unobtrusive, the mosque is full of clues to the nature of religious life. It expresses in structural form the pattern of the Muslim faith. Its most conspicuous features are the minaret, the *mihrāb*, "niche," and the *minbar*, "pulpit." These serve respectively the call to prayer, its direction and unity, and its interpretation. They correspond to three roles belonging to the mosque personnel—that of muezzin, *imām*, "prayer leader," and *khatīb*, "preacher." In large and well-endowed mosques these are usually different individuals. They may also be assisted by others such as the *muwaqqit*, who keeps the hours for the muezzin, the *qāss*, who relates stories for instruction and devotion to the faithful, the *qāri'*, "reader," who chants the Qur'ān, and, perhaps, a *muhtasib* to supervise the morals of the community. In the more modest mosques these offices may be performed by the same individual at different times.

The duty of the muezzin, in this context, needs no further description. The earliest call to prayer seems to have been given from the rooftops of the Prophet's quarters in Medina or of other near-by houses. Traditionally, the first muezzin was Bilāl, an Ethiopian. The minaret, though admirably suited to the call to prayer and itself, in some forms, a kind of stabbing summons to the upward direction of life, may not have evolved only for this religious function. It no doubt incorporated features of the Christian architecture absorbed through conquest. Its name, "place of light" or "fire" suggests that it may have had strictly utilitarian origins, as a watchtower for fire signals. Christian history reminds us, too, that towers had their attraction for ascetics and devotees. There is record of at least one outstanding Muslim theologian who owed much to the seclusion of a minaret.[7]

But whatever the diverse factors, architectural and otherwise, contributing to its evolution, the minaret is the muezzin's world. It is the vantage point of a devotional appeal. The artist may find in it an occasion for an exquisite theme. But the man with a mission in words is its master. When the minarets began to go up one by one, in the fifteenth century, around the ancient church of Saint Sophia in Istanbul, they marked the edifice as indubitably Islamic. The minaret everywhere serves to identify on the landscape the community of the faith of Muhammad. Its form is a silent embodiment of the oral summons that it houses.

The *imām*, however, within the mosque, is a more important official: he leads that to which the muezzin only calls. The term *imām*, in Sunnī Islam, designates the leader who stands in front of the assembled believers, to ensure unison in the prayers. The congregation follows him in the recitals and prostrations. The *mihrāb*, "niche," which the *imām* faces, marks the *qiblah* toward Mecca. It is always empty, though its walls may be exquisitely adorned with tiles and texts. The recess serves as a focal point that sets the faces of the faithful on the line to Mecca where they find spiritual rendevous with the rest of their fellow Muslims. By the *mihrāb* the congregation is consciously set on one of the radii from the gravitational center of Islam.

Like the minaret, the *mihrāb* may also have derived from non-Islamic factors similarly subdued. The earliest traditions suggest that a spear, thrust into the ground, sufficed to mark the direction. But when churches were taken into Islam, the numerous niches in familiar use for statuary or episcopal thrones seemed to suit the need. Emptiness was all that was required to baptize the old into the new and to proclaim the iconoclasm and equality of Muslim devotion.

Similarly the *minbar*, "pulpit," gave the mosque a rostrum for exhortation and preaching, in which earlier forms were readily adapted. The characteristic Muslim pulpit is a projection at right angles to the main wall, often adjacent to the *mihrāb*, with steps leading upward through a screen or curtain surmounted by a lintel. The preacher faces down the steps from the platform at the top and addresses the assembly without a reading stand. His words are seldom read from a book or notes, though carefully prepared. The spacious areas on both sides of the *minbar* give ample scope to the artist in calligraphy and design. Sometimes the *minbar* is retractable, being provided with wheels in order to be pushed into a recess when not in use. For the sermon by the *khatīb* is a weekly institution—at the time of the noonprayer on Fridays. At other times the shaikhs and readers recite or catechize from lower, less pretentious, desks or platforms, on which they squat in closer audience among smaller groups. Several such low rostrums may be seen in any sizable mosque. In populous cities the visitor will often find such instruction in progress.

The place and function of the mosque sermon in Muslim religious life needs to be more fully investigated. The discourse is generally hortatory rather than discursive. It does not so much defend the faith as commend it: it encourages to practice rather than to apology. The underlying assumption seems generally to be that believers know what they believe but may be forgetful in the fulfillment of their duties. The nonbeliever is never present to listen, so the sermon is never directed toward an outsider. This fact has deeply influenced the form and temper of the average preacher. His discourse is usually divided into two parts, the first and much longer section beginning with certain conventional openings and containing the substance of the theme, the second following as a brief peroration, after a pause.

Many mosque preachers follow a calendar sequence and fit their themes to the significance of the season or approaching festival. They may also comment widely on current political and social affairs, though the liberty to do this has been strictly curtailed in certain areas of late because of the delicate nature of mosque-state relationships.[8] Nevertheless, the close connection between the preacher's duty and social life is traditional. The *minbar* was in early Islam the place of caliphal pronouncements and sometimes of judicial and other judgments. The sermon has often been an instrument of public education in particular points, even in emergencies of public health. It has also been a means of political indoctrination or propaganda. This was natural in a society when the mosque was the chief place of assembly amid a population that was largely illiterate and where there was no sense of any incompatibility between worship and other affairs.

Much contemporary criticism of the mosque-preaching in the past concentrates on this point of its subservience to ruling authority and its function as a means of governmental control. Other critics deplore the lack of originality displayed by many preachers and trace the neglect of the mosque by some sections of the population to the stereotyped form and content of the sermon. There is impatience when the preacher repeats pious platitudes and demonstrates that he is incapable of any adequate intellectual or spiritual wrestling with the realities of the world as at least some of his hearers know it. The need for improvement of the mosque sermon is widely felt in responsible circles and there have been a number of manuals in the recent past seeking to grapple with it.[9] The ultimate future of the preacher in the life of Islam would seem likely to turn upon the adequacy of theological education.

The following sermon from the *Dīwān*, a published collection of 'Abdallāh al-Marāghỹ of Cairo, may serve to illustrate the manner and content of a mosque discourse. The theme is "faith in God":

Praise be to God, who guides the hearts of His chosen ones by faith, and makes tranquil the hearts of His elect in confidence. I bear witness that there is no god except God. In His dominion nothing occurs save by His willing it. I bear witness that our Lord Muhammad is the Apostle of God, whose resolution was not weakened by adversities.

O God, bless and preserve and be gracious unto our Lord Muhammad, his people, his companions, and those who follow him.

God Most High has said in His glorious Book: "Those who believe in God, their heart is guided, and God is in all things most knowing."

You who worship God: faith is the devoting of the heart unto God and acceptance of what God has revealed to His prophets. It is belief in His determination and will. It is a breath from the spirit of God, by which He confirms in their trials those who sincerely believe among His worshipers. It is a torch lighted from the light of God, irradiating in the hearts of the chosen ones among those who love Him. Faith has signs that point the way to it, and conviction has indications that guide humanity toward it. God most High said: "Those believers whose hearts glow at the mention of God, and whose faith is increased when His verses [signs] are read to them, those who rely upon their Lord and perform the prayers and give generously of that which we have bestowed upon them, these are the true believers indeed. They have honor with their Lord and forgiveness and gracious benefits."

These are the indications of the true faith: the fear of God that impels a person to magnify Him and extol Him, meditation on His signs which stimulates him to trust in His promise, reliance upon God leading him to conformity to His decree, so that he reverences Him in his prayers and is obedient in his alsmgiving. God will increase him in rank and forgive him his evil deeds and bestow upon him gracious blessings and guide him in the path of the upright.

You worshipers of God: how wondrous it is that everything belonging to the believer is good. It is only so for the believer. If some good fortune befalls him, he gives thanks and it becomes a blessing to him. If some misfortune, he is patient and it becomes a blessing. A gift does not make him negligent, nor does catastrophe anger him. That is how Muhammad was. God tried him with blessings and he received them with great gratitude. He tested him with calamity and he met it with splendid patience. He went one day to the people of Al-Tā'if to preach to them the message of his Lord. They stoned him until the blood flowed. He took refuge in a vineyard and sought shade there. Then he turned unto God and said: "O God I plead before you for the feebleness of my strength which has been patient with men. O You, Most Merciful, You are the Lord of those who acknowledge weakness. You are my Lord. It is not your anger that is upon me. I will not care anything of it."

Such also was the life of his companions, the believers.

They did not weary of the animosity of the unbelievers and did not despair at their seeming victory. They drew out of failure the means to success, and out of disaster a road to victory, taking refuge with their Lord in loyal resolve, and entire confidence. They it was who hearkened to God and to the Apostle after wounds befell them. They it was to whom others said: "Truly, men have gathered together against you; so fear them." But that only increased their faith and they said: "We have considered God and the grace of the One we trust." So they overcame by grace and favor from God and no evil touched them. They followed a course well-pleasing to God who is the Lord of great goodness.

O you worshipers of God, faith guides believers, both as individuals and communities, to bear hardships, however great they may be, and to clear open the way to a happy life, however difficult be its attainment, and to the performance of religious obligations, however arduous. Hardships reward believers with rest and quiet and confidence. Difficulties repay them with strength and courage. Acts of worship make them grow in faith.

Fasting is half of patience. Patience is half of faith. How great is our need in this life of a disposition that will implant fasting in the soul. It will nourish the feeling of mercy and train the power of the will and purpose, and lift man to the loftiest character. Prayer is a link between the servant and the Lord, and between the believer and all fellow believers. Pilgrimage means mutual awareness and mutual good will, sacrifice, patience, and fortitude. *Zakāt* is goodness, liberality, righteousness, and the payment of debt.

Then fear God, you worshipers of God, and lay hold of the bond of faith, for that is the strong tie of God, gathering believers into one mind. Take pleasure in God's blessings and find your beauty in God's glories. May God cause quietness to descend upon you and bring your hearts unto unity.

Tradition records that the Apostle of God said to his companions: "Ask me anything you wish." A man cried: "O Apostle of God: What is faith?" He said: "Sincerity." "And what is conviction?" and he said: "Honest dealing."[10]

Despite the criticisms directed against him from several sides in Islam, the preacher still has an influential role in the community. On his lips religion becomes articulate and something of its daily meaning is expressed. Though there are powerful factors working in the direction of secularity and irreligion, the mosques are frequently crowded and listeners overflow on to the sidewalks where loudspeakers relay the discourse. Even in Turkey, where the pressure of a laic state had been strong for three decades, a revival of mosque attendance has marked Islamic renewal, not least in Ankara itself. If, then, the *khatīb* is far from enjoying the prestige he once wielded, he and his art maintain a vigorous continuity with the great past and have still to be reckoned with in the understanding of Muslim religious life.

Certain other features of the mosque as an index to Islam deserve attention. The notable lack of seats strikes the Western visitor—though it is by no means so strange to the Eastern Christian. More significant still is the total absence of a special sanctuary or altar. Two large candlesticks may flank the *mihrāb*, but their meaning does not hold a central place. Long lines of pillars support the flat roofs, or wide expanses of carpeted space stretch beneath a soaring dome. The Qur'ān is everywhere the theme of decoration. A clock will often be found in a prominent position. Small folding stools that serve to support the reader's copy of the Qur'ān are about the only movable furniture. In some mosques a balcony or gallery runs along one side or even around the structure. Outside the mosque proper is a wide *sahn*, ''court,'' unless the mosque is small. Here stand the fountains in open cisterns or under cupolas with columns. If the mosque is famous, it may boast some celebrated tomb of patriarch, traditionalist, exegete, or ruler. Behind a grille or under an ornate canopy, a sarcophagus will be found. Around these shrines the visitor may see candles, ribbons, and other decorations, placed there by the faithful at times of remembrance or invocation. In small local mosques the memory of some saint, *marabūt*, may dominate. Signs of special veneration then become more evident. For popular Muslim devotion has not seldom broken out of the strict rigidities of orthodox theology to find satisfying popular forms by which to express and arouse itself.

For all its wide variety, however, the mosque has a clear unity of function pervading and constraining all its architectural diversity. This unity arises in the last analysis from Islam itself and has been deepened by the fact of pilgrimage. In the great ages of mosque-building, travel was frequent and extensive. Masons, designers, craftsmen, and ceramicists traveled from center to center, on their long way to or from Mecca, studying the edifices they saw, noting details, and comparing skills. They learned in this way how to combine their artistic tastes with the requirements of the faith. Such luxury as they might allow themselves was transmuted into forms at least basically subdued to the dictates of dogma. Carpets on which the faithful prayed could be richly dyed and patterned; lamps by which they recited the sacred text could be lavishly inlaid with gold and silver; domes that symbolized the overarching unity could be elaborately adorned with color or gold. These were compensations for the prohibition of statuary, ikons, and pictorial art. The mosque, then, can be seen as the majestic synthesis of prevailing religious dogma and a worshipful art that accepted its limitations creatively. Nowhere can the soul of Islam be so movingly read and pondered as in its hallowed precincts.

VI

A study of the religion that the mosque expresses would not be complete without some reference to its principal historical division. Early in its career, Islam suffered a serious schism, dividing it into two major groupings called Sunnī and Shī'ah. This is not the place for a detailed exposition of the factors involved, or of the other subdivisions into which both, but Shī'ah Islam in particular, are divided. The context of devotional life seems to be the most appropriate area in which to set a brief explanation of this duality in Islam, though originating factors were political as well as theological.

Sunnī Islam follows the rule of the orthodox *Sunnah*, "path," of the Qur'ān and the (Sunnī) Tradition. It believes in the validity of the historical Caliphate and in the utter finality of the prophethood of Muhammad. Shī'ah Islam holds that 'Alī, fourth Caliph, cousin and son-in-law of the Prophet, should have been his immediate successor and, therefore, disallows the first three Caliphs and the *de jure* status of the subsequent Umayyads and their successors. The dark family tragedies of the house of 'Alī, culminating in the massacre of Husain and his retinue at Karbalā' in A.D. 680, gave to Shī'ah Islam a background of martyrdom that shaped its whole theology. Devotion to the tragic three—'Alī, Hasan, and Husain—evoked religious attitudes to which Sunnī Islam has remained for the most part a stranger.

In its main areas in Iraq, Iran, Afghanistan, the Yemen, and India, Shī'ah Islam is devoted to the memory of the Prophet's family and sees in its story of death and defeat a drama of re-demptive sacrifice. The celebration culminates in the Muharram rites when the tragedy of Husain is re-enacted with intense emo-tion. Here, more than anywhere in Sunnī Islam, the Shī'ah Muslim comes to grips with the mystery of suffering and grapples with areas of meaning the average Sunnī ignores. Descriptions of Shī'ah devotion in its supreme festival are readily accessible.[11]

What is of importance here is to appreciate the underlying rea-sons for the deep contrasts in Shī'ah devotional life. The crux lies in the contrasted Shī'ah concept of the relation of the divine reve-lation to humanity in time. Shī'ah Islam believes in Muhammad as the culmination of prophethood. But whereas the Sunnī be-lieves that the succeeding centuries enter into the Muhammadan revelation through the Qur'ān and the orthodoxy of the possess-ing community, Shī'ahs believe that it is mediated to the genera-tions through *Imām*s, without whom its relevance cannot be known. These *Imām*s do not replace the Prophet or impugn his finality. Rather they are the indispensable media of the under-standing of the truth the Prophet proclaimed. It is through them, and them alone, that he is made contemporary. The truth is not possessed in an orthodox continuity of retrospective education. The community is not the repository or guarantor of valid under-standing in reliance upon the prior documentary sources. The guarantee lies in the *Imām* who is thought of as an emanation of the divine light and of the wisdom of God in the time of his life.

Whereas the term *imām* in Sunnī Islam simply signifies the leader of the mosque prayers, habitual or actual, in Shī'ah Islam the *Imām* is the agent of the divine illumination of the age. The succession begins with the Prophet and 'Alī and his sons and passes down to the number of seven (in some Shī'ah sects), or to twelve (in others). By virtue of its more immediate sense of divine revelation, Shī'ah Islam has shown much greater tendency to sectarianism and schism. It is subdivided into many forms, one of the most notable being Ismailism. Its doctrine of the Hidden *Imām* gives rise to speculative excesses far more readily than does the disciplined orthodoxy of Sunnīs. Shī'ahs have their own traditions and separate schools of law. Many racial and cultural tensions can be read into this central schism and the cleavage goes very deep. New sects such as Babism and Bahaism arose in the nineteenth century from Shī'ah Islam, carrying some of its ideas into wider disparity.

The issue between Sunnī and Shī'ah ultimately concerns the relation of dogma to devotion and of the eternal universal to the temporal particular. Is the individual believer related to Muhammad as the place of final revelation, backward through the generations? Or does that essential truth break upon the believer anew in more contemporary occasions of new radiance and articulation? Shī'ahs have affirmed the latter. What they have lost in schismatic divisiveness when compared with Sunnīs, they may have gained in devotional immediacy and the sense of urgency.

Though devious and proliferating in many of its forms, Shī'ah Islam has often greater spontaneity and intensity. It has escaped the aridity and formalism that have periodically afflicted the Sunnī segment. It has shown more hospitality, or been more exposed, to esoteric confusion. Under its influence many non-Arab elements have come to coalesce with original Muslim forms. Because of their doctrine of the sinlessness of the *Imāms*, Shī'ahs look much more largely for intercession and mediation.

Relations between Sunnī and Shī'ah have varied through the centuries. The more extreme sects, carrying their doctrines of emanation to a point where the supremacy of Muhammad is denied and he comes to be merely one in a series, have naturally aroused the strongest antagonism. Shī'ahs in general have much ground for hatred when they relive the agonies of Husain or remember such episodes as the defeat of their own Fātimid Caliphate by that earnest Sunnī, Saladin, or the bitter zeal of the last great Mughal, Aurangzīb. On the other hand, there have been many efforts to draw the household of Islam together and to develop its underlying common heritage. But devotionally it would seem that an irreconcilable difference of mood, emphasis, and emotion divides the two.

VII

If Shī'ah Muslims represent a plea for greater immediacy of the soul to truth than Sunnī Islam provides, the same is true of the long and deep tradition of mysticism, the Muslim forms of which are known as Sufism. It is in this area that the devotional achievements of Islam as religion are greatest. Sufism has a long and checkered history. There were times in the later centuries when it did more to conserve and perpetuate Islam than did orthodoxy itself. Its beginnings go back to the Prophet who is claimed to be by some Sufis the supreme exponent of disciplined mystical ecstasy. The Qur'ān, in this view, is then the greatest product of the Sufi approach. This understanding, sustained by many texts capable of such interpretation, justifies the Sufis in asserting a direct intimacy with the truth such as outrages or dismays the orthodox custodians of the faith.

The strong development of Sufism, associated with such teachers as the Brethren of Purity and Al-Muhāsibī in the ninth and tenth centuries of the Christian era, largely came in protest against the increasing formalism of Muslim theology. Whatever elements in primitive Islam served to give it positive generation, it drew strength from the failure of the orthodox to satisfy the demands of the devotional spirit. The mystic, being always suspect to the custodians of dogma, seeks the attainment of divine knowledge by a contrasted attitude to the deeds or documents of the historical faith. Mysticism believes in an alternative way to truth, beyond reason and revelation dogmatically defined. It discounts what Muslim theology calls 'aql, "intellect," and naql, "transmitted truth," and concentrates on kashf, "discovery," in which the meaning of faith and truth is given in experimental immediacy to the seeking soul. The insight is the reward of a path to knowledge that involves moral discipline and ascetic life. This Sufi way, tarīqah, is understood to consist of stages, the three main grades of which are the murīd, "novice," the sā'ir, "traveler," and the wāsil, "attainer."

The conditions of knowledge are, for the Sufi, primarily spiritual, not intellectual. Muhammad is the exemplar of the path. He exemplifies faith as an attitude rather than dictates it as a dogma. The Qur'ān likewise is a textbook in the method. The findings to be valid must be the Sufi's own. But because they are experimentally known, they cannot be readily defined in intellectual terms. "Come where I am; I can show you the way" is the mystic's call, not: "Believe what I teach, I can tell you the orthodox truth." As such, Sufis represent at once a protest, an aspiration, and a goal. Their very lack of rational concern and some of the forms of their technique are liable to lead them into aberration and bring their purpose into disrepute. Some Sufi doctrines of passivity and the Sufi veneration of saints have occasioned no little apathy and crude superstition. Sufism has suffered from its own excesses and is reproached by many modern reformers. Yet even these critics, Muhammad 'Abduh, for example, and Iqbāl, have themselves owed not a little to Sufi influence in their upbringing.

In its finest forms Islamic mysticism has inspired the greatest devotional literature in Islam. There is the celebrated poetess Rābi'ah (died A.D. 801); Al-Hallāj, the Persian writer (crucified in A.D. 922); Al-Ghazālī; Ibn al-'Arabī, "the greatest mystical genius of the Arabs" (died in Damascus in A.D. 1240); his contemporary, the famous Jalāl al-Dīn Rūmī, author of the immortal *Mathnavī*. The writings of these and lesser leaders are becoming increasingly available in translations and anthologies for Western readers.[12] They are living testimony to the vitality of the tradition to which they belonged. The student may find in their most eloquent expression the characteristic Sufi intensities: the yearning after the knowledge that is absorption; the joy of penetration beyond the shell of selfish selfhood into wholeness; the price of discipline and the meaning of temptation; the purity and poverty of the ardent spirit; the disinterestedness of valid love; the stations and states of the progress of the soul; the anticipations of illumination and the climax of *fanā'*, where the soul transcends itself and its search in passing into love.

The most notable external feature of Sufism is its organization into orders for the better fulfillment of its purposes. These orders became a profound factor in the whole life of Islam. They resembled economic guilds or fraternities, and gave a cohesion to Muslim social life that often outweighed the mosque and orthodoxy in local importance. The orders gathered around first the person and then the reputation of some great founder, whose devotions they used. The most famous of the orders were the Qādiriyyah founded by 'Abd al-Qādir al-Jilānī (1078-1166); the Suhrawardiyyah, named after Shihāb al-Dīn al-Suhrawardī (1144-1234); the Shādhiliyyah, deriving from Nūr al-Dīn al-Shādhilī (1196-1258); and the Maulawiyyah, from the title of Maulawī, given to the author of the *Mathnavī*. Numerous other orders and innumerable offshoots developed throughout the world of Islam.

Their rituals differed considerably but all in some sense used the technique of *dhikr*. The dervish is no doubt the most familiar image to the Western mind in this connection. *Dhikr* is the use of rhythmic recitation and rhythmic movements of the body to induce the sense of abstraction from the physical world that the Sufi seeks. Repeated ejaculations of *Allāh* or *Subhān Allāh* or the words of the *Fātihah* serve to sever attention from the senses and concentrate it on the thought of God. That the practices of the mystics have encouraged charlatans and rogues is a familiar denunciation. But the scandalous excesses of some should not blind the critic to the force and fervor of restrained and disciplined mysticism. For all the tensions they have set up in Islam, the Sufis have not seldom been its salvation. Among their humblest devotees one may still find a rare quality of spiritual desire and a sensitivity of soul to God, life, and eternity.

Here, from a Sufi manual, or rather, scroll, of devotion carried in the long robe of an unknown artisan or in the camel holster of an unnamed cameleer, undated and timeless, is a translated extract. It breathes an unmistakable, religious self-awareness that knows both repentance and confidence, entreaty and adoration:

O Lord, open to us Your mercy and clothe us, O Lord, in the most excellent robe of guidance and prayer. Be glad, O God, at Your greatness . . . and let the sighing of our tears flow, O God, into Your awful worship. Correct, O God, in me the allurements of evil for the sake of my entreaty. O my God, if Your mercy had not shown me the good way, then who would have led me unto You in a plain path? . . . If Your aid had forsaken me when self and Satan struggled with me, then truly Your forsaking would have left me in misery and loss.

O my God, I knocked at the door of Your mercy with the

hand of my hope. I fled unto You, seeking refuge from my multiplied sins and I hung upon the borders of Your garments with the fingers of my trust. So pardon, O God, the wrongs I have done, the evils and the sins, and rid me, O God, of my evil state, for You are my Lord and Sovereign, my reliance and my hope, the goal of my desire in my calamity and distress.

O my God, how will You reject a worthless one who takes refuge with You fleeing from his sins? Or how will You disappoint one who implores guidance of Your excellence with entreaty? Or how will You cast off one who longs to drink of Your waters? No! You will not . . . for Your door is open to the seekers and the homeless. You are the end of our search and the goal of hope, O my God.

This is the Sufi's *Alaika tawakkaltu*, "Lord in Thee have I trusted"—one of the most familiar phrases in the religious life of all Islam.

V

THE ISLAMIC ORDER FOR HUMAN SOCIETY

I

The second clause of the double summons that the minaret lays upon Muslims because of their confession of God and the Prophet employs one of the most inclusive concepts in the Arabic language. With the imperative *Hayya*, "Come!," it demands an alert response to what it calls *Falāh*. "Come unto the good" it cries—the good, implicit in the revelation already acknowledged. It is the good to which worship leads and for which the Muslim is enlisted in the ranks of the believing. *Falāh* is not, then, some pietistic abstraction or the indulgence of a private sanctity. It is the true state of well-being, the prosperity, of the people of God, fulfilled in communal existence and realized in social life. "Come unto the good life." "Alert yourselves in mind and will to the authentic well-being of Muslim humanity, achieved within the Islamic order." Such is *Falāh* as the muezzin proclaims and defines it.

It is a term to set the mind strenuously to work and well calculated to serve as the ruling idea in any careful exposition of Islam in its external meaning for human society. What, as the Muslim sees it, does Islam mean for the political, economic, and social areas of human life and relationship? What is the *Falāh* to which those under Islam are bidden? How is it conceived as to its content? How is it to be expected as an actuality? To these questions and some, at least, of their answers in historical Islam we must now turn.

As familiar as the prayer mat to the traveler among Muslims is the doctrine that religion pervades all life to the student of Islam. Repeatedly in classical dogma and in current apology the reader comes upon the fact that Islam is totalitarian. It does not distinguish between duty as a believer and duty as a citizen; between what is owed to God and what is owed to society. All social responsibilities are religious in character and religion is fulfilled in what ensues not only in the mosque but also in the market. There has been a marked tendency to interpret Islam as unique in this respect, though these attitudes often derive either from a misunderstanding of the distinction between religious and secular elsewhere or from incomplete scrutiny of their "identity" in Islam. But the fact remains that Islam sets out to be an inclusive system in which the relation of the person to God pervades also one's relation to one's fellows.

Falāh, then, exists for the muezzin as a concept. The ideal revelation is in hand. In its light believers see light. God has sent the knowledge of the divine will and in its obedience and fulfillment the good life for humankind is to be attained. Those attitudes of mind and soul that relate uniquely to God in worship and have been described under "prayer" have their counterparts in attitudes toward the world of one's fellows within Islam. *Īmān,* "belief," has as its corollary *Dīn,* "deed," including manward as well as Godward obligations. True Muslims are they who "perform," because, and as, they believe. Such "performing" covers not only the ritual prayer, fasting, and pilgrimage but almsgiving and all that it implies. It symbolizes responsibility toward one's fellows. Islam, as proclaimed from the minaret, is *Falāh* as well as *Salāt,* the *laborare* of goodness as well as the *orare* of worship. Just as in Christian terms the word "service" may mean a good deed or an occasion of worship, so in Islam the obligation of religion means behavior as well as belief. "The pillars of religion" in

Islam involve not only creedal confession but the recognition of God in all realms of human conduct. *Falāh*, as a word, seems to have obvious kinship with Hebrew and Syriac terms for "cult" or "prayer," though its immediate Arabic sense is "good" or "success."[1]

This comprehensive quality of Islam is epitomized in the historical form of its genesis. From the moment persons and tribes became physically, as well as spiritually, tributary to Muhammad in Medina, Islam was an external as well as an internal loyalty. This post-*Hijrah* amalgam was repeated and intensified in the subsequent expansion of Islam. The new faith did not spread as a religious understanding enjoining submission to "the powers that be." Rather it came superseding those powers with impressive rapidity and finality. To become a Muslim was to become a subject; those who remained non-Muslims were the more subjected. When Islam conquered, rulers were changed. Heraclius or the heirs of Khosroes went; 'Umar, Mu'āwiya, Al-Mansūr came.

This pattern of external dominance was only the outward form of the inward fact. Islam was not an account of human relationship with God that could coexist with a variety of political expressions. Rather those political expressions gave way to the Islamic. The Caliphate became the symbol of a trusteeship of Muhammad's definitive prophethood and of a perpetuation of his model rulership. Both were permanently fused together and remained ideologically intact until the twentieth century. It is in community, in political expression and political sovereignty, that Islam is realizable. The true law in the custody of the true community is the condition of the true society. The ideal state of affairs, the muezzin's *Falāh*, demands the proper ideology under the proper conditions. The law that defines the one also establishes the other. We may perhaps go so far as to say that within the Muslim perspective religious ideology not simply requires but *is* a communal order realizable by political sovereignty within the life of this world. This is the ultimate meaning of law in Islam and of Islam as law. Even the phrase "Islam as law" is ambiguous, however, because it may imply that Islam could also be, in a parallel sense, something else. It is just that something else which the term "Islam as law" is here meant to rule out. Properly conceived, the historic religion is a total way of life, known and learned from divine disclosure and attainable in political, social, and economic existence, by human beings on earth.

II

Though the definition proposed just above would not coincide with some expressions of the contemporary Muslim mind, these should not take priority over the exposition of the classical meanings. Turning to an attempt at a summary of them, it seems reasonable to divide the study of *Falāh* into two parts: definition and actualization, the "what" and the "how" of the ideology that is Islam.

The underlying incentive of Islam has always been to *do* what God willed. The ultimate human status before God, that of the *'abd*, "slave-servant," points to deed rather than to contemplation. The definition of humanity before God is an active relationship. Though this does not obviate theology, it means that Islam is finally, and more characteristically, concerned with what the Lord requires in moral deed.

The ground and form of that requirement is revelation. The Qur'ān is interpreted as validating human reason as an instrument for tracing the majesty of the divine *mind* in the universe of nature. But reason is not an appropriate means for the discovery of the divine *will*, except in a confirmatory sense. God is the author of the law by which we acknowledge the divine sovereignty. God shows the path in which we should walk. Rational ethics or political science or economic theory—as the product of human logic, argumentation, dialectic, or pondered experience—do not, theoretically, exist in Islam. The basis of human conduct and organization is revelation. Only in writing the lesser points or the "by-laws" into the fundamental "constitution" for human life, given in revelation, have these human systems any validity.

The true form of the family, the state, the economy, are discoverable in the divine will. We are not meant to argue for democracy on the ground of inalienable rights; or for laissez-faire on the principle of the greatest happiness; or for mutual help as proper to the human mind; or for beliefs because they work; or for any one of the multifarious pros and cons of utilitarianism, pragmatism, libertarianism, egalitarianism, and all the other forms of political or ethical theory. What is right for human society has been revealed in the divine law committed to the trust of the Islamic community. Some in recent times would open the door to theorists on the grounds that some points of human organization are too detailed and insignificant to be worthy of revelatory action on the part of God.[2] But this tendency to confine revelation to major principles and elevate it beyond the level of the meticulous is foreign to the historical mind of Islam and is a modern innovation.

Law, then, as the secret of *Falāh* comes in revelation from God. But it still requires definition in the manifold of human activity. Revelation as a process is consummated once and for all in Muhammad. This fullness of revelation is the Qur'ān where the divine law is recorded and known. The Qur'ān, as the first and ruling source of law, is the definitive court of appeal as to the meaning of what is good. But Tradition interpreted and enlarged the meanings of the Qur'ān and so became the second element in the structure of Muslim ideology.

Tradition tended to proliferate under the double impetus of external need and interior veneration. Much came into the Muslim heritage of obedience in this way from the customs and cultures of conquered territories. Muhammad became the posthumous repository of many ideas and practices that Islam had neither will nor power to eradicate from the behavior of its new devotees. But there is little evidence that elements incompatible with crucial Muslim teachings found any such entry.

For the rest, Islam sought to give sanction to new ways and patterns of behavior in the positive form of traditions about its supreme human leader. If the expanding community was in a real sense legislating in an expanding manner for itself, it did so in the name of its great earthly architect. The fact that things must be believed to turn upon prophetic precedent is no more than a measure of the veneration in which revelation and its agent were regarded.

When such communal "legislation" outran its validities, however, and distorted the historical memory, there arose the problem of correction, which was undertaken by the great traditionalists. When the mind of Islam was uncertain about the legal validity in any area of its traditions, the authority of the great schools of law was the practical answer. How far their edit-ing succeeded it is almost impossible to determine precisely. Perhaps it is unimportant. What matters is the general validity of this second "Muhammadan" source of access to the mind of God.

For all its multiplicity of traditional sources, law was still incomplete. The Qur'ān and the valid traditions alike did not suffice for the regulation of the behavior of the community. Inas-much as that behavior required revelatory criteria and directives, other sources of ideology continuous with the first and second had to be evolved. The structure of Islamic law is generally re-garded as complete with the establishment of two other regulative sources, *Qiyās* and *Ijmā'*, "analogy" and "consensus." Intricate and sometimes bitter controversies raged around these concepts, their limits, and their functioning. These, however, are the task of the historian rather than that of the expositor.

III

Analogy can be readily understood. It is a principle of exten-sion of Islamic law on the basis of a likeness in two situations, one of which was specifically provided for in the Qur'ān or Tradition. The inclusion of the other—analogous—situation might then be reasonably inferred from the first. Thus, if the Qur'ān prohibits the use of wine, the prohibition might be understood to include other intoxicants that had similar effects, their avoidance also being presumably the intention of the prohibition. The schools required careful definitions of what was properly analogous within the terms of the point being argued and differed somewhat as to whether the intention had to be explicit or simply inferred. The dangers involved in analogy made it suspect in the eyes of some who disallowed it altogether.

Of much wider range and subtlety was the concept of *Ijmā'*. Reliance on consensus goes back to the Qur'ān and to tra-ditions—some of them disputed—underlying the notion that truth is safe with the community. Individualism is heresy. The private person it is who goes into untruth. The whole is not likely—according to some statements, is not able—to stray uni-versally. Put in its most daring form, consensus means that Islam is what Muslims define it to be. In the more modest and circum-spect view, it means that there is a source of security in the com-munal mind. The Muslim community is not likely to go long, or far, into a position that is not validly Islamic. In some such form, though its organs of expression may differ, reliance on the com-munity is characteristic of, indeed necessary to, all religions.

Consensus is not conceivable or proper except in a complemen-tary relation to the documentary sources. It affords a principle of development in Islam whereby a new attitude, or a new require-ment, can gather the force of law and hence the sanction of "reve-latory" status, through its acceptance in general by those who believe. After God and the Prophet, the Community. They, in whose custody of worship and conduct the truths of the religion have been entrusted, may be reasonably accepted as a frame of reference, a court of appeal, for the validation, or otherwise, of what is truly and authentically Islamic. This, it should be clear, is not democracy as such. It is not majority opinion statistically as-certained. It is the attainment of a common mind on a particular point, the legal recognition of an existing state of affairs—or of opinion—that has come to be in the community, in an area of former silence and present compatibility vis-à-vis the Qur'ān.

The schools again have differed profoundly on problems asso-ciated with consensus, but most minds of good will have been ready to accept its sanctity. There has been no general reluctance to allow *Ijmā'* on the grounds that it has resulted in law just as binding as the law that came down from heaven. Some have sug-gested that consensus may be a hidden form of the sin of associa-tion: it results in a product that becomes a part of the Sharī'ah equal with what God spoke. The exaltation of the humanly ori-ginated to the level of the divinely originated might be *Shirk*, "idolatry." But these fears have been largely disallowed, a fact that indicates the importance that law attributes to the commu-nity.[3]

Consensus does not arrive without stimulus and direction. The community is a large and somewhat indefinite entity. Its mind, especially in what is novel or problematic—obvious areas for *Ijmā'*—comes only through pioneers, through individuals who propagate creative thoughts. Most consensus starts with minori-ties; it may even start with heretics. It is a process of becoming, or

of thinking, that someone must originate. And when it is originated it is manifestly not consensus. Yet if only consensus validates,
how can a pioneer opinion ever be launched? How can a consensus ever legitimately arise? It cannot be, without coming to be,
and cannot come to be legitimately, without being.

To confront this dilemma, Islam developed the much more
controversial notion of *Ijtihād*, the means to *Ijmā'*. *Ijtihād*
means, in its technical sense, enterprise or initiative. It involves
diligence and implies great effort, either to understand or to discriminate the right action in any general issue. It is usually held
that a *mujtahid,* one judged capable of *Ijtihād,* qualifies only on
the ground of prolonged grammatical, legal, and theological
training. The *mujtahid* was not an administrator of law in a court,
but a scholar learned in all its niceties and so capable of reaching
conclusions that might commend themselves to a general consensus in the course of time. In this way the lacunae in Islamic
ideology or in the Sharī'ah might gradually be filled and the
documentary sources made complete.

Ijtihād as a means to an ultimate consensus was valid only when
it did so eventuate in public approval. Just how wide such approval had to be, or when it could be understood to exist, were
matters on which definitions varied. The ways in which the
mujtahid could function were also a theme of long controversy.
Some allowed a relatively wide freedom to what was called *ra'ȳ*,
"expert private opinion." Others held that this could be practiced
only under certain limits.

There was the principle of *Istihsān*, whereby the legist considered a certain course of action good, somewhat after the manner
of Western equity. There was *Istislāh*, by which a position could
be validated for its soundness, not in general, but in respect of
public welfare. There was also *Istishāb*, in which the argument
went back toward analogy and found validity for a course of action by associating it with a provision in the Qur'ān or Tradition.
But these nice technical points of detail cannot be treated adequately here. Their variety is only a measure of the desire to ensure that even the competent experts should reach conclusions on
new rulings only under strict safeguards.

Some authorities denied *ra'ȳ* and *Ijtihād* altogether, asserting
that the documentary sources were sufficient, or preferring to

make them so by crude invention of traditions. In any event, *Ijti-hād* was understood as limited to the realm of law and had no competence over dogma. There was much discussion as to whether *Ijtihād* was a permanent function, whether "the door of *Ijtihād*," as the phrase was, remained open. Or was *Ijtihād* a kind of self-curtailing process less and less needed as the Sharī'ah was steadily completed by its exercise? The steady parallel emergence of ever new demands, especially in modern times, tended to render the latter view untenable. But many held it with great tenacity, claiming that *Ijtihād*, having fulfilled its entire duties and having made possible, through *Ijmā'*, the completion of the perfect law, was no longer an available function in the Islamic community. This controversy still continues, and meanwhile the complexities of life make ever more necessary the new judgments the old mind so much fears.

On a conservative hypothesis, those fears are perhaps justified. The idea behind *Ijtihād* and *Ijmā'* clearly has very wide potentialities. It can be developed into an inclusive principle of change on the ground of the majority mind and extended to many areas of inconsistency with the traditional teachings of the Sharī'ah. It is, in fact, being so used, tacitly more often than avowedly, in the present scene. Most Muslim nations have considerably modified their civil and criminal laws, in the name of the popular will, expressed in representative parliaments or otherwise. Such changes are claimed by their champions as Islamic in a spiritual sense. They are valid because the community attests them as desirable.

When appeal in this way is made to the spirit, as contrasted with the letter, of Islam, it is evident that the criterion of what is authentic becomes much freer. The community, therefore, assumes a much more crucial role, which is often definitive rather than complementary. Such reinterpretation of what Islam means and requires may be seen as the modern form of *Ijtihād* and as a new concept of the *mujtahid* role, even though those who make the changes do not invoke it.

In the classic past, however *Ijmā'* via *Ijtihād* was only a fourth and subordinate source of ideological definition. And it was not valid on the democratic principle of the majority, but in the assumption that the community mind was a correct clue to the voice of God, where that voice had not otherwise spoken. This, then, is the structure of Islam—the Qur'ān, Tradition, *Qiyās*, and *Ijmā'*, shaping the holy Law that prescribes the conduct and measures the responsibilities of true Islam. That law was "totalitarian" in the sense that it pervaded all of life and had authority over all realms. Admittedly, there were many areas of behavior where it was indifferent and it left many options, not reprehending or commending possible lines of action. It did not seek to be inquisitorial or burdensome. It recognized the natural desires and frailties of humanity. In some realms it spoke absolutely; in others permissively. But nothing was exempt from it that it saw fit to include.

Before we turn to the actualization of the Islamic law so defined it should be noted that historic Sunnī Islam relies upon four great schools of law that grew up in the second and third Muslim centuries and gathered to themselves an authority that has ensured their perpetuity. Other schools flourished only fitfully and fell away. Shī'ah Muslims follow their own schools.

The first and largest of the Sunnī schools is that of Abū Hanīfah, centering in Baghdad. One of his chief pupils was Abū Yūsuf, the famous casuist of *The Arabian Nights*. Mālik ibn Anas founded the Mālikite school in Medina and established its authority in the central role of Medina in the tradition and government of Islam. Muhammad al-Shāfi'ī, personally the greatest and most gifted of the founders, built the Shāfi'ite school, with Cairo and Baghdad as its main centers. He was a skillful mediator between competing positions. The fourth and least of the schools, the Hanbalites of Ibn Hanbal, represented a conservative extremism such as Al-Shāfi'ī failed to reassure. Al-Shāfi'ī contributed most to the establishment of *Ijmā'* as a valid, formal source of Muslim law. He was one of the most remarkable figures in the whole history of jurisprudence. The diffusion of the leading schools varied considerably from time to time and from dynasty to dynasty. Their historical vicissitudes are not our concern here. In many centers of jurisprudence and legal lore they coexisted in varying strength.

The individual Muslim, as well as the individual judge and lawyer, belongs to one or other of the schools. Opinions are divided as to the limits of movement from one to another. Intriguing as the details are, the point of relevance here is that the schools represent the historical form of Muslim law or communal ideology as it is interpreted, taught, and defined by authority. Areas of diversity are many but small. What is common is great and serious. The schools are, so to speak, the focal points of the communal recognition by Islam of divine guidance for human life. They are organs for the definition of what that guidance means for the Muslim, wherever time and circumstance have needed its restraint and constraint. They are the lexicographers, we may say, of applied law; the grammarians of the divine mind or word or will.

Such definition is, in a sense, an ongoing process, for new situations require new relevance from the ancient law. These aspects call for discussion below, under the theme of actualization. It is in the realm of practical attainment that problems of redefinition most plainly arise. It is in facing the question "how" that inquirers are often sent back to the question "what" for new scrutiny. For historical purposes, this exposition of the organs of definition and of the sources of ideology must suffice. How the Muslim law is realized in community must now be studied. It will be clear that we are concerned with the social and the political. The Godward areas of Muslim duty—worship, fasting, and pilgrimage—have already been considered. These have, it is true, their social import and this will be implicit in what follows. "Come to the good life." The law defines it. What does obedience entail?

IV

We shall be following the order of presentation of many a recent Muslim author if we turn at once to the third of the pillars of religion, *Zakāt*, the "obligation of almsgiving." One of the basic principles of Islamic ideology is embodied here. It is the principle of social responsibility by which those who have possessions are obligated to concern themselves about those who lack what they enjoy. It distinguishes ideally between essential possession and actual possession. The former is the right and stake of the community in what anyone owns; the latter is de facto ownership. It teaches that what is mine belongs to the community in the ultimate reckoning. I, as a possessor, must remember the "not mine" aspect of what I call "mine," and give this recollection practical shape by donating a portion of it for public use. Only so do I validate what I retain. Private property is recognized on the condition of private benevolence. This is *Zakāt*, as interpreted in Muslim social thought.

Zakāt takes its honored place with witness, worship, fasting, and pilgrimage among the five pillars of Islam. It has clear Quranic force. *Zakāt* is frequently linked with *Salāt* as one of the first, confirming obligations of the new Muslim. "Perform the prayer and do the poor-rate" is the formula of submission (Surah 2.43, 83, 110, 117, 277, etc.). Those who withhold the poor-rate are a class synonymous with idolaters (Surah 12:7). *Zakāt,* as serving to identify the Muslim as such, is noted in Surah 58.12, 13.

The root idea of the word "*zakāt*" may be purification. But whatever may be the etymology, there is no doubt of the understanding of the institution. Property that recognizes no obligation in and beyond possession is contrary to the law. The Qur'ān uses an alternative word for alms, *sadaqāt*, which is nearly synonymous and introduces the idea of rightness and friendship. But *sadaqāt* (plural) are wholly voluntary.

On the basis of Quranic injunction and traditional exhortation, the practice of almsgiving became a basic social institution in Islam. It figured in the life of the community from pre-*Hijrah* days. Meccan Surahs enjoin and describe it. After the *Hijrah* the emigrants had great need of the charity of the Medinan Muslims. The pattern for the integration of more and more non-Muslim Medinans and their tribal neighbors into Islam is given in Surah 9.103: "Take alms of their wealth wherewith thou mayest purify them and mayest make them to grow and pray for them." There is no doubt that giving confirms believing: it dramatizes effectively a new allegiance. It may also express an otherwise inarticulate repentance.

The use of *Zakāt* when received in the early community was varied. It was distributed for the relief of the poor and needy, for parents, widows, slaves, and orphans, and was also utilized in military ways, for the furtherance of the *jihād* and, in certain circumstances, for the inducement of allegiance. It is meant to provide the means for progress "in the way of God."[4] By and large, however, it was the internal soundness, rather than the external expansion, of the Muslim community for which *Zakāt* was meant, though the former is often a most important condition of the latter.

This is not the place to outline the intricacies of detail into which this subject divides. The portion of the payment of one's possessions varied widely from time to time and also in respect of different forms of property—land and its produce, wealth in gold and money, merchandise and the rest. Some taught that *Zakāt* should comprise everything above a stipulated maximum retainable for legitimate self-support. Abū Dharr, for example, a notable Muslim teacher, invoked by exponents of the welfare state today, is said to have required that believers should give up everything they did not need. But the generally prevailing view fixed a limited percentage—10, 5, or 2.5 percent, for example—beyond which the believer was not required to go.

The agencies for the collection and distribution of *Zakāt* payments also varied from time to time. In early days the state played a large role. Mosque personnel frequently provided an obvious agency for this purpose. It was sometimes claimed that *Zakāt* could be paid directly by the rich to the poor. But general considerations made it preferable that the transaction should be publicly supervised and administered. When *Zakāt* was officially levied as a tax, it still hinged to a great degree on individual declaration of property. Just as the will to pay was its final sanction, so the will to avoid payment could discover numerous means of evasion and could offset much laudable exhortation.

Though incumbent or required (as distinct from *sadaqāt*, which were voluntary and which could be used for needy non-Muslims), *Zakāt* was, nevertheless, not always physically compulsory. In modern times, with far-reaching fiscal changes supervening in all Muslim nations and with the rise of state schemes of social welfare, there has been an insistence on the fact that such taxation is not technically *Zakāt*. Taxation is not confined to Muslims but falls on all citizens, whereas *Zakāt* is a Muslim ordinance. Muslims, therefore, who pay taxes that are used in part for social welfare must not suppose that they are absolved thereby from their *Zakāt* duty. The Government of Pakistan so ruled when it agreed to foster the payment of *Zakāt* by the sale of *Zakāt* stamps in Government Post Offices. Pleas from some quarters that taxation by the state in the interests of the poor of itself constituted *Zakāt* were disallowed.[5]

Technicalities apart, *Zakāt* is understood by almost all apologists as the basis of an ideology of social responsibility. It is the institutional witness to the duty implicit in ownership. Thus when fiscal policy in the modern state undertakes to bring about economic equality through graded taxation, welfare programs, and related measures, it is fulfilling the ideal to which *Zakāt* bears witness. Though Muslim believers may still be obligated to pay their poor-rate, they have the satisfaction of knowing that the witness of its continuity has shaped the concept of all taxation and made the state actively cognizant of poverty.

This third pillar of religion is, likewise, a main support in the Islamic case against the evils of both capitalism and communism. It renders the first innocuous and the second unnecessary. It does away with the sting of both by depriving Marxism of any legitimate argument against property and depriving property of its scandalous features. Owners who truly recognize, in an active sharing, the debt their property imposes on them vis-à-vis the community obviate the criticisms that an exploiting capitalism evokes.

Thus the raison d'être of communism is destroyed at the root, and capitalism, by the same token, is disciplined into validity. Some exponents of the meaning of *Zakāt* have gone so far as to say that communism is sufficiently disproved on the sole ground that if it prevailed payment of *Zakāt* would be impossible. Capital cannot be destroyed without the elimination of the institution—*Zakāt*—that humanizes it. The further point is frequently made that *Zakāt*, when practiced, reverses the vicious spiral that Marx identified as the inner contradiction in capitalism. *Zakāt* transforms it into a happy spiral. For distribution of alms stimulates popular purchasing power and thus quickens the market, augments production, boosts profits, and so finally rewards the payers of *Zakāt* and gives them a still greater income out of which to disburse again.

A crucial assumption about human nature is implicit in this understanding of *Zakāt*. As Muslims see it, the institution of alms solves what is at issue between the great rival philosophies of this century. Islam, it is believed, has always had the secret. But there remains the question whether it has taken the real measure of the communist critique. It answers, with charity, the communist denial of the right to possess. It solves the problem of poverty by leave of the rich, where Marx proposes to solve it by their liquidation. His insistence on the necessity of violence it counters with the efficiency of exhortation and religious obligation.

The Qur'ān makes it perfectly clear that hoarding is hateful to God. Monopolists and cornerers of the market will be punished in hell. Islam demands economic justice and social neighborliness. *Zakāt* wants all to understand the sovereign principle: "To have is to share." Only giving cleanses keeping. Property is a trust. The community is the context of value. As these precepts are followed, the Islamic good life is actualized. Society is rescued from the militant robbery of communism and from the cynical robbery of benighted and untempered capitalism.

V

Two other factors in the actualization of Islamic ideology should be noted as a postscript to *Zakāt*. The law of inheritance in Islam, though of great intricacy and diversity in its details as interpreted within the various schools, makes, in general, for division and impedes the concentration of large capital wealth in individual hands. The Qur'ān and the *Sunnah* give specific direction for the division of personal wealth after death. No bequests of a testator can override or alter their provisions. Any transfer of property outside the provisions of the law has to be made during life and actually vested in the recipient before death. No will could be accepted that bequeathed property to legatees beyond the allowable proportions or by the deprivation of legitimate recipients.

This was in conformity with basic Quranic legislation on inheritance in Surah 4.12ff. But an earlier verse in Surah 2.176, enjoining on testators the equitable bequeathing of their property to their parents and kindred—a verse sometimes held to have been abrogated by Surah 4.12—has been used of late to justify new legislation that makes possible testamentary gifts without the consent of legal heirs, in partial liberation from the earlier stipulations. These new interpretations of what is in the public interest, however, only serve to emphasize the long-standing practice, still hailed by apologists, by which inheritance becomes a means of distributing wealth, and so, in turn, a part of the Islamic crusade against the excesses of capitalism.

The definitive Quranic passage gives males two-thirds, females one-third—this being an advance on pre-Islamic Arabian practice. Heirs on the paternal side take precedence over heirs on the maternal side. There is no primogeniture; sons are treated equally. It is this fact, together with the recognition of numerous secondary heirs who might have been ignored in a free bequeathing, that has given Muslim inheritance its significance as a deterrent to excessive concentration of capital. When this has been regarded as unfortunate, there have been attempts made to surmount it by constituting an estate as a religious *waqf*, "endowment," the administration of which could be more readily—and freely—determined.

In addition to legislation on inheritance, there is the familiar Muslim prohibition of usury. In Surahs 2 and 3 the Qur'ān strongly condemns *ribā'*, or—in the generally accepted sense— the making of gain without due return or compensation. A careful distinction is made between usury and legitimate profit. One of the passages concerned, that in Surah 2, is in fact a spirited reply to those who tried to get away with usury under the plea of fair profit. Muslim economists have discussed and defined the distinction with great pains and ingenuity. It is suggested that the only legitimate form of return for wealth is where investors are personally involved in the enterprise and seek no guaranteed return on their investment. It is asserted that modern banking, commerce, and capital development are perfectly feasible on this basis.

Instead of the present system of stock market transactions, where investors are entirely out of relation with the enterprises that use their capital and from which they demand to receive assured gains, Islam envisages a direct relation of capital to enterprise in such a way as to make gains not usurious but legitimate. If a road or a bridge is to be built, for example, the government or the company should invite specific participation from those with money to invest. They must be consciously linked with the work in hand and be rewarded from the fruits of that particular scheme. When the bridge or road is complete, the profits from tolls and the like are distributed proportionately, when all demands of construction and maintenance have been met.[6]

Whether this concept of economic "involvement," as the only valid condition of financial profit, is feasible under modern conditions is for economists to say. The idea of "zero interest" is the Muslim form of valid investment profit. Banking also should be made to conform to the same pattern. For interest to be legitimate, it must be dissociated from usury and linked only to the valid meanings of profit. The ramifications, as indeed the viability, of this approach cannot be estimated here. What matters is the ideology—the demand that all the operations of finance shall be carried out in terms of uncompromised profit only. The ideal is the form in which Muslim economics seeks to shape in practice its conviction that there should not be exploitation and that the will to work, not the will to make money work for you (presumably to somebody else's detriment somewhere), is the true economy. "Come to the good life," whatever it finally means, does not mean the hardly concealed gambling of stock exchanges.

Zakāt and the forms of inheritance and the prohibition of usury together constitute the main elements of Islamic economic teaching as both an ideal from which direction can be found and an active means for realizing what is right. It is hardly necessary to add that these three are corroborated by many Quranic and traditional passages calling for probity, honesty, and integrity in social and commercial relationships. The Qur'ān is understood to teach the main bases of economic planning in what one writer calls "four postulates"—economic trusteeship, economic cooperation, limited private property, and state enterprise. Islam learns in the Qur'ān that God is against the covetous and that trade should be always in fairness and good will.

The overarching truth of God's sovereignty means that humans, properly understood, have no right of exploitation. "Not one of God's created servants" says Sayyid Qutb, "has the power to cut off any man's provision, or to withhold from him any part of that provision." The fear of God is the final assurance of reverence for law. In honoring God, we fulfill what such honor demands in our human relationships. "The basic principle," says the same writer, is "that there is an all-embracing identity of purpose between the individual and society, and that life in its fullness is interrelated."' The invitation "Come to the good" has in some way a force in itself that facilitates a response.

VI

It is clear, both within Islam and outside it, that the actualization of the muezzin's *Falāh* is not possible only through economic provisions and moral exhortation in the holy law. That law may be meticulously and validly defined so that ignorance, as the archenemy of the good, is eliminated. Yet full obedience tarries or falters. The principle that no one has the right to exploit their neighbor does not of itself suffice if some should wilfully assert such a right. Though they may possess no rightful power to do so, they may exert de facto power. There may be an all-embracing identity between the individual and society. But that identity, if axiomatic, is not automatic. Individuals in their recalcitrance can refuse to recognize its ideal existence and proceed actively on the contrary hypothesis. The question, therefore, of the actualization of the good necessarily leads us into the realm of the political. Islam has thought long on the relation of the order of the state to the *Falāh* of the call of the minaret.

The urgency and inclusiveness of this issue is, of course, implicit in the very concept of law as the instrument of good. For law always involves enforcement or sanction in some sense. How does law come to be fulfilled? It cannot be indifferent to the question. For if its will is seriously thwarted or its directives flouted, its inherent authority will sooner or later be undermined. A law that remains permanently unobeyed becomes a dead letter. The very vitality of law as law depends on active obedience. Should the law then be equipped with means whereby defection can be punished, insubordination checked, and conformity ensured?

There is a tendency in some modern circles in Islam to answer this question, in the last resort, with a reluctant no. It is felt, if not always very clearly expressed, that somehow a moral, religious law cannot be served by force. Obviously in some respects every society will and must punish its disturbers and every system its criminal rebels. Such punishment is necessary for the protection of basic rights and securities. But beyond this, the high moral desiderata of a fully religious ethic cannot be suitably compelled —according to this viewpoint. The nature of obedience is so often inward; its compromises subtle and inaccessible to evidential scrutiny and court procedure. Moreover, the quality of an obedience that is not morally spontaneous and free is questionable. The good, in other words, that can properly or feasibly be compelled is of a limited and often rather negative kind. The full law of Islamic ideology can appropriately proceed only by religious sanctions and by the force of purely moral persuasion.

There is much to be said for this view and it underlies in part some recent pleading for the separation of religion and state. It comes near to the distinction, made in some faiths outside Islam, between two orders or levels of human life—that of the political realm where feasible, enforceable standards of behavior can be legally defended and applied, and that of the spiritual order where goodness must arise through moral and religious forces, to which law may bear witness but which law cannot actualize. This is not to argue two standards of equal validity, but two standards of accountability—a lesser one that courts can apply and a higher one over which conscience and God must preside.

On this basis, some in Islam today distinguish between feasible, "secular" criteria of a citizen's accountability, on the one hand, and the full free vocation of the true "religious" Muslim on the other. The first need not be thought of, on this view, as un-Islamic. It may partake of the spirit of Muslim culture. But it will not pretend to be achieving the full meaning of Islam, for that is the law of a goodness that cannot be compelled and yet remain itself.

Despite its force, however, this line of thought, though it may prevail one day, is clearly uncongenial to the historical Muslim mind. Its account of Islam is not one that would commend itself instinctively to the Muslim centuries. The emphasis has rather been to refuse the distinction upon which this view proceeds. There ought not to be two realms of the good. Islam, as a law unto good, should be attainable within the political order. This has been instinctive and characteristic from the beginning.

But such a decision only sends the mind back to the problem of the external condition of the good that the law enjoins. The historical answer, at least in theory, was the Caliphate. Islam originated as a politico-religious expression and by the Caliphate intended to remain so. Muhammad founded a state; he did not merely launch a religion. Perhaps even that distinction is unsound. We should perhaps say he launched a religion in founding a state. Through the Caliph the nonprophetic functions of the founder were perpetuated, the prophetic ones being already completed. The Caliph was the acclaimed guardian of the Sharī‘ah, and though he stood under it and was its creature, he insured the conditions under which its application was possible. The Caliphate stood for the headship of an ideal empire in which the perfect amalgam of faith and society that the Prophet had attained would be perpetuated for all time.

Unfortunately the Caliphate early fell on evil days. After near perfection under Abū Bakr and ‘Umar, it suffered the misfortune of the aged ‘Uthmān and later of the Umayyads. They suppressed the true elective principle and introduced features disloyal to the Prophet's example. This made inevitable a distinction between *de facto* and *de jure* authority. The necessity of this distinction in itself made clear that the external ideal was not being maintained. In subsequent centuries the Caliphate became the center of unhappy and often inglorious controversies. By the eighteenth century important stretches of Islam found themselves under the rule of non-Muslim powers in a complete reversal of what Islam had always envisaged.

Only slowly and with great travail has the alternative political answer to that situation emerged, and a great debate, as indicated in chapter 1, still continues. Alien authority has now for the most part been terminated and Islam has digested the new principle of nationalism. Some of its writers, however, protest that nationalism is ultimately incompatible with Islam and that its acceptance is only a temporary stage designed to ensure freedom from interference within which the new form of Islamic politico-religious expression will be evolved.[8]

VII

This leads at once to the consideration of current ideas of the Islamic state, as the external means to the Islamic ideology. For some, in line with the alternative considered above, the Islamic state is—no more, no less—a cultural expression. The Islam it safeguards and embodies is simply the recognition of the values of Islam through institutions and laws that reflect its spirit. Religion is then understood in a way that could readily admit of a multireligious state, if circumstances require it. Islam, on its God-directed side, becomes an individual's religious relationship, generally informing the national heritage but creating no dogmatic requirements for the state itself. Laws will not have to satisfy any considerations other than the sovereign will of elected assemblies. The right to elect and be elected will not turn upon any religious criteria. The Muslim as such will be an equal citizen with any non-Muslim who is also a citizen. The Islamicity of the state is cultural, general, spiritual, not militant or divisive.

This reading of the state takes us back to the position on law and the good earlier outlined. If the future is, possibly, on its side, certainly the past, and, for the most part, the present, are not.

Champions of that past understanding, on the other hand, seek to give it a viable present form. They look to the kind of state in which there will be some degree of identity between the historic Sharī'ah and the forms of conduct in all realms. They are looking for a new expression of the sovereignty of the Sharī'ah in the name of the sovereignty of the God who gave it. This leads in turn to the ideal of theocracy—a term about which there is much confusion of thought. Inasmuch as it incorporates within itself so many of the issues at stake, it is well to explore the Muslim sense of the term carefully.

In the bare literal sense of the word, there never has been and never can be a theocracy in human affairs. For God is a spirit, eternal and divine. God does not sit immediately in any national senate or upon any political throne to rule. God's reign is, by divine ordering, within a viceregency which is ours as human. Islam has always recognized this truth. God is in heaven; government proceeds on earth. Theocracy, then, in any feasible sense, must mean divine authority in and through human institutions. In its barest sense, it could mean a perfunctory acknowledgment of God by rulers and ruled who did substantially as they liked. But such an interpretation is neither sensible nor Islamic.

Does theocracy mean, then, a form of divine sovereignty applied by those who speak for God? If so, who are they? There are times when some Muslim accounts seem to suggest this. In one sense Muhammad's own authority was such a sovereignty. So was that of his worthy successors. But later successors disqualified themselves and left the locus of theocratic rule still to be sought. Moreover, even when true successors ruled, they were themselves subject to the holy law whose servants and creatures they remained.

A more suitable answer would be that Muslim theocracy is really the sovereignty of law divinely revealed. The community stands under God because it stands under God's law. This is the Muslim confidence. But still the theocracy, in practice, remains incompletely defined, for the law needs interpretation. Are the interpreters agents of the theocracy? If so, how are they constituted and attested? Does authoritative interpretation make them somehow lords over God's heritage? This is what some have feared and others have claimed in the long controversies.

Does theocracy really mean shaikhocracy? Or should it mean nomocracy—the rule of an inviolate legal tradition? Or is the divine sovereignty self-renewing and dynamic in a sense that makes it ill-served by a static law? In which event, perhaps the community of obedience is the true organ or repository of the divine mind, which alone is worthy to rule? When this view is taken, opinion may still differ as to the forms through which the obeying community truly functions as arbiter of the divine will.

All the current debate on actualizing Islamic ideology in Islamic society revolves around these questions. What is clear to most who attempt to answer can be stated in this way. Islamic polity must be based on Islam. The ideals of the Qur'ān and the Prophet are sufficient to it. The business of the Islamic state is to serve these Islamic concepts. Islam demands the entire allegiance of the believer and the state should ensure as best it may that those demands are satisfied.

Beyond that, there is division. Some would have the organs of state as free as possible, developing a creative obedience to Islam with an overall court, somewhat like the Supreme Court in the United States, to determine whether particular legislation was inconsistent with the Sharī'ah. Others would tie the state very firmly, in both constitution and life, to the traditionally interpreted Sharī'ah in the hands of the 'ulamā'. For some, the Islamic state is a matter of long definition and plain adherence; for others a realm of valid experimentation and reconstruction. The issue of this fascinating debate on how to understand theocracy cannot be here foreseen. It is all the time proceeding. The whole discussion is indeed a running commentary on the muezzin's invitation. *How* is one to come?

The answer thus far is: by adherence to the economic institutions of Islam and the principles they teach; by the aid of the Islamic state as the political form of a true theocracy, however determined. Deep-thinking Muslims, however, realize that there remains a question beyond these answers. Just as the economic realm led into the political, so both lead into the spiritual. The demands of this realm have been with us already in discussing true political forms. But they need some further thought at this point if all the muezzin's implications are to be clear.

VIII

Zakāt teaches responsibility. The Islamic state seeks to provide the framework for obedience to the Sharī'ah. What of human response? "Come ye." If the good is made plain and made possible, what else delays it? Here any realistic social order encounters the problem of human nature. Much Muslim thought is aroused at this point. Numerous writers criticize the existing Islam in the name of the Islam that ought to be. Or better, they incriminate unworthy Muslims in the name of a proper Islam. They are aware of Muslim un-Islamicity, if the phrase may be permitted.

Some are persuaded that the solution is more vigorous state compulsion. The falling short of the actual when compared with the ideal is due to external circumstances. These can be identified throughout history. For some writers the true Islamic society has never actually existed since the Prophet's death, or since the Caliph 'Umar. External reasons, varied and unfortunate, have always obviated the true achievement of Islamic ideology. The more these factors are dealt with, the more that ideology will come into its own.

Others seem content with a potential perfection, or prefer to state the ideal in neglect of the actual. Thus Sayyid Qutb, already quoted, writes that the duty of alms habituates the Muslim until such payments become "a natural part of the will of the wealthy."[9] He wrote thus in a land where, seven years after this sentence was penned, a strong internal revolution broke out to abolish long-standing and grievous extremes of wealth and poverty, which are still uncorrected.

But such neglect of the realistic does not obtain everywhere or with the same authors all the time. True to its ultimate concept of law as the means to good, Islam finally leaves the problem to conscience within and exhortation without. "When reverence for God," writes Sayyid Qutb, "is not in conscience, then there is no safeguard: for the law can always be deceived or evaded, and the ruler, the judge, or the people cheated."[10] Persons, in the end, must respond to obligation; they must recognize and accept responsibility. Otherwise, even the law itself will be somehow imprisoned in nonfulfillment. Here is a clue that should be taken further still—further, that is, into a radical exploration of human obduracy. But writing on the Islamic social order usually turns from this region back toward a new confidence in the conformity that ought to be, a new effort to serve and stimulate it, in every way possible.

Much emphasis in this connection is naturally laid on education. The means to the good in Muslim ethical thought has always been closely linked with sound habits and an amenable disposition. Ibn Maskawaihī, for example, one of the most noted of the ethical writers in Islam, insisted on the necessity of wise habituation. Like the Greeks, whose ethics in the pre-Stoic periods Muslim moral philosophy so much resembles, Ibn Maskawaihī sought to inculcate the good life on the condition of proper environment, native inclination, and educative discipline. In all three respects he modeled himself largely on Aristotle.

The basic conviction that ignorance is the root of evil and that, therefore, knowledge is virtue was the common ground. When such a point of view encounters the problem of insubordination and rebellion, it is inclined either to minimize its essential seriousness or find a way through it in still more vigorous education, concentrating on the human material that is most promising in the circumstances that are most hopeful.

This is the reason that explains the frequent citation of traditions, not only in mosque sermons but in the many manuals of political and economic theory, in the pamphlets of the *Ikhwā al Muslimū* and the writings of such teachers as the late Abū-l-'Al-Maudūdī. It is not simply that the passages quoted embody the right doctrine. It is also that the example is stirring and evocative of obedience.

At times in this literature the outsider senses in the writers an apparent unawareness of the wide disparity between the situations covered in the tradition and those in which contemporary Muslims find themselves. A tradition that the Prophet proclaimed communal rights in water, pasture, and fire is understood as enshrining in principle the idea of state ownership and nationalization. Practices of self-discipline or gracious largess in the Caliph 'Umar adumbrate modern forms of social conscience.

Exhortation from history is an important element in the Muslim response to the burden of actualization. For, as one writer puts it, Islamic idealism is not merely an "ethereal minstrel":

> It is a concrete plan for Islam, not merely Aristotle's philosophizing, that good citizens of a state ought to be good men too. Each member of society, embued with the right spirit of righteousness (cf. Surah 2.177) is intended to develop a dynamic personality. . . . The Islamic blend of rich subjectivity and powerful objective urge will guarantee not only the use of man as an end, but the reaching of the goal of ideal civilization. But before that, much leeway has to be made up toward salvaging the guiding subjectivity from the morass of disuse and unmeaning use, and establishing convincing records of objective welfare.[11]

There we must leave the matter of human nature, its recalcitrance and obedience. The road from ideology to reality, from law to life, from knowing to doing, passes inevitably through the narrow portals of the human heart. The good in general goes no further than we are willing to come into it in particular. Whether the God behind the good has anything more to do in this situation than is effectuated in law, we cannot ask in this context. The minaret calls; *Falāh* invites.

IX

As a postscript to this discussion of the Islamic order for human society, it is appropriate to summarize briefly the main features of marriage and the family in Islam. For the family is the first context of the individual, the earliest school of habits and, therefore, a crucial factor in the struggle for the good. The clearest enunciation in the Qur'ān of the status of husband and wife is the passage in Surah 30.20: "And one of His signs is that He created mates for you from yourselves that ye may find rest in them, and He established between you love and compassion. Verily therein are signs for a people who reflect."

The reader of the Qur'ān is here invited to contemplate the relationship between the sexes in marriage as a clear evidence of a gracious providence—a clue to the mystery being found in worship. But Islam has never gone to the point of understanding marriage in such a sense as to make monogamy essential to its nature. "They twain shall be one flesh" is not taught. Rather the possibility of a plural marriage relationship is evident from the oft-quoted passage in Surah 4.3.

It reads: "If ye fear that ye cannot do justice with the orphans, then marry as pleases you, two, three or four women: and if ye fear that ye cannot be equitable, then only one, or that your right hands possess [i.e., female slaves]. That will be more suitable to prevent you from doing injustice." Though this passage was for centuries—and in places still is—taken as a clear allowance of up to four wives, much modern exegesis considers that it is a virtual prohibition, in that it puts a condition on plural marriage that is, ideally, unattainable—equality of treatment to plural wives.

Opinions differ as to what is meant by equality—equality of financial and temporal provision or precise and constant equality in emotional regard. The first would be perfectly feasible; the second manifestly not. Those who take the second view consider that, an impossible proviso being attached, the passage in effect forbids more than one wife. "The mere suspicion," writes Mahmūd Hoballāh, former director of the Islamic Center in Washington, "that the husband may not be absolutely just in his feeling and in his treatment of his wives makes it illegal for him to marry more than one wife.''[12]

But this interpretation, if it be the sound one, still leaves the matter open to experiment. There is nothing in the passage to check a husband who believes he can attain equality of treatment. He is left as the sole judge. If he fails, it will be a *post facto* failure and then the marriages exist. There is nothing in the passage to suggest that it would be a violation of obligation to an existing wife for a husband even to think that he might duplicate her. This would be total, not virtual, prohibition, founded on the belief that the gift of the self in marriage is by nature inalienable and incapable of being concurrent. This Islam does not teach.

Though the plurality of Muhammad's wives to almost thrice the maximum mentioned in Surah 4.3 has inevitably affected Muslim concepts, it is explicitly stated in the Qur'ān that it is not exemplary. Most exegetes and biographers insist that there were peculiar reasons in the Prophet's situation—the need to provide for widows of fallen warriors, the multiplication of desirable examples, the political aspects inseparable from a ruler's matches. They also point out that Muhammad was faithful to Khadījah throughout their marriage and that his subsequent wives, except 'Ā'ishah and Mary the Copt, were not virgins.

Though it is customary, and perhaps sound, to think of plural marriages as necessarily insecure or unhappy, it should not be overlooked that many Muslim homes, where they were practiced, were often close units of loyalty and honor. The evils of plurality and feminine seclusion are many, but some husbands have built their relationship on the Muhammad-Khadījah pattern and have practiced tolerance and benevolence. It is in this sense that the best minds understand Surah 2.228: ''And men are a degree above them [women].'' The male is superior in physical powers and has protective duties. The same verse says that women have equal rights in kindness.

There are numerous passages that enjoin modesty in both sexes and gentleness in relationships, though corporal punishment is noted in the Qur'ān as permissible in disciplining a wife, when all else has failed. Marriage needs headship and this is the role of the husband. ''Men are the protectors and maintainers of women be-

cause God has given the one more strength than the other'' (Surah
4.34). The woman for her part is to appreciate that realm in which
men are weak and she is strong, and not flaunt or display physical
attractiveness beyond the limited circle of the immediate family
(Surah 24.30–31).

The marriage contract in Islam is public and requires the matu-
rity and marriageability of the parties, though they need not necessarily be the contractors. It is not intended to be limited in time,
but the form of the contract does not refer to death as its only
terminus. One passage, in Surah 9.28, has been understood to
approve *muta'*, ''temporary marriage,'' on the part of strangers
temporarily away from home in commerce, war, and the like. But
the exegesis is not unanimous.

The purposes of marriage are generally defined as procreation,
unification of families, mutual cherishing, and purity of life. The
new relationship is not less, not more, important than that of
blood relationship.

The marital bond is dissoluble at will by the husband. But of all
the things that God permits, divorce is the most hateful. It should
not be determined rashly. When the marriage relationship for any
reason has become undesirable, it may be terminated. No other
cause need be shown than that the desire has lapsed. The reason
why the initiative in Quranic law lies with the man has been stated
as follows by the former president of the Muslim Board of Elders,
Jerusalem:

> Since the man is sounder in judgment, and more capable of
> self-control, and the one who has to pay the alimony, Islam
> has given him the right to dissolve marriage. Yet he is ad-
> monished not to divorce unless it is absolutely necessary, for
> that is hateful to *Allāh*, and a good Muslim would not want
> to displease Him. The woman is liable to abuse such a right
> since she is temperamental and emotionally unstable. . . .
> Yet Islam has permitted the woman, on concluding wed-
> lock, to ask that the matter of divorce be the same for her as
> for the man. Furthermore the woman is permitted to seek a
> *qādī* to help her divorce, if the man has mistreated her or
> been too miserly.[13]

An increasing number of both men and women would dispute this analysis of reasons. The inequalities in divorce are being diminished by new legislation in many directions. Moreover, even in respect of the old masculine freedom there are several Quranic exhortations or provisions that check its worst excesses. Couples are encouraged to think again and the divorced woman is to be treated fairly and not hindered from remarriage, after due time. There are also provisions about the custody of the children of broken unions.

Some quarters argue that divorce is a necessary evil and that the Muslim view of reasonably ready dissolubility is realistic. Certainly its incidence is widespread in the Muslim world. Because of the view of dissolubility inherent in marriage, the relationship between the sexes is much more fluid, within law, than where Christian concepts have some sway. Plural marriage is steadily diminishing due in part to economic and social factors. But consecutive marriage still falls short of the best in monogamy.

This is not the context in which to discuss further the Muslim view of the place of women in society. Vigorous feminist movements bear witness to the struggle that is being waged to establish equal rights and opportunities in every realm. They have evoked a variety of counterstatements from conservative minds, sometimes in tactical retreat, sometimes in unqualified opposition. As noted in chapter 1, the whole theme is a continuing debate. The relative obligations of woman to home and to society, and the appropriate opportunities for each, are areas of the good to which the muezzin invites and which await contemporary definition from those he addresses. The realm of womankind is perhaps the most formative of current issues and one that is certainly fruitful in controversy.

It has been a deliberate purpose here to refrain from discussion of the darker sides of polygamy and the harem in history. Our study had been Islamic ideology rather than the Muslim situation at any given time. We have been at pains to understand the good of the minaret's call, *Falāh*, in this final area of human relationship—the area that begins the determination of all others. What that relationship has been at its best and what it may still mean in changed times should be sufficiently clear from the fundamental interpretation, out of which all its other aspects flow.

Thus, in all the realms of its relevance Islam calls Muslims unto good, as husband, father, son, as wife, mother, daughter, as merchant, citizen, friend, as believer, confessor, worshiper. It enjoins on them an ideal of human interrelationship built on a divine. What the minaret utters puts the world into its own perspective. When the perspective is understood and followed, the world is in harmony with the muezzin. And where, because of secularity, preoccupation, or carelessness, this does not happen, the minaret still stands on the landscape. The culture it gave birth to remains as formative in life as its symbol is conspicuous. In all circumstances of the relationship of its people to its message, active or passive, eager or reluctant, Islam through its muezzins continues to invite: "Come ye to prayer, come to your true well-being. God is most great, Muhammad is his Apostle. There is none save God." Our other task in this book is to discover what its invitation to the Muslim should mean for the Christian.

Part III

MINARET AND CHRISTIAN

Readers have thus far explored the meanings of the call to prayer, as they address those who belong, with the muezzin, in Islam. Unless the foregoing study has entirely failed of its purpose, they have entered in some measure into the inner fullness of the Muslim summons.

What follows is based on the conviction that there is a call within the call to Muslims which the non-Muslim ought also to heed. The muezzin certainly intends it so. The witness of God and the Apostle is clearly not meant only for believing ears. Islam addresses the entire human race. It is out of our comprehension of its import for ourselves that our answer must be made.

It is, of course, possible to relate ourselves to the Muslim call to prayer wholly in the realm of the academic. Islamics is that branch of study which takes its subject matter from the vast historical reality called Islam, even as ornithology occupies itself with birds and forestry with trees. Within Islamics there are fascinating realms of specialization offering a lifetime of satisfaction for the philologist, the architect, the historian, the theologian, the lawyer. The impulse to such scholarship about Islam is plainly increasing. Its history is long. There have been many who in response to it have looked out upon the world of the minarets and, falling under its spell, have become travelers, scholars, grammarians, writers, at its behest.

But for all its painstaking service to the understanding of Islam, scholarship in Islamics is not a final response to the muezzin. The mosque does not exist to be admired, or the minaret to dominate a landscape. Nor does the Qur'ān expect the devotion only of calligraphers. A purely artistic or academic interest in historical religion fails to do it justice. If Islam speaks of God and for God imperiously, God cannot be greeted with a mere agreement to study Him. This truth does not invalidate the scholarly duty to understand, to analyze, to explore Islam. It only affirms that such a duty remains partial even when it is perfectly discharged.

Many in recent years have been prepared to go further than this academic relation to an enduring phenomenon in human affairs. Their impulse has come from a sense of the cruciality of the times and the potential relevance of Muslim beliefs to their own apprehensions and aspirations. Islam has come to seem for them an obvious factor of importance in cold wars. Association with Muslim states and diplomats of the United Nations brings home the place and potency of the Muslim millions and Muslim meanings in the world of today. A growing interest in the muezzin is apparent, in his message, his reception, his background, his outlook. This topical concern seldom goes so deep as that of the scholar, though it seeks a relationship that is more than knowledge. It moves in the direction of association—anticommunist, pro-democratic, mutual monotheist, and the rest.

Understandable as this attitude is, it still falls short of a satisfactory response to the fact of Islam. It rests finally on incomplete criteria. It does not strive to penetrate Islam with genuine objectivity. It is motivated too largely by utilitarian attitudes. It is looking for allies rather than inwardness. Its standpoint is the significance of Islam for the West, rather than the meaning of Islam for Muslims. The self-preoccupation of this attitude is liable to preclude its coming to a valid relationship. It does not face the demands the minaret makes upon Muslims, or relate itself to their response to those demands. It needs to take with a more objective seriousness the concepts within the summons, to go deeper than interest, prudence, or policy into areas of spiritual communication.

But when we reach that realm we are beyond Islamics only, and beyond external common interests, into true mutuality. The Muslim has become for us more than a source of knowledge of religion, more than a potential ally. And we, for our part, have

*become more than students, more than observers, more than tac-
ticians in internationalism. As such, we must bring, in all honest
openness, the faith by which we ourselves live and understand. It
is the relationship thus ensuing that this third part has in view, in
bringing together minaret and Christian. The shape of this religious, Christian relationship to contemporary Islam must first be
briefly set down, before the duties to which it calls can be made
plain.*

vi

MOSQUE AND MEETING

I

Arabic-speaking Muslims refer to the mosque not only as a *masjid*, "place of worship," but as a *jāmi'a*, literally, a "gatherer." It is a place of assembly. The day of the week when, at noon, this assembling is imperative is called *yaum al-jum'ah*, "the day of assembly." These verbal significances serve to remind the reader that Islam is meeting and that, as such, the mosque is its most characteristic ground. The muezzin, it may be said, is a herald of encounter.

The mosque is exclusively the meeting place of the faithful. The non-Muslim may admire its architectural glories and study its meaning at any time other than the weekly assembling. In some countries, it is true, prevailing conditions make it impolitic to visit mosques even for this purpose. At the Friday noon hour the outsider is present only on very rare occasions and under unusual circumstances. Nevertheless, the mosque remains a gatherer: the minaret proclaims an invitation that has no limits of race or background.

161

If one cannot become an habitué of the mosque without first being a Muslim, this is a possibility that is always open. The muezzin means to be taken seriously when he calls to worship and the good. If his summons is primarily an interior exhortation and not an exterior evangel, the whole impact of the faith and culture he symbolizes is certainly open to acceptance. Mosques, then, are for meeting in the ultimate, as well as the immediate, sense. One of the first acts of the Prophet in Medina was to build a mosque. There, in the years that followed, numerous converts, Medinan and tribal, "met" Islam.

Christians who seek to meet Islam in the fullest sense and to do justice to its content in the realms that, as we have insisted, go deeper than academic comparison or orientalism, find themselves faced with an exacting task. As they follow the cadences of the muezzin they hear terms—God, apostle, witness, prayer, good, sovereignty, unity—already familiar to them in a Christian context. Here are words already full of associations bound up with Christ, in whom, for the Christian, the fullness of their significance is reached. When Christians listen earnestly to a call they must regard as more than merely "interesting," they can hardly fail to relate the good in Christ—salvation, God's saving health, transformative forgiveness, and newness of life—to the good of the muezzin's call to prayer. They cannot escape the relationship of their own coming to God through Christ to the Muslim call to surrender. Their convictions about the Apostles of the New Testament must bear upon their attitudes to the Apostle of Islam. Prophethood as they have known it in Isaiah and Jeremiah must shape them as readers when they come to the Qur'ān. The degree of their sincerity in their Muslim relationships will be the measure of their inward loyalty to the insights by which they themselves act and react religiously.

One cannot have a religious relationship that begins by neglecting religious criteria. If Christians are to meet the full meaning of the mosque with the hospitality it deserves, they cannot begin by behaving as if Christianity were nonexistent. Inevitably sincerity of conviction means that the insights of one faith become the norms by which the contents of other faiths must be judged.

It is precisely here that the supreme difficulties of the present exposition lie. In bringing together minaret and Christian in this whole discussion, it is assumed that there is a mutuality of significance between them. In proposing the mosque as a place of meeting, of Christian meeting, it is believed that they cannot remain in mutual exclusion, if both are to be loyal to their essential nature.

What such meeting involves on the Muslim side cannot be inwardly set down by any but a Muslim. Though the traditions of mutual alienation are long and persistent, there are elements, Quranic and otherwise, that point decisively in the direction of openness and concern. Nor are signs wanting that some sincere Muslims are now susceptible to the appeal of items of Christian faith to which there has been a traditional hostility. Moreover, the Muslim conviction of finality and ultimacy, involves, as it does for all who hold such claims, a reverent awareness of everything that is so consummated. It ill becomes the ultimate faith to spurn the insights or neglect the assurances to which it claims to have done the fullest justice. There can be little doubt that, within the general duties Islam has to its own claims, the areas of Christian belief are the most serious and the most searching.

But it is only the reverse side of the situation with which these pages can properly aspire to deal. Muslim attitudes to Christianity are the inward responsibility of the contemporary Muslim. What follows here is rather an attempt to see and to express the form of a Christian meeting with or at the mosque, to reflect upon what is implicit when Christians come within spiritual earshot of the minaret. Their first, perhaps inarticulate, reaction may well be to wish that they had never done so. For the more they penetrate into the world of meaning that waits for them there, the more they realize the exactingness to mind and spirit of what they confront.

That point of realization, however, is also the point of no return. Once the measure of the involvement of things Christian in things Islamic has been taken, there is no evading its demands. Christians remain haunted by the obligations to an interpreting fidelity and patient expression. They may at times feel almost where the friend of Hamlet found himself in the sequel to the words:

> If thou hast ever held me in thy heart
> Absent thee from felicity awhile,
> And in this harsh world, draw thy breath in pain
> To tell my story.

For here indeed in Islam is a harsh world, harsh to some of the Christian's tenderest convictions, a world that disallows the Cross and strips the Christian's Master of his most tremendous meanings. Yet the harshness has to be transcended, for much of it is well intentioned. And in any event the story to be told is safe only in the custody of those for whom every antagonism is an opportunity. For that, precisely, is the heart of the story itself.

So we must proceed by holding resolutely together the springs of our duty and its demands, for they arise in the same context. Not to care about Islam would not be to care about Christ. To hold back from the fullest meeting with Muslims would be to refrain from the fullest discipleship to Christ. Valid Christianity is interpretive Christianity. Wherever there is contrariety there is obligation and, likely, there are clues. Nor is the Muslim situation, for the Christian, contrariety alone. There are wide areas of positive mutuality that it is a joy to explore and enlarge.

There are tremendous questions inseparable from a glad acceptance of what Islam in measure portends, questions of the "how" and the "whence" within the good the minaret declares. How does humankind come to the good? Is its being identified for them the sum of their need in relation to it? How are we to conceive the sovereignty in God that we proclaim? Is worship the obligation of servants only, or does it also involve the relationship of love? When we recognize the mighty prerogatives of God, must we not the more explore how they are active most divinely? It is these, and many other, themes that make the intelligent, reverent confrontation of Islam and Christianity so profound an exercise in religion. The only condition of its authentic fullness is that it should be deep and honest, and uncompromised by vitiating motives.

But lest the whole enterprise of Christian-mosque meeting be dismissed as a sentimental indulgence for theologians, it may be well to recollect its deep practical significance for the present day. Christian mission and all its intellectual and spiritual corollaries are no idle pursuit, isolated from the realities of contemporary life. Urgent practical issues impinge upon it; to these it relates itself vigorously. In being concerned for a worldwide expression of Christ, the Christian mind is involved inextricably in the major issues attaching to one-worldness in our day.

II

In his definitive fashion, the great lexicographer Samuel Johnson once remarked that outside Islam and Christianity all else was barbarism. One need not subscribe to this outrageous dictum to acknowledge the immense role in human affairs played by these two great monotheisms of the Near East. Both stand heir in part to the earlier traditions of Judaism, but each has far surpassed it in the extent and variety of their diffusion. Both have shown a consistent capacity to transcend racial and provincial boundaries, and to root themselves in a diversity of lands and communities. Together they embody the religious terms of reference by which vast numbers of contemporary humanity and crucial areas of human relationships are shaped and informed. There can be no doubting the urgency to affairs of their mutual attitudes, and their distinct quality both of belief and action. For they constitute two predominant households of faith in a world increasingly alive to the dangers of its disunity.

Neither mosque nor church, then, can properly disregard the religious bearings of the present predicament of states and nations. Witnessing to their faith in the true dimensions of life, they take their place in a world that is afraid to make war and unable to make peace. The pains and perplexities of coexistence lie upon all nations, a coexistence that has been dictated as a necessity by science, but has not yet been defined by politics or safeguarded by the moral will.

In this precarious context no self-respecting religious expression can evade its duty to demonstrate the meanings of its conviction about God and humanity and nations in the global dilemma. Religions themselves appear to some observers as part of the very divisiveness which must be overcome. Does the coexistence of peoples require the coexistence of religions? Does the latter, in turn, require total abeyance of missionary expression? Would that, again, involve a radical reassessment of the concept of witness as inseparable from valid faith?

How do expressive religions metamorphose themselves into tacit religions? Stars become planets when they are cool enough no longer to shine by any light of their own. Must religions, somehow, do the same? Will they still thereafter be religions? Will their transfiguration into incommunicative and introverted entities effectively serve the guidance of bewildered humankind? Assuming it to be feasible, may we not in fact be retrogressing thereby to something resembling the old household deities, when gods were worshiped as tribal preservers and no effort was made to believe in the commonness either of the gods or their societies? Shall we truly serve supranationalism, transnationalism, or whatever it is that we know not yet how to describe, by abandoning the will to universality that underlies the sense of obligation to witness? The diversities of religions may have in fact contributed to the disunity of the human race. It is true that there are ways of religious relationship that provoke or exacerbate human resentments. But will a divided world truly be served by self-preoccupied religious faiths that continue to deal with the same themes but do so in timid isolation?

The present context is not the one in which to pursue these issues with the fullness they deserve. The immediate point is only to urge that the obligation of religious systems to the contemporary malaise is inevitably an obligation toward each other. They can no longer remain physically sheltered in an alienation bridged only by the curious or the aggressive. Indeed, technology has compelled both them and their worlds into adjacence and mutual involvement. It is a commonplace that science is transforming the world into an uneasy neighborhood. Neither habitat nor heart can escape the increasing physical oneness of a globe where distances are less and less, and intrusivenesses more and more. But the physical interpenetrations of human diversity are far from being the only compulsion to mutuality. The meeting of faiths is not to be seen as a prudent conformity to external necessity. It is rather the obligation of their nature and their ancient sense of the metaphysical oneness of humanity. For that must be the spring of guidance when physical forces impose an externally common predicament but do not of themselves illuminate its nature or undertake its burdens.

In this vocation there can be no doubt that Christianity and Islam have each a crucial place. Their territorial and cultural seclusions are largely at an end. Transcending as they already do the barriers of race, language, and geography, they must take up the spiritual seclusions that still persist within their widely spreading households. Their duty in the total situation of today must in large measure hinge upon their duty to each other. If the mosque is truly to be a "gatherer" for its people, it must reach out into the realms of Christ within the Church, into the travail and the confession of Christian humanity, of Christ's disciples through nearly twenty centuries. If they, in their contemporary allegiance, are to be worthy of their Master and Lord, they must go out in reverent and fervent expressiveness to the place of Muslim assembly, to the home of the Muslim soul.

III

The chapters that follow are concerned with aspects of this task. Some attempt will be made in them to define and argue the shape of the Christian obligation. But out of what fundamental convictions does that obligation arise? Having justified the impulse to meeting by reflections drawn from our present point in history, it will be well to set it also in the more ultimate context of the faith that feels it. For ultimately the nature of the Christian mission takes its rise from the nature of the Gospel. The church is sent because Christ came. The Gospel as such has no native country. Its historical "beginning," as the evangelists affirm, was truly in Palestine, where "Jesus came preaching." But if the events so initiated are seen as the activity of a divine redemptive purpose at work in the world, then the fruits of that redemption belong indifferently to all humanity. There are no Palestinian or Western monopolies in Christ. The eternal Gospel of a world-inclusive love can never be treated as a piece of Anglo-Saxon privacy.

The description of mission as religious egoism may have some validity in relation to some of its disloyalties. But the abeyance of mission would be the supremely damnable egoism, for it would argue a proprietary right in that which is too big to belong to a few, and too inclusive to be arrogated to some alone. The Christian Gospel in its worldwide expressiveness proceeds upon convictions about the nature of God and of humankind that cannot be localized.

To attempt, therefore, to finalize its significance in ourselves is to disqualify our allegiance. To believe in Christ at all is to acknowledge him a universal Christ. Because he is requisite for all, he is perquisite to none. The Christian mission is simply an active recognition of the dimensions of the love of God. Christ belongs to us only because he belongs to all. He is ours only by virtue of his universality. To think otherwise would be unpardonable presumption.

This sense of an obligation as wide as one's sense of relevance confirms itself when it is obeyed. One discovers that all other religious faiths are diversely and variously concerned with just those areas and issues of life and death, of time and mystery, with which the Christian faith concerns itself. Parallels are plentiful in the interrogative aspects of religions. They are present also, fruitfully, in the indicative aspects. And if these grammatical similes may be extended, points of meeting also offer themselves in the imperatives of religion.

The uniqueness of what the Christian finds in Christ does not mean or argue the exclusiveness of everything Christian. On the contrary, the ruling concepts of Christianity—where the human is the vehicle of the divine, and God and humanity are in a living relationship, in law and revelation, in compassion and rebellion—necessarily recur, sometimes in articulate, often in inarticulate, form in the other religious faiths of the world.

Those who go out humbly with Christ into the world of all peoples will discover the multiple but constant relevance of what they take. Moreover, the transactions of such expression are mutual. It is the ruling conviction of the ecumenical movement within contemporary Christianity that it takes a whole world to understand a whole Christ. Those who bring Christ are not vulgarly universalizing their own culture: they are conveying what, when apprehended, both they and their hearers learn. If the claims of the Gospel are valid, it could not be otherwise. For those who take only themselves may not expect to do more than teach. They who take Christ are in a state of perpetual discovery. And the discoveries they make are made through the discoveries they enable.

In the end it is this abiding conviction of relevance that shapes the Christian mission and also makes possible a truly adequate response to the contents of other faiths. It is for just this reason that the minaret represents a genuine call to the Christian. Away with the thought that it is improper to bring them together. Away with the Muslim suspicion that the Christian could only take cognizance of the mosque like some conspirator spying out enemy terrain. Away with the un-Christian arrogance that thinks of the Muslim world only as something to be conquered by a Western religion.

The muezzin from his minaret calls his hearers to come to grips with life. The earnestness of his *hayya*, "Come!" is also in the Christian Gospel. He invites others to a relationship with God and to an attitude toward their fellows. He stands ideologically upon revelation. His concern is for a world in which the reign of God obtains. He acknowledges himself the trustee of what is greater than himself. In all these respects the elements of Christianity are not only and altogether contrasts. Contrasts there are, sharp and ineluctable, as we must see. But there are terms about the same things and confrontations with the same reality. To go into this world of the mosque in the name of one's duty by Christ is not to be an enemy; no misconceptions, Muslim or Christian, should be allowed to make it seem so. For mission is grounded in relevance and the bearers of relevance are never aliens. If the inward demands upon their hearers of the relevance they bring make bearers sometimes in appearance disturbers, the disturbance has to do profoundly with what the Muslim faith itself is all about. To embrace and then fulfill the wide dimensions of these disturbing but tremendous relationships is the Christian answer to the summons of the muezzin.

The muezzin is not a theme for fascinated sentiment. He has not arisen from a museum. He is not merely part of a picturesque setting created for tourists. He is a man in earnest, a voice with an imperative. If we respond to him with equal seriousness, we shall not silence or suppress the meanings we have learned in Christ of the very things for which he pleads or for which he speaks. The more fully we do him justice, the more inevitably we involve him, and so ourselves, in the significance of Christ. For us that involvement means expression. Who shall say all that it involves for him?

Here, then, is the Christian summons to the fellowship that links the centuries in allegiance to Muhammad and proclaims itself from dawn to sunset each successive day. What does this Christian vocation mean in the light of the manifold moods and aspirations around the minaret today? Ascending with the summoner to prayer, how do we survey the life that spreads below him? Descending again into the bustle of multitudinous humanity, which through the waking hours the muezzin punctuates with prayer, what are we constrained to say? How shall we explain to the worship the minaret enjoins the worship we owe to God in Christ? How shall we take the meanings of Christ into the summons from the mosque?

vii

THE CALL TO UNDERSTANDING

I

With notable frequency Muslim writers of various schools have joined to salute Thomas Carlyle and to accord him a unique place in their estimate of English literature. The fact might be surprising were it not that he began, in his *Heroes and Hero Worship*, a new chapter in Western interpretation of the Prophet Muhammad. The very limitations of Carlyle's appraisal, when tested by the standards of Muslim dogma, make the Muslim welcome all the more significant.

In "The Hero as Prophet" Carlyle was at pains to vindicate Muhammad from calumny, but this did not mean that he was ready to consider a personal acceptance of Islam:

> We have chosen Mahomet not as the most eminent Prophet: but as the one we are freest to speak of. He is by no means the truest of Prophets: but I do esteem him a true one. Farther, as there is no danger of our becoming, any of us, Mahometans, I mean to say all the good of him I really can.

In doing justice to the Prophet of Arabia and his role in history, Carlyle adopted a manifestly non-Islamic hypothesis. "A man of genius," he saw in Muhammad, "an earnest confused voice from the unknown deep," whose utterances were "the Alpha and Omega of his whole Heroism," in "a bastard kind of Christianity, but a living kind." When he went on to speak of the Qur'ān, as he knew it in Sale's translation, he found it

> as toilsome reading as I ever undertook. A wearisome confused jumble, crude, endless iterations, long windedness, entanglement . . . insupportable stupidity, in short. Nothing but a sense of duty could carry any European through the Koran. We read in it unreadable masses of lumber, that perhaps we may get some glimpses of a remarkable man.

Carlyle's vindication is clearly far from being admissible to orthodoxy. "The confused ferment of a great rude human soul" is hardly a Muslim account of the holy Qur'ān. The thesis that Muhammad was great by the standards of his day and race is dubious praise for one whom Tradition makes an exemplar for all time and all humankind.

The eagerness that approves Carlyle becomes more comprehensible, however, when his views are seen against the background of animosity and innuendo he repudiated. For he initiated a transformation long overdue. "Our current hypothesis about Mahomet," he wrote "that he was a scheming impostor, a Falsehood Incarnate, that his religion is a mere mass of quackery and fatuity, begins really to be now untenable to anyone." If Carlyle's account reads more passionately than would now seem necessary after a hundred and more years, his strictures on the ignorant and malicious critics, his generous recognition of earnestness and sincerity in the origins of Islam, were unusual enough in the generation for which he wrote.

Lingering memories of the ultimate frustration of the Crusades and implacable hostility to the Ottoman Turk in a later day had bequeathed to Christendom a temper of bitterness in which the wildest calumnies were circulated. Dante had made Muhammad a heresiarch, and later writers dubbed him a sensual impostor. He appeared in the guise of a frustrated cardinal who revenged himself on the Christian world, when disappointed of the Papacy, by inventing a rival religion. He was a fabricator and a devil who swindled many women and was finally eaten at his death by swine. Mammets were images of Muhammad allegedly worshiped in mammetry by Turks—in the most anti-idolatrous system known to history!

This is not to say that generations of simple Muslims were innocent of all un-Islamic superstitions, or that everybody in Western Europe was ignorant of the historical character of Islam. But informed honesty was rare. A preacher in the reign of James I characterized Muhammad as "that cozening Arabian whose religion, if it deserves that name, stands upon nothing but rude ignorance and palpable imposture . . . a subtle devil in a gross religion . . . a monster of many seeds, and all accursed."[1]

The satisfaction of Muslims over the efforts of Carlyle may be taken here as a sign of their hunger to be understood and recognized. But to examine what such understanding involves is to be prepared for deep-rooted and abiding suspicions. When Muslims approve of Carlyle they do not abandon mistrust and resentment. Rather their interest in citing him is often to justify their retention. The depth of this suspicion in many quarters has to be realistically appreciated if it is to be finally abated. It can be dissolved only by positive attitudes that make reparation and win understanding by displaying it.

No Christian thought about Islam, then, can properly start with querulous complaints about suspicion and ill will. It must resolve to surmount prejudice wherever found and brace itself to correct error, restrain bitterness, and dissipate antagonism. It begins simply with the will to understanding, divested of susceptibilities that would compromise its purpose and alerted to its own duty of inward integrity. Foregoing the impulse either to excuse or upbraid, we must seek an openness of soul and sensitivity to all that is deepest in our fellows.

What is it to be a Muslim in the world of today? Part of the answer has been attempted in the chapters in Part 2. Such was their purpose. But the Christian concern must go beyond the effort of understanding represented by the most careful study of books and documents, into that which these can only serve. For

Christians are ambassadors of a person-to-person relationship. They are debtors to their fellow mortals. They must surpass the limits of merely academic knowledge. More than students, they must learn to be in some measure participants. As bearers of "the Word made flesh" they must strive to enter into the daily existence of Muslims, as believers, adherents, contemporaries. This is the prerequisite of being understood and the first element in their response to the significance of the minaret.

II

We begin with those aspects of being a Muslim that are most to the fore in the external scene, before attempting to penetrate into the inner meaning of personal Islam. "Community" may be an inadequate word, inasmuch as Islam, notably in Pakistan, has gone beyond communalism into nationalism. But there is hardly a better word available to express the consciousness of otherness deep in the Muslim mind and soul, whatever precise political or cultural form is chosen to implement it.

Dār al-Islām and *Dār al-Harb* is a fundamental distinction running through all humanity: the household of submission to God and the household of non-Islam still to be brought into such submission. The militancy long attached to the division has been reinterpreted in many quarters. But the sense of otherness abides. The household of Islam is aware of itself as a community which belongs together and does not belong elsewhere. The cleavage is to some degree softened by the necessities of contemporary life, by common factors in world society and current technology, by the sharing of common ideals of democracy and progress. Contemporary Muslim political leadership speaks often in the language of the West.[2] Moreover, such affinities of thought and outlook reproduce basic similarities between the Muslim and the Christian patterns of philosophy in the Middle Ages. Even when engaged in bitter polemic, Muslim and Christian controversialists in those centuries moved on a similar plane of thought and held many presuppositions in common.[3] It has often been remarked that Islam belongs to the Western side of any East-West division of human history. Its place is with the Hebrew-Greek tradition, not with the faiths of Asia proper.

Nonetheless, despite these aspects of Islamic participation in the stream of Western history, it remains true that Islam conceives of itself as unique, as a community of belief and culture that is essentially different. This sense of otherness, moreover, is often strongly felt vis-à-vis the Western world, in whose heritage from Abraham to Aristotle Islam intellectually belongs. Nor is it seriously weakened, much less jeopardized, by the obvious diversities that lie within it.

It would, of course, be foolish to forget the manifestly varied quality of the Muslim world from Marrakesh to Jakarta, from Tashkent to Zanzibar. Nor must our poles of contrast be only geographical. There is a far cry from the impoverished peasant of Baluchistan to the affluent citizen of Lahore, and from the Nuba Muslims of the Sudan to the erudite scholars of Al-Azhar. Economic, cultural, racial, physical, historical factors divide and subdivide the vast and teeming household of Islam. Even individuals often feel within themselves a division of soul to which they are compelled by contemporary change. It is little wonder, then, if Islam is endlessly diversified and if the very definition of Islam itself, or of the Muslim, becomes in some quarters problematical.

Yet for all the elements of variety, there is a peculiarly tenacious quality about the continuity and identity of Islam. The current Egyptian revival of letters may assert, as Taha Husain does, that Egypt belongs to the Mediterranean world and that the task of its educational systems is to produce a good Egyptian citizenry rather than serve the purposes of antiquated Muslim theology.[4] But Egypt remains Muslim. Pakistan asserted its Islam in a national form that sundered the household of Islam in India. But it insists, in self-defense, that a division that would exclude no Muslims and embrace no non-Muslims was impossible to draw; that Pakistan serves by its existence those whom it does not include; and that only so could the essential otherness of Islam be asserted and expressed. Thus Islam proclaims itself unique even when it resorts to a principle of nationalism that would seem to belie the Islamic universal. Though Pakistan embodies a principle of exclusion that cuts it off from Muslims, this is the paradoxical price of the principle of inclusion by which it affirms a Pakistani household of Islam.

The partition of India and the genesis of Pakistan are by no means the only examples of how the principle of nationalism has been appropriated to the expression of Islamic otherness. The Pakistani became such, not with the idea of being less like the Egyptian or the Turk considered as Muslims, but with the idea of being forevermore unlike the Hindu considered as a physical neighbor. It is in this sense that Muslims see no inconsistency in the growth of a national expression. It is, they believe, a nationalism devoid of the bitter divisiveness of European nationalism. The fact that the old caliphal unity of Islam has been destroyed implies no diminution of the essential spiritual oneness of Muslims, however they may now be organized politically.

Cynics and realists may be inclined to question this interpretation. Certainly no concrete scheme of Muslim world-federalism is on the horizon. Whatever may be true ideally, centripetal forces are very potent today. Even within the more homogeneous Arab world, forces of unity are compromised by personal and dynastic rivalries and suspicions, which the common hostility to Israel has some part at least in abating. The political disunity of the Arab world, despite strong Muslim preponderance in the population except in Lebanon, is the more remarkable in view of the fact that the frontiers of many of these states were drawn as recently as 1920 by Western powers, themselves divided, in alleged pursuit of the adage *divide et impera*. Arab Muslim political behavior since seems to require us to rewrite the adage: "Ceasing to rule is not ceasing to divide."

Nevertheless, in the circumstances of the contemporary world, the failure of the household of Islam to achieve any outward form of unity higher than a fragmentary nationalism need not be interpreted as implying any essential failure in the consciousness of Muslim singularity in the face of the non-Muslim world. Islam may have baptized to itself some of the forms of political order which, in parts of the West, are associated with religious neutralism or indifference. But it has shown a steady capacity to harness those forms to its own world of ideas. Even where nationalism needs to be sensitively aware of the rights and participation of non-Muslim minorities, it makes no compromise of its essential Muslim character.

Moreover, even in Turkey, where, it may be said, the concept of the laic secular state made the greatest inroads into Muslim ideas of state and religion, in the five decades since Kemal Atatürk, Islam has shown a surprising resilience and power of continuity under change. Rash would be the observer who presumed to deny that Turkish Islam, for all its vicissitudes and upheavals, remains a recognizable, virile, and sustained Muslim phenomenon. There are, indeed, those who see in recent Turkish history, not a disruptive change in Islam, but a conscious experiment that never ceased to be Islamic.

Be that as it may, there can be little doubt that, for all the political diversity of its existence today behind national frontiers, Islam is no less self-conscious and singular than it ever was. *Dār al-Islām* is still a meaningful concept and an abiding reality. And though the political and the national forms of the present day seem to belie much of Islamic history, Islam itself has demonstrated its capacity to survive in the contemporary political order with no essential loss of identity. Perhaps we doubted it could be so only because we conceived of Islamic unity in terms of empires and caliphates. If these have departed, the community they once ruled remains.

Though we are accustomed to investigate survival capacity in relation to the political order, because that order is so much in our ken and in our daily press, it is equally apparent on the social and tribal frontiers of Islam. African Islam must here provide the obvious example. Writing of the slow assimilation of paganism to Islam in the horn of Africa, J. Spencer Trimingham remarks: "Although at no single point in the process can anyone draw a definite line and set up a boundary stone inscribed: 'Here paganism ends and Islam begins,' there is a stage where one can say thus: 'This man is a Muslim and not a pagan.' "

Though elements in pagan life persist in the new allegiance, its Islamic quality is definitive. Trimingham continues:

We often find fierce loyalty to Islam combined with utter ignorance of teaching and complete laxity in the performance of even primary religious duties. They may not know how to pray, but they divide mankind into believers *(mu'minūn)* and unbelievers *(kāfirūn)*. We may find it difficult to distinguish between their customs and manner of life and those of pagans if we examine them in isolation, yet if

we look at their life as a whole, we shall find that it is
Muslim. . . . The test is a psychic one. Some subtle factor in
their outlook on life has changed. Pagan life sanctions have
been changed into Islamic sanctions. Although they may
believe in a vast realm of spirits, they now believe in only
One God. . . . The only possible criterion is *to know
whether they themselves claim to be Muslims.*[5]

If and as they do, they are inexorably identified with an Islam that
slowly re-creates their entire existence.

Whether, then, on the fringelands of its contacts with paganism, or in the strongholds of its history, we find a community
of faith, worship, and allegiance recognizably itself—persons
claiming to be Muslims through an almost endless variety of
otherwise diversive factors. It is this "sense of being Muslim"
that is the first quality with which our enterprise in understanding
must grapple.

III

The immediate corollary, explaining so much else, is the awareness of what, as Muslims, they are *not*. Identity also spells antipathy. The Egyptian Muslim is not a Copt, the Indonesian
Muslim not a Christian, the Sudanese Muslim not, essentially, a
pagan. Cairo is not London, nor Teheran New York. Islam, in a
word, is not the West. Nor is Islam Hinduism, nor Buddhism.

It is manifestly the Western directions of this sense of otherness
which are most serious and exacting for our purposes here. The
ultimate incompatibility of Islam with Hinduism, or "In-
dianism" as some more passionate writers describe it, was demonstrated in the creation of Pakistan. Islam, it was there believed,
could not validly survive in an all-Indian political unity, despite
sincere guarantees and numerous urgent reasons pointing toward
such unity. There could be no clearer assertion as to the unique
and separate quality of Islam over against the other religious systems of Asia. In Indonesia, the Philippines, and elsewhere in
the Far East, Islam maintains, under much variety, its essential
distinctiveness. But what may be called its Asiatic religious distinctiveness is intensified in relation to Europe, the West, and

Christianity, though Islam is historically much closer to them.

There has always been a peculiar susceptibility to tension in the relations of the two great monotheistic faiths, for reasons deeply rooted in Muslim origins and expansion. But our concern is with the immediate, present aspects of Muslim otherness in relation to the West and to nations considered to be Christian. It must not be thought that the adaptation of many Western forms of political and social life signified either a passive or a hospitable attitude toward the West itself. Rather the nationalism into which the West has educated the Muslim East means a sharpened quality in the sentiments of thoroughly independent peoples.

It is this that explains the urge to political neutralism so evident in the Arab world, the desire to be outside the conflicts and the powerblocs, the assertion of noninvolvement in the quarrels and legacies of the West. It explains the tendency to negativism and isolation. Only with difficulty do nations pass from the negative attitude of reproaching and evicting the foreigner to the positive and constructive attitudes of mature self-responsibility. Ayatollah Khomeini is a symbol of the mentality that transforms legitimate grievances and valid antagonism into hysterical and self-frustrating hatreds. The retrospect of imperialism is so near, memories so long, and bitterness so painfully allayed. Criticism is slow to turn from its favorite external targets to an inward cleansing.

IV

For all these manifestations of readjustment, and for the basic aspirations of which they are the surface evidence, Christians need and must bring a wide and warm understanding. Not deploring that their task is difficult, they must undertake cheerfully the burden of being on many counts suspect. Is it to be wondered at if a Christian of British or U.S. origin encounters obstacles in any ministry in Christ among, e.g., Egyptians? Would it not be surprising were it otherwise, given the legacies of a century? But to enter on such an exacting mission without first entering into the soul of those to be served is worse than futile.

Not only for its assurance and its confidence does this Muslim nationalism need to be patiently understood. Sympathy is demanded for its problems. Its pathway is not all clear and confident. It is beset with many uncertainties and dilemmas. In several countries of the Arab world the pattern of parliamentary government applied in the post-Versailles period proved a dubious blessing in all the circumstances. Urgently needed reforms in land tenure and fiscal measures necessary to correct extremes of wealth and poverty were not effectuated in any adequate form, as long as the institutions of democracy were manipulated by wealth in the interests of the status quo. Necessary reform eventuated only by the intervention of military leadership and the abeyance, temporary or otherwise, of constitutional forms. Such regimes may represent far more truly the will of the people, but they do so in departure from the recognized forms of constitutional democracy. Though the immediate present reaps benefits long overdue, the question of the forms of power is fraught with great future consequences. Thus the exhilaration of newness and confidence is allied with experimentation and venture.

For Arab Muslims there is the massive problem of Israel. What this has meant on the physical side concerns us later. As a deep bitterness in the Arab soul, it is an abiding factor in the contemporary situation. It is important that we be able to see and to suffer it in the terms in which the Arab knows it and to pierce through the tangle of historical controversy to the emotional reality experienced among the neighbors of Israel.

Israel from the Arab point of view is an intrusion. The justice it represents for fundamental Jewish aspirations, denied or tormented in the European world, is achieved at Arab expense. The virility of the Zionist state, the circumstances of its establishment, the revelation of Arab disunity and failure, the fundamental insecurity as to the future, combine to make Israel a supreme test for Arab leadership. The justice and the futility of the demand for repatriation; the injustice and the hard finality of the displacement; the Arabs "attacking" as defenders in 1948; the Israelis as "defenders" invading in 1956, 1967, 1978, and 1982—these are the bitter paradoxes of the struggle. If Israel is not to remain a kind of national ghetto, it must find a means to coexistence with the Arabs. If the Arabs are ever to recover from the Arab tragedy of Israel, they must make terms with it. Otherwise their future will be perpetually mortgaged to their past.

Entangled in these exacting spiritual decisions, to which Israel as a state compels the Arabs, are bitter reactions against other parties in the shaping of events, the British Mandatory and the United States in the United Nations. If the historian who would be impartial finds it difficult to unravel the story of these years, it is little wonder if its victims read it as they find it in their lives, their broken homes, their disrupted souls. History as one knows it in one's own person is always more compelling than history as it may be written in the cold analysis of documentary research.

If there have been few issues in our time more charged with emotion, more confused by competing interests than "Palestine," the first duty of the Christian servant must be an imaginative sympathy for those who pay in their persons, with their property and their bewilderment, the human cost of those events. The instinct to recognize resolution, ardor, toil, and tenacity in the creation of Israel only makes more imperative a wise and patient understanding of the Arab sense of loss, of defeat, of humiliation, and of wrong. Sentimental as such understanding may seem in the eyes of cynical politicians or partisans, only the assurance of it in the Arab soul, as a debt recognized by the conscience of the world, could begin any redemption of their history.

If meanwhile negativism, the search for a scapegoat, blind nostalgia, and sullen resentment persist, the fault will not be wholly Arab. There are peoples in history, it would seem, for whom events are more than usually unjust—the Poles, the Atmeni, the Jews in Hitler's Europe. Not to see that the Arabs of Palestine are now among that number is to have failed to recognize what Israel means. The consequences in the Arab world are a desperate factor in contemporary Islam.

V

The dilemmas of the modern age, however, are not all of them political. One of the changes noted in chapter 1 is the educational duality running through the Muslim world. Schools and universities under state supervision and control attempting a general modern education inclusive of new sciences have all too little in common with mosque schools and universities that conceive of education as the means of continuity for a religious heritage through the generations. There is education that seeks the future and education that hails the past.[6] These contrasts are reflected not only in institutions but in individuals, and so call for discerning relationships on our part. Christian ministry must discriminate wisely between unfaith and secularity, skepticism and the drift to irreligion on the one hand, and on the other the mind that closes itself to defend itself, the faith that is at once insecure and assertive. In the contemporary literature of Islam, where these tensions are reflected, an understanding can best be sought. We must labor to appreciate what Islam means to its people, both as a legacy from the past and a vocation in the present. We must be prepared for interpretations, by Muslims, of the meaning of their Islam, as varied as themselves, and for a new alertness of outlook. Much of the old apathy and lethargy had physical causes for which science has remedies. An awakened agricultural population will be a factor of vast import in the years ahead.

This review of factors in the orientation of the Muslim to non-Islam is by no means exhaustive. The sense of unique community and consequent otherness, its confidence and its stresses, the political and social issues, the Arab meaning of Israel, and accelerating material change—these are the most obvious. They are offered only as a measure of the task of understanding to which the Christian is called, in regard to Muslims in their external relationships.

VI

We must, however, go beyond external circumstances if we are to penetrate into contemporary Islam. Being a Muslim, which is what we seek to understand, involves much more. It is imperative that we strive to think ourselves into the interior life of Islam and to appreciate the inwardness of its external problems. Such a purpose calls for steady effort and imaginative sensitivity.

Such understanding must have its tools. Among the first is a deep acquaintance with language and literature. Early generations of the modern missionary church possessed not a few scholars of stature in the field of Arabic study, whose successors in the present day are, it would seem, fewer and feebler. The Bible in Arabic, the centenary of whose completion was celebrated in

1966, remains a monument to the pains and erudition of Dr. Eli Smith, Dr. Cornelius Van Dyck, and their associates. It has established itself in the affections of evangelical Arab Christians throughout the Arab East, and such need for revision as it now has derives partly from improved renderings of Biblical texts since their time, and from a proneness for arabicized Hebraisms, rather than from serious failure on the part of the translators themselves.[7]

From Henry Martyn to Samuel Zwemer, the Christian Church has produced a notable series of missionary Arabists—notable but always too few. The tasks of each generation fall, justly and inevitably, upon the representatives of each. We in ours have great need of the consecrated scholarship which knows that dictionaries and diction, vocabulary and syntax, have much to do with the faith of "the Word made flesh." Fascinating fields of study and of achievement are open to those who can find their way from the kingdom of God to a grammar and back again to the kingdom.

The difficulties of the Arabic language have been often overrated, though it is well not to begin by minimizing them. But students who do not expect fluency via a phonograph or competence in one year can find ample compensation for the tedium and the troughs of their Arabic adventures. Their increasing reward will be steady mastery of a beautiful instrument, a language of fascinating structure, strict phonetics, and consistent behavior. As they extend their range, they will be able to see, from within, the response of a language to the demands of new times and new themes. Arabic literature of the present day is in the process of an interesting revival and adaptation. In proportion as literacy increases, its vigor will no doubt discover new forms. The current debate between the classicist and the modernist will find appropriate solution.

If this seems too remote an enjoyment for beginners, they may at least allow the "distant scene" to sustain the painful present. Temple Gairdner's *Phonetics of Arabic* may well deter them at first with its frightening illustrations of the Arab mouth, the workshop of spoken Arabic.[8] They will discover that they need much more throat energy than English requires. But slowly the sounds and the syntax will yield to them. Even if they never become so fluent that Arabic might be taken to be their mother tongue, they will at least have entrance to the Arabic mind, both past and present. Stiff enough to be challenging, satisfying and rewarding enough to spark enthusiasm—such is Arabic with its tantalizing invitation to would-be speakers. Nor do they lack a wealth of aids. Perhaps the perfect Arabic teaching manual will never be written, but there are a growing number of good ones.[9] As for the vagaries and varieties of the colloquial language, they can rely upon cooperative tutors in their own area. The discipline of classical study will pay rich dividends in mastering the dialects—though the reverse is not generally the case. But the common speech will open doors everywhere—as the Greek of the New Testament has shown.

Was it unguarded enthusiasm that prompted the idea that every Christian ministrant to Islam should aspire to be an Arabist? For the theological aspects of our relationship, that ideal is imperative. To discover the Qur'ān in its untranslatable character and to feel the pulse of Arabic literature from Al-Mas'ūdī to Taufīq al-Hakīm is an ambition no missionary should dare to abandon. But it may be allowed that in Pakistan, Iran, and Indonesia, in Turkey or Malaya, Arabic for certain types of service may be unnecessary. But in each of these territories there are new and growing national literatures. If old in heritage and wealth, Urdu in Pakistan has an emerging literature in the era of Pakistani independence. Persian studies are a vast area in themselves, second only to Arabic in their importance for the understanding of Islam. Turkish in the 1920s suffered a rude, but—as many believe—salutary break with its traditional script, which marked a new chapter in its long history.

Everywhere in Islam, literature—the index of the literate mind —is alive with new aspirations, new issues, new impressions. Christians who intend serious communication cannot absolve themselves of the duty to enter into and to apprehend this literature. As long as their own expression, whether in preaching, in conversation, or in print, remains non-Arabic and Western, they are to that extent failing to make articulate a universal Christ.

It should not be thought, however, that English has no place. Indeed, the desire to learn English has often proved, and will no doubt remain, an important point of contact with younger

Muslims. There will be many opportunities of ministry for those who are unable to master Arabic or any other Muslim tongue. Those who are born to English should recognize their immense good fortune in having easy access to the language in which so much of contemporary science and life are accessible. We have neither wish nor right to withhold or disallow what this language might mean to those who seek to know it. There is also a wealth of Christian thought and writing in the English language, properly a part of the universal treasure of Christian experience and truth, to which access should be widely available. We do well to see in the aspiration for English fluency a means to larger aspiration for the knowledge that belongs to human right and dignity. To help others to it may, therefore, be a Christian purpose. But any easy reliance upon English on our part, any assumption that the natural interest in it of many to whom we go, absolves us from the duty of knowing them in their own tongues, any disinclination for the toils of disengaging ourselves from English for their sakes—these must be forsworn. The bearers of the Word of God must everywhere be students and users of human words.

Our duty, however, is not merely with language as grammarians present it. There is also the duty of attention to proverbs, to local lore, to stories and familiar heroes. Dr. Eugene Nida in his *God's Word in Man's Language* has illustrated from many lands the necessity of being able to translate not only the word but the idiom. "Behold I stand at the door and knock" must become "Behold I stand at the door and call," in an order of things where thieves knock to ensure that the house they intend to rob is empty, whereas true friends are glad to be recognized by their voice.[10] Examples are legion. In the Arab and the Muslim world this area of meaning is especially urgent. There is a problematical contrast between much of the Arabic of Christianity and the Arabic of Islam. It arises in part from the contrasted concepts upon which the two faiths diversely proceed. The Arabic of the Qur'ān differs widely from the Arabic of the New Testament. Much needs to be done in the field of vocabulary alone, if there is to be effective theological interpretation. It is imperative, therefore, that Christians strive to enter as fully as possible into the Quranic world, with the painstaking ambition to know it from within. This does not mean that Christian Arabic will ever be recognizably Quranic.

It does mean that there must arise a Christian Arabic to which readers of the Qur'ān will be more readily drawn. Only Arabs can produce it. But for us of the Western churches is the duty of recognizing, in the implicit strangeness of Christianity and the difference of Islam, the large effort involved in "knowing and being known."

VII

Language, vocabulary, idiom, and concept lead us progressively into specific fields of Christian study in Islam. The relationship of the individual Muslim to the Prophet Muhammad is the first. In his person and his story meet the ideals and aspirations of Muslim peoples. His posthumous role in shaping Muslim society and fashioning Muslim ethical ideals is second only to his living role in transmitting from God to humankind the Book of divine disclosure. He is the point of final, culminating divine contact with humanity, represented in the Arabs. He is the focal human point at which the divine will is translated into religious law, for the blessing and guidance of humankind. From his devotion to vocation arises the asceticism of the Sufis in Islam. Muhammad and his people (*āluhu*) are bound together inseparably. Through him the world of Islam finds the crux of its creedal and moral relationship with God. What the Prophet means in the convictions of innumerable Muslims must be apprehended with discerning sympathy if we are to mediate the Christian meaning of Christ to the Muslim sense of Muhammad.[11]

Effort is no less imperative when we turn to the Qur'ān. Essentially the Qur'ān is prior to the Prophet, though historically it comes to earth through him. As the speech of God it shares God's eternity. But its place in the interior life of Islam does not turn upon theological reasoning alone. It is established by centuries of veneration, by generations of being a "people of the Book." Its familiar surahs are recited at birth and in bereavement, repeated in the crises between, and breathed in the long piety of all the generations. The superstitious and the ignorant have charmed away evil with portions of the holy Book. Children of the mosque schools through the centuries have washed their slates and cherished the water so made sacred. The Qur'ān has been their grammar and their literature. Its chanting is the chief music of the worshiper. Its sentences are the chief adornment of the mosques. The centrality of the Qur'ān has made calligraphy the most characteristic form of Muslim art. Its memorizers have been those who alone were qualified to pass into further realms of legal study. Commentary on the Qur'ān has been since Al-Ash'arī the main activity of Muslim theology. The periods, the reiteration, the warnings, the refrains, of the Qur'ān have been the constant companions of the devout for fourteen Muslim centuries.

If some thinkers in Islam today have come to look upon the Qur'ān with some modifications of the older theology and tend to think of it in less supernatural terms than their forebears, this has not altered its place in their affections. An Indian Muslim leader of the 1920s records how he rediscovered the power of the Qur'ān while a political prisoner. "Ever since," he writes, "this book has had the invariable effect of intoxicating me with its simple grandeur, its intense directness and its incessant flow of motive power for the manifold activities of life."[12] He holds that to soak oneself in its sentences is to find all the philosophy one needs for life and death.

An illustration from another witness may be cited from a narrative of Arab dhows and Arab sailors in the Red Sea and the Persian Gulf. The English author spent several months in one such craft between Aden and Zanzibar. He describes the daily prayers of the crewmen and the frequency and evident reverence with which they listened to a Qur'ān-reader in their midst:

> I found the timelessness of things and the utter dismissal of the modern world were easy to become accustomed to. The only book on board was a copy of the Quran, in which the passengers often read. When he came to a good part, Hamed would often call a small group together and read aloud, in a very pleasant and well modulated voice, and they would discuss whatever they read for hours. They seemed to find perfect content in this book and never tired of reading it. Sometimes one or another of them would chant chapters from the Quran from memory.[13]

It would not be difficult to multiply such examples of the place the Qur'ān occupies in the devotional and mental life of the Muslim. When every allowance has been made for secular pressures, the holy Book of Islam remains among the most continuously formative volumes in human history. Those who would bring into the ken of its people the deep content and meaning of the Bible as the record of the mighty acts of God must surely aspire after a patient understanding of the Book that comes between.

VIII

In the inner life of the contemporary Muslim is a deep sense of the Islamic past, sometimes nostalgic, but always a factor in the current scene. "The past in the present" might well be the theme or title of an analysis of Islam today, and the issues it faces. The sense of history and what it involves constitutes yet another area where discernment and sympathy are imperative.

Muslims are keenly conscious both of the glories and the twilights of that history, though they are not always of one mind in identifying them. Primitive Islam, the times of the Prophet and of Abū Bakr and 'Umar, the first two caliphs, are the days of the pristine purity. In that period may be sought the true patterns of Islamic rule, even the prototype of socialism and the welfare state. There is less assurance about later periods.

For those who are concerned with splendor rather than with entire fidelity to the primitive qualities, there are the golden glories of Umayyad Damascus, of Al-Mansūr and Hārūn al-Rashīd in Baghdad, of Fātimid Cairo, of Salāh-al-Dīn, of the Mughal Emperors and Sulaymān the Magnificent among the Ottoman Turks. Through political vicissitudes runs the stream of science, philosophy, medicine, and astronomy. There are great names— Al-Fārābi, Ibn Sīnā, Ibn Rushd, Ibn Khaldūn—to whom Western thought is much indebted. Al-Tabarī, Al-Bīrūnī, and Al-Rāzī have a secure place in the advancement of knowledge.

Despite the restraints upon creative art in Islam, there has been a great tradition of builders, designers, and craftsmen. The Muslim world contains endless wealth of architectural beauty and "sermons in stones." How diverse, for example, are the minarets: what riches of design and adornment, of proportion, color, line, and structure have been invested in their purpose! Imagination can give us ready entry into a Muslim sense of the past insofar as it may be mediated through its monuments.

Muslims' awareness, however, of the past greatness of their faith is not only a happy indulgence in the awareness of a community that transcends time. It is also, in some degree, a painful problem. For that sense of history includes the knowledge that somehow it has not always gone aright. Muslims feel themselves part of a chosen people, in that to them and theirs has come the supreme favor of God. They are not among the *mushrikūn* and the *kāfirūn*, the "idolators" and "unbelievers." Being the ultimate community of God, the destiny of Islam is to lead the world and to manifest the success of the divine election. In its greatest periods, Islam believed it attained these expectations. In its triumphant origins as an imperial religion Islam conquered large portions of the two existing Empires, the Byzantine and the Persian, within a single decade. Within a century of the Prophet's death, the faith had been carried victoriously across the Pyrenees in the West and the Oxus in the East. Then, indeed, God was with Islam. Things, then, were as they should be.

But in later times it seemed that God in general history had half forsaken Islam. The Caliphate fell on evil days. At times there were at least three competing Caliphs. It was true that conquerors of Muslim hearthlands coming out of Asia—Seljuk Turks, Mongols, Tartars, Ottoman Turks—sooner or later became Muslims. The Islamic heritage might change its political masters but it always emerged religiously and culturally dominant.

In modern times even this comfort became dubious. In the eighteenth and nineteenth Christian centuries the historic lands of Islam came increasingly under the domination, if not political, certainly economic and cultural, of Western powers representing a non-Islamic faith. India fell from a position of hegemony in Islam to be the "vassal" of the East India Company and then of the British Crown. Victoria occupied the heritage of Akbar and Aurangzīb. Ottoman Turkey, looked at from the West, was the sick man of Europe. It seemed as if the course of Islamic history had gone awry, as if the God of the Prophet had forsaken his people, as if the divine protection had miscalculated.

To make the plight of the Muslim even more painful, there came the Industrial Revolution and the steady growth of applied science giving immense advantages, in world relations, to those few European nations, and later the United States, that by happy coincidences of history and geography enjoyed a protracted head start in the race to technology, leaving the whole remaining world in relative backwardness and exploitability. This was the Europe which had barely preserved itself from Islam, on its western approaches in the eighth century and its eastern in the sixteenth; Europe which had languished in barbarism when Muhammad lived in Arabia; Europe which owed its Greek philosophical and scientific education to Arab, or rather Muslim, schoolmasters.

For the Muslim of the nineteenth century it was not simply that the Muslim world was far behind Europe in scientific advance, but that it was an old tutor bettered, indeed humiliated, by a recent pupil. Though the debt of Europe to Muslim science was perhaps idealized by these interpreters, there was enough truth in that reading of the situation to leave the average Muslim bewildered, resentful, and uncertain. This mood produced many understandable, if sometimes, ill-conceived, reactions, from the Indian Mutiny to Wahhābism.

In this long perspective of Islamic history, it is wise to see in much of Muslim thought and action in our time the urge under God to rectify the past, to put history in harmony again with Islamic destiny, to recover the success and the leadership proper to the household of Islam. In so far as that urge prospers in its purpose, so much the more are assurance and confidence restored to Islam. The creation of Pakistan was perhaps the most conspicuous example of the attempt to recover the historic nature of Islam, to retrieve the un-Islamic in Muslim history. But what Pakistan meant is reproduced elsewhere in Islam beyond its borders. No outsider can enter into the present-day mentality of Islam without appreciating the nature of its relationship with its past. There is the recovery of one past, the appropriate, and the retrieval of the other past, the inappropriate. Both emotions are powerful present factors.

IX

This distinction leads into a final aspect of interior Islam, suggested in chapter 1. The Muslim mind is not able to find complete unanimity as to the identity of the appropriate and the inappropriate in its own past. There is general agreement that the one is loyalty and the other decadence. But what is the loyal and what the decadent? And why? And how did the latter come to be?

These questions are differently diagnosed according to whether the observer is conservative or "modernist." There is a strong tendency to blame the decline upon *taqlīd*, the spirit of traditionalism, and uncritical veneration. Iqbāl, in his diagnosis of Islamic weakness, identified this petrification as the true cause of failure and called for a new dynamism to replace it. In this he was supported by numbers of other critics in all parts of the Muslim community. There is nothing wrong with Islam; what is wrong is worthless Muslims, is the reiterated cry. The new dynamism, however, with its call for freedom from ancient exegesis, from conservative commentary and static interpretation, is not always recognizably Islamic, at least in the eyes of those who fear an avalanche of reinterpretation, sweeping away their old mental securities. It is one thing to reproach unworthy Muslims; another to decide in what precisely their reproach lies. Were they too literal or too lazy? Too hidebound or too venturous? Is the way back the way forward? Have Muslims been disloyal in departing too little from the letter or from appealing too much to the spirit? To correct what is wrong do we need to shake off authority or to reassert it?

Muslims are divided in their answers to these questions. Some are inclined to blame the shaikhs and 'ulamā', others to vindicate them. Some regard reformers as too drastic; others as too timid. A great debate is in progress about the "why's" and the "whither's" of Muslim diagnosis and destiny. Examples are on every hand. It is not simply the fact of the debate, but the larger question it raises as to recognizable organs of development, or valid reform, in religion. Who is ultimately to determine what is legitimately altered and what not?

To this most important issue, *Ijtihād* is not a complete answer, hedged about as it is by many provisos and suspect in the eyes of many. Would it be unfair to say that the Muslim mind in general tends to be disparate in its attitude and can rest content with a number of different truths and attitudes, without bringing them into strict cohesion or inclusive rational order? Moreover, since Al-Ghazālī and the twelfth century, there has been a general tendency toward authoritarianism and away from intellectualism in Muslim theology. This has produced an attitude of caution and an abeyance of many urgent questions that come with accumulated pressure upon Muslims of today. It may be said that finally Islam is what Muslims believe. But this leaves one searching for a definition of the Muslim. One cannot say "Muslims are they who profess Islam" if one does not wish to be arguing in a circle.

Our desire for communication with Muslims, then, must reckon with the fact that Islam itself is undergoing a process of redefinition. There is bewilderment in some circles, assertiveness and extravagant claims in others. We must be ready sympathetically to hear Islam equated with true democracy, perfect socialism, innocuous capitalism, and abiding peace. We must be prepared to understand what a prominent leader had in mind when he wrote: "I do hope I am a Muslim." It is the view of one Muslim editor that there is more (true) Islam in the United States and Britain than in Pakistan! It would, of course, be entirely unjust to stand by Lord Cromer's famous (and foolish) dictum: "Islam reformed is Islam no longer."[14]

We have neither right nor desire to insist that Islam remain perpetually what we have at one time thought it was. Like all living things it changes, adapts, "decomposes to recompose." Though never ceasing to be recognizably itself, it can often puzzle us with what that self is and is becoming. If it puzzles us, how much more it must puzzle, distress, or vex, and yet exhilarate, those who feel the burden of these changes because, unlike outside spectators, they are internal adherents.

The realization that Islam is on the move is no small element in our Christian duty of understanding and discernment, in our would-be relationship in Christ with the peoples of the minaret. The call of the muezzin to the Christian demands first an attentive ear. It also demands a willing hand, and to that we now turn.

viii

THE CALL TO PARTICIPATION

I

Many Muslims would insist that there is too much participation already in the affairs of Muslim society on the part of faiths outside it. Any call to participation, therefore, is ill-meant and undesirable. Religious and cultural self-sufficiency has always been instinctive to the Muslim mind and never more so than in the current context of national revival and the assertion of autonomy. All cultures are liable to a healthy jealousy for their own identity with a lively suspicion of alien intrusion into their own proper responsibility. The long sanctions of the Islamic past and the provocations of more recent history reinforce that sentiment. Muslims feel that they have suffered too long from the inroads of outsiders and need to hold fast their protective resentments, not least against the West. It will be important to take the measure of these deep emotions as the first duty of any intelligent involvement from outside.

Involvement there is bound to be. The question about it has long ceased to be "whether"; it can only be "how." Whatever the emotions may be, interpenetration of cultures, and so of the

193

faiths informing them, is inescapable. Technology has seen to that. The differing "calendars" in regional histories, the disparity in resources and capacities across the continents, make it certain that cultural and religious privacies are at an end. There is manifest truth in the paradox of the "global village." Humankind has never before shared a world so inexorably common. Yet villages can never be global and the globe never a village. Particularities persist. There is no world citizenship; inasmuch as the world is not *a* city. These insistent and indispensable identities, which religion helps to shape and reinforce, struggle all the more to secure themselves against the menace they sense in a surrender to the cosmopolitan.

Christian participation in the life and welfare of Muslim communities requires a steady realism vis-à-vis this deep-seated rejectionism, tempered by a patient sense of how inter-involved, even so, all things must be, whether it is a matter of local Christian minorities who share nationality, or of expatriates mingling with local industry, science, expertise, education, and the rest, in the setting of contemporary change. The very fact that participation of some kind is inevitable makes its creative achievement the more difficult. Whatever the tenure of the non-Muslim within the Islamic situation—professional, social, technological, incidental, or official—the will to be relevant and available to its human needs and issues faces a testing variety of obstacles to be surmounted and much hard skepticism about the fact and the possibility of good faith.

Why this is so should be evident from the broad survey undertaken in chapter 1. The purpose of the present chapter is to take some soundings of the complexity of intercultural relationships on Muslim ground, then to see how far traditional patterns of Christian ministry and mission have been superseded, and finally to take stock of how continuing Christian vocation could be understood and fulfilled and what the circumstances may be both of human need and genuine opportunity, in which a due obedience to Christ through a serving compassion may still be attained.

II

Ayatollah Khomeini's characterization of the president of the United States as "the great Satan" may sound a vulgar caricature to American ears.¹ Yet it expresses in stark honesty the workings of the mind of a threatened identity. Under the Shah, in the words of Amir Taheri, Iran had become "an economic giant and a political dwarf." Being an economic giant meant a welter of new weaponry, demanding an influx of Western technicians and with them a dangerous medley of influences capable of eroding traditional values and consigning Iranian meanings to alien submergence. The menace was made all the more galling by reason of its Iranian conspirators, seen as stooges of the Western invaders. Nor did talk of "progress" in technology justify the price paid in forfeited dignity. Ideological purity was more urgent than technological development. Xenophobia, for the Ayatollah, was the only right form of Islamic identity, given the unforgiveable machination of the foreign factor. The latter's much vaunted "democratic ideals" would be rendered pointless once a popular cultural revolution had taken due toll of invaders and ousted all their works. Such passion, even savagery, might seem fanatical, inexplicable, vindictive, irrational, to the average Westerner, caught unawares and confounded by its sudden eruption. But within it lay many readily predictable features of the human psyche expressed in the religious collective.

Those dramatic events in Iran represent in extreme form the tensions deriving from intrusive new wealth and new sophistication, coming from external origins and provoking disruptive local consequences, throughout the Islamic world. It is not that, in the long perspective, science and technology are unfamiliar or uncongenial to Islam. Quite the contrary. Much of Western competence in near modern times stands on the shoulders of Muslim scholars and scientists of their golden middle age. But the contemporary range and incidence of technology are emphatically Western in their purview and their ethos. The receiving world has had to accommodate them against a background of political disadvantage, economic exploitation, and social vulnerability.

Even where the response is absorptive rather than explosive, as for example in the Gulf States and Southeast Asian Islam, it remains guarded and defensive. Education is a vital field in this regard, for it is situated at the point of continuity, or discontinuity, between the generations. If old values are to be maintained, they must survive the impact of a new-style familiarity with assumptions about human nature and society that the earlier traditions did not confront. Sociology is an obvious case in point here, for it imports into faith and tradition the disconcerting dimension of "social conditioning" and relativizes "truth" into the given "plausibles" determined by the context. There have been calls for a purely Islamic sociology that would counter such forfeiture of religious certitude.[2]

There are exacting demands here and temptations to hasty, emotional, or shortsighted reaction. One source of reassurance is to carry the issue into vigorous counterattack and denounce the Western mentality as the unhappy victim of its own secular trends. It is assumed that Islam is well constituted to accept the outward facilities and products of scientific technique, while firmly rejecting the presuppositions of the science that produced them. Muslim concerns about education clearly recognize the danger from Western-style sophistication to orthodox, traditional Islamic beliefs and values. But many seem to think that the danger is met by a simple insistence that Islam unites everything under "religion," rejects "secularism," and must carry through a complete dewesternization of knowledge.[3]

The fact that, whether blandly or deeply, Muslim thinking is obliged to take critical account of the West only proves how far participation has gone. Attitudes that assume exemption from its problems—intellectual and social—only entangle Muslims more surely in them. They may assume that they have wiser, stronger resources in the stuff of their faith, but precisely for that reason they must recognize the real dimensions of contemporary existence to which those resources must relate. Criticism or superiority cannot be both honest and escapist. To deplore secularity or to see a true Islam immune from it is to be obligated to define and achieve that true Islam in a secular time. Just as "there is more to myth than the instant need to demythologize,"[4] so there is more to secularity than an immediate warrant both to dismiss and denounce it.

"The mote in the eye" is, of course, easy to identify by Easterners looking to the West. It is right that they should redress a distorted vision from the opposite direction. Professor Said's book on orientalism (though written, paradoxically, from the warm security of Western academia) illustrates the point well.[5] He writes with a Middle Eastern *animus* to reproach the perversity, as he sees it, of Western scholarship about Islam. This he finds wholly the tool of economic and political interests, making it subjective, wishful, and inept. It could hardly, he avers, be otherwise, inasmuch as so much academic funding comes from governmental and commercial sources with their own interests. Academics, he insists, have quite failed to maintain a scholarly integrity in face of these debts and pressures. The result is a Western image of Islam that is superficial, sensational, and unworthy.

The wise response to such strictures—and they are also directed to specifically Christian studies—will be to ask for a radical realism about vested interests all round and for a true awareness of the complexity of the world in which *all* have to search for integrity and wisdom. It should be recognized that there *is* sincerity in at least some ventures into Islam from outside.[6] But such recognition had better come by its merits than by its protests. It may be that incriminators, however partial, may progress to the wider relevance of their analyses, which, for all of us, are readiest when they concern the alien and the outsider.

In the long involvement of being on the receiving end of external factors of power and change, Muslims have every reason both for resentment and realism. But these can also be lively educators of internal situations if they are not blunted by self-justification on either side of the relationship. The more Islamic economics, for example, wrestles with the problems of nonusury in modern financing,[7] or Islamic sociology with the sanctions of collective beliefs, or Islamic education with the future of the past, or Islamic historians with their elucidations,[8] the more open their Islam must be to its inner meanings and, with these, to its outer relationships. Its responses can be only its own. But they will not be responses if they ignore the wider world. Any Christian sense of participation in them, in whatever form, must turn wisely on that openness and hope to serve it.

III

Many of the old forms of Christian action in Muslim lands have been taken over by the state or have been rejected by Islamic nationhood. But it is fair to say that they had a long and honorable history. Scattered across the Muslim world were scores of homes of healing and halls of learning in which generations of Muslims found both health and knowledge. Hospitals in Gaza and Galilee, Peshawar and Kermanshah, were known by the names of devoted physicians and surgeons whose reputation wove a living legend of compassion around a circuit of villages. Schools and colleges nurtured to literacy and leadership a long sequence of Muslim youth in the Arab, Asian, and African worlds. Institutions, now nationalized and secularized, left their legacy of educational or medical concern and ideals to a situation they notably stimulated even to their own supercession. It is, in part, the destiny of all such ministry to health and to truth to make itself dispensable, or to entrust its relevance elsewhere. But while these ministries endured they embodied a significance that only the unimaginative could deny. In a near half century of eye surgery Dr. Henry Holland of Quetta removed 65,000 cataracts from the eyes of Pathans on the northwest frontier of Afghanistan.

Such "saving health"—to borrow the psalmist's phrase—was, and is, inseparable from the biblical, Christian understanding of "salvation." The term excludes an idea of welfare that takes no account of forgiveness and grace. Christians are not called to organized philanthropy dissociated from the love of God in Christ. Nor are they called to a rescue of the soul that ignores society and sickness. "Saving health" means the fullness of personal life—of body, mind, and spirit—in the redeeming intention of God. The physician, the nurse, the midwife, the teacher, the agriculturalist, have therefore taken their place in the Christian concern for the world. The loving compassion within their skills, working with Christ, is part of the meaning, and impact, of the kingdom of heaven. It exemplifies the gift and character of him who said: "I am among you as one who serves." The spiritual meaning of salvation is discovered in its earthly incidence. Its proper association with a faith affirmed, far from being intrusive or improper, is the surest tribute to the human dignity given under the sovereignty of God. That "Jesus came healing," "Jesus came teaching," is no invalid precedent for those who bear his name.

While insisting on the inseparability of body and soul, ministry and faith, in the Christian liability to one's neighbor, it is clear that we must recognize in many areas a termination of the former privileges of service. That is all to the good inasmuch as local, national responsibility for health and education has come into full charge. State resources, once marshalled and applied, can be far more efficacious—not to say, in affluent areas such as the Gulf, far more commodious—than foreign and voluntary agencies could be.

There may still be specific aspects of health thus far inadequately covered by public and state agencies, such as psychiatric care, or care for the mentally disabled, or research into the local incidence of diseases, where Christian *diakonia* can still play due part with acceptance. But increasingly and gladly the major field is yielded to other hands. Situations where the slender resources of isolated mission hospitals were the only succor over wide territories are changing, though in some places they persist.

This termination, entire or partial, of the old patterns has two welcome consequences. It enables Christians to share *with* Muslims the many problematics of active compassion, both practical and ethical, and invites them to search and refine the integrity of religious teaching and spiritual values. Further, it relieves the Christian of the onus of an accusation that often accompanied missionary compassion and in the last quarter century often reached bitter proportions. It was that the juncture of service and witness, so instinctive to classic Christianity, involved a kind of religious imperialism, an exploitation of the sick at their most vulnerable, and a dire compromise of genuine humanity.

It was the fact of the accusation, rather than debate about its truth, that finally mattered. For in such issues of strong emotion what is so believed becomes a fact of the situation. It does not suffice to protest that to see evangelism as capitalizing on human disadvantage is a travesty and far from the nature and intention of the church. Travesty it remains. But not for those who see it with other eyes. Their anger may misread. We need, in turn, to beware of not misreading what it alleges and why.

It will not suffice to note that multitudes of the critics' fellow nationals have seen the facts another way. Nor could the issue have been solved by forbearing to witness, for that would betray the Christian's deepest trust and fail the world at a deeper point than its disease or poverty. Abandoning *diakonia* would have left the evangelist, like the priest and the levite, "passing by on the other side." Jesus refused the temptation to be merely breadmaker. But he did not commit himself to the proposition that persons shall not live by bread at all. Yet service in his name has always been in need to remember his own warning: "You seek me because you ate of the loaves," and so to dissociate works of service from any impulse to discipleship other than free response to truth perceived. Perception, nevertheless, could not be feasibly divorced from evidence, however frail, of how truth might go hand in hand with love.

Thought on the dilemma of ministry and its implications, as meant or as read, has been overtaken, in large part, by the new situation. But suspicions persist and it is well to appreciate their depth, for they attend all those other contexts of participation across frontiers to which this chapter is moving. They were reviewed in a conference between Muslims and Christians held in Chambésy, Switzerland, in 1976, on the subject of their mutual experience of mission, da'wah, at the hands of the other. It had about it a frankness that made it something of a cause célèbre.

Muslim speakers, in differing degrees of sharpness, called for a moratorium on all Christian mission in Islamic areas and, further, for corporate penitence for the sins of proselytism by which Muslims had been assaulted and provoked. A final agreed statement sought to distinguish proselytism and propaganda from genuine and appropriate concern for the expression of truth as the sincere witness desired to bring it. But even in its formal, and mutual, repudiation of ulterior motives, the conference found it difficult to escape a besetting preoccupation—on both sides—with *amour propre* and the more subtle vested interests to which all religions are liable.[9] These can be overcome only in a willingness to go beyond postures, whether incriminatory or conciliatory, and allow the issue, for all of us, to deepen into an honest search for what the roots of compassion must be in God and ourselves. That brings us back to questions of faith, but only *within* the duties and tasks of human community wider and larger than the custodial faithful whose institutional "interests" can rightly be only those of servants to all.

That the Chambésy Conference had to struggle so painfully with its tensions illustrates the problem of establishing (as one speaker put it) "a code of missionary behavior" for two essentially missionary religions, not to say also a confession of what it called "reciprocal repentance," which also raises the vexing question of how "reciprocal" it could, or should, be. There is, for one thing, no consensus, on either side, as to what might be appropriately missionary and what not. Both have a wide divergence of activity and organization, with elements in no way amenable to common counsel, still less to control. Untidiness and disparity are likely to continue, though, we may hope, within an increasing respect for the dignity and the sensitivity of the other. Often the factors which exacerbate and distort are those that stem from political or communal pressures, as, for example, bitterly, in the Philippines and Lebanon.

These factors need to be firmly separated from the essentially religious issues, despite the paradox that it is impossible to do so. In this, of course, lies a profound question as to what religion "essentially" is. It is perhaps in the readiness to be led, realistically, into that sort of ultimate question that the best hope for religious honesty—not to say, authenticity—may finally lie. For, in the last analysis, any presentation of faith must have within it, though perhaps inarticulate, the question of what faith should be, of what it should say for itself, and why. To that extent all witness, from whatever direction, involves itself, however passively, in final themes as to meaning and mystery, however far those themes may be foreshortened, compromised, or evaded in the convictions it offers. In that sense even a clamor of voices may come to wisdom more contritely than an enervating indifference.

Mission, from whatever quarter, respects conviction and exists to commend its own. But commendation today has to coexist with that of others. The unresolved question is what that does for our convictions. It can be resolved only in mutuality and in humility. It is only in mission that truth comes to its own crisis—a crisis from which the very thrust of mission can all too easily exempt it. A faith, such as Islam or Christianity, that is denied if not commended, cannot be satisfied merely to coexist. Yet only in coexistence can it pursue its commendation.[10]

IV

Our study must turn from these deep waters of how and why about faith and mission to persons and roles by whom and in which faith and mission consist and happen. Given the steady and probably irreversible recession of the old patterns of healing and education already noted, it is clear that present and future commendation of Christian faith can proceed only through general participation in the spheres of day-to-day living and working in the contemporary scene. The question is how to turn physical participation into spiritual and personal communication, whether it be in the exchanges of fellow nationals of different faiths, or whether it be in the presence to each other of expatriate and local elements through whatever circumstances of employment, emigration, or interaction.

In the latter case there are many obstacles to the achievement of genuine witness and Christian expression. Oil technicians in Saudi Arabia are hardly likely to find deep rapport with their context in terms outside their professional skills. Language and cultural otherness will impede them even if the will is present. Nor will a host community take any will for witness kindly. Rather it will assume that relationships will be strictly functional—an assumption confirmed by the very circumstances of housing and the patterns of tenure. Personnel in aid programs, development service, advisory roles, and the like, are, for the most part, necessarily engrossed in their tasks and functions, and often disallowed relationships outside them. Personal faith is not readily communicable in such situations and tensions are quickly aroused if ventures are made.

At worst those tensions could follow the lines of the earlier rejectionism to which institutional communication was liable, especially if it is suspected that "tentmaking" Christians have been deliberately sponsored in evasion of visa regulations that would have excluded them had they been avowedly missionary. Muslim resentment has been expressed where this has been suspected.[11] It is important that there be no subterfuge in Christian relationship. The "tents," whatever skills or tasks they entail, must be real. But, given legitimate presence in or by them, it would be odd, even inhuman, and certainly un-Islamic, if they were to be denied all personal significance. Islam itself, across the centuries, has communicated its witness through merchants and seafarers. Whether into Southeast Asia or by trans-Saharan caravans, it has been a faith of "tentmakers." Onlookers have asked the meaning

of *Salāt*, or interrogated pilgrims en route to Mecca, or questioned the devout in the keeping of Ramadān. Islam, then, could
hardly fail to respect articulate Christians in the expression and
practice of their faith in the setting of Muslim residence.

Ideally we should also be aiming for an end to the kind of incubus which impedes a full and free expression of faith by minorities
and aliens. Islam has nothing to fear and everything to gain from
open attitudes subject only to courtesy and public order. The idea
of territorial exclusivism is an anachronism in the world of today.
The familiar bond between faith and identity is worthier and
more resilient when it admits of hospitality.

It can be no proper part of any faith to reduce its immigrants,
whether transitory or permanent, to mere functionaries of its
economy or operatives in its infrastructure. To do so would conspire with the secularity Islam otherwise so strongly deplores in its
assessments of the West. Will it do to characterize Westerners as
incurably materialist and yet confine them to wholly material relationships? Their temptation to be true to stereotype will be
strong enough, given all the complexity of their tenure, without
the connivance of the resolute theists who are their hosts. And
they, in their turn, are not lacking the temptations of secularity
and growing numbers of those who succumb to them.

Given the audible Christian in a hearing situation, participation, otherwise spiritually barren, will yield endless themes and
occasions of exchange. It will be wise, as in the parables of Jesus,
not to let controversy preoccupy, but to draw out thought and
recognition from the immediate context of shared experience.
Our responsibility under God for our competences in technology,
how these relate to a creaturely care for the sacrament of creation,
the task of personal conscience in the power structures of the
state, the making or unmaking of human destiny in the arena of
the world—all these, and many more, present themselves to lively
souls in converse about faith.

When at dawn the muezzin calls *Hayyā ilā-l-falāh*, "Come to
the good," what may it mean in the working day of the engineer
sinking artesian wells and reshaping a whole society in a crucible
of petro-dollars? Or for the cost surveyor in league with rapid
urbanization for a shifting and disconcerted population? Or for
an advisor conjuring up new techniques and devices which may

well conduce to neglect of worship and disinterest in God? Or to a medical person administering the skills and mysteries of a contemporary hospital? Or to a volunteer busy with a literacy project that may make decision necessary in a score of issues hitherto dormant for the illiterate, about the communist diagnosis of the human being and labor, the blandishments of sexual freedom, or the puzzles of an unequal world? As with Jesus, so with ourselves, much of the impact of the Gospel comes most surely in tandem with awareness of daily life. When these doctrinal themes emerge—the main concern of chapter 10, below—this, rather than bare controversy, will be their wisest ground.

All this, of course, presupposes not merely "tentmakers" but peacemakers, trust-makers, sense-makers. It calls for a quality of sincerity, intelligence, and patience that may be far to seek. But it seems clear that it is this sort of Christian presence across the world—open, compassionate, and expressive—with its legitimate occasions afforded by the need and the supply of skills and human means within the fair exchanges of the working world, that provides the best hope of Christian communication. By the timings of history, if nothing else, cultures and faiths with them are immersed in these relationships in the market of humankind. They demand our utmost to redeem them. Many Muslims today, not least in the Arab world, are minded to read a providence of God in their new dimensions of power, of autonomy, of oil, of neutralism. Will Christians be at fault if they also read a circumstance to which they should respond?

V

Participation as a fact to be thus deepened into a vocation, to be made a spiritual transaction as well as a physical adjacence, is, of course, by no means confined to ex-patriate Christians of Western provenance. It has been there all the time in the local minorities, some of whose members are also involved in the export and import of technical functions—Palestinians in the Gulf region, Copts outside Egypt, Indians in further Asia. Recruitment of personnel is by no means limited to Western sources. Pakistani Christian nurses, for example, are in great demand in Muslim hospitals. Areas of conspicuous wealth and concurrent development draw in large numbers of workers to service their economies. Such influx has helped to diversify the Christian presence and to stimulate the traditional relationships between local Christian minorities and their Muslim majority communities.

Dhimmī, "tolerated minority," status under Islam has long made for a pattern of quiescence in ancient, local Christianity around the mosque. Traditional tolerance allowed only a freedom to remain, to teach the faith only within the family, so that adherence became a circumstance of birth and continuity that of a closed community. There was no freedom to express faith, still less to recruit to it, outside that circle of one's origin. Over the centuries the churches came to accept this version of themselves. Indeed, they had no other option. It was a tradition that abjured theological exchange and, when it did not ghettoize the mind, reduced participation to mundane affairs. It dies hard even now when ecumenical stimulus has notably emancipated attitudes and fostered initiatives. Tragically, Lebanon, which for a variety of reasons was the most promising of settings for Muslim/ Christian meeting, has been overtaken by events that have bitterly denied and destroyed its promise. Their legacy will be long and harsh. Yet their utterly tragic quality only makes plain how inescapable participation is. Conflict is the desperate measure of the refusal of cooperation, the ultimate index of the criminal futility of religious exclusivism, inflicted or endured, the final nemesis of the *dhimmī* system breeding the neuroses of fragmentation.

It is relevant to this whole context to note how Muslims across Europe are experiencing their own minority dispersion in the last quarter century. It is an experience not congenial to the characteristic assumption of Islamic history that Islam, being the final revelation and accustomed to statehood, would always occupy the place of power. Turks in West Germany, Pakistanis in England, North Africans in France, and a variety of Muslim peoples scattered elsewhere in Europe come up against the problems of minorities vis-à-vis cultic forms, cultural occasions, nurture in the faith, and legal status, analogous to those faced by local Christians inside Islamic states for generations. As with Muslims in the subcontinent of India, sundered from Islamic citizenship by the creation of Pakistan, this condition serves to focus thought on the essential nature of religion when it is no longer politicized. It also alerts the mind to issues of tolerance as only psychic or other insecurity can appreciate them. These new dimensions of reciprocal experience, rightly apprehended, can be useful in deepening the participation between us.

The presence of Muslims, too, in the length and breadth of the United States and Canada, though differing on many counts from that in European countries that have never avowed *e pluribus unum*, likewise entails an intriguing shift in Christian awareness. In earlier generations, mission meant going to others. It was, as the word goes, "overseas." It involved "foreign parts." Changes of recent decades have brought representatives of that distant concern right into our domestic scene, our local context. Western cities have impressive mosques. Modest ones may well be found across the street. Muslims in Britain are believed to outnumber Methodists. When, as it were, the tables of participation are turned, how should we understand the meaning of mission? Even the etymology of the word is somehow awry, for there is no more "sending."[12]

Much more than etymology, too. Genuine hospitality, sensitivity, understanding, and ensuring of rights are certainly vital. But what, in the discipline of these duties, of evangelism? In principle Christians are never absolved from the sharing of Christ. They have no authority to privatize the Gospel. Christian hospitality to all communities cannot rightly argue their exclusion from the deepest factor in its making—namely, the love of God in Christ. It does not bring an authentic relationship if it has first neutralized its character. To have neutralized one's own faith in the imagined interest of relationship is probably to have also neutralized the other's. And how, then, is the other truly welcomed?

If witness, in this way, is inseparable from hospitality, it has to be consistent with it. Many minorities suffer—as indeed Christians have in Asia—from acute psychic insecurity. They cling even pathetically to familiar things. "How, they ask, shall we know it's us, without our past?"[13] Religion is a major factor in their continuity, a large element in their comfort, a crowning asset against their risks. Evangelism insensitive to these considerations may easily be counterproductive. Some would say counterindicated. It will seem depredatory, threatening. It will usurp family loyalties, embitter relationships, jeopardize both past and future.

And it can readily provoke a responsive triumphalism, an obduracy that hardens into enmity, or merely the suspicious unease that spells estrangement.

Black Islam in the United States, for some of these reasons, is a case in point. Orthodoxy would insist that in truth it is no Islam at all, for it made itself the focus of black racialism, broadly on the thesis that because Christianity was largely a "white" religion, antipathy to whites could well adapt to its ends the faith historically associated with otherness vis-à-vis the Christian world. But the adapting made a travesty of Islam. The most moving proof of this is the *Autobiography of Malcolm X*.[14] But the tight discipline of Black Islam, the total extinction of the past of all recruits, their change of name, their sworn allegiance to the leader, the association of all the evils and ills of black society with a white conspiracy, and an eschatology of revenge—all these sharply exemplify what can happen to religion when it is prostituted by communal fears and sectarian aggression.

There is, of course, much more to this example than a reminder of religious dangers. Witness must be positively *within* participation. It will reassure, not for any merely tactical reason, but out of genuine respect and the ability to think and feel as if one were the other. It will relate its expression of God in Christ as closely as possible to the great positives of Islam, which have to do with divine sovereignty, human creaturehood, our charter to be over nature under God, and to all those deep spheres of human finitude and wistfulness that we know in common. It will proceed as far as it can from the Muslim's Qur'ān, without contentious issues about status and loyalty.[15] It will draw sympathetically on every potential of Islamic spirituality and let the preoccupations of Muslim doctrine be, as far as possible, the context of Christian meanings. It will seek this expressiveness through all the practicalities of human neighborhood generously pursued.

VI

Such open practice of human neighborhood on the ground here and now must include a sharp sense of the history of not so human neighborhood there and then in the past, as it survives in collective memory. If, outside the Muslim community, we are concerned for the call of their minaret about "coming to the good," we must be alert to the negative participation we already have in all that impedes their answer. We are implicated in many of the ills and wrongs that their quest for well-being, *Falāh*, must overcome. Right prospect turns on honest retrospect.

What must impress the sensitive observer of Islam today is the degree to which its preoccupations derive from external relationships, which reach far back. Its response is, and cannot be other than, its own. But the inner decisions and conflicts about the response are always relational. They are responding to non-Islam historically confronted via politics, culture, and events. The problem for the concerned outsider, and certainly for the Christian, is how to relate to Muslims in *their* answers, out of the community we so evidently have with them over the questions.

What has happened in Iran is a most obvious and painful example, leading for the time being to very bleak conclusions. Another, similarly sharp, but at more analyzable range, was eloquent in the writings of Frantz Fanon, the West Indian who made Muslim Algeria his adopted country and whose philosophy guided its revolution. In his *The Wretched of the Earth*[16] and other writings he grounded his whole revolutionary theme in antipathy. He saw imperialism not only as political usurpation but as psychic conspiracy. Minds as well as peoples had to be decolonialized. Alien empire had required a total subservience of spirit and not simply a physical acquiescence in powerlessness. Thus violence was a positive liberation and not only a negative instrument to dislodge the colonial power. In making repudiation absolute, violence was itself the experience of liberty. Fanon was, therefore, totally opposed to the sort of cultural hospitality that Leopold Senghor, president of Senegal, exemplified in his determination—and ability—to belong across frontiers and possess a double culture.[17] In Fanon's logic this was merely to africanize the servitude, to leave the essential imperialism intact, and to make political "independence" illusory. It was to connive with self-deception.

It may be argued that, at a price, it succeeded. Satan, so to speak, did cast out Satan. Algeria was freed. But then neither is Senghor's Senegal a colony still. There are large issues in the contrast that we have to let rest in this context. The immediate point is the undeniable participation of Islamic decision in areas of meaning and action externally defined and constituted by relations from without. Frantz Fanon, for his part, had—at least through the 1960s—a steady fascination for much Palestinian thinking, minded to find in the Algerian success a transferable precedent for the Palestinian struggle. Much of the marriage of violence and necessity that his logic required has characterized the Palestinian will to "liberation." Nowhere has the legacy of an external history been more bitter than for the Palestinians.

Whether in Israel, on the West Bank, or in dispersion, theirs is a deepening experience of deprivation, indignity, frustration, insecurity, expropriation, and tragedy, to be laid squarely at the door of the current version of Zionism in grave compromise of its founding vision. Yet that version is itself the legacy of a Jewish sense of deprivation, indignity, frustration, insecurity, expropriation, and tragedy, undergone elsewhere and now finding opportunity—as former victims are liable to do when role reversal makes them victors—to secure itself remorselessly. But, also incriminated in that sequel as we now observe it, are the duplicity of the Balfour Declaration, the tactical ambiguities of Zionist intentions, the self-interests of international politics, the pressures in the United States, the rivalries of Arab states, and a whole cycle of longer history oppressively possessed by propaganda.

The Israel/Arab encounter symbolizes most painfully of all the theme of Islamic decision within a *Sitz im Leben* externally constituted and externally referred. Action is, to date, a matter of reacting. Decisions are located in relationships. In the Indian subcontinent Muslims for generations knew and learned themselves in the world of Hindu neighborhood, with all its subtle quality. The decision for Pakistan was one form of the reaction; the shape of Indian Islam since partition another. Likewise in the African scene. Africa sets its own unique imprint on all that it absorbs. Muslims are no exception.

Nor of course is there anything exceptional to Islam in this liability to wrestle with what is external to itself. No faith enjoys exemption. It is rather the intensity and the direction which we must be at pains to understand. For Muslims, in reaction, often try to turn the frames of reference around and require the non-Muslim to confront Islamic meanings in their challenge to non-

Muslim meanings. This is happening on many counts, for it is both a deep psychic emotion and instinctive to faith. Either way, the question for all—and central to us here—will be how best to make the resulting community of situations (for such it is) positive, versatile, frank, and articulate.

VII

One very obvious area of this community of situations is that of Marxism both as philosophy and as political science. It is present at once in the actual confrontation of superpowers and their proxies, or intended proxies, in border realms of their range. It is there for Southeast Asian Islam in the adjacence of China and its communist control of one quarter of humankind. It is there, too, in the inner strains of the Iranian revolution and in the Soviet occupation of Afghanistan. It provokes many questions that, in the West, often fail to surmount more vulgar forms of self-interest and obtuseness, about how far Marx and Islam are compatible, how securely "democratic" is Islam, how responsive are Muslims to the logic of communism, given the unacceptable contours of capitalism. At what point are the latter defined?

That there is, deeply, in Arab and Muslim tradition a place for the *vox populi* is evident. In Saudi Arabian, and other, practice, there is, for example, the *majlis*—the "sitting" or "court" where a ruler hears petitions and is personally accessible to anyone with a grievance. A sort of consensus against, if not always for, change *can* be determinative. The Qur'ān affirms that "their proceeding is by counsel among themselves."[18] There is also the potential, if also contentious, institution of *Ijtihād,* "enterprise," tending via consensus, *Ijmā',* toward the emergence of a popular will. But these are likely to be sharply circumscribed, especially in Shī'ah Islam. 'Alī Shari'ātī, the philosopher of the Iranian Revolution, laid great emphasis on *al-nās,* "the people," and certainly their role in the streets was vital to the Ayatollah's cause.[19] But Ayatollah Khomeini himself conceives of the people strictly within the interpreting and controlling aegis of the "clergy," and the "clergy" firmly within the theory of the *Imām.*[20]

Questions about the "democracy" of Islam may well not be the ones most urgent to ask in this context. What of Islamic attitudes to Marx? There is certainly no sympathy for the notion of the withering away of the state. Statehood has always been seen as inseparable from the ethos of Islam as a highly politicized faith, inaugurated by a prophet-ruler. But the state has not in fact "withered away" in the communist order. Islam might be said, in part, to share the optimism of Marxist eschatology, with its sanguine notions of human evil as "capitalist" and "bourgeois" rather than human and general. It is easy to be hopeful about solutions if one has been naive about analyses. Islam, by and large, lacks the kind of radical sense of sin in society that belongs with Christian diagnosis, taught by the New Testament and Good Friday.[21] On the other hand there is much in the Qur'ān to challenge the soft utopianism of the Marxist classless future, as well as the materialist "dialectic" that undergirds it. Then, of course, Islam is insistently theist and deplores the consigning of worship to supercession as merely an epiphenomenon of the economic system.

On the other hand, as with all religions, there have been in Islam those aspects of listlessness, apathy, and craven tolerance of wrong that led Marx to reach his famous dictum about religion as "the opium of the people." Yet, "the cry of the oppressed" has also been there and "real despair"—features of the religious scene that gave Marx his noble sense of pathos and his drive not merely to study society but to change it. That dynamism, some Muslims have said, aligns him significantly with Muhammad who, by very different canons, was a tremendous architect of change, both social and economic. It is feasible to extract from Muslim tradition about Muhammad pointers to some communal ownership of vital necessities—for example, in his day, wells, oases, and herds. Quranic inheritance law, too, serves to preclude large capital buildup, as does the prohibition of usury, varied as its interpretation may be.[22]

In these and other ways it has been popular in places to argue affinities between Islam and Marxist economic theory. But with its philosophical bases loyal Muslims could find no loyal alliance. On all these counts, whether arguably congenial or abhorrent, there can be no mistaking the fact of Marx and his legacy as significant and evocative of new external elements in what the Muslim mind has to confront. Communism, therefore, is an important dimension in the community of situations relating Christians with Muslims.

VIII

Imaginative literature, poetry, and the novel are a vital index to contemporary Muslim experience and for the will to understand it from outside. There are, for example, elaborate novels, such as Jabrā Ibrāhīm Jabrā's *Al-Safīnah* ["the Ship"], which explore the enigma of the self and individual passion with the sort of subtle, and even desolating, absorption in personal mood and tangle that characterizes much Western "stream of consciousness" writing.[23]

More significant on a larger canvas are the many fictional, or autobiographical, studies of Muslim sojourn in the West. A pioneer in this field was Yahya Haqqī's *Qundīl Umm Hāshim* ["the Lamp of Umm Hāshim"], in which the Cairene, Ismā'īl, studies eye surgery in England, returns to Egypt, and suffers deep humiliations through the clash of his skills and the traditions of local piety with its simple faith in the healing properties of the oil in the lamp of the mosque. Ismā'īl finally marries Fātimah, around whom the story of his pride and fall and riper wisdom is woven.[24]

Hamidou Kane's *L'aventure ambiguë* traces a similar story with greater subtlety of presentation, moving between the warm, mystical spirituality of Senegal and the cold, logical modernity of Paris.[25] The narrative ends tragically when the tensions of two incompatible personalities, taut within a single character and sharpened by contradictory loyalties, prove inconsolably shattering. In both cases the strain between divided worlds is the more ironic because of the expectation and fascination that initiated the broken ventures. These and many kindred stories epitomize in personal terms the pain and perplexity involved in living out of a sacred past into a secular future, striving to conserve the one and to concede the other. They express the ambiguity at the core of *Falāh* itself and how to come to it.

Our obligation to imaginative literature takes us not only to this two-world experience but to social criticism in the heartlands of

Islam. Tāhā Husain, the most influential figure in Arabic letters this century, turned his pen effectively to the portrayal of social ills, notably in his *Al-Mu'adhdhabūn fī-l-Ard* ["the Oppressed in the Land"], a series of vignettes that might be loosely compared to James Joyce's *Dubliners*. He draws moving portraits of earth's suffering folk as he has observed them. The evil he sees in society he makes the reader see in the pathos of those caught in its toils. Each individual is representative; imagination only fills out the canvas. There is the village girl who marries, at her father's insistence, into an unhappiness that ends in suicide. One day she goes with her waterpot to the river but does not return. All the promise of her beauty is blighted by a system that thwarts the natural course of love.

The story of Qāsim, too, ends in a watery grave. He is a consumptive fisherman who goes out to another day of his weary, daily struggle for existence. On the way, in the early dawn, he hears the muezzin calling that prayer is better than sleep. Through his mind runs a prayer his brother, a skaikh, has taught him about the remembrance of God. He performs the prayer in the mosque and that day the heavens smile: he catches a superb fish, which a youth helps him to carry to the house of the man who buys it. Overjoyed with success, he goes to the market to buy food for his wife and daughter, anticipating their delight. "Carrying his body more often than it carries him," and spending his waking hours in wonted listless despair, this is indeed a day of days. But on the night of his success, his seventeen-year-old daughter Sakīnah is seduced by his brother-in-law, a man of pious reputation and a pilgrim to Mecca, but a dealer in bribes and a despiser of the poor. Qāsim finds his wife Ammūnah shattered by shame and grief. He seeks the river never to return. The dawn muezzin greets the silence of the daybreak but Qāsim is beyond hearing. A compulsion of wretchedness drives him from the world. The tragedy makes no more than a ripple on the surrounding surface of indifference.

There is also the story of Sālih, a village lad, who is always punished at school. Being poor, he has no sweets or melon seeds with which to bribe the helper of the blind schoolmaster. The burdens of poverty never lift from his shoulders and at the close he meets death at a railway crossing. In a chapter entitled

"*Sakhā*" ["munificence"] Tāhā Husain, in sardonic vein, pillo-
ries the callousness of the well-to-do, wrapped and lulled in their
own luxury. He means the reader to multiply across the whole
"earth" of these "oppressed" the toll of human suffering. He
prefaces his collection of stories with the dedication:

> To those who are consumed with the passion for justice,
> Whom fear of injustice makes ever wakeful,
> I address this study.
> To those who come by what they do not need,
> To those who do not come by what they need,
> Is this narrative addressed.[26]

Such burden of conscience in the litterateur could be quoted in
all the major literatures of contemporary Islam. Stories of pathos
and poems of protest are one thing; active, adequate measures
another. These have to recruit, equip, and deploy the ecologist,
the engineer, the agriculturalist, the doctor, the public-health re-
searcher, the nutritionist, the relief worker—all the technicians
and tacticians of the muezzin's "well-being." But these in their
turn reach into the resources of religion—to interpret sexuality, to
guide parenthood, to relate village to city, to curb exploitation, to
inform political power, to call evil by its name, to consecrate the
good earth and human dignity, and so to arrive at a right worship.
None of these issues, though poignantly national, can be confined
in national responses. They ramify into obligations that no body
politic can discharge in separation, or leave to the harsh law of the
market, in privatizations of plenty inflicting privatizations of
poverty, within the state or across the hemispheres. Faiths and
their cultures, doctrines, and disciplines are still far from breast-
ing the developments of world history.

Alongside the burden of conscience in imaginative literature in
the Arab world, in Turkey, Pakistan, and more distant Asia,
there is a deeper problem still, in which we must participate. It has
to do with the uncertainty about religiousness at large. We are
accustomed to the fanatical image that may itself be, paradoxically, proof of the point. Not that misgiving is widespread or
more than rarely explicit—given the strong tenacity of Muslim

loyalty. Yet it emerges and does not need the significance of numbers to command attention.

Concern here is not with the sort of outspoken skepticism argued by Sādiq Jalāl al-'Azm in his *Criticism of Religious Thought in Islam*.[27] Rather it is with the kind of heart malaise discernible, for example, in the Egyptian novelist Najīb Mahfūz. Alongside an implied social criticism and a sense of human pathos goes a sort of Kafkaesque somberness—even despair—about human ways and institutions, not least those of politics. His longest work, *Awlād Hāratinā* ["Children of our Quarter"], puzzles its way into the perplexities of the human order, or disorder, by imposing on the Cairo suburb and its conflicts the dark enigma of "the old house," the abode of the mysterious Gebalāwī, analogue for God. Gebel, Rifa'a, and Qāsim, a sequence of prophet-leaders, surrogates for Moses, Jesus, and Muhammad, try their hand successively at organizing the quarter on behalf of Gebalāwī. They all fail and their followers hive off into further faction. Finally a magician, Arafa, surrogate for technology, penetrates the secret of Gebalāwī and kills him. In a subtle and elusive web of narrative, Najīb Mahfūz beguiles his readers on several levels and leaves them with a tantalizing sense of the chronic unease of humanity, the divisive haplessness of religion and of belief in God, as somehow a conspiracy of fear, illusion, hearsay, and hope.[28]

This writer's habit of elusiveness is sufficient index to the inner temerity of his thinking. It would be idle to assume that his dubieties were general. But he is evidence enough that the mental gropings of European and American writers, of Kakfa, Camus, Beckett, Hemingway, Sartre, and Koestler, have found register within Islam. Kāmil Husain, in much more sanguine vein, had nevertheless something of the same doubtfulness of the amenability of humankind to the necessary wisdom or of the capacity of human collectives, especially states, to achieve personal good. He justified religious faith for its psychic efficacy rather than for its objective truth.[29] The work of Jamal Khwaja, of Aligarh Muslim University, might be cited in the same vein.[30]

It is prudent to keep such voices in perspective; it would be careless to ignore them. If they indicate, within their own authentic setting of being Muslim, a register of experience akin to what

Christians have encountered at longer and larger range, then they must belong with that participation in response that we are called to make. To "come to prayer" is, for some, to explore this terrain, to reckon with everything that counterindicates the summons.

There is one other area of imaginative literature which is crucial for any search to participate in the throes of contemporary Islam—the literature of Palestinian resistance. Unique in its own quality and origin, it is also symptomatic of the unresolved trauma of suffering to which Islam, or more properly the Sunnī expression of it, instinctively relates from within assumptions of power and requital, not of tragedy and redemption. Palestinian experience in the birth, consolidation, and enlargement of the state of Israel has undergone more than half a century of deepening frustration, personal tribulation, collective humiliation, exile, and dispersion. It has been paying the corporate price for such restitution as Israel may be thought to have attained for Jewish tragedies at other hands and on other soil. Real and costly as that vicarious situation has been, Palestinians have been able to find no clue to read it in those terms. What politics or nationhood would have done so in their place, with Israeli self-justification so insistent?

But what cannot be forgiven, or forgotten, must be spoken. Hence a deep and eloquent Palestinian literature—largely a Muslim literature—of which the sole representative there is space for here has to be Ghassān Kanafānī and his grim story *Rijāl fi-l-Shams* ["Men in the Sun"].[31] Heavy with multiple symbolism, it tells of three men, Palestinians, and their attempt to cross the desert to seek employment in Kuwait. They have to negotiate border posts, the hostile desert, and the slyness of their "brother" Arabs. They trust their luck with the driver of a water tanker— sexually impotent by reason of war wounds—who volunteers to secrete them in his water tank until they are inside Kuwait. Trivialities and inanities delay the driver at the border post and, when he eventually opens the tank to release them, they are dead. He wonders why they did not bang on the inside of the tank and, after rifling their clothes, dumps them on the garbage heap. Its powerful protest is all the more telling for the fact that its author suffered a violent end when a terrorist bomb exploded under his car in the Beirut sun. There is no need to elaborate the allegory, triple victims of a triple heartlessness of exile, enmity, and desertion, all "in the sun."

IX

All the foregoing is no more than the scantiest suggestion of the human need that the minaret everyday witnesses, and from within which it calls to prayer and to the good. There was much to be said for citing it by literature rather than by statistics. Statistics are the business of officials and governments, where responsibilities, as we have said, essentially belong. Much has changed about the occasions of participation since the earlier version of this chapter was written in the mid-1950s, for the first edition. In some areas, notably in Africa, wide doors are still open for the Christian surgeon and the Christian educator. It is urgent that those doors be imaginatively entered with the sort of life commitment that characterized earlier generations. Where, widely, it is no longer so, intelligent Christian presence, in all the settings afforded by the intermingling of parts in the human whole, has to educate itself into the feel of what it is to fear and hope, to think and pray, to doubt and seek, as Muslims do, and translate that education into wise and careful ministry.

In 2 Timothy 1:7, the writer assures Timothy that God has given to them both "the spirit of . . . a sound mind." He uses a splendid Greek word, *sophrosyne*, which philosophers might understand as "a mind whose thoughts are safe," having in view the Greek virtue of moderation warning against excessive, ill-balanced—and so, dangerous—thoughts, thoughts that might ruin the one who indulged them. Greek wisdom was always prudent. But there is a richer meaning to *sophrosyne*. It is "the possession of saving thoughts." These are not concerned to be safe, but to save. There is no point in the "oil and wine" until we "come where people are."

ix

THE CALL TO RETRIEVAL

I

Among the great faiths of the world Islam is unique in its relationship to Christianity. Though indebted in part to Christian parallels, Islam has proved in history the supreme displacer of the faith of Christ. Displacement of an earlier by a later religion is no unusual phenomenon. The Church of the New Testament called itself "the new Israel" because it believed itself heir to the promises of the old, and found in its experience of Christ the grace and truth that achieved by fulfillment the law that came by Moses. In the theological expression of this relationship to Israel, the New Testament sees the Jew in Christ offered the consummation of his inheritance by that in which a separate Jewishness is superseded. This as the Christian sees it is displacement by fulfillment.

Islam holds a similar conception of its relationship to the Christian faith—though with no sustained effort to show how Islam does better justice to the meaning of Christianity than Christianity does itself. The Qur'ān offers no theology of a Christianity made ultimate in Islam, as the New Testament does of a Judaism fulfilled in Christ and the Church. But the claim is made that

Islam represents what Christianity should have been and failed to be. Islam is the correction of what is erroneous and the more perfect expression of what is legitimate in the religion of the followers of Jesus.

There is a familiar Muslim parable of three caravans that set out across the desert. The first halted and encamped while the other two went on. By and by the second halted and encamped, leaving the third to complete the journey alone. The caravans were, respectively, Judaism, Christianity, and Islam.

Islam, then, as Muslims see it, has arrived, whereas Christianity has fallen short. If, therefore, we wish to know what the religion of the Prophet Jesus was truly meant to be, we go, not to the existing Gospels, which are themselves corrupted by the disloyalty of Christians and the deviations of their impure faith, but to the Qur'ān. It is common in some Christian circles to speak of Islam as a "Christian heresy," but for Muslims the "Christian heresy" is Christianity itself. Islam claims that in its historic faith the Church has misconstrued the mission of Jesus. Inasmuch as these "errors" involve the central points of the Christian understanding of Jesus—his Incarnation and his death upon the Cross—the issue admits of no reconciliation. The Muslim sees Islam as correcting Christian "distortion" of Jesus and of God. Christians see Islam as disqualifying the heart of their understanding of both.

Among the factors contributing to the rise of Islam was the failure of the Christian Church. It was a failure in love, in purity, and in fervor, a failure of the spirit. Truth, as often before and after, was involved to its hurt in the spiritual fault of its trustees. Islam developed in an environment of imperfect Christianity and later by its own inner force gathered such strength as to become, and remain, essentially at odds with the pure faith beyond the imperfection.

This is the inward tragedy, from the Christian angle, of the rise of Islam, the genesis and dissemination of a new belief that claimed to displace what it had never effectively known. The state of being a stranger to the Christ of Christians has been intensified by further failures of love and loyalty on the part of institutional Christianity in the long and often bitter external relations of the two faiths through the centuries.

It is for these reasons that the call of the minaret must always seem to Christians a call to retrieval. They yearn to undo the alienation and to make amends for the past by as full a restitution as they can achieve of the Christ to whom Islam is a stranger. The objective is not, as the Crusaders believed, the repossession of what Christendom has lost, but the restoration to Muslims of the Christ whom they have missed. All that the minaret both says and fails to say is included in this call to retrieval as the listening Christian hears it.

This chapter concerns itself with Islam from this angle of its unawareness of Christ, and with the Christian responsibility for that awareness. Its twin topics are: Muslims as strangers to Christ, and the Christian sources of Muslim estrangement. We take up, as it were, the study of a veil, of a process of obscuring by which the fullness of Christ has been lost.

The two disciples on the road to Emmaus, in St. Luke's story, mistakenly took Jesus for "a stranger in Jerusalem." The Christian who seriously contemplates Islam is led sometimes to a similar, but sadly unmistaken, question: "Are you always a stranger here?" The days before the advent of Muhammad are commonly called by Muslim historians *Ayyām al-Jāhiliyyah*—"The Times of the Ignorance." They were dark and sad because of what was yet unknown. As the Christian sees it, there is a *jāhiliyyah* still within Islam—a *jāhiliyyah* about Jesus.

II

Most Muslims would probably protest at once that they are very familiar with the name and the prophethood of Jesus Christ, and that they are far from unaware even of the Christian account of him, for it is the duty of their faith to repudiate a part of it. They know well the Jesus they acknowledge and enough about the Christian account of him to refuse it. How, then, are they strangers? If we press the matter, we intend no reproach—except upon ourselves. We mean only that the question compels a deeper investigation. We begin with Jesus Christ and his Church in the present assessment of Muslims and move backward in history in order to come finally to the circumstances of Muslim "Christian" knowledge in Muhammad's day.

The study of Muslim society entitled *Social Justice in Islam,* by Sayyid Qutb, referred to above, in chapter 5, ends with a final assessment of Muslim duty in relation to communism and capitalism. In the course of this discussion the writer remarks that Christianity is opposed to materialism, but he adds:

> Christianity, as far as we can see, cannot be reckoned as a real force in opposition to the philosophies of the new materialism: it is an individualist, isolationist, negative faith. It has no power to make life grow under its influence in any permanent or positive way. Christianity has shot its bolt so far as human life is concerned: it has lost its power to keep pace with practical life in this and the succeeding generations, for it came into being only for the limited and temporary period between Judaism and Islam. When it was embraced by Europe owing to specific historical circumstances, and when it proved incompetent to keep pace with life as it developed then, Christianity confined itself to worship and to matters of the individual conscience, ceasing to have any control over the practical affairs of life; for it had not the power to persevere, to develop, or to grow. Christianity is unable except by intrigue to compete with the social and economic systems which are ever developing, because it has no essential philosophy of actual, practical life.[1]

There is no need to suppose that the writer here is malicious, or willfully perverse, nor yet that he is preparing the ground by contrast for the perfect social system of Islam. The ignorance of Christian thought and history displayed in his dismissal of Christianity *is* ignorance, sharpened perhaps by instinctive animosity. The faith that believes God incarnate is truly far from "isolationist," for it believes in a divine involvement of love in all our human needs and hopes. Nor can it be rightly called "negative," for its positive ethical commands are love toward God and one's neighbor. Nor is its worship a private obsession.

Worship in Christianity is that context of Godwardness in which alone both the person and society are fully and securely alive. How shall we describe as "individualist" that which lives in the fellowship of the Holy Spirit and that robbed even the most stubborn divisions of the ancient world of their finality? "In Christ there is neither Jew nor Greek." And not the ancient world only. Has the writer forgotten, ignored, or simply not heard of William Temple and F. D. Maurice, Wilberforce, Shaftesbury, and Livingstone, and other exponents of the social meaning of Christianity in both thought and action? And then there is the writer's sense of history. What are the "specific historical circumstances" by which Christianity came to Europe? Was St. Paul's response to the Macedonian call "isolationist" and St. Augustine's vision of the City of God "individualist"?

Here, however, we are not concerned with refutation; only with the measure of unawareness. We must avoid the easy temptation to vindication. For these misunderstandings will be set right, not so much by argument as by a constructive effort to discover and correct the sources from which they come. Assertiveness such as this is not overcome by its like, but rather by the patiently objective. Here are not simply arguments to be refuted: here is a tragedy to be redeemed. What matters is not that Muslims have thought ill of Christianity but that they have misread the Christ.

Sayyid Qutb, sadly, is representative enough. A score of Muslim depreciations of contemporary and historical Christianity could easily be cited. The Christian Church is incurably compromised with hypocrisy and vested interest. The Christian ethic is vague, impracticable, otherworldly. It has set impossible standards of moral purity—and every form of corruption, prostitution, and vice has flourished behind its idealist façade. Better the sound, moderate, feasible sanity of Islam, with its recognition of the weaknesses and limits of human nature, than the futile idealism and real shame of Christian society. Christian history, likewise, is a sordid record of compromise and bigotry, broadening out into the proliferating sins and scandals of Western civilization. Christianity is jejune, effete, misguided, and discredited. Its origins are erroneous, its story tarnished, its energies spent.

III

The disqualifications of Christianity are carried into theological realms and involve considerable discussion and devalidation of the New Testament. Prominent in this area of Muslim criticism of Christianity is the Ahmadiyyah movement, or rather movements, which developed in Indian Islam in the last quarter of the nineteenth century and were named after their common founder, Mirzā Ghulām Ahmad. In the present context, it may be appropriate to discuss his legacy briefly, though it would be misleading to see in him and his followers a representative expression of Muslim criticism of Christianity. The reason for citing the Ahmadiyyah attitudes is that, though they go further than orthodox Islam approves, they provide a measure we cannot ignore of the extent of Muslim unawareness of Christ.[2]

Mirzā Ghulām Ahmad claimed to be a renewer of Islam and in the opinion of many Muslims laid claim in some ambiguous sense to prophethood—an issue that contributed to the division of his followers, after 1915, into two sections known as the Lahore and the Qadiān (now Rabwah) Ahmadiyyah. The former, interpreting their founder's claims modestly, have tended to come steadily closer to orthodoxy. The latter have held to the idea that their founder was a "prophet" or at least a "renewer" capable of being succeeded by a caliph. They are still governed by hereditary succession from him. Their community was obliged to move from Qadiān to Rabwah when the partition of the subcontinent left the former outside Pakistan. But they still look back with great reverence to their old localities. Both groups have engaged in extensive Muslim missionary work and have mosques and representatives in many parts of the world.

Among the factors behind Mirzā Ghulām Ahmad's activity was a sense of the need of Islam for revival and a belief that it suffered from a certain inferiority consciousness vis-à-vis Christianity. Islam needed to be more militant and assertive, and to rid itself of a sense of positive relatedness to Christianity. To achieve this he was prepared to jettison certain Islamic beliefs that, in his view, compromised the standing of Islam in relation to Christianity, and thus to make some sacrifice of orthodoxy in the interests of a more vigorous anti-Christianity. He was stimulated in part by the presence of Christian missionaries in his locality and in part by the sense of Muslim subservience to British rule in the India of his time. In pursuit of his resolve that Islam must be cleansed of a lingering excess of respect for Jesus, he sought to eliminate those traditional beliefs, which had come into Islam after its expansion, relating to Christ as returning from heaven to the world in order to subdue anti-Christ and bring in a Muslim millennial state of bliss and righteousness. Though embedded in orthodox faith, these beliefs regarding a future role for Christ were traditional and not Quranic. Mirzā Ghulām believed that Islam would be more robust without them.

As for the Qur'ān, what it actually said on the point at issue could be reinterpreted. The Qur'ān quotes Christ (Surah 19.33) as referring to "the day I die"—which Muslims have understood as applying to a postmillennial death, yet to occur, because Christ did not die on the Cross. In the famous passage (Surah 4.157) the Qur'ān says of the Jews: "They did not kill him, they did not crucify him, he was resembled to them," meaning that someone else, made to look like Jesus (supposedly Judas), was crucified in his place, and Jesus ascended into heaven. Instead of the orthodox belief that Jesus was never actually nailed to the Cross ("they did not crucify him"), the Ahmadiyyah interpretation affirms that Jesus was so nailed and later taken down, still living, and laid in the cold tomb. Thus they did not succeed in killing him by crucifixion. He revived in the tomb, escaped, and later journeyed east, to die at a great age in Kashmir, where, near Srinagar, his tomb may still be seen. This is what the Qur'ān means by the phrase: "the day I die."

By means of this interpretation it is possible to retain Quranic authority for a view of the Cross that rejects not only Christian history but also much Muslim tradition. Though the Lahore group has corrected its unorthodoxy on points relating to the status of the founder, it has sustained these interpretations of the role of Christ and shares them with the Qadiānī group, whose publication *Jesus in Heaven on Earth* expounds and argues this view in considerable detail.[3] There can be no doubt that the attitude widens the gulf between Christians and Muslims to the degree that it displaces or modifies the veneration for Jesus in Islam that derives from traditional expectations centered in him. Islam had retained a second-advent Jesus though it lacked a crucified and risen Jesus. The effect of the Ahmadiyyah movements, as far as they succeed—and they are very vocal—is to distance Islam still further from a Christian view of Christ.

It should not be thought that this of itself makes all Ahmadiyyah writers derogatory of Christ as a leader. Some of them, it is true, have carried their anti-Christianity to a point of vilification far removed from characteristic Muslim attitudes, suggesting, for example, that there is something unsavory about the relationship of Mary Magdalene to Jesus, that he was offensive to his mother in the wedding feast at Cana, and that the cry on the Cross, "Why hast thou forsaken me?" was cowardly and pathetic, even ignominious. This derogatory attitude to Jesus is checked, and in many cases excluded, by the Muslim recognition of him as "one of the prophets." Nonetheless, insofar as the Ahmadiyyah movements have changed Muslim attitudes toward Christianity, they have done so in the direction of greater alienation and a more rigid Muslim self-sufficiency. Where, as here, a serious compromise of Muslim orthodoxy has been made, it has not been done to facilitate Christian relationships but to aggravate them.

This brief discussion of the Ahmadiyyah movements is evidence of our immediate argument, that there is a state of not knowing in respect of Christ. "Behold I stand at the door and knock," he says. But some in Ahmadiyyah put more bars to the door, or withdraw further into the shuttered house.

IV

If the Ahmadiyyah movements must be seen as arming a state of unawareness against what might dispel it, there are other forces too. Disinclination to look beyond Islam, complacence and self-sufficiency, animosity politically engendered but religiously operative, misconceptions about the West—all help to complicate and perpetuate the state of strangeness to Christ these pages argue. A few examples should be cited.

One of the great leaders of Muslim India in the decade after the First World War was Muhammad ʿAlī, advocate of all-Indian unity and of Pan-Islam, a thinker to whom the idea of Pakistan, or any "Islamistan," would have been anathema. During his imprisonment under the British, he wrote a "fragment" he intended as a personal introduction to a much larger work on the Qurʾān and Islam that he was never able to complete after his eventual release and reabsorption in political activity. *My Life—A Fragment* is a moving piece of Muslim autobiography from which we have earlier quoted in discussing the place of the Qur'ān in Muslim life. When Muhammad 'Alī takes note of Christianity, in *My Life—A Fragment,* he is sharply, almost disdainfully, hostile. The classic expression of Christian faith in the decisions of the Council of Chalcedon, he argues, makes too great a demand upon our credulity. At the same time the liberalism of modern Christianity has left that old faith almost unrecognizable. Islam is saved all this confusion by its simplicity. The Apostle Paul had no knowledge of, or care for, the teachings of Jesus and evolved of himself a doctrine of Christ which had no historical validity. "The only trace of the Christianity of the disciples of Jesus and the members of his family left after the fourth century was to be found in certain Jewish rites like circumcision practiced in Abyssinia."[4] The New Testament is a broken reed and the Christianity that runs through St. Paul, Athanasius, Aquinas, Luther, Wesley, and Kierkegaard is an imposture.

The unawareness that is evident here as to the historical discussion of Christian origins by scholars within the Christian tradition is not unique among Muslim authors. Their interest in the internal theological debate in Christianity is a natural consequence of the fact that the Muslim view of Christ is there involved. But unhappily few, if any, Muslim thinkers have penetrated into the Greek New Testament or opened themselves to the convictions that, arising from historical scholarship, point strongly to the authenticity of its general witness and the unity of its presentation. They have been too easily content with what has seemed to confirm their prejudgment. We are in great need of trying to stimulate a Muslim study of the New Testament that will face responsibly all it contains.

A pioneer Muslim study of Christ in the Gospels created some expectancy that the time might have arrived. 'Abbās Mahmūd al-'Aqqād in 1952 published his popular *'Abqariyyat-al-Masīh,* of which an abridged version appeared in English under the title "The Genius of Christ."[5] It has had a wide circulation and shows deep reverence for its hero. Much space is given to the messianic concept in history and to the birth and teaching of Christ. Muslim metaphors are used to illustrate the meaning of Christ's words, and stress is laid on the importance of the disciples. But the author draws back from any commitment as to the Cross, ignoring the sense of final suffering running through so many parables and sayings of our Lord, and declaring that beyond the point of Christ's arrest in the garden nothing assuredly historical is known. Thus he bypasses the Cross and Resurrection and attributes the spread of Christianity to the zeal of the disciples and the suitability of their message to the world of that time. Though the work is in popular format, it represents a sincere and reverent attempt to comprehend Christ within a Muslim frame of reference. It is an interpretation of the Gospels without the climax that brought the teaching to its consummation and generated the Gospel that made the Church. It is a tribute that nevertheless insists: "Come down from the Cross." It is, therefore, for all the welcome interest it shows, a measure of the distance that many Muslims, even with good will, still maintain from the Christ of Christianity.

Another noted Egyptian writer, Muhammad Husain Haykal, onetime president of the Egyptian Senate, prefaces his long and painstaking *Hayāt Muhammad* ["Life of Muhammad"] (1935) with certain remarks on the Christian faith. Christianity he characterizes as unfitted to be the religion of the West, by virtue of its ascetic renunciation. Christian antipathy to Islam is entirely due to doctrinal errors: to the substitution of trinity for unity; to the idea of redemption as incompatible (as it is thought to be) with belief in a Day of Judgment; and to the assertion of Christ's being divine.

There is little point in multiplying witnesses if the fact is clear. A popular Indian Muslim's biography of Muhammad, Khālid L. Gauba's *Prophet of the Desert,* underlines it sharply. After remarking that Muhammad was practical and successful, the author observes:

Poor Jesus Christ expressed the noblest sentiments on charity and forgiveness; thus upon the Cross, persecuted and crucified, he forgave his enemies—"They know not what they do." But it was never in Christ's good fortune to have his enemies reduced to impotence before him.[6]

Reflection on this verdict will surely provide the measure of the extent to which Muslims are unaware of Christ. The writer here is clearly discounting him on the wrong counts. The supreme glory of Christ has become something that renders him pathetic. It is not simply that Christ goes unrecognized in the hidden majesty of redemptive love, but that the criteria of majesty are devalued and "good fortune" given precedence over "great grace."

These are the attitudes that await the patient ministry of Christian interpretation. For all their incompleteness and their intermittent bitterness, they are evidence that Jesus is not unknown. Yet neither is he known: the secret of his significance remains undiscovered. The part, in fact, obscures the whole; the partial truth, blind to the full truth, becomes at the same time untruth. It withholds more than it gives and forestalls its own completion. This situation between Islam and the Christ of Christianity is what demands retrieval.

V

If we have tried to sense that situation by reference to a few recent writers who represent the general mind, we can also let it kindle our imagination by historical reverie. A geographical journey can impress it on our minds as well as can an excursus into books. So much of the area of Muslim predominance in the world was once Christian. The minaret stands often in the very precincts of a departed Christianity and in some cases mosques are transformed cathedrals.

When Damascus capitulated to the forces of the second Caliph, 'Umar, in A.D. 635, the great Cathedral Church of St. John the Baptist was divided into two parts, and half the churches of the city were taken over for mosques. For some seventy years the Cathedral housed the two religions until Walīd I (in whose reign the Muslim armies crossed the Straits of Gibraltar) decreed its complete absorption into Muslim use. When the Christians appealed, his successor, 'Umar II, was advised by his Islamic lawyers that the former Christian half, taken into Muslim prayer, could not be alienated to Christian use again. There was a symbolic truth in that uneasy and impermanent partition, as well as in the ultimate Muslim possession of the whole. For a partition there truly was—a barrier between the rite that read the Gospel, commemorated the Cross, and epitomized the fellowship of the risen Christ, and the rite that prayed facing Mecca and understood God according to the Prophet Muhammad.

Ousted in two stages from the Cathedral in Damascus, Eastern Christianity everywhere gave ground to Islam—not territory alone, but numbers, vigor, vitality, and tradition. It persisted, isolated and introspective, in a constantly growing Islam that had all the prestige of success and victory. This is not the place to tell in detail the story of the submergence of the Christian Church in wide areas of Asia and Africa, including its own birth lands and the cities of its early splendid story—Jerusalem, Antioch, Alexandria, Carthage.[7]

If the old and oversimple thesis that Islam was spread by the sword needs modification, so does the popular counterstory that the faith from Arabia was a tolerant option freely chosen. It is true that Islam was capable of considerable toleration and that it was prepared, on conditions, to allow Jews and Christians to remain what they were. It is also true that when active persecution did occur it was the work of particular Caliphs and of local fanatical officials, not representative of the best in Islam. The idea of a sword at the throat of every Christian, imposing islamization, is a crude and overdrawn picture. There were the martyrs and there were the dispossessed; fear and discrimination played on the motive of vulgar passions. But there was also the possibility to continue as a Christian if one was ready to pay fines, wear distinctive dress, surrender some of one's churches and never build new ones, and suffer indignities and curtailment of opportunity—unless one had a craft or a skill of which society or government had need. If Christianity did not persist in more robust quality, the fault was not wholly with Islam.

At the same time it is important to keep clearly in mind the imperial form of Muslim expansion and the essential contrast in the fashion of the world outreach of original Islam and original Christianity. The latter did not attain imperial status for three centuries, during which it was, in the main, a persecuted minority, recognizing and paying its civil duty to the Roman empire and defying it only where it found that empire incompatible with its first allegiance, as in emperor worship. Christianity was a faith to which, after three centuries of almost overwhelming odds, an empire turned.

The history of Islam, by contrast, contains no Constantine. Muhammad was from the outset its Constantine as well as its Prophet. From the time when Islam established itself as a city-state in Medina, it was a form of rule as well as of worship. It came upon the Eastern world not simply as a creed but as an allegiance, a state, and a sovereignty. Its tokens were not baptism and the bread and wine; its tokens were prayer and the caliph. It would, therefore, be both unhistorical and un-Islamic to suppose that when multitudes of Christians, in ancient Christian bishoprics, turned to Islam, they did so merely out of intellectual persuasion and never out of prudential realism, or that what they accepted was a creed only and not also a conquest.

But our immediate concern is the nature of the retrieval that this history imposes on Christianity today. Let it be clear that the retrieval is not territorial. Christianity is not a territorial expression. The retrieval is spiritual. It aims not to have the map more Christian but Christ more widely known. We are not concerned with the comparative strength of Islam and "Christendom" but the absolute loss of Christ. The retrieval to which we are called does not mean reconverting mosques into cathedrals, but giving back the Christ. The external tokens of his displacement are important only because of the displacement they symbolize. To restore Christ transcends all else.

If, then, we make a brief mental visit to the areas of such displacement, it is to feel the force of this aspect of our duty to Islam. Take the Sudan. How many Christians in America or Britain would spontaneously think of it as a Christian country, or of a Sudanese Christianity other than that planted by recent missions in the pagan south? But Christianity had its first contacts with black peoples in the earliest days and there was a Nubian Christianity with its capital at Maqurra from the sixth to the fourteenth century. It may have been an isolated and at times impure Christianity, and the reasons for the Muslim penetration and displacement, seven centuries after Muslim success in Egypt, may not have been entirely external. But, for all its imperfection, that Sudanese Christianity had deeply affected the life of a vast region of Africa. Its disappearance left Ethiopia the last remaining representative of a Christian Africa. J. Spencer Trimingham, who surveys this history in his *Islam in the Sudan* has this footnote to his narrative:

> Remains of red brick Churches of the Alwa [Christian] Kingdom exist at Soba, Rudis, Elti, Kutranj, Kasemba, Bronko, Hassa, Haisa, Kamlin, Arbaji, and Sennar, on the Blue Nile and at Qataina on the White Nile.[8]

Ezekiel might have added: "Can these bones live?"

Remains, no doubt more familiar and no less eloquent, lie across North Africa. Tertullian, Cyprian, and Augustine made North Africa a classic Christian world. One of the justly loved writers on the Christian relationship to Islam, Constance E. Padwick, reflected in a "North African Reverie," on the living appeal of its shattered past:

> Standing . . . amid the forest of broken pillars that represent the Christian basilicas of Roman Carthage, one tastes the victory of Islam as though it took place only yesterday. . . . Those broken columns, all that is left on earth of a Church of many bishoprics, speak to Christendom with a voice shattering to complacency. . . . Here it was said to the Church as it was said to the Virgin Mother of old: "Yea, a sword shall pierce through thine own soul also that the thoughts of many hearts may be revealed."[9]

Today the few and scattered representatives of the Christianity that once found passionate expression on that southern Mediterranean shore are engaged in reparation. Their task is to utter anew the faith and love that once lived within these ruins and so to break the silence of the centuries. It is to wake the echoes of an ancient history and make them vocal in the accents of today, to build again the worshiping community beside the old basilicas. Here, exemplified in Barbary, is the call to Christian retrieval that comes in the very silence of the Christian past around the minaret.

Where the Christian past has unbroken continuity and the faith lives side by side with Islam, as in most of the Arab world (outside Arabia), in Ethiopia, and in Turkey, there is still a partnership of

Christian reparation with the ancient Churches. Centuries of Muslim predominance have not left a continuing Christianity untouched. The price of continuity has been a certain introspection and a habit of aloofness. The relationship of the Western Christian to Eastern Christianity will call for consideration below, and mention of the question here is made only lest it be supposed that tasks of reparation are confined to those areas where a former Christianity has altogether ceased to be.

VI

We merely *illustrate* what is meant by retrieval when we take stock of Muslim writing about the Christian faith and ponder its displacement in many historical territories. These are only symptoms and parables of the Muslim unawareness of Christ. To *know* it in itself we go to the Qur'ān and the place of Jesus in Muslim revelation. Here is the longer of the two largely parallel passages relating to Jesus' birth as found in Surah 19.16–34:

> Remember Mary in the Book, how having withdrawn from her people to a place eastward and secluded herself from them, We sent unto her our Spirit and he appeared unto her as a perfect human being. And she said: "I seek refuge with the Merciful from thee. If thou art one who fears God [leave me.]" He said: "Indeed I am a messenger of your Lord unto thee to bestow upon thee a pure child." She said: "How shall I have a son when no man has touched me and I have not been a harlot?" And he said: "So has thy Lord said: 'It is an easy thing for Me and in order that We may make him a sign unto men, a mercy from Us.' It has been so determined."
>
> Thus she conceived him and withdrew with him to a remote spot. And her travail-pains drove her to the foot of a palm-tree, crying: "Would that I had died 'ere now and become oblivious in oblivion." Then he [the child?] called to her from beneath her: "Do not grieve: thy Lord has provided beside thee a flowing stream. Shake the trunk of the palm-tree towards thee for the ripe fruit to fall. So eat and drink and be gladdened. If you see any human person tell

him: 'I have vowed a fast unto the Merciful: I will speak to none this day.' ''

And she brought him to her folk, carrying him [in her arms] and they said: ''O Mary, this is a shocking thing you present us with! O sister of Aaron, thy father was not an evil-doer, nor was thy mother a harlot.'' She motioned towards him. But they said: ''How can we address one who is a child in the cradle?'' And he said: ''I am the servant of God. He has brought me the Book and made me a prophet. He has blessed me wherever I be and has enjoined on me prayer and almsgiving as long as I live; and [made me] honorable towards her who bare me. He has not made me a miserable lordling. Peace be on me the day of my birth, the day of my death, and the day of my resurrection alive.''

This was 'Īsā, son of Mary—the true saying concerning which they are dubious.

The passage goes on to deny that the one so born is in any sense the Son of God—an unfitting notion. The parallel passage in Surah 3.35–60 gives further details about the birth of Mary herself and of John, son of Zachariah. Repeating that Jesus is, like Adam, only man, it puts into his mouth the words: ''I have come unto you with a sign from your Lord. I create for you out of clay the likeness of a bird, I breathe into it and by God's permission it is a bird. I heal the blind and the leper and I raise the dead by God's permission and I proclaim unto you what you may eat and what you may store up in your houses.''

This bare and somewhat enigmatic statement is almost all the Qur'ān knows of the ministry of Jesus in the Gospels and of his parables. Surah 5.112 refers interrogatively to Jesus and a table of food from heaven, perhaps dimly echoing the feeding of the five thousand or the Last Supper, or simply transposing the like question once addressed to Moses. It should be noted that the Qur'ān throughout refers to Jesus by the name 'Īsā, corresponding to the Esau of the Old Testament. Though there are many theories relating to this name, its use remains a mystery.

Christ is, then, a prophet, a teacher, a healer of the sick, a spirit from or of God. To him is given the Gospel—not the good news about God in Christ, but a book of words or preaching, which the

Qur'ān does not anywhere reproduce, except in very occasional references, such as those to the camel and the eye of the needle and alms given in secret. The only element out of the background of Jesus' ministry, apart from his healing, is the fact of opposition, in face of which he relied upon his disciples, for whom the Qur'ān has a high regard. But it presents no picture of Jesus' education of those disciples, nor does it allow that the opposition to Jesus issued in his crucifixion. Indeed, this is specifically denied in vehement terms along with the whole idea of the Incarnation. Thus the ascension of Christ is an arbitrary kind of exit from the human scene.

There are certain passages in the Qur'ān that might be regarded as conciliatory toward Christians. Surah 5.82 says: "Thou wilt find the nearest {of humankind}, in affection, to those who believe, those who say: Lo! We are Christians. That is because there are among them priests and monks, and because they are not proud." But there are other verses bitterly denunciatory of Christians and of priests. Surah 9.30–31 reads: "God Himself fights against them. How perverse they are! They have taken, as lords beside God, their rabbis and their monks and the Messiah, son of Mary, when they were bidden to worship only one God." It is hard to resist the impression that Muhammad's attitude changed when he discovered that his claims failed to receive the hospitable welcome he had first expected from the people of the earlier book.

The foregoing is a summary of all that the Qur'ān contributes to a knowledge of Jesus Christ. Allowing for repetitions of warnings against his divinity and the duplication of the birth narrative, it could be written in three or four pages. Though there is much fuller material in Muslim traditions—much of it derived from Christian sources during the expansion of Islam—it is concerned mainly with eschatology and adds nothing that is expressly excluded by the Qur'ān itself. The chief note in the traditions about Christ is that he was a homeless wanderer, *Imām al-Sā'ihīn,* the preacher who had nowhere to lay his head, but the final nature and the ultimate quality of this homelessness are all unknown.

If one sought a single justification for the Christian mission to Islam one might well be content to find it in the Quranic picture of Jesus of Nazareth. It is not simply what the picture fails to tell, vast as that is, but also what it disallows. Worse than the silences are the vetoes. A partial portrait can be filled out. But what if it has negated in advance its own completion? For love of Christ, retrieval must be made.

Consider the Quranic Jesus alongside the New Testament. How sadly attenuated is this Christian prophet as Islam knows him! Where are the stirring words, the deep insights, the gracious deeds, the compelling qualities of him who was called the Master? The mystery of his self-consciousness as the Messiah is unsuspected; the tender, searching intimacy of his relationship to the disciples undiscovered. Where is "the way, the truth, and the life" in this abridgment? Where are the words from the Cross in a Jesus for whom Judas suffered? Where the triumph of the Resurrection from an empty grave? There is in the Qur'ān neither Galilee nor Gethsemane; neither Nazareth nor Olivet. Even Bethlehem is unknown by name and the story of its greatest night is remote and strange. Is the Sermon on the Mount never to be heard in the Muslim world? Must the story of the Good Samaritan never be told there? Must the simple, human narrative of the prodigal son never mirror there the essence of waywardness and forgiveness? Is "Come unto me all you who are weary . . . and I will give you rest" an invitation that need not be heard, and is Jesus' taking bread and giving thanks a negligible tale? Should not all humankind be initiated into the meaning of the question: "Will you also go away?"

In sum, must not the emasculated Jesus of the Qur'ān be rescued from misconception and disclosed in all his relevance, in words, deeds, and sorrows, to the plight and aspiration of all humanity? To do this is what is meant here by retrieval. Our concern about assaying it will surely measure our own estimate of who and what he is—the Christ who questioned his disciples on one crucial occasion: "Who do men say that I am?" The answer matters, to Christ and to all the world. We have no right either to suppress the question or to neglect the response. Rather, inseparable from our Christianity, is the duty so to bring others to Him who asks, that they may answer for themselves.

VII

Unhappily the Islamic ignorance of Jesus goes back to Christian failure, so that retrieval is also restitution. Could Christ otherwise have been so obscured and lost to sight and knowledge?

Does not the New Testament inseparably link the fullness of Christ with the Church which is his body, in the sense that the one instrumentally depends upon the other? "The light of the knowledge of the glory of God in the face of Jesus Christ . . . this treasure in earthen vessels." So run St. Paul's metaphors. The loss of Christ necessarily argues a delinquent Christianity. Arabian and Eastern history confirm the fact.

In the analysis of that tragedy we must begin with the Christianity in which Islam first developed, "the dimness," as C. E. Padwick has it, "from which Islam drew at its beginning so blurred, so veiled, an outline of the Son of Mary—mysteriously born and lord of many a miracle, but not of love's paramount miracles of the divine Incarnation, the Cross and the Resurrection."[10]

The Qur'ān took up and laid the sanction—and sanctity—of divine revelation upon misunderstandings for which the Church must bear its measure of responsibility. Misconceptions as to the Trinity and Jesus make clear that Muhammad was hardly in a position to know at first hand the authentic Christianity of the New Testament. The Christians, with the Jews, as "Peoples of the Book," may well have been, as we have seen, the historical source of the germinal idea that blossomed into the conception of "an Arabic Qur'ān." But the full witness of the Christian book seems never to have been available to him. Certainly the Bible did not then exist in the Arabic language, and the Greek, Syriac, and other versions could have been open to him only indirectly, through personal contacts.

However we may decide the question of Muhammad's illiteracy, noted in an earlier chapter, it seems clear from the contents of the Qur'ān that Muhammad's knowledge of Christianity was wholly oral in origin. It also appears that either the range or the quality of those contacts was insufficient to constitute an authentic encounter with Christ. It is true that we must also take account of the originality of Muhammad himself, the yearning for an Arabic answer from heaven, for an "indigenous" revelation, for a direct, divine message to the situation in Mecca. All these are factors that might have been in effect, even if Muhammad had enjoyed the fullest opportunity to know the purest Christianity.

The facts, or at least some of them, seem patently to reproach

Christianity itself for Muhammad's belief that God in the Qur'ān was superseding it. Could his antagonism have been wholly Arabian self-assertion? Could it have sprung only from Muhammad's will to be a prophet? For at the outset that will was not consciously formed. Could it have been only Muhammad's growing communal confidence that made him independent of all parallel sources of ideas such as Jews and Christians? For he had at least begun, or so it seemed, by being in debt to them. If the displacement of Christianity was not due only to these motives, must there not have been other factors for which Arabian Christianity was directly to blame? Islam was generated as a new faith because of the conviction that a new one there must be. But why?

Christianity on the borders of Arabia was torn by ecclesiastical disputes that poisoned theological controversies. It was embittered by partisanship and compromise. The Ghassānids and the Hīrā Christians on the Syrian and Iraqi frontiers of Arabia were responsible for some Christian penetration, but they occupied buffer areas in uncertain relation with Byzantium and Persia. The southern Arabian Christianity of Najrān and Yemen is known to have suffered much persecution and did not succeed in making any lasting foothold in the Hijāz itself.[11] The pre-Islamic Arab poets refer to Christian hermits, Christian wine, and Christian bells. Does the conventional paganism of poetry alone explain why Arab Christianity produced no religious literature of its own? The ancient poetry of Arabia offers no conclusive evidence that Christian ideas had made any abiding impression upon the Arab mind and heart.

Ideas of a divine judgment, of a revealed book, of resurrection, and of the divine will were present in the Jewish-Christian background. They came to fervency only in the intense conviction of Muhammad, a conviction so intense that it received them as a new divine action of inspiration, displacing their old guardians and diverging widely into a new entity. Perhaps in the formative years of Muhammad's quest a more virile, a less dubious, Christianity could have satisfied his sense of need and obviated the great "other" that Islam became. We cannot tell. We should beware of reproaching Arabian Christianity in a situation in which so much is obscure. But the new religion did emerge and as it hardened into self-sufficiency Christians had no longer any means of demonstrating that Muhammad had misunderstood their teachings. It became part of the very dogma, not to say the vested interest, of Islam that Christianity was now replaced.

VIII

The rise of Islam will always remain a painful puzzle for the Christian mind. Mystery must always surround the genesis of so great a phenomenon. But Islam is the only great post-Christian religion and as such was not generated in isolation, either geographical or mental, from the Christian world. That world, therefore, can never exonerate itself from responsibility. To define that responsibility in detail is impossible. How to face the fact of it is now the question. For whatever we may learn from the failures of other generations to be the Church, we have to strive to be it worthily in our own. We have also to recognize that more Christians than those contemporary with Muhammad have compromised their Christianity and perpetuated Muslim antipathy. Only two major areas of exemplification can be considered here.

The first belongs to the twelfth and thirteenth Christian centuries, the era of the Crusades. Though it is almost seven centuries since the Latin Kingdom of Jerusalem collapsed (A.D. 1291), Islam is still conscious of the crusading temper of that Latin Christianity as a bitter tradition. This lingering sense of wrongdoing in the Arab East is a reproach for which in the Christian Church we should be thankful, inasmuch as it is a recognition that the Crusades were a piece of Christian history unworthy of the name and treasonable to the cause of Christ. It is of course easy to adopt a superior attitude of criticism vis-à-vis the Crusaders, who from 1096 to 1291 strove to recover and retain the fields of Palestine for "Christian" powers. A complacent and comfortable critic may forget the sacrifice, endurance, and valor of numberless volunteers, whose bones were left to rot on Anatolian roadways and whose spirits languished in frustrated sieges. The Crusades were served with a devotion that, had it been as wise and true as it was fervent and undaunted, would have blessed the Eastern world.

But devotion was ill-served, misused, misguided, and betrayed. The Crusades were generated in contradiction and pursued in ambition. The relations between Western and Eastern Christendom and between individual leaders within the Latin forces were, for the most part, lamentable. Sacrifice was demanded and sacrifice was squandered. Duplicity, self-seeking, stupidity, and plain human frailty besmirched the name of the Church. In numbers the Crusaders were at a disadvantage; their main military asset was the dividedness of their enemy. Once the great Salāh al-Dīn (Saladin) had consolidated an energetic and resourceful resistance, the Latin Kingdom was doomed, and its fall proved in the end an irretrievable disaster.

That final frustration, however, only confirmed the Christian confusion of mind in which the Crusades were conceived and pursued. The really important matter was not the possibility of pilgrimage but the obligation of witness. Christ's concern was, and is, for men not monuments, for souls not sanctuaries. What had been lost, and remained lost, to Christendom, was nothing to what had been lost, and remained lost, to Muslims. The gain of Jerusalem had no merit to supplant the giving of Christ. But these insights few saw. The Crusades were a mistaken gesture of a disloyal Christendom:

> *Deus vult*—of that they were sure. What then does he will? The deliverance of "those holy fields"—yes, and hence enmity to "the Paynims." The literature of the period gives us glimpses of what were the jokes of a crusading army in a camp where a Baldwin or a St. Louis prayed—tasty tales about serving Paynims with pork or even with bits of roasted Paynim—probably no better and no worse than the talk of other armies, but far from any saving thought on behalf of Muslim souls.[12]

There were contemporaries with great saving thoughts, notably Raymond Lull, who, in his oft-quoted words, saw ". . . many knights going to the Holy Land, thinking they can acquire it by force of arms." But they were rare. The multitudes failed to recognize that "he who loves not, lives not" and that the only way to serve Christ and the world is by "the pouring out of tears and blood." If Lull's vision measures by contrast the tragic misguidedness of the Crusades, they in turn measure the dimensions of Christian reparation. The Crusades did not merely postpone an authentically Christian answer to Islam. They intensified both its urgency and its difficulty. History has not yet outlived the legacy of their reproach.

IX

Indeed, history has in part repeated that legacy. The Crusades may seem very far away. Much nearer our own time there have been other forms of "Christian" disservice to the faith. The Western world no longer advances on the Eastern in the name of religious repossession of forfeited sanctuaries. But for almost two centuries the science, industry, and commerce of the West have steadily permeated the world of Asia. Nations belonging to the continent of Europe—Britain, France, Belgium, Holland, Portugal—established themselves as the governing powers over wide areas of Asia and Africa, taking advantage of the protracted head start that circumstance and ambition had given them in the pursuit of empire and trade.

What matters here is not the details of that story but how it seems in retrospect to numerous Muslim peoples who have now broken free into their own nationalism. The retrospect is naturally conditioned by their struggle and their aspiration. They tend inevitably to identify Christianity with the lands where it was traditional and whence material and political domination came. That identification in the absolute sense is, of course, false. Its falsity, as we shall note elsewhere, is one of our large tasks of interpretation. But the responsibility of Christianity in "Christendom" we cannot seek to escape. The faith of the Christian Church, as Muslims have read it in the behavior and the attitudes of Western powers, Western commerce, and Western culture has been deeply and sadly obscured, sometimes entirely dimmed. Insofar as the faith acting—as it only can—through Christians failed either to correct those relationships where it could, or repudiate them where it could not, it is involved in a compromise that demands retrieval. It may be argued that no generation of the Church can bear more than its own immediate burdens. But this does not release us here and now: in the solidarity of Christian fellowship, those past delinquencies have entered, and do enter, into our own burdens.

The past as the past cannot be undone in the present. But part of our present duty is the correction of the past. We have to carry the burden of what the Church has been, of what it has failed to be, and the burden of what the Muslim supposes Christianity to represent. Examples of the need of reparation in detail would mean writing again the history of East-West relationships, as well as trying to disentangle what resulted from Christian disloyalty and what from Western rejection of Christianity. That would be impossible. Muslims, anyhow, are not likely to make the distinction. They know, perhaps, that government inquiries into vice in Teheran have traced it in part to the influence of American films; that low Western journalism has inspired a flood of similar publications in Cairo and Beirut; that flaunted Western wealth has broken down many old conceptions of commercial integrity among Muslim merchants; that the "invisible exports" of the Western world—secularity, indulgence, cheap love, commercialized sex—are all too visible in their impact upon the Eastern mind.

Trade relationships on the part of the West have been too often conceived in terms of markets, not of persons; of sales, not of society. Diplomatic relationships are liable to be preoccupied with bases for our defense or the global contributions of others to our security. In too many ways Westerners tend to be condescending or patronizing, so that even their good will is suspect and their genuine sympathies misunderstood. Emotional susceptibilities on the other side have no doubt some responsibility. But no Christian, who considers seriously the combination of contempt and fascination with which the Muslim East regards the West, can doubt that if Christ remains in so urgent and so deep a sense a stranger, the fault is plainly ours.

We may perhaps adapt the words of Jesus' question to Philip the disciple: "Have I been so long a time with you and yet have *they* not known me?" In the New Testament understanding of the Church, the Christ of all the world comes to belong to humanity through witness only in proportion as his Church belongs to him in loyalty. "Let not those who seek you be confounded through me'' cried the psalmist. The fear that they may be—the fact that they are—must be ever with us. Perhaps another question may be borrowed. ''Do you understand?'' Philip the deacon asked the man of Ethiopia. Today he might have answered: ''How can I, if some man misguides me?''

All that should be said about retrieval as an aspect of the Christian duty to the peoples of the minaret leads directly into the very heart of the matter. The surest way to repair what we have been is to tell who Christ is. Estrangement will best pass in the presence of the Stranger. Retrieval leads into interpretation.

X

THE CALL TO INTERPRETATION

I

"Rescue a word . . . discover a universe" suggested an eminent Cambridge New Testament scholar to his hearers, in preaching before the University. "Can we bury ourselves in a lexicon," he continued, "and arise in the presence of God?"[1] Dictionaries are, indeed, places of unexpected wonder for all who have felt the fascination of words, not least the Greek lexicon that serves New Testament study. All words, in fact, have histories, and some of them extraordinary adventures. Who would normally connect the attic of his house, a place of discarded things, with the Attic architectural glory of ancient Greece, or "bunk" with a constituency in North Carolina, whose representative felt he had to speak for it even if what he said was nonsense? How many remember that "oxen" and "beef," "pigs" and "pork," are words which go back to the Norman Conquest of England, when the Saxons became the herdsmen and swineherds who kept the beasts, and the French Normans ate the meat? So the animals have Anglo-Saxon names and their meat French names.

History is hidden in language. Meanings may subtly change

until they almost reverse their originals—like "comfort" and "security" and "simpleton." For words are meaning being exchanged. They are the counters of intellectual intercourse. A given language agrees upon a particular sequence of letters written, or sounds uttered, to convey a certain sense. When the print says "man" or the speaker cries "fire!" a particular impression is conjured up in the mind of readers or listeners. They have at once a mental image that the word has inspired within them at the behest of the mind intending that result. Words are the highways of the traffic of ideas, sentiments, emotions, and relationships, and the work of the world is done by them.

The trouble with a foreign language is that the symbols are not part of a familiar system. They are to the listener a sequence of meaningless sounds, to the reader a jumble of indeterminate shapes. The art of translation is to take over what was carried in one agreed frame and to convey it in another. No meaning is received save in terms of what is already known. The word is the point of exchange.

These considerations, obvious enough in themselves, illuminate that most comprehensive of New Testament descriptions of Christ as "the Word." The English Bible has wisely used the capital letter. As the Christian faith understands and receives him, Christ is "the Word of God." He in himself constitutes what God wants to say. God, that is, engages in speech, and is not content that there should be a barrier of silence and, therefore, of unknowing between God and humanity. Whereas the ultimate speech of God for Islam is prophecy, "sealed," as the phrase goes, or accomplished, in Muhammad, the speech of God for the Christian is personality—a human life in all the revealing human situations, the Person of Jesus Christ in the flesh, whose antecedents, character, history, and meaning for us are sufficiently recorded in the Bible. The Bible thus becomes a secondary "word"—the written word preserving and expressing the incarnate. There is the Life that reveals; there is the history that describes. The latter is the means to the continuing accessibility of the former.

Thus the Bible is very differently conceived from the Qur'ān, where the revelation is essentially the "scripture" written. But the immediate point is that God is understood to have spoken. As both Muslim and Christian agree, it takes God to reveal God. God must say what God has to say, though the task may be deputed to servants, to prophets, to seers. But what they say must be intelligible to the human world; otherwise no meaning is conveyed and the speech, if it is spoken, is nevertheless not heard.

Christianity rests on the conviction that the surest method of revelation is personal; that the unmistakable terms of divine disclosure for us are human life. So in the mercy of God the life was lived, the deeds were done. We need make no mistake about God after we have known Christ. "He that hath seen Me hath seen the Father" was his claim.

Using, then, the image of human life, God's self-revelation was uttered in terms already within our ken, in a manger and village carpentry, in synagogue and field, in Gethsemane and Emmaus: God the Interpreter and the Interpreted. The very substance of human life has become the vehicle of the divine. Listening to this language we discover God. We learn what God intended for humanity. "The Word was made flesh" (John 1:14).

But like all other speech this divine Word can be silenced by inattention, by indifference, by being out of range or mind. So it is that what God says may go unheard and unknown. This is variously true of us all. We have seen in the previous chapters something of the particular form of Muslim "unawareness." The Word divinely spoken stands in need of a witnessing expression. We have to "rescue the word and discover the universe" of God's revealing love, in Christ. We are called to be interpreters of God's self-interpretation. A phrase in St. Matthew's Gospel may serve us here: "Thou shalt call his name Emmanuel, which, being interpreted, is God with us" (Matt. 1:23). "Being interpreted" is a mighty condition. It stands between everything and nothing. It is the hinge upon upon which "Emmanuel" turns. For "God with us" is not simply a statement. It is a conviction. More than an announcement, it is an experience. Unless it is heeded, pondered, and believed, it might as well have never been. Meanings not conveyed are meanings frustrated.

The amazing reality behind and within the Christian mission in the world is this task of interpretation. Our duty is to carry over the Word that God has uttered, to be the translators of God's speech into the language, the idiom, and the minds of ordinary mortals. Our words are to be the servants of the Word, our lives of his life, our persons of his Person. Others are to take from us their knowledge of him from whom God would have them take their knowledge of God. There is the sequence, "Thou in Me and I in them," with the purpose "that the world may know that Thou hast sent Me" (John 17:23).

The Christian interpreter of the Word which is Christ must learn to face all obstacles and subdue them to the master purpose. What is worthy of all acceptation must be capable of all acceptation. The interpreter refuses to believe that the language of God in Christ is beyond anyone's understanding, given patience, lowliness, resourcefulness—and the Holy Spirit. Every wise translator will be indefatigable in seeking clues in all areas of life, and patient with all contrariety, knowing that wherever there is opposition there is also relevance. Indifference, on the one hand, or conscious "difference" on the other, obliges us to find a way in.

Islam is particularly calculated to test the mettle of Christian interpreters: it forces them to a radical and patient expression of their faith. By the very vigor and cruciality of its objections, Islam compels the Christian to delineate Christ more deeply. The grounds of misunderstanding must be made the theme of more patient exposition. Every difficulty must be made an opportunity.

This interpretation involves a person-to-person relationship. The situations discussed in chapter 8, "The Call to Participation," may provide the framework and the occasion. But the progress or the contagion of the kingdom of heaven is "soul by soul." We cannot institutionalize the world into God's kingdom. Nor can we fulfill our ministry except by an intimate relationship with ordinary people. For they are the crux of the Gospel. As Christians we are committed to the infinite significance of the person.

The metaphor that describes our task is that of a shepherd and sheep, pastors and people. We are called to a tender solicitude for the minds and wills of others. The Word that is Christ has to come into their vocabulary. So we must study what they mean in all the moods, the overtones and undertones, of their existence. It is our life task to make bridges into their minds. This means being near enough to be heard; getting near is a large part of our problem. But our first confidence must lie in the worth of the story, if only we serve it as it deserves. "Hearing comes," said the Apostle, "by the word of God" (Rom. 10:17). Only when something is apprehended is it being communicated.

What, so understood, are the main contents of Christian interpretation to the peoples of Islam? Five important areas immediately come to mind in a sequence that is "automatic." They are (1) the Christian Scriptures; (2) the Person of Jesus; (3) the Cross; (4) the Christian doctrine of God; (5) the Christian Church and a Christian society.

A. Interpreting the Christian Scriptures

II

There are two excellent reasons why interpretation should begin here. The first is that Muslims have an instinctive sense of "holy books"—the highest and greatest of which is the Qur'ān. They expect religion to have this "scriptural" quality. The second is that ultimately all presentation of Christ and of God must hinge upon the Biblical and, particularly, the New Testament expression. A large part of our task is to bring the Muslim to a patient and hospitable perusal of the Gospels and the Epistles.

But these two sound reasons also locate for us the supreme difficulties. The nature and role of the Christian Scriptures in Christianity are so strangely contrasted with the Islamic role of the Qur'ān. The strangeness is not merely that of vocabulary, important as the distinctions are between Christian and Islamic religious Arabic. There is a much more inclusive unfamiliarity persisting beyond all problems of language and textual translation.

Muslims who address themselves to the Bible find a variety of books of independent authorship, stretching over more than a millennium. Within the New Testament they find four different Gospels, and a sequence of various Epistles. All are in evident contrast with the holy Book of Islam, which came via one human instrument, through some twenty-three years of Meccan and Medinan history. It is difficult to comprehend why there should be four Gospels, when the Gospel, or *Injīl,* entrusted by God to Jesus the Prophet was a single book, though now no longer extant. The assumption is immediate that because there are four, none of them is valid. Indeed there is a widely current Muslim explanation: The early Church lost the original Gospel given by Jesus and several leaders set themselves to making good the deficiency, with the result that they all differed and they were all wrong.

Involved in the question is the larger one about what the Gospel in fact is. On the Muslim view of revelation all prophets are bearers of words from God, understood to be entrusted to them in complete form, not as a result of a divine enabling of their mental and spiritual powers, but as a verbal transmission from heaven. Thus the teaching of Jesus, properly understood, is a body of words, now lost, but happily safeguarded in the culminating revelation of the Qur'ān. This view does not envisage a gospel in, as well as through, Jesus—good news of a divine initiative for human salvation in his presence in the human world and his history there. It is, of course, upon this latter concept of the Gospel, the Gospel of God in Christ, that the character and the very possibility of the Gospels according to the four evangelists rests.

On the Christian view, it is not only comprehensible, it is desirable, that the significance of that life and death should be recorded as it impressed itself upon minds within the Church. The Gospels bring a cumulative witness to a central figure without conspiring to eliminate secondary divergencies. They arose in the heart of the church to perpetuate its saving memory of Christ when time was thinning the contemporary generation and the wider world beyond the Palestinian was entering the fellowship. Thus their existence is in no sense a gesture of recovery that failed, but an act of affirmation that was achieving its universal purpose. They exist not to replace the irretrievably lost words of Jesus, but to report his significance—words and deeds—as a glorious possession.

To take across into the Muslim mind this truth about the Gospels is a primary duty. It has another aspect. The Qur'ān for Muslims is the word of God to Muhammad immediately reproduced for human hearing. It is not what others reported Muhammad to have said as a prophet. Such reports constitute Tradition and are, as we have seen, of lesser status, though indicative of the divine will. But the Qur'ān does not go through the mental under-standing of reporters, any more than—as understood by ortho-dox Islam—it goes through the conscious processes of the Prophet's mind. It is more assuredly God's if the human element is in entire abeyance.

Not so the New Testament. Though the Gospels undoubtedly contain verbatim accounts of what Jesus said, there are many places, not least in St. John, where the evangelist merges imper-ceptibly into his material. There is condensation and editing; there is choice, reproduction, and witness. The Gospels have come through the minds of their authors and, in deep measure, through the mind of the Church behind the authors. They repre-sent experience and history. They are history told out of the expe-rience to which it gave rise. This may be seen as eminently suitable, distinctly appropriate. For "the Word" is a captured significance, a realized meaning. To have Christ as the Church found him is to have Christ more validly than he could be had in some hypothetical and unattainable abstraction. For all history is experienced fact and cannot escape the interpretative element. Such interpretation might be suspect if it were uncongenial, un-sympathetic, as an abstract record that had not participated. But the New Testament has escaped this danger and enjoyed its con-trary by the very involvement of the writers in the impact and meaning of what they report. We have, then, to help the Muslim conceive of a divine revelation that is primarily personal, not oracular; that proceeds by enabling, not overriding, the minds of its writers; and that gathers into its written "word" the compre-hension of the hearing of the Word incarnate.

III

In this context, also, we must present the Epistles. On the hypothesis of the Qur'ān they must be deeply mystifying, even inexplicable. How can personal correspondence be divine revel-ation? If St. Paul chooses to address himself to Galatia, how can that constitute a piece of a preserved volume in heaven? The objection is worth facing because the content of the answer is so rich.

The Epistles in the New Testament are the clearest evidence that Biblical revelation cooperates with human experience in order to complete and fulfill itself. The revelation is not simply of a law to be followed, or a set of facts to be believed, or even a history to be accepted. It is the offer of a relationship. It *brings*, it is true, a law to obey and involves facts and history, but it *is* essentially a relationship to be received and experienced. Its doctrine of God means fellowship with God; its doctrine of human nature means repentance, forgiveness, and regeneration. All that it proclaims and asserts, it offers and imparts. It is proclamation unto experience. Thus what it means cannot be expressed out of connection with its reception. In the Epistles, therefore, we find St. Paul and others explaining the converts to themselves, showing them in detail the nature of their faith, its impact upon their character and their behavior, its meaning as a break with the past and as a promise of the future.

The evangel *recorded* in the Gospels is *experienced* in the Epistles. It is out of that experience, analyzed and elucidated in the Epistles, that the Gospel records were written. Herein is the essential unity of the New Testament. Christians, as the earthly product of the faith, the human consequence of the divine grace, are in this sense part of the revelation. To explain them, to discipline them, to describe their making and their behaving, is the work of the Epistles. In them the nature of what God says is being apprehended, not by divine dictation to a scribe, but by apostolic education of the early Church, under the Holy Spirit, into the meaning of its own life and the shape of its proper fellowship. The divine communication is completed in the representative description of its actual consequences in human destiny, both personal and social, as those consequences were to be seen in Corinth, Rome, Ephesus, or Philippi.

Another reason why an apostle's correspondence can take its appropriate place in the volume of revelation involves a further point, applicable to the Bible as a whole and not least to the Old Testament. This is the "occasional" nature of Biblical revelation. It is rooted in history and in particular events. It arises out of representative situations. St. Paul may be dealing with questions peculiar to Corinth (idolatrous meats in the market place), or to Galatia (the temptations from the Judaizers). But the principles on which he bases his discussion are abiding. The instance illustrates their application, and may well recur, in recognizable, if not identical, form elsewhere. If not, the principle remains. Those churches of the Epistles, with their problems and vagaries, are to be regarded as symbolic. The apostolic attitude to the "occasion" has a relevance beyond it. For the occasion is inclusive of much more than itself. The Epistle to the Romans belongs to more than the Romans. Even the letter to Philemon, so intimately personal, has an ageless relevance beyond the issue of Onesimus, the slave who ran away.

Here is the pattern. Without the instance, the universal might be mere abstraction. Apart from the abiding truth involved, the instance would be ephemeral and negligible. In the concrete universal, in the significant particular, comes the down-to-earth revelation. It is not only precept but demonstration. It not only enjoins but saves. The Biblical revelation borrows endless "occasions" of human existence that in them it may representatively reveal the pattern of the kingdom of heaven. How appropriate this is to the faith that believes the Word to be made flesh, how remote and mystifying to Muslims until interpretation facilitates their understanding.

"Occasions," too, explain much of the Old Testament. H. G. Wells in his *Short History of the World* impatiently complained that the Bible spent too long rehearsing the story of a very insignificant people with a very undistinguished succession of kings. What he failed to see was that the Biblical interest in Israel was, among other things, illustrative of the doctrine of humanity. Events are recorded from Abraham, through the Exodus, in the exile and beyond, not because they exhaust what is significant in the human story, but because they are representative of human waywardness and because their particular sequence has its place in the preparation for redemption in Christ.

Inasmuch as Biblical revelation turns on events, and events in history are potentially innumerable, it proceeds by inclusive selection. The relation of God to all history is made clear in a particular history. A special history prepares and introduces that which illuminates and redeems all history. So the Bible covers not the two decades of a single prophet's ministry, but the eighteen or so centuries between Abraham and St. John, between Ur of the Chaldees and the Isle of Patmos. Its revelation lies in the varied, always selective, always representative, reaction of humanity in rebellion and in obedience to the divine will and word.

Thus the greatest prophecies are incomprehensible apart from historical occasions. Amos is not to be understood apart from the iniquities of Omri and the rise of Assyria. "Can two walk together unless they be agreed?" (Amos 3:3). It was events that made clear to Amos in Tekoa how the historical causes producing a punitive Assyria were controlled by the righteousness that required the retribution of Samaria. The domestic tragedy of Hosea illuminates the divine relationship with a harlot nation. Jeremiah, Isaiah, and Ezekiel are prophets who must be measured and understood against the background of history. They are the interpreters of particular events so that all history may be understood.

Likewise the Psalms, as poems of lament, complaint, fear, or dismay, will hardly seem to a Muslim what God could have supposedly revealed. But in their accumulative witness to the meaning of God in human life they communicate the "felt" significance of the truth that God willed humans to understand. As they wrestle with their situation in the context of what they know of God that knowledge is enlarged and deepened by God and brought to light and life for all who read. The revealing process, so to speak, enlists and allows the mental and spiritual capacities of particular persons through whom it addresses the minds and spirits of all persons. And when the Psalmists are lifted into exaltation and doxology, their witness is to the apprehended meaning of the truth made known. Theology passes into doxology, which is its most communicable form. If the Qur'ān contains no Psalms and little history and is the fruit of only one prophetic experience, that fact is the measure of the difference in the Biblical and Quranic concepts of revelation, and so in turn of the extent of our interpretive task.

Much more might be said in this context. It must suffice to add one further point about the nature of Biblical revelation—its honest realism in describing human weakness. Whether it be the story of Abraham or David or the portrait of the disciples, they are there, as Cromwell might have said, "warts and all." No attempt is made to hide their shortcomings or minimize their frailty. In this they are a measure of the humanity that God would redeem. Inasmuch as we perceive them to have been "men of like passions with ourselves,'' we may have hope and faith for ourselves. Though most Muslims are well aware of human frailty because of the doctrine of the compassionateness of God and so are prepared for human weaknesses, they do not readily associate these with patriarchs and prophets. The Qur'ān, moreover, emphasizes very strongly the difference between Islam and non-Islam in terms of belief. The *muslimūn,* or believers, are "the gainers;" the *kāfirūn,* or disbelievers, are "the losers." Though there are strong moral distinctions in the Qur'ān, they normally follow distinctions of creed. Thus there is less tendency to recognize any inward wrongness within the community of the faith. This is natural in a revelation concentrating on law. Whereas law condemns all that is outside it and approves what is within it, redemption proceeds upon a sinfulness from which all suffer and from which all may be redeemed. This aspect of the Biblical understanding of humanity under God may be one of the most important and difficult notes in a Biblical ministry to Muslims.

IV

It is evident that all these are points arising from the contrasted concepts of revelation upon which the Qur'ān and the Bible proceed. The interpreter of the one to the readers of the other must, however, take note of certain duties resulting from the Muslim attitude to the Bible. The Qur'ān contains material belonging to the same history as the Old Testament. It speaks of the creation and the fall, of the patriarchs and the law. It includes the two lengthy descriptions of Christ's nativity already noted. This fact of Quranic involvement in Biblical history and the claim of Islam to be the culminating revelation, gathering into itself all the pre-Islamic prophets from Adam to Jesus, have naturally given rise to a state of acute tension between the heirs of the two Scriptures through the centuries. The main and positive Christian task just described is complicated by much interscriptural controversy. Though this must be kept in due perspective and never be allowed to monopolize the business of interpretation in this field, the points at issue cannot be ignored.

Where there is variety or discrepancy in either Old or New Testament history between the Bible and the Qur'ān, the Muslim explains it under some form or other of the doctrine of corruption. The differences in patriarchal story, for example, are not to be explained in terms of Muhammad's sources of knowledge or his didactic purposes. They are explained in terms of a distortion in the present (i.e., the canonical) versions of the original. This is emphasized, according to orthodox Islam, by the disparity between the Quranic picture of Jesus and that in the New Testament. Muslims reason that Jews and Christians, who in Arabia so manifestly failed to recognize and accept the mission of Muhammad, were not fit custodians of their own Scriptures. Quite evidently they tampered with them in various directions, suppressing what would have made them confirmatory of Islam and obscuring the true nature of their identity with the Qur'ān. The Muslim does not pause to consider that no *consciously* anti-Islamic corruption in fact occurred: the Canon was made final three centuries or more before Muhammad's mission. And unconscious anti-Islamic perversion is hardly an intelligent hypothesis.

But on the Muslim view, the point is that the Biblical Scriptures do not square with the Qur'ān; that their true original form did so square; and that, therefore, corruption has occurred. It does not matter that the alleged original form is irrecoverable. The Qur'ān embodies it sufficiently. The Muslim position thus begins with a hypothesis that is beyond proof or disproof, a hypothesis that ends where it begins. The Qur'ān is the infallible book. All other true Scriptures agree with it. The Biblical Scriptures, as they are, do not agree. Therefore they are corrupted. But their corruption is offset by the Quranic embodiment of what they ought to contain.

Only a little imagination is necessary to appreciate how difficult it is to penetrate this closed circle of thought. To insist as we must that the Canon of Scriptures has not undergone any change since the fourth century and that it then recognized documents long established is sound history. But it makes little impression on dogmatic prejudice. If the two holy Books are not the same, so much the worse for the Biblical. As scholars and historians, our task is to draw at least some in Islam into more objective and scientific attitudes toward the problem of interscriptural relations. There are signs of some hope in this direction, but the path is not easy: the whole issue of what Quranic revelation is, and is not, will be found to be involved.

V

Imagination need go only a little further to realize the bearing of Christian textual and other criticism upon this situation. Educated Muslims are not unaware of the prolonged discussion in Christianity about the Bible. If very few have ever penetrated firsthand into that discussion or taken pains to acquire the necessary Hebrew and Greek disciplines that it requires, many have heard of Renan, Strauss, Bauer, and Kirsopp Lake. Not a few Muslim apologists welcome the suggestion that perhaps historical Christianity ought rather to be called "Paulinism." They are familiar with the hypothesis that a simple Galilean teacher was unwarrantably transformed into the Christ of the creed—a hypothesis that, if established, would coincide in large measure with the Muslim picture of Jesus.

This involvement of the Quranic Jesus in the discussions that have so long occupied Christian and secular scholars in the New Testament field has naturally sharpened Muslim interest in their studies. But unfortunately it cannot be said that the interest has yet produced a full or sustained study of Christ in which all the accumulated evidence on the subject is sifted and assessed. Rather the Muslim attitude in general has been to take the mere fact of this New Testament criticism as demonstrative proof that the Christian scriptures are unreliable. Not understanding the demand for utter scientific liberty behind such studies, most Muslims conversant with them assume that quite evidently even Christians are all at sea about their Scriptures. Muslims accept without more ado the indication that the New Testament lacks the undisputed validity of the Qur'ān.

Furthermore, they find the numerous versions of the Christian Scriptures bewildering and suspect in their multiplicity a confirmation of their doubts. It must be remembered that Muslims began only in the second quarter of the twentieth century to take kindly to Quranic translation in non-Islamic languages, because numbers of non-Muslim translators had been at work. Consequently the Muslim mind does not readily appreciate variant ren-

derings of Scripture, or the idea that the essential revelation might
require the suggestiveness of different versions before it is fully
understood. We hope that with growing realization of how language is related to thought, these grounds of suspicion about the
Bible will diminish and disappear. But meanwhile they persist as a
source of unthinking surmise that the Christian Scriptures are
somehow not what they claim to be.

There are certain other sources of misunderstanding when we
try to express the Christian possession of the Scriptures to
Muslims. One has arisen in the course of Christian missionary
insistence on the Bible in the past. It concerns the fulfillment of
prophecy. Early Christian apologists from Al-Kindi and John of
Damascus used the argument that whereas Christ was propheti-
cally foretold, Muhammad was not. The argument was popular
down to the nineteenth century, and, to Christians using it, it
seemed valid and undeniable.

The Muslim counterargument, however, was not far to seek. It
relied in part upon corruption and affirmed that prophecies about
Muhammad were lacking only because they had been suppressed.
But some of them escaped suppression. The Old and New Testa-
ments do contain foretellings of Muhammad. The corruption of
these Scriptures is not total. They have their valid parts and
Muslims are ready to adduce them on the basis of the essential
oneness of all scriptures. The Qur'ān itself exhorts Muslims to
consult those volumes antecedent to the Qur'ān. In doing so, they
believe themselves able, and also commanded, to identify those
passages in the existent Bible that can bear positive Muslim exegesis. They will gladly demonstrate to Christians where their own
Bible foretells, describes, and commends Muhammad.

So it comes about that there is considerable Muslim exegesis
of the Old and New Testament in a Muslim sense. It is as if the
writers say: "Far from being unprophesied, Muhammad is amply
foretold in your own scriptures." The exegesis involved may often seem dubious and remote, but given the Muslim presuppositions and a certain inventiveness, it can be given some semblance
of plausibility. These Muslim interpretations of the Bible make a
further demand upon Christian patience and ministry. Hindi and
Parsee Scriptures have also been used in the same sense.[2]

The most painful and inclusive example of the problem is the familiar word translated "the Comforter" in St. John's Gospel: παρακλητος. It has the same consonantal sequence as the Greek word περικλωτος, meaning "one worthy of praise." There is not the slightest textual reason for reading περικλυτος instead of παρακλητος in the New Testament. But the root from which the name "Muhammad" is derived in Arabic, together with its other forms—"Ahmad" and "Mahmūd"—means "a praised one" and corresponds roughly with περικλυτος. It has, therefore, been suggested, and it is widely held in Muslim circles, that the promise of the Paraclete refers to Muhammad, the Prophet to come. The change of the vowels by which "Paraclete" came to be read is then an example of Christian perversion.

This charge and the Muslim alteration have no textual basis. Nor does the sense of the passage bear the Muslim rendering. It is well to remember that the interpretation arises, in the end, not from exegesis but from presupposition. However painful the necessity, the Christian must cheerfully shoulder the task of distinguishing clearly between Muhammad and the Holy Spirit, and of appreciating how it comes about that the Muslim can be so confidently confused on this point.

There remains one further point to be kept in view when trying to relate the Christian Scriptures to the Muslim mind. Some differences between Islam and the Biblical faith may be explained by the former as due to abrogation. This is the doctrine that later revelation supersedes earlier revelation—a view held to obtain even within the Qur'ān itself.[3] Some Biblical statement may be entirely free of corruption, and yet be no longer valid. The full implications of this doctrine are too wide to discuss here. It explains the Muslim confidence that the Bible has nothing to add to the Qur'ān and that the latter is sufficient without the former. One need not defer too seriously to a faith that one's own has surpassed.

The Bible is from this point of view a treasure unexplored because it is thought of as possessed. It is a prisoner whose case cannot be pleaded, because it is thought to have been already decided. In this situation, the Christian must rely on the inherent worth of the Scriptures and press for a new attention to their contents. It may be that even faith in abrogation can be persuaded to show critically the sense in which the abrogated is perfected in the abrogator, and to study the former if only for this purpose. In any event, the Scriptures are capable of proving themselves an unpredictable treasure—a prisoner who, like Paul, can make a hearing even in bondage. But in this case it can hardly be appreciated, without the intelligent and discerning service of those who appreciate how great "a prince imprisoned lies."

B. INTERPRETING THE PERSON OF JESUS

VI

"He does not beget and is not begotten," says the Qur'ān (Surah 112:3) in formal rejection of the doctrine of Christ as the Son of God. To allow such doctrine is to "associate" a man with God, to deify the human and so lift it to the status of the worshipful, which belongs only to God. It is to commit the supreme sin against the basic assertion of the Muslim *Shahādah*, or "Creed," that there is no god except God. Though the Qur'ān allows the virgin birth of Jesus, it is implacable in its opposition to the belief that the one so born is divine.

Here, then, is another area of Christian interpretation with no escape from its demand. A simple reassertion of the Christian doctrine of Christ will not suffice. Nor do we circumvent the difficulty by transferring the emphasis to doctrines of God. For these, as we shall see, are inevitably involved already. Indeed the doctrine of Incarnation is already a doctrine of God and is rejected by the Muslim on that ground. Islam does not so much resist the faith of Christ as "God manifest in the flesh," because it is unsuited to Christ, but rather because it is unworthy of God.

We do not, therefore, dispense with the problem of explaining Christ to Muslims by taking what some might call a "theocentric" approach. Rather, the more effectively we are "theocentric" the more we find the problem with us. It was not for nought that Jesus said: "You believe in God, believe also in me" (John 14:1).

Nor again can we escape the problem by shifting our emphasis to the human Jesus. To concentrate only on elements in Jesus that Muslims can at once accept is to fail Jesus himself. We cannot leave him in Galilee as if he were no more than a prophet, when he himself refused to stay there, but went on to Jerusalem to be crucified by those who would not have molested a mere prophet. We cannot interpret him apart from the terms of his own understanding of himself. These include those claims that gave rise to the faith of the Church in his divinity.

Moreover, to be content only with the prophet-teacher would not be to do justice to the Muslim's need. The Christ Jesus of the historic faith is an inescapable figure. It is he we must present to the world of Islam, in the fullness of his relationship to the sins and bewilderments of humanity and in the fullness of his relevance for our understanding of God. Yet how we are to do this remains a problem and a burden. We must learn to communicate at all costs what it is to us to recognize in Christ the incarnate Savior, and we must do so in terms that Muslims can understand.

Our first step, no doubt, will be to convey to them the character and personality of Jesus as seen in the Gospels. Our surest way, supposing we have overcome the scriptural difficulties just outlined, will be to acquaint Muslims with the New Testament narrative. Difficulties of expression await us in all of them. St. Mark, for example, begins with the phrase "Jesus, the Son of God." The Muslim anathema springs at the very first verse. This is unavoidable: the evangelists wrote from the standpoint of a matured faith. It is possible, and in some contexts wise, to use selected passages that allow Muslims to make contact with Jesus without immediately provoking their resistance. But we do well to indicate that such passages are selective and introductory. They may well defer, they can never supplant, our fuller task.

Our final confidence must lie in the fact that the disciples and evangelists themselves came to their full faith as to the identity of Jesus from their experience of him before and apart from those convictions. Our aim will be to lead Muslims by the same path: to let them begin where the disciples began. The final explanation of the personality can hardly antedate its discovery. No Muslim is more a monotheist than were Peter, James, and John in Nazareth. We shall not err if we suppose that the order of Muslim experience will be the same as theirs. "What manner of man is this?" is a question Jesus is capable of compelling upon every generation, however predisposed it may be against the ultimate answer. Let us wait patiently. The confession: "You are the Christ, Son of the living God" is not the outset of faith. We have no New Testament right to require orthodoxy before we have presented Jesus.

The measure of what the presentation involves has already been indicated in the discussion of the Quranic Christ. Enlarging greatly that account by all those aspects of Jesus that remain unknown to Islam, we may lead into the Christian faith as to who he is. We must remember that the revelation of divinity is also the revelation of humanity. Christ is, to us, the measure of that fullness of human life which is the divine intention and is actualized when the human is perfectly related to the divine. It must be made clear that the Christian doctrine about Jesus is not an imposition upon the facts, but rather a conclusion from the facts. It must be our desire and prayer that Muslims so become acquainted with the real Christ that they come to understand why Christianity has explained him in terms of the historic creeds. The whole faith as to Christ must not be left to seem a mere dogmatism or a piece of doctrinal subtlety, but rather a reasonable and legitimate ground of explanation.

It is the Holy Spirit, through the Scriptures and the Christian commendation of Christ, who leads the mind into the conviction about Jesus that compelled itself upon his first disciples. Our purpose is to put all in the way of those facts and on the path of that experience by which believers first learned to speak in awed tones of the Son of God. The faith about Christ must never be dissociated from him whom it explains and from whom it derives. What we are concerned first to communicate is not a doctrine but the experience that shaped it.

But when we have done all in our power to acquaint Muslims with the real Jesus and his words and works, his meaning and ministry, we still have to explain the faith about him from the godward side. If we are compelled in the earthly presence of Jesus to acknowledge a divine quality, the meaning of this human manifestation of God still has to be related to what we believe about God. Or, in New Testament language, what is meant by referring to God as "the Father of our Lord Jesus Christ" (Eph. 1:3).

The answer must be stated as far as possible in terms that the Muslim already understands: the double belief about God—that

God reveals and that God is sovereign. We do not, at the outset, introduce the concept of divine love or the attendant mysteries of the divine will. We can be well content with the two basic Muslim affirmations about God—that God reveals and that God is sovereign.

It cannot be overemphasized that the Christian understanding of Christ is the Christian understanding of revelation: "God who at sundry times and in divers manners spoke in time past unto the fathers by the prophets has in these last days spoken unto us in his Son" (Heb. 1:1). "By the prophets," "in the Son"; these are the preparatory and the culminating phases of the same enterprise of revelation. Against a background of interpreted history and into a concrete situation came a human life, a personality, bringing into final focus and into unmistakable form the revelation of God. It was a revelation that was verbal in that he taught and preached, actual in that he lived and suffered, personal in that *he* was involved, and not only what he said. This aspect we can perhaps describe as "situational." Bethlehem, Galilee, the Well of Sychar, the Temple at Jerusalem, Bethany, and Golgotha brought in to demonstration the character of the person.

This, according to Jesus himself and the faith he generated, was the divine strategy. It may well be that Muslims will not accept this account of the matter. But it is our first duty that they should know what it is they reject. They look upon our faith about Christ as an imposition upon the human teacher that offends against his place in the economy of revelation. But in fact it *is* his place in the economy of revelation. It would be blasphemy to turn a human teacher into God; but to recognize that fact is not to deny that God in Christ might come to teach. The sad fact about Islam is that it has refused the Christian faith about Christ on the wrong premise—on the basis, that is, of something which that faith does not assert. We have not made a teacher into God; we have believed that God undertook in Christ the education of humankind as to God.

It must be made plain that the faith about Christ is set in the same confidence in divine revelation which Islam holds, but represents a different concept of how revelation is achieved. Here, perhaps, it may be added that it takes God to reveal God. This profound truth finds some echo in Muslim thought itself in the saying that "God reveals himself by, or in, himself." If God is personal, knowledge of God must be a personal revelation. God can never be only propositional. One does not know a friend as one knows Euclid's fortieth proposition, for a friend is more than a fact. "Who God is" lies deeper than the fact "that God is." And the "Who" cannot be fully known except by divine self-communication. Words, teaching, ideas, propositions must become the Word—experience, fellowship—before revelation is complete. It is this ultimate of revelation which Christianity finds in Jesus. God in revelation is God in Christ. Revelation is not simply recorded in a book; it is embodied in a person. Is it not more fully, more appropriately, more effectively, revelation for that reason? The question may not be readily appreciated by the Muslim accustomed to the idea of a Book as the point of revelatory impact. But it must be made clear that what Christians believe about Christ belongs to the same realm of belief in a God who does not leave humanity in darkness. The difference lies in a contrast in belief as to how God most fittingly dispels it.

When we speak of "God the Son" we mean God in the act of revelation. When we speak of Beethoven the musician, or Leonardo da Vinci the artist, we mean them in their full personality in a particular capacity, which does not preclude their having others, but yet involving them wholly. It is necessary in the Muslim context, though not in the Christian, to insist that the expression "Son of God" excludes all paternity in the physical sense. On Christian premises the latter is unthinkable. The phrase means that Christ is God in divine self-revelation, an activity that begets or generates a historical personality, wherein what God is in revelatory love, God is also known to be in revelatory action. The Father begets the Son in the sense that God's "will" to reveal is translated into act. But all is of God and from God and by God. God is at once revealer and revealed—the Father and the Son. By this faith in Christ we recognize simply that when God reveals God, what he gives us is himself. Our faith in the divinity of Christ is not, as the Muslim has believed, an affront to God, an offense against the divine unity, the supreme doctrinal sin for Muslims. On the contrary, it is the genesis and the ground of our faith that the one living and eternal God has been self-revealed.

VII

We turn now to the second fundamental conviction of Muslim theology—namely, that God is sovereign. This too constitutes an objection to the Muslim mind that can and must be turned into an explanation of the Christian doctrine. Suppose, as we have argued, God engages in self-revelation. Is it likely to take form in human life? Would not this be unworthy of the divine glory? So runs the opposition in Muslim thought, with its constant sense of a great gulf between the divine and the human. It is true that the gulf is bridged: otherwise, there would be neither revelation nor religion. But God bridges it by intermediaries—by archangels and angels, by prophets and teachers who are the means of sending down law and guidance for humankind. In this understanding, God sends rather than comes; gives rather than brings. To conceive of God in Christ is for the Muslim mind an unworthy thought. God does not become man. It would imply something unthinkable of the divinity. Muslims have resisted the Christian interpretation of Christ on these grounds in the belief that they are safeguarding the divine majesty.

Faced with this contradiction the Christian is compelled to look more closely at the sovereignty that is protected in this way. Are we right in forbidding anything to God which he does not forbid himself? If God is truly greater than all will there be things God will not do that we can identify and "forbid"? May we perhaps be in the position of prescribing limitations to God, or of defending the divine sovereignty in ways God does not approve? May we be limiting God's sovereignty in the very act of, supposedly, defending it? These are the questions that arise. Is an enterprise of revelation, in its most appropriate form for humankind, an act unworthy of God? Must God not be left to determine the steps of the divine purpose and shall we say no? If so, then we can never say that the Incarnation could not be. If it cannot be denied as a possibility, then any claims of occurrence cannot be ruled out in advance. They must be investigated as a matter of historical evidence. Such investigation brings us back to Christ in human history.

The burden of all these questions, put into the affirmative, is that what the Muslim desires to assert—namely, divine sovereignty—is in fact most gloriously in effect in Jesus Christ, the Word made flesh. For is that sovereignty truly sovereign if it fails to take action against the empire of ignorance and evil in humankind? Thought on the Incarnation here merges imperceptibly as it must into the Cross, because it was for redemption that God visited humankind. When we present Christ we ask Muslims to believe not less but more in the undefeated sovereignty of God. To believe that God stooped to our need and weakness is not to make God less, but more, the God of all power and glory. With all patience, born of faith in this very sovereignty, we must invite all to seek and find in Christ the demonstration that God is God alone, and that all contrary powers are gloriously vanquished and subdued.

The term *islām* means the submission of the believer to the law and will of God. It is a relationship in which God must be all in all. God being "all in all" is the New Testament summary of the whole meaning of Christ. In either case the sovereignty and the submission belong together. Recognizing in Christ the divine initiative of love manifesting its supremacy over all that otherwise would enslave us, Christians make their submission. It is a submission of worship and of confession. It is their *islām* and Bethlehem is where it begins.

Our concentration here on the two Muslim themes of God as revealing and ruling does not mean that there are not other clues in Islam to the interpretation of God in Christ. These two are central and must be related to whatever else we have been given in trust. Though God's relationship to humanity in Islam is basically that of law, a deep sense of the divine mercy and favor is also there. It has been intensely developed in Sufism. The Qur'ān itself speaks of Muslims as being those upon whom God has been gracious, "not those with whom Thou art angry" (Surah 1.7). God is the merciful, who both cherishes and bestows mercy—a mercy that many Muslims down the ages have sought with strong entreaty and penitent petition. We must learn to relate what we find in Christ to all those aspirations, to the Muslim yearning for what lies beyond law, to forgiveness, renewal, and true piety. It may be said, in general, about the divine mercy, as Islam conceives it, that it remains unpredictable. It is bestowed freely and in relation to the practices of Muslim religion. But it does not come forth to embody itself in a redemptive enterprise, or to articulate itself in inclusive events where it may be known indubitably.

The Islamic belief that God is merciful admits of no doctrine of assurance, or of sonship, so that Muslims could say, "We know that we have passed from death unto life" (1 John 3:14). "It may be"—"it may well be"—is the language they must use rather than "it is." We have, therefore, to present Christ as the focal point of the divine compassion, the place where the divine mercy fulfills itself in history, through one who is both its pledge and its means, one in whom we know God as forgiving and ourselves as forgiven. The assurance this active mercy allows us is not presumption. For it is God who, in Christ, leaves us no room for doubt. But, considered as the token of an ever dependable mercy, the Incarnation is inseparable from the Cross, whither we must now turn.

C. INTERPRETING THE CROSS

VIII

"They did not kill him, they did not crucify him, it was made to appear so to them" (Surah 4.158). So runs the Qur'ān in its familiar disavowal of the crucifixion. Once again Christian interpreters have to begin from an explicit rebuttal of what they have to proclaim, and once again they must somehow turn resistance into understanding. But how?

In what follows it must be insisted that we have neither space nor intention for any comprehensive exposition of the Christian faith regarding Christ crucified—"the power of God unto salvation." Rather the aim is to investigate how best to bear witness to it in face of the Muslim rejection. It is implicit throughout that we must affirm the fact of the Cross always in the same spirit in which Jesus himself suffered it. We cannot champion the Cross by attitudes which, had Christ taken them, would have meant there would be no Cross to proclaim. If we say, "In this sign conquer," it must be only the victory of meekness.

It is well to begin with the actual circumstances in the life and ministry of Jesus from which the crucifixion developed. The

Qur'ān does not dispute that the Jews desired to crucify Jesus. The fact that they resisted him strongly and resented his words is another inst⁓nce in the Muslim mind of that hostility on the part of gainsayers to which all the prophets from Noah to Muhammad were exposed. The Qur'ān stresses that the messengers of God are always rebutted by unbelievers, whom God in the end outwits and defeats.

It is important to keep in view this fact of opposition to Jesus on the part of his contemporaries, even though the Qur'ān does not explain the underlying sources of it, in its profound silence about the content of our Lord's teaching. For this hostility shaped the situation from which Jesus was rescued, it is said, at the last from would-be murderers who crucified someone— possibly Judas Iscariot—whom they were made to mistake for Christ. Another suffered the full brunt of a hostility that was intended for him.

But why this belief in a divinely arranged escape? Why this strange rescue of the Christ? Here, it must be said, motives are not historical but dogmatic. It is not that the Muslim is confronted with strong evidence that Jesus in fact circumvented death in this way and that someone other than he was substituted at the arrest and beyond. On the contrary, there is no such evidence—despite the efforts of several in the Ahmadiyyah movement to find it in Kashmir. Rather the origin of the assertion about the history lies in the presupposition that hostility to the prophets should not succeed in slaying them. Such a climax would be a divine failure to sustain them and corroborate their message. Such a failure would be unthinkable. Noah, Abraham, Moses, David—all saw the confusion of their opponents and the vindication of themselves. Muhammad, though rejected by the idolatrous Meccans, lived to capture Mecca and destroy the idols. So also Jesus. God will not, cannot, allow faithful servants to suffer ignominy, or allow their detractors a final triumph. So Jesus did not suffer. It was more appropriate to the nature of things, divine and prophetic, that Judas should have taken his place—a proper end for him, a manifest outwitting of the Jews and a fitting climax for Jesus. How far indeed from the sense of the Gospels and "the cup that my Father has given me."

Truly, here is a gulf to be bridged by the interpreter—but one whose sources are in prejudgment, not in history. A recent Muslim writer on Jesus in the Gospels remarks when he comes to the Garden of Gethsemane, "Here the role of history ends and the role of creedal faith begins."[4] He means that what happens after the arrest, history does not tell: faith, perhaps credulity, takes over the story. But history is plain enough. If Muslims do not follow it, it is because their prejudgment has intervened arbitrarily to break its course and to disallow what it wills to reject.

There was opposition, as we have seen. If its culmination in Christ's being crucified is a subsequent invention (as it can be only if it is not fact), did the Church invent the faith that made it, creating the history that in fact created it? Was the historic Church, of which Islam must and does take account, constituted only in the teaching of Christ? Were the disciples only preachers of an ethic and not also bearers of a life out of death? Why then the Holy Communion commemorating, from the beginning, sufferings that never happened? And why did the new Sunday, for "the third day" of the Resurrection, become the first day of the week? Is historic Christianity, in short, explicable on the hypothesis of a substitute crucifixion?

But the whole matter goes deeper still. Apart from accounting for the Church and its genesis in faith in the Resurrection after the Cross, there is the deeper question that takes us beyond history into the thought of God, from which the Muslim rewriting of the Cross derives. What are we to say of the nature of a God who behaves in this way or of the character of a Christ who permits someone—even if a Judas—to suffer the consequences of an antagonism his own teaching has aroused against himself? Is this kind of victory the worthiest in prophets of God? The antagonism is there, on the Muslim hypothesis. The question is: What does God do, what does Jesus do, with it?

The answer unmistakably is that Jesus suffers it. The Muslim reinterpretation offends deeply against all that the Gospels disclose about the self-giving of Jesus, his awareness of the inevitability of suffering, and his surrender to its necessity. "The Son of Man," he said, "must suffer." From beginning to end, he resisted the temptation—in the wilderness, on the road, in the garden, even on the Cross itself—to avoid the climax, to abandon Jerusalem, "to come down from the Cross."

The Quranic account has turned those temptations into history—or rather has abolished them, in a surrender to the easy way, with divine intervention or collusion. It has thus made havoc of the manifest continuity between what Jesus taught and what Jesus suffered. Though far from its intention, it has discredited the message in thus discrediting the messenger. In conforming Christ to its own conception of the successful prophet, Islam has robbed him of himself, transformed him into an unrecognizable Jesus. It affirms that someone else was made to resemble him. Rather—more tragically—he no longer resembles himself. The Jesus of the Gospels is undiscernible in the shadowy figure who is made to quit the path of his own teaching and his own *islām*, or "surrender," to the redeeming purpose of God. Truly here at the Muslim Cross we must say, as was said of old: "They know not what they do"—as true of philosophical rescuers as of Roman soldiers.

But what also of the character of God? The God of the Muslim Cross—of a substituted sufferer and an abstracted prophet—is a *deus-ex-machina* God; a God who turns the tables, opens the trapdoor, and confounds all foes; a God who deals not in the sure, if slow, processes of a moral order where love wins by suffering, but in the arbitrary assertion of the inscrutable. Yet it must be remembered that the Muslim rewriting of the crucifixion story is thought to be in the interests of God's glory. God, it is held, cannot be honored in the victory of a prophet's foes. He cannot be thought not to rescue his servant from the hands of his enemies. So the question moves into the realm of what is most appropriately divine, what is most truly consonant with the divine glory. Indeed, we may say, what makes God God and glory glory? How is God characterized as God? So deep do the issues go that are raised by the Muslim attitude to the Cross. It may be that the most we can do at the outset is to clarify what is here involved and simply let the issues stand. For beyond this point, argument is inappropriate. We are left with simple witness and the conviction we cannot enforce but only explain that "God was in Christ reconciling the world unto himself."

IX

Beyond controversy, then, what does explaining involve? How does the Cross save? What is the meaning of the Resurrection? How was "God in Christ"? All witness to the faith of Christ crucified must surely speak out of the experience of salvation. We must show what the preaching of the Cross has meant in our own lives and proclaim the discovery of power and peace that has been made by multitudes through the faith that Christ died for them. Here Bunyan's pilgrim, with his burden unloosed at the Cross, becomes the parable of its significance in all the centuries. The terms in which this truth is expressed may differ, as do the New Testament metaphors themselves—liberation from bondage, ransom from sin, illumination of darkness, deliverance from evil, translation from enmity, and the rest. But whatever the language, the unanimity of confession leads to the Cross as the place of the transaction.

Our task is to bear witness among all peoples to the fact of the power of Christ crucified in transforming human souls, breaking the entail of wrong and emancipating formerly selfish lives into the service of God and humanity. Behind every enterprise of Christian *caritas*, behind innumerable lives of sacrificial ministry, obscure or famous, lies the attractive and compulsive power of the Cross of Christ. Islam must share with all, in this witness. The question, "How does Christ save?" must be answered out of the experience that he does.

Yet Muslims have a right to an honest explanation of what Christianity believes about the relation of the Cross to its consequences in human life and character. For this we must invite them to return to where we began—to the opposition of ungodliness, which, as we have seen, Islam admits but deprives of its climax. Christian history believes that Jesus suffered the full length of that hostility, and that he did so willingly, as the price of loyalty to his own message. Jerusalem was the stronghold of those bigotries and evils against which in his teaching Christ had set his face. How, then, could his teaching remain out of relation to its most marked antithesis? Christ refused to stay in the safety of

Galilee and went up to Jerusalem. But his going there—he being what he was and Jerusalem what Jerusalem was—could not but be costly. "Behold," he said, "we are going up to Jerusalem and all things that are written concerning the Son of Man shall be accomplished" (Luke 18:31).

This final and inclusive encounter Jesus faced, in full loyalty to his own doctrines, not rendering evil for evil, or countering hatred with guile. Out of it only the Cross could emerge if Jesus was not to unleash violence, appeal to force, or make himself a king. Either he would withhold his witness or incur its consequences. Either he would resist those consequences by the only kind of action open to the resister, or he would suffer. These alternatives are plain and clear in the consciousness of Jesus in the Gospels. He chose to suffer. The Cross, as an event, is no artificial scheme. It is what happens when a love like Christ's encounters a world like Jerusalem.

Herein Jerusalem is the prototype of all. The Cross bore a superscription in Hebrew, Greek, and Latin. The human forces that made it what it was, as a human deed, are common to all humanity. A coalition of dark but representative human sins accomplished the death of Christ. There were political and personal sins of convenience and security in Pilate; ecclesiastical sins of prestige and pride in the chief priests; social sins of compromise and brutality in the mob—all necessary to each other as allies in an evil deed. It is this representative character of the Cross as something persons did that is so clearly stamped upon the story. We recognize Pilate, Judas, and Caiaphas in our own hearts and in the soul of all peoples. It happened in Palestine, but it was what the whole world did. The governor and the soldiers may have been Roman, the accusers Jews, but it was humanity in its wayward-ness to which they belonged. All understanding of the Cross must begin with the actual history and must recognize in the event, as a human deed, the representative expression of what human beings do in their wrongness. Before we can really participate in the Cross as redeeming, we must see ourselves involved in its revelation of humanity. It is the place where we discover what kind of persons we are—we and our fellows.

But if the Cross was in these ways the representative human deed, it was also the act of Christ. How did he behave confronted with the worst that humans could do? In fidelity to the course he had freely chosen, he endured the Cross and suffered the contradiction of sinners against himself with forgivingness on his lips and in his heart. And from that forgivingness forgiveness flows. Had Jesus died in resentment or in blasphemy, in imprecation or sullen silence, there would have been no redemption. Only by bearing does the redeemer bear away the sin of the world. The words from the Cross—words that would never have been uttered had Jesus allowed himself to be mercifully stupefied by the gall on the reed—illuminate the inner nature of his passion and proclaim the Cross as a supreme deed of redemptive sacrifice. Truly "with his stripes we are healed." Here we find a quality of love that makes an end of evil because it freely takes all its consequences upon itself. In revenge and hatred evil is perpetuated. In pardon and long-suffering it finds its term. For those who will acknowledge their inclusion here, such redemption means a new beginning, where "the old things have passed away."

The meaning of the Cross as the redeeming deed of Christ will always defy a complete expression in theology. We can only put ourselves in the way of its fullness. The majesty of Christ's suffering must be somehow communicated: his self-giving; his insistence on going to Jerusalem; his refusal to take ample opportunities to escape; his preoccupation with prayer, not flight, when Judas was already plotting his arrest; his silence before Pilate when a few words could have set mob uproar loose; his patient acceptance of the necessity of the passion as the price of love. All these take their place in the story.

The Cross was no afterthought, no sudden tragedy. It was the conscious choice of Christ. It was what Christ did with his mission in the world, and with the accumulated evil of humankind. As the perfect fulfillment of the one, it became the effective redemption of the other. If the Cross shows us what we are, it shows us unmistakably what Christ is. To disallow this climax, to save Christ from the Cross and forbid the Cross to Christ, is to sunder what Christ, in being himself, has forever joined together.

Christian faith about the Cross goes on to believe that they were joined together in Christ's obedience because they were also joined together in the eternal purpose. If the Cross is to be seen as the act of humanity and the act of Christ, it is also understood in

Christianity as, in a tremendous sense, the act of God. "God was in Christ reconciling the world unto himself" (2 Cor. 5:19). Christ's obedience in the Cross is the fulfillment of the Father's will. All lies within the love of God. To see this is to be preserved from all mistaken theories that conceive of Christ as somehow placating a propitiating God from without, as if God needed some persuasion to the forgiveness of sinners. No! Rather the suffering of Christ expresses the divine love already active toward sinful humanity. In every evil situation love must suffer.

The great prophets saw this truth clearly. Jeremiah in some measure experienced it in his own person. The great sufferer for his people, described so graphically in Isaiah 53, was said there to have been "wounded for our transgressions." He was a vicarious sufferer because he took upon himself, in all their pain and sorrow, the sins of his generation. The love and sacrifice in which he suffered accorded with the very nature of God, so that it could be said: "The Lord has laid on him the iniquity of us all" (Isa. 53:6). Evil matters to God. It matters beyond our imagining, to God's holiness and compassion. Wherever by love an evil situation is redeemed, God is there. In Christ at the Cross that whole divine concern for human waywardness, bearing its consequences in a great single deed, is seen in cosmic fullness. "Behold the Lamb of God who takes away the sin of the world" (John 1:29). The mercy of God accomplishes the forgiveness of the world within the pattern of suffering that the divine nature—love—necessitates: a redeeming act cannot be other than a suffering act.

All who have sought to express this truth have come to a sense of the poverty of words and find themselves cast back upon the inclusive saying: "God was in Christ reconciling. . . ." The Cross is finally what God does, answering what humanity did there, and accomplishing the divine purpose in what Christ did. All preaching of the Cross is thus the proclamation of the inward meaning of humanity's act, Christ's act, God's act, meeting in a single event, where for all time the nature of sin and the victory of grace are disclosed.

X

What else may help us, under the Holy Spirit, to convey this "word of the Cross" to the Muslim? The power of the story itself;

the illumination of the great Old Testament prophets of redemptive suffering whom Islam neglects; the recognition in Islam that forgiveness is at once better and harder than revenge.[5]

We must insist that there is nothing of truth in the thought that it is immoral for one to suffer for another. It happens. And when we are ready to submit to its power and live in its terms, it redeems. We must also banish all idle thoughts about the interplay of wills. Would there have been no Cross if Judas had not been a traitor and Pilate a coward? If not, are their treachery and cowardice responsible for the redemption of the world? These thoughts arise from misunderstanding of the inter-will character of this event and indeed of all events. The Cross has to do with sin. Sin sets the situation, but what love does in that situation pertains to love alone. One cannot rightly attribute the genesis of Islam to the idolaters in Mecca.

In segments of Islam there are far-reaching ideas of sacrifice, notably among the Shī'ahs, and the sense that suffering innocently borne marks a place of divine favor and power. Thus the remembrance of 'Alī, Hasan, and Husain may help to illuminate in some measure the Christian awareness of the Cross. The tragedy of Karbala, when Husain and his retinue were massacred, is interpreted in Shī'ah passion plays as a voluntary and redemptive sacrifice for the sins of Muslims. Husain is pictured as having acquired intercessory powers on behalf of his people by the effusion of his blood, and the thought of his resignation to death stirs deep devotion.

But to mention these aids to interpretation is to realize that in truth the Cross has no parallel. It may be best to wait for those who are strangers to its meaning to see it by its own light. In other senses perhaps the very contrast is the clue. In the main body of Islam, apart from the Shī'ah and Sufism, the assumption has generally been that God's cause triumphs manifestly. The battles in early Islam are almost uniformly explained by Muslim writers as necessary to the survival of Islam. Had they not been undertaken, the infant faith would have been destroyed. The hypothesis clearly is that force is valid in the Prophet's hands and name. So ultimately Muhammad rode into a prostrate Mecca and by that victory clinched the submission of the tribes. Jesus in Jerusalem chose to refuse external patterns of success. They were within his reach and to his hand. He rejected them for the way of the Cross.

This contrast must be understood by all who would enter into the meaning of the Cross. It is all the more marked because the situations of Jesus in Jerusalem and Muhammad in Mecca are in some measure analogous. Both faced an opposition to religious truth based on prestige and pride. Both were rejected as upstarts, disruptive of the status quo. The Pharisees and the Quraish—though otherwise highly contrasted—are thus far alike. But there the similarity ends. Jesus did not conquer Jerusalem. He suffered outside its walls. The Cross became his throne.

It is necessary to present this contrast tenderly and without reproach. Until it is understood, the Cross as the key to the kingdom of heaven can never be seen in its fullness. There are some Muslims who think Jesus pitiable in his very choice. But such voices are rare and might well be rarer had not Christendom so often taken the oppressive way and forsaken the pattern of the Cross. Freed to draw by its own force, the Cross remains the magnet of human souls. When the contrasted patterns of Christendom are cited, let it be remembered that, though these reproaches must have their reckoning, it is the Christ of the Cross whom we are calling others to seek and find. Faiths must surely first be understood in their architects before they are assessed in their followers.

This, then, is the word of the Cross by which the Church lives. There always remains about it that which to some is an offense and foolishness. The recognition of the Cross as the place of pardon and peace, of divine mercy in action for human remaking, comes only in the Holy Spirit. Our task is to be wise and patient instruments of that Illuminator of the hearts in whose light human beings see light and through whom they recognize as the lover of their souls the one who suffered and rose again:

> Hath He diadem as monarch
> That His brow adorns?
> Yea, a crown—in very surety
> But of thorns.

XI

What of the Resurrection, inseparable from the Cross, both in Jesus' anticipation and in the faith of his Church? Islam believes in a resurrection yet to be. When the Qur'ān reports the infant Jesus speaking of the day of his death, it refers to the future. Jesus did not die and without the Cross there is no victory. Ours it is to explain the Resurrection as the issue of the nature and quality of Christ's death. An event of unmistakable significance, it corroborates, vindicates, demonstrates, the ultimacy of the love in which Christ died, the inclusiveness and finality of his victory, and the identity of the sufferer himself. Because *he* died *as* he did, he rose again.

The Resurrection is not an arbitrary finale to a situation that otherwise would have been different. It is the intrinsic victory of Christ as crucified and of the Cross as Christ bore it, a victory that seals human redemption and opens the doors of eternal life. It is the coming of the king of glory into his own, having proved himself the king of love. Jesus and the Resurrection thus became the apostolic Gospel.

No doubt there are matters of historical evidence that need to enter into the presentation for it was certainly not on the hypothesis of a resurrection yet to be that the Church was generated.[6] But important as these are, the crux of the interpreter's duty lies in the Cross where we have concentrated our thought. Was not Jesus recognized as risen because the disciples saw "the print of the nails"? To bypass the Cross is to remain unaware of Easter. The garden where there was an empty tomb is not reached save by way of the garden of the agony. We must strive to lead Muslims back to that interrupted pathway if we would bring them to the opening of the everlasting doors.

D. INTERPRETING THE CHRISTIAN DOCTRINE OF GOD

XII

There is a prayer in Surah 20.27–28 that might well find an echo in the heart of a Christian who strives after an interpretation to a Muslim of the Christian understanding of God: "Loose the knot from my tongue that they may understand what I say." For here Muslim susceptibilities are so many and Christian expression so difficult.

In one sense the interpretation in this exposition has already been made. For it is impossible to discuss the Christian Scriptures, the person of Jesus, and the Cross without involving and being involved in doctrines of God and making them explicit. True as this is, there is need to gather together the full theological implications of these themes and present them concisely and in line with Muslim attitudes. In so doing certain other important points may be clarified.

It is, indeed, only this truth of the implicit theology that has allowed us to defer specific discussion of the doctrine of God until now. Whereas in his call to the Muslim we followed the muezzin in beginning with the affirmation of the divine unity whence all else derives, we are here content to take up the same theme as a sequel to other topics. This is not to suggest that God is not prior and supreme, the eternal source of all things. It is simply that Christianity believes the divine fullness to be known in context, in action, and in history, and that, therefore, thought on these may be the nearest and surest way to thought on God.

Our exposition does not make God an afterthought. It follows the order of all personal knowledge, moving inward through experience to fellowship and through grace to faith. In the order of being, God is before all else. In the order of knowledge, there is much that properly precedes a full awareness of God. God is the origin of our knowledge of him. But within that knowledge God is a culmination. We come to know one who always was and eternally is. In any discussion of our coming to know God, we begin with what he has done in order to move toward what he is. The Muslim *Shahādah* itself expresses its great dogma in the form of a disavowal of an earlier and erroneous idea. It is impossible for any doctrine to begin *in vacuo*. The New Testament presupposes the Hebrew background, and the creeds presuppose the New Testament valid.

In turning, then, to study the Christian doctrine of God we are exploring our own presuppositions when we discussed the Scriptures and Christ. There are at the outset two serious sources of misconception. The one is a misapplication of the criterion of simplicity, the other a misconception about terms.

XIII

It is widely thought, and often said, that the Christian doctrine of God is unnecessarily complicated, abstruse, and subtle. ''The

Father incomprehensible, the Son incomprehensible, the Holy Ghost incomprehensible, the whole idea incomprehensible," as one wit had it, making crude havoc of the Latin meaning. The Christian faith about God, it is argued, is finally unintelligible: it collapses under its own intricacy. This view can be found expressed in numerous places in contemporary Muslim literature. Not a few Westerners who have embraced Islam, whether travelers, like H. St. John Philby in Arabia, or disciples of Ahmadiyyah missions and mosques in the West, explain their decision in such terms. Christianity they did not understand, because its central doctrines were confusing and elaborate. Islam is readily intelligible and entirely simple. Muhammad 'Alī, in *My Life—A Fragment*, earlier quoted, declares that for Islam a postage stamp would suffice, as far as theology is concerned. "There is no god but God and Muhammad is his Apostle" *is* the dogma of Islam, and it makes no great call on its believers' powers of thinking or their credulity.[7]

In view of these attitudes, it is important to make clear that the Christian doctrine of God is not intricate for the sake of intricacy, nor are the issues implicit in its formulation artificial and unnecessary. It is also important to consider the criterion of simplicity here assumed. "Simple solutions," A. N. Whitehead once declared, "are bogus solutions." Be that as it may, the higher the theme the less likelihood there is that it can be adequately formulated in simple terms. This is not to deny to the simple and the unintellectual their awareness of God, or to overlook that such awareness may often come nearer to God than does philosophic disquisition. Nor is it to deny that Church Fathers and theologians, like all experts, have not sometimes fallen into excessive love of their own pursuit of theological learning. This is not the place to attempt a definition of the necessity of formal theology to religion—though it may be observed that it would hardly be Islamic to deny it. But we are concerned to insist that doctrines of God are not properly to be evaluated by the criterion of simplicity—itself a mischievous notion as long as it remains undefined.

The simplest statement, such as "God is one" or "God is love," is simple only in the sense that subject and predicate are simple words and there are no complicating clauses. These simple statements, however, have a profundity no sincerity can evade or conceal. What the demand for simplicity in these realms is in danger of becoming, perhaps unwittingly, is a demand for abeyance or, worse, disavowal, of thought. This should be resisted at all costs. Even a little reflection surely makes it clear that doctrines of God are not commendable merely by their ability to fit on a postage stamp. Definitions are not quantitatively evaluated.

It seems necessary to make this point plain. The definition of a brick could conceivably be simple and being simple would supposedly be brief. But the faith about God, though it might conceivably be brief, could hardly be always simple or necessarily be valid because it was either brief or simple. Simplicity is too nebulous and undefined a quality to be, in this bare sense, a sufficient criterion of a sound theology. To insist on this fact is not to imply that theologians have never been tedious, or that Christian doctrine has never been clumsily expounded. It is to argue that properly understood the Christian doctrine of the Trinity is the formulation of revealed knowledge and personal experience, the continuity of which as a spiritual reality could be safeguarded only in this way. It is easy to join with Carlyle in ridiculing Christendom divided over a diphthong in its definition of Christ. It is profounder to enter with patience into the issue involved and to appreciate that no faith can live in or by a truth it is unable or unwilling to express.

Part, then, of our Christian task in this realm is patiently to dissipate the erroneous notion that Christian theology is a piece of dispensable subtlety encumbering the simplicity of true theism. Muslims need to be awakened to the profundity of their own simplicities and the relevance of what they consider Christian extravagancies. Differences of view about God cannot properly be compared on the ground of comparative simplicity—not if God is truly their subject. The question must always be resolved into: How articulate is the simplicity? That question is only another way of asking: How adequately profound is the doctrine?

XIV

This leads to the second point—the misconception about terms. The Christian faith in God as Father, Son, and Holy Spirit is not a violation of faith in God's unity. It is a way of understanding that unity—a way, the Christian would go on to say, of safe-guarding that unity. Perhaps our largest duty with the Muslim mind lies just here. For the Muslim, faith in God as Father, Son, and Holy Spirit does violence to the divine unity. For the Christian, it expresses and illuminates the unity. The Muslim sees the doctrine of the Trinity as incompatible with belief in the unity of God. The Christian finds these not merely compatible but inter-dependent. The issue, understood in Christian terms, is not Trin-ity and unity, but Trinity and atheism. The Christian faith in God is defined in this way as the form in which such a faith is finally possible in this world of mystery and evil.

This claim will be the burden of the exposition that follows, when it is hoped it will be sufficiently sustained—though, clearly, no full presentation of the Christian doctrine about God, either philosophically or historically, is possible in this context. If our aim is to help interpret that faith to Muslims, we must begin with this plea that the Muslim estimate and ponder the Christian Trin-ity not as a violation of unity, but as a form of its expression. We cannot proceed except on the understanding that we are both firmly and equally believers that God is one. We both stand squarely in the Hebrew tradition: "The Lord our Lord is One Lord." We are not discussing theism and tritheism. Christianity is concerned only with the first. Muslims who debate tritheism are not discussing Christianity. Where we differ is over how to define and understand the divine unity. What lies outside that issue is irrelevant to Christianity.

Here, before we go further, let it be said that "debate" about God is unseemly. It is un-Islamic and un-Christian as long as it is querulous, assertive, or doctrinaire. We are not concerned to bring cases to victory but minds to meeting. Though, where rea-son is involved, we have a right to be discursive and a duty to be positive, it is clear that thoughts of God should never be competi-tive thoughts. Over all theological partisanships must be heard the rebuking cry: "Who is this who darkens counsel by words without knowledge?" (Job 38:2).

Our aim must be to mediate in intellectual converse and strong charity the fullness of the faith by which we live. Our plea must be to be understood for what we believe and not for some travesty of it. Our patience must undertake to differentiate the faith and the travesty. And let no one suppose that the issues are unreal or that they can be avoided. If we shirk or silence them in the realm of God, they will meet us elsewhere, wherever we turn. We must banish the suspicion that a conspiracy of silence would serve peace better. But when we venture into word and colloquy, we must remember that the theme is God.

Why, then, do Christians believe in Father, Son, and Holy Spirit—one God? What do Christians mean? Answer is possible here only in the barest terms. Two themes of thought about the Christian doctrine of God are suggested: its experimental origin and its propositional form.

XV

God, as we suggested above, came to be known for what God is from experience of what he does. Action and relationship become the clue to personality. We do not say only that the doctrine of the Trinity is a summary of the activities of God, for undoubtedly it is much more. What we do say is that those active relationships are indicative of God's being and nature. The first fact about this developing sense of God in active relationship with the world is that it was experienced by those who were as adamant about the divine unity as are the best of Muslims. Indeed the fundamental protest made by Muhammad against Meccan idolatry was implicit in the whole ethos of the Hebrew and Christian tradition. Muhammad's iconoclasm was desperately valid and necessary in the Arabian context. It had no validity, however, as a disallowance of Christian dogma, because that dogma could in no valid way be identified with paganism. The fact was that the Christian community had made the same revolt as Muhammad in its own ancestry and context centuries before Muhammad made it in Arabia.

The Apostles, then, and the Church Fathers were not thirsting to multiply deities when in the historic faith they interpreted their Christian experience. They began, as Muhammad began, with God, with *Allāh*, one Sovereign, Creator, Sustainer, Provider, and Lord, ruling and revealing. They knew that the universe derived from God's creative fiat. They understood creation to mean that God's responsible will underlay all existence, not merely originally but from moment to moment. They recognized that God sought an entire worship and obedience in which lay the secret of human good and human happiness. They knew that human life stood under the law of God and they believed that this law had been revealed and entrusted to a community of people—which people they were—which was to practice and commend this law as a truth for all mankind.

In all these points they were akin to the Islam which Muhammad's mission constituted in the fresh enunciation of many of these truths. It is true they spoke of God as Father only occasionally and tentatively. But they knew him as sovereign Lawgiver and merciful God. Their worship and doctrine recognized God's lordship and they entertained wistful hopes of his historic intervention in pursuance alike of righteousness and mercy.

In this context Christian faith was nurtured. These were the suppositions of Christ's own teaching. They were axiomatic to Christian theologians in and beyond the New Testament. From this point we move into that profoundest of all sayings: "You believe in God, believe also in Me" (John 14:1). The Greek original allows either verb to be indicative and either imperative. What matters is the intimate connection between faith in God and faith in Christ, between believing in Jesus and believing in God. Whence does this connection derive? Why is the nature of God such as to issue in something like the person and mission of Christ? Why is the fact of Christ inseparable from a final understanding of God?

We can discern a twofold answer. God is by nature revealing. God's will to reveal, being at once righteous and merciful, means also—in this world—a will to redeem. In our treatment of the Christian Scriptures we noted the Muslim-Christian conviction that God is made known to us in divine self-revelation, because God is related to creation in law and in love. God does not leave us in ignorance, or fail to bring to our reason the light of the divine will and purpose and nature. In the Christian understanding this revelation is finally personal and consummates all its words into a Word that lives and moves and has its being in our human ken. But further, this revelation—if it is of a living God—intends fellowship. God will not simply tell us what, but show us who, God is. Revelation bringing God to us and us to God in knowledge means communion. The end of law is obedience; the end of education, understanding; the end of revelation, knowledge. God is not an idea; nor can God be obeyed, understood, or known merely as an idea. God for Muslims and Christians, in their common if contrasted traditions, is a God who seeks worship and intends fellowship. Revelation overcomes not merely darkness, but distance.

At this point the Christian understanding of God encounters the fact of evil. The revealed law is manifestly flouted and the revelatory purpose frustrated by human recalcitrance. The world in its history is defiant of God and goodness. This theme is interwoven in the Biblical revelation of God as also a revelation of human nature in its waywardness. The possibility of such a tragic reality is implicit in the possibility of fellowship. For we would not be creatures capable of responding to the divine goodness that comes to us in revelation unless we were also creatures capable of becoming rebels against that goodness. Love and obedience cannot be compelled and remain truly themselves.

Christianity, therefore, sees the possibility of sin as involved in the human-divine situation as we know it, both in the idea of revelation and in the reality of human conduct. It proceeds from this possibility in thought to the reality in fact. It seeks to learn what God, the sovereign Good, does in response to our lostness and disobedience. It finds the answer in Christ. It believes that all faiths, not least Islam, should be alive to this reality of insubordination, of disobedience, of un-*islām* in human history.

It needs, perhaps, to be added for the Muslim's thought that the Christian belief in real human freedom to be and remain rebellious is not inconsistent with faith in the ultimate sovereignty of the divine goodness. We have seen elsewhere something of the concern of Muslim theology on this point of the interrelation of the divine and human wills. Suffice it to say here that a genuine, though limited, human freedom even to defy God, although it helps to explain historical realities, does not compromise God's reign or unity, inasmuch as God's permissive will allows and controls the situation in which human defiance can occur, and inasmuch as the very possibility of such defiance is implicit in the greater purposes of revelation and grace.

But the remedy of evil is more important than its genesis. If we are potentially defiant and actually rebellious, what of the law that revelation sends down, as the token and measure of the divine will? Shall it remain permanently flouted? Must not the revelatory purpose take cognizance of our legal and moral non-submission? Can God remain sovereign apart from redemption? Must not recalcitrant humanity be brought somehow through its disobedience into that fellowship and love of the good of the law which is the purpose of human existence and the crux of the human predicament?

This is the final meaning of the whole idea of Messiahship, of God's intervening in history to put us right and to renew the thwarted purposes of righteous law. The ideal of that correction varied widely as long as it was in prospect. When Christ came, fulfilling and transforming it, it was seen to mean suffering and the crown of thorns. The significance of Christ as the anointed Redeemer—born, teaching, suffering, dying—is the most formative element in the Christian doctrine of God.

Christians in the generation after the Resurrection understood the Godward significance of their experience of Christ. They discovered the truth of his claim: "Whoever has seen me has seen the Father" (John 14:9). That God was in Christ was the only adequate hypothesis on which they could express and transmit what their experience of Christ had meant to them. So they spoke of him as "the Word made flesh," "Son of Man" and "Son of God," "the Captain of their salvation," "the Author and Finisher of their faith." Theirs was not the language of polytheists. They were not idolaters. They were responding to a profound experience of God. They could find, as monotheists, no other ground on which to explain what Christ had been to them and had done for all humankind.

God was not less God, not less one, by this belief; only more so. For the sin and disobedience that formerly frustrated God's purpose and defied law, and, uncorrected and permanent, would have constituted a contrary force not subordinated to good, had been triumphantly overcome, in a way that no punitive judgment could do. It is out of this realm of deed that Jesus had said to Jewish monotheists: "You believe in God, believe also in me." Can we in our turn finally believe in God sovereign and supreme without believing in some such enterprise as that of "God in Christ reconciling the world to himself"?

This is the truth we have in mind when we speak of the experimental origin of the Christian faith in the Trinity. But the experience went further. It generated another fact. For this faith brought a new unity into humanity. It also entrusted new tasks of witness and proclamation. It was the occasion of a new joy and a new release of power and peace. The redeeming work of Christ on the Cross had its counterpart in redemptive transactions in human souls. The goodness the law intended now became a personal delight. Christians found themselves transformed into a new likeness. Forgiveness brought a sense of joy and obligation. Moral power was released in human hearts and a great new phenomenon appeared in the world, described as fellowship in the Holy Spirit. This was so manifestly continuous with the earthly life of Christ that Christians attributed it to the same source. It was so evidently of God that it was recognized to be God's. This new accession of understanding and joy was no less a divine activity than the suffering and teaching of Christ himself. God was evidently not only over humanity in creative sovereignty and for them in redeeming love. God was also in them and with them as an abiding Presence, "the Holy Spirit proceeding from the Father and the Son."

This divine activity was not, of course, discontinuous with the divine guidance and inspiration of the prophets and patriarchs. But now in the wake of Christ there seemed to have come an age of the Spirit that, although anticipated in its nature, was new in its fullness. For this reason Christians came to recognize that they must make room in their theology for God's ever present activity in their minds, their affairs, and their hearts. They had a vitality not their own, inexplicable by circumstances and not deriving from genius of theirs. For ordinariness was their hallmark.

It may be worth observing that the Qur'ān recognizes in measure the sort of divine relationship to humanity that underlies the Christian doctrine of the Holy Spirit. The Book itself is God's speech. God sends messengers and spirits, to whom the divine counsel has been spoken. There are intermediaries between God and the world of time and sense. Clearly these communicative activities of God are differentiated from creative activities. We have at least to think of God in different capacities. The basic contrast here is that Christianity takes these activities and gathers them into its understanding of the nature of God. When we speak of God the Spirit, we refer to God in this activity. Though God may use agents and instruments, it is finally God who is using them.

In this sense the doctrine of the Trinity is no more and no less than the concept of God as being in relationship with humanity, God whose will sustains, whose love redeems, and whose Spirit orders and indwells the world of human life. A God out of relationship with us is certainly not theism, or monotheism; still less a God with whom religion, as Islam and Christianity know it, can have to do. But God in relationship is precisely what we mean by the doctrine of the Trinity—God so truly and unmistakably in relationship with us that we take the pattern of that relationship to us as the clue to the divine nature. What else, what better, should we take?

This, then, is the experimental origin of the Christian faith as to God. The genesis in experience cannot be too strongly emphasized. The Christian Fathers were not armchair philosophers, sitting down to evolve nice metaphysical theories. Their faith, when formulated, solves many outstanding philosophical problems but does not exist for that reason. It is profoundly significant that the sweetest and perhaps the earliest statement of this Christian faith places it in the context of experience where theology ends as it should in doxology: "The grace of our Lord Jesus Christ and the love of God and the fellowship of the Holy Spirit be with us all evermore" (2 Cor. 13:14). "For through Christ we all have access by one Spirit unto the Father" (Eph. 2:18). "Glory be to God most high."

XVI

Few would deny that belief needs to be formally defined. Only so can it be safeguarded from misunderstanding. Only so is it secure for future generations. The basic assumption that what God is can be formulated from what God does, made by the early Christian theologians, would seem to have been a sound one. Dogma serves the needs of more than will admit it. The Church was profoundly right in requiring that its understanding of God in the experimental realm should be taken also into the definitive realm. The Christian community sought to embody in creedal shape the nature of its experience, that all generations might enter into the same communion of saints—and of mind.

The whole story cannot be done justice here. We must be content with one fundamental principle and some simple observations. The principle is that we must strive to introduce the Muslim heart to the faith within the Christian doctrine by the same path that the Church itself followed. We are to bring others to God in Christ, before we can justify to them what creedally we believe about him. Our duty is to demonstrate and communicate an awareness of the grace, love, and fellowship which are the human consequence of what God is. But we will not evade the intellectual tasks implicit in the creedal forms. A few observations may be apposite.

The Christian Trinity is God the Father, God the Son, and God the Holy Spirit. It does not consist of God, Jesus, and the Virgin Mary, as there has been a tendency among Muslims to suppose.

The terms "Father" and "Son" have no physical significance and are used analogically. The divine solicitude for humankind in ignorance and sin "begets" or generates the activity of redeeming love that is evident in the historic Christ. That "God was in Christ" rather than that "Jesus was God" is the classic expression of this truth. James Denney sets out the distinction clearly when he writes:

> The word "God" as a proper noun identifies the Being to whom it is applied so that it can be used as the subject of a sentence; but it does not unfold the nature of that Being, so that it could be used as the predicate of a sentence. In the formula "Jesus is God the Son" . . . "the Son" introduces the very qualification of God which makes it possible to apply it to Jesus. In the same way . . . in saying that Jesus was "God manifest in the flesh," "manifest in the flesh" serves the same purpose.[8]

The writer adds that the Fathers of Nicea and Chalcedon "would have pronounced the bare statement that Jesus was God to have been as far from adequate to the whole truth they were desirous of expressing as the bare statement that he was man." The phrase "God the Son" means God in self-revelation in the person of

Jesus, "God with us" taking perfect humanity into the divine revelatory purpose and giving to us that of which we may say, "This is the Lord: we have waited for him, we will be glad and rejoice in his salvation."

There is absolutely no reason to insist, as some Muslims do, that the term "Father" necessarily implies paternity in the physical sense. No one using the phrase "alma mater" wishes it to be understood that the college or university has a womb. Terms are used for their rich significance in those senses in which they can appropriately be predicated. It goes without saying that God does not have children as human beings do. This, however, does not invalidate the use of the deepest analogy known to human life—the more so in that all fatherhood and family is the idea of God and takes its name, according to St. Paul, from God.

Is the doctrine of the Trinity against reason? It may transcend our complete rational comprehension and also elude philosophical discovery. But once revealed, it is certainly open to the fullest exploration the mind can attain. If mystery remains, beyond the reach of thinkers, this is not to say that their ambitions have no place. Theists have no need to be ashamed of the intellectual bearings of their faith. It illuminates many of the otherwise unanswered questions of philosophy. It is well to remember that rejection of this doctrine on the grounds of mystery does not rid the unbeliever of the mysterious. The Christian doctrine lies precisely at the point where the supreme mysteries belong. If we reject that doctrinal account of them, we still have the mysteries on hand. It is sometimes forgotten that although the onus is always on belief to make good its claim, there is a similar obligation for skeptics to validate their unbelief. It is a false assumption to suppose that they have any easier task, and blindness to suppose they have no task at all. No doctrine can be justified on the ground that it is mysterious. But if the mystery is taken hold of and becomes luminous, then such doctrine may well be standing with the truth.

Reflection makes it clear that the idea of the divine unity cannot be enforced in a mathematical sense, and that enforcement in such sense is the ground of most Muslim antipathy to the Christian Trinity. The higher we proceed in the scale of being, the more rich and varied are the unities we encounter. Mathematical units, such as stones or a unicellular organism, are low in the scale of values. In constructing a straight, solid wall, the bricklayer may lay any brick that comes to hand, because they are all alike and interchangeable. They are mere units. Not so the components of a flower or the parts of the human body. Here we have larger unities with differentiated parts. Human personalities are the richest and most diversified unities within our experience. William Shakespeare or Abraham Lincoln were individual persons but what wealth of diversity lay within them.

If the order of ascending unity reveals increasing fullness, who shall say that the unity of God is not the richest and the greatest of all? Certainly we cannot disallow the doctrine of the Father, Son, and Holy Spirit on the ground that these add up to three. Was not Muhammad prophet, husband, leader, and exemplar? He was, no less, one Muhammad. On whatever other grounds Muslims feel disposed to disagree with the Christian understanding of God, it cannot validly be on the ground that it is not a doctrine of unity. For the only sense in which it can be thought not to be so is the one completely inappropriate—namely, the mathematical.

A bare unity, philosophically understood, is a barren one. We have seen something of this problem in discussing the relationship of the Qur'ān—created or uncreated—to God. Creation, to be meaningful as a loving transaction, must originate in a purpose that is already love within itself. We cannot say that "God is love" and also say that "God is solitary" or, in this solitary sense, that "God is one." Entire transcendence is in the end a blank agnosticism. The Christian faith in the Trinity only carries further the truth implicit in the Muslim faith in revelation and judgment. It is the Christian form of belief in a God who has real and meaningful relation with humanity and the temporal world.

The formulation of the Christian doctrine of God was not a formulation of men in exercising a philosophic or scientific capacity, but in their capacity as the redeemed. As the creedal side of the saving enterprise of God, it should be set always in the center of its origin and of its abiding meaning. "God is most great" says the Christian *takbīr*, "because God has become the Redeemer." God's lordship is both an experience and a hope. "Blessing and glory and wisdom and thanksgiving and honor and power and might be unto our God forever and ever" (Rev. 7:12).

XVII

There is perhaps one final question. Our attempt to interpret so far fails its glorious theme, is compassed about by so much weakness, and beset with so many pitfalls and discouragements, that the temptation to desist is ever present. Can we seek to build our Muslim relationships on less exacting grounds? There are many areas of nontheological intercourse and mutual enterprise that may be more fruitfully developed. Let us leave the irreconcilable.

But no! Though we may begin and build confidence and expression in less pressing realms, there is no properly Christian interpretation that is not concerned to give to all persons the knowledge of God in Christ. The most tenacious and most widespread worship of the one God in human history and the world today, outside the Christian communion, has surely the most eloquent claim to the knowledge of "the God and Father of our Lord Jesus Christ."

Idolatry is far from being, as Islam supposed, the sole or even the most serious disparagement of the divine unity. Pagan idolaters multiply gods in ignorant ideas of celestial coexistence. But sinners who deify themselves or their ambitions dethrone the one God. Their challenge to the divine sovereignty is more heinous and more defiant. To refute idolaters is one thing. But it should also mean a passion that God should be all-in-all over every other challenge of evil and hate. The Christian tradition believes it has been given in trust the knowledge of just such a divine sovereignty, reigning and to reign, in the majesty of redeeming love. The tragic irony is that Islam has mistaken the historic expression of that faith for a refined piece of the polytheism it was created to denounce. To find such a faith in such a situation is surely to make the fullest interpretation imperative.

E. Interpreting the Christian Church and a Christian Society

XVIII

From the contemplation of our duty toward Muslims in the realm of Christian faith in regard to God and Christ, the Scriptures, and the Cross we pass now to the realm of the Christian society and the Christian Church. Here also massive misunderstandings confront us. Some derive from the implications of misconceptions already studied, and others from the ambiguities of Christian history. As before, so now, our conviction is that occasions of misapprehension must be made themes of expression. All that can be attempted is a brief discussion of aspects of the Christian Church that are central to Christian definition and Muslim interpretation.

The nature of the Church is to be understood in the light of the nature of the Gospel. It is what results from the divine initiative of grace in Jesus Christ. He had gathered around him a nucleus of disciples who were both learners in his teachings and servants in his compassion. He bound them closely to his person and taught them to center their faith and devotion upon his identity as the Messiah. This recognition had first to undergo the supreme test of the crucifixion, an event that seemed to give the lie to all their hopes, but in its issue both transformed and fulfilled them. The concept of the Christ, first tentatively, then triumphantly, confessed by the disciples bound them in spirit and heart to the long expectations of the people of Israel. They saw in its fulfillment their own "social" continuity with their forebears in a continuity of hope and yearning.

It also bound them and their long antecedents in Israel to the whole community of faith resulting from the recognition in Christ of God's enterprise of human redemption. The initial group of disciples became the apostolic circle, born into a new solidarity of conviction and fellowship by the Resurrection. Jesus the Master was still the personal center and focus of their devotion. Yet now it was Jesus the Lord, so named and understood, not in the partial knowledge and therefore incomplete discipleship of the months between their enlistment and his death, but in the total assurance and commitment generated by his passion.

It was in this sense that the Resurrection brought the historical Church into being. Legatee of the hopes and many of the patterns of the old Israel, and heir also to Christ's law and example, it was the new community of redemption resulting from the acknowledgment of Christ as Lord. Energized and guided by the Holy Spirit, it became the instrument in the world for the diffusion and demonstration of the good news of God. Almost three centuries elapsed before empire or government capitulated to it. Its essential nature as a community in, and yet not of, this world, a society within society, a fellowship deriving from divine grace and human response, was by that time fully apparent.

This community of belief and fellowship was in a state of perpetual wonder at itself, exploring in its Epistles the meaning of its own genesis and the secret of its true being. Entrusted with the ancient Scriptures, it became the matrix within which the Gospel tradition was set down for the guidance of all the generations and for the lands that had not known a contemporary Christ. It described to itself through its Apostles' correspondence the meaning of its new life, the secret of its calling and its destiny. It knew itself heir to the promises. It was the body of Christ and a covenant society founded on the divine mercy and pledged to show forth the praises of its Lord. It was at once a building for the habitation of God through the Spirit and an organism in which Christ, his truth and compassion, would still be active in the teaching and service of the world. It was an earnest of the meaning of the kingdom of heaven, the token in community of the power and the wisdom of God in Christ. It united the past of preparation with the present of realization. It lived to bear both into the future of humanity.

Embodying the meaning of the ages, it was also set for the healing of the nations. Its fellowship transcended the most obstinate divisions of the ancient world. In historic decisions the Church broke away from the limitations of the Hebrew synagogue without sacrificing its debt to the Hebrew nurture. It welcomed Greek and barbarian into its life, and came to use many of the concepts of the Greek mind to describe and define its creedal faith. In pursuit of this openness of hand and mind, it spread in widening evangelism across the Near East and into adjacent Europe, Africa, and Asia. In responding to the dimensions of the love of God in Christ, it learned more of its own nature.

Those Epistles and the subsequent Gospel histories of the Christ, who had made their writers and readers what they were, came to establish themselves as authoritative Scriptures in the mind of the Church. This process of recognizing authoritative status, which was later finalized in canonization, did not endow those writings with authority or establish the Church as somehow superior to them. Rather it was a recognition by the community of their inherent authority.

Both Church and Scriptures together stood under the fact of Christ—Master, Savior, Lord—from whom both derived their being, the one as the written, the other as the institutional, consequence of all that he had been and was. But just as the writings argued readers and so a possessing community, the possessing community likewise argued a history and originating facts, and so in turn a Scripture and a record. The Scriptures were in the custody of the Church only because the Church was itself in the custody of the facts of the Scriptures. It gave the writings circulation; what they described gave it existence.

The understanding of revelation upon which this relationship of Scripture and community rests has already been discussed. To the question: Did Jesus intend a Church?, by which some Muslims have been attracted, the answer must now be clear. If his purpose was to teach and redeem, a continuing institution of hearers and redeemed seems inescapable. This is not to say that Christ intended everything that historical churches have become. But it does mean that the relationship of disciples and believers to him involved their relationship with each other, not simply as an agreement to associate, but as a corporate communal reality inseparable from a common allegiance. Faith is necessarily fellowship. To be in Christ is not to be solitary. Jesus as teacher had taught his hearers to say "Our Father. . . ." When they entered the meaning of his passion they found a new fullness to that implicit sense of community.

Muslim tendencies to disallow the Church belong to the partial Muslim awareness of Jesus and would find their answer in its enlargement. But such tendencies are not universal. Many Muslim writers, in line with certain Quranic passages, lay great stress on the disciples and picture them as the devoted disseminators of his words after his removal from the earthly scene. This view picks up the Church after the hiatus of silence (where the Cross stands) and sees a continuity between a Galilean prophet and the Apostles. But it must be asked whether the shattered disciples after Good Friday recovered their nerve and became evangelists only in terms of a Jesus who had eluded death and was no more with them. The incredibility of such a hypothesis has been suggested already in the discussion of the Cross.

XIX

Apart from these Muslim attitudes to the historical origin of the Church, there are recurrent questions about its relation to human society at large. In this realm there are issues at stake that are deep and urgent. The interpreter has to renounce contrasted distortions. Muslims, as is well known, rejoice in their conviction that Islam knows no separation, ideally, between faith and society, between believer and citizen, between doctrine and culture. Islam is a practicable and feasible religion relating to the whole of life. Several aspects of this quality we have studied above in chapter 5, "The Islamic Order for Human Society." We have seen the general Muslim repudiation of "religion" as something distinguished from "the secular," from government and from the everyday, as if it were a private affair concerning only the soul and God.

There are aspects of this Muslim understanding of Islam that, properly understood, belong also to Christianity. There are other aspects that, unexamined, betray serious naivety in the analysis of human nature and society. Their patient examination can be greatly served by a simple exposition of the Christian case. Here perhaps more than anywhere else we can most profitably dispel misunderstandings and at the same time deepen the level of realism in the discussion.

Many Muslim writers, past and present, upbraid Christianity for its failure to discipline and control Western civilization. It has not checked imperialism or corrected exploitation. It is, on the contrary, implicated in aiding and abetting Western dominance in the world. Even its missions are seen as a form of religious imperialism.[9] Other critics proceed upon a somewhat different hypothesis. Christianity, for them, is not so much reproached for involvement in Western mischief and selfishness, as for noninvolvement. Christianity is absolved from positive implication by the contrasted charge of aloofness and withdrawal. It is a religion of high ideals and absolutist ethics, impossible of attainment in this human world. Society then goes on in partial lip service to its ideals, but with little or no actual obedience. The faith itself, meanwhile, nourishes its ethics in individual seclusion or "monastic" isolation. Christianity, therefore, has not so much failed civilization as proved itself incompetent to try. In either case the faith of the Christian Church is wanting because it does not put the world to rights.

Any Christian attempt to face patiently the issues here involved might begin with a historical investigation of the debt of humanity, East and West, to Christian ethics, Christian love, and Christian sacrifice. But this of itself would not be a complete answer. Nor would an explanation of the failures of institutional Christianity in the world as due to inferior Christians, or disloyalty and nonpractice within the Church, suffice to meet what is here at issue. We must be both radical and realistic. We cannot claim all that is worthy, compassionate, and true in Western civilization for the credit of Christianity, and explain the contrary as arising from neglect of Christianity.

It is a Christian principle to be radical with ourselves and to take the diagnosis of sin into religion itself with no areas of spirit or mind immunized from the reproach that calls to repentance. We must recognize what failure implies for the religion so failing, and not seek evasive exoneration in reprobating its confessors. For what the confessors are, or are not, is part of the record of the religion and some clue to its nature.

Beneath these considerations lies the heart of the matter. The Church is conceived in the New Testament as a society within a society. It is never properly thought of as coterminous, within history, with the whole of human society. "Christendom," though the term has some validity, is not, in the final analysis, a Christian concept. The Church is an *ecclesia*—a called-out community. It is built upon the idea and the fact of redemption. It, therefore, involves an analysis of human nature as wayward and sinful. This waywardness is redeemed and corrected in Christ into newness of life, on the condition of faith and commitment. "Any who did accept him he empowered to become children of God. These are they who believe in his name" (John 1:12). There is the "natural" person in recalcitrance and the "spiritual" person in regeneration and pardon. The former no doubt penetrates into existing churches. But the Christian understanding of how human nature is put to rights is that it happens personally and through faith.

Goodness and truth and love, then, are not actualized in terms of the "natural" person, but of the person made new. The transaction is conditional upon repentance and faith and is perpetuated in discipleship. These conditions of the transaction, being personal, are not social. Christianity belongs to and inheres in persons who believe. It is never coterminous as such with any given society.

Many social institutions, laws, customs, practices, habits, concepts, ideals, and norms may become "Christian." Christian truth relates to them imperatively. But they become so only derivatively from the Christian conviction and Christian regeneration of the persons who shape or inhabit them. Thus the unit of Christianity, that in which it inheres, as fire in coals, is not society, but persons in society. Things are not the final locus of Christianity; persons are.

Thus the Christian fellowship of persons discipled to Christ as Master and Savior is within, not identical with, a total population. It is always in nature, if not in fact, militant, antiseptic, regenerating its fellows as far as it can and resisting what is unChristian in its context as far as it may. It does not expect to identify itself with the whole. Not that it does not so desire, but because parts of that total aggregate withhold the vital allegiance that alone constitutes a Christian person.

The Christian distinction between the regenerate and the unregenerate derives from a sense of the radical nature of human wrongness and the conviction that the true faith cannot be compelled. Response can be given or withheld. In the degree to which persons withhold it, they count themselves out of the kingdom it offers. The kingdom in love will never let them go, but it will never compel allegiance. Allegiance to this kingdom can only be given.

This distinction between the natural and the spiritual is basic to a proper understanding of the Church. The Gospel of grace does not suppose that humanity is perfectible by law. It cannot assume that because a revelation of law is given, the heirs of that revelation are by that fact a perfect society. A community that confronts men and women with an all-out decision cannot at the same time be a community that recruits them all. Christianity, then, is not a political expression. Realist Muslims have recognized that Islamic law has not at any prolonged time in history evoked a true society.[10] There has always been disparity between what was and what might have been. But Islam in general insists that the disparity is incidental. Those who have divine guidance as the clue to their life under law ought to be organized as a political expression and should be able as such to constitute the perfect human society.

The Christian mind, by contrast, believes that the society of the redeemed will always stand within the community, militantly, not identical with the whole. That whole, the secular world, must be free to organize itself. If we try to assume its conversion, it will belie our facile complacence. We cannot by legislation or assertion identify it with Christ. Its recalcitrance has to be recognized as part of its freedom and has to be confronted patiently with the conditions of its retrieval. We only deceive it and ourselves if we suppose that no conditions exist.

This fundamentally is the reason why the Christian faith recognizes an ultimate distinction (and in that sense a separation) between the Church and the state. The distinction is the counterpart of its understanding of a world in need and God in divine grace. The "separation" does not connote the nonrelevance of Christ to life; it does not mean abdication of responsibility; it does not indicate indifference; it is not a withdrawal into a private and self-regarding piety; it is not dereliction of social duty. It is a refusal to regard men and women as being in no need of redemption, or the kingdom of heaven as unconditioned by repentance and a new heart. How patiently the meaning of this relation of the Christian community to human society as a whole and to the criteria of goodness must be unveiled.

XX

Such a patient interpretation may serve to illuminate the fact that a totalitarian religious identification of faith and the state is not so realistic as is sometimes supposed. Whenever religion is equated with the powers of this world, the quality and worth of religion are inevitably reduced. It is by calling persons out of their ordinary levels rather than by hallowing them as adequate that they, and indirectly their society, can be worthily transformed. This is part of our witness to Islam. The New Testament conceives of Christian life as more than we can manage—by ourselves. It is the gift of grace and the fruit of salvation.

It is imperative, however, at the same time to make entirely clear that the Christian Church is not indifferent to society and that the doctrine of redemption does not write off the "secular" world as hopeless and forsworn. On the contrary, its confidence in a redemptive purpose that has entered and is ever entering into history has the great "future tense" of hope. The redeeming Christ here and now brings the pledge of a sovereignty that will subdue all things unto himself.

The Church is not pessimistic when it is radical; nor piously preoccupied when it proclaims conversion. Christianity is not concerned merely with the eternal destiny of the individual. Nor is faith a private affair between the soul and God. To belong to Christ is to take up the Cross, to undertake costly responsibility for the world, to bear witness against social evil and strive for economic justice on all sides. To recognize that changing social conditions does not of itself change human nature is not to be indifferent to changing them. To appreciate that "things" as such can never be all that they should be, apart from the men and women who shape them, is not to be careless about how "things" are. Christianity is not to be written off as pious irresponsibility. On the contrary, disciples who acknowledge their own redemption by the Cross are summoned to assert the rights of their Redeemer over the whole of life. The righteousness that saves them is an active righteousness. In Christ we learn to take responsibility for our neighbors and for everything that shapes their lives— social, political, economic, and international.

The Christian's faith in the Incarnation means that humanity is called to be expressive of the divine nature. There could be no greater travesty than to suppose the Christian faith is either aloof from, or unfit for, a deep social conscience, fulfilled in action. We seek no exoneration from responsibility for Western wrongs and evils on the ground that they are no concern of the Christian faith. Rather we recognize failure in our moral duty.

The truth just outlined—that the Church does not look for a

full redemption of society apart from faith—does not mean we establish a universal alibi to excuse disloyalties in all our great, if subordinate, tasks of social militancy. We do not the less seek to humanize and hallow laws and institutions, because we seek finally to save the soul. Those who write Christianity off in this respect have not begun to understand it.

The clarification of the Christian's role in society should help to illuminate some interior problems in Muslim thought at the present time when a great debate is in progress. Does the "totalitarian" religion aim to dominate society and insure obedience by state authority and enforcement, or does it seek to permeate opinion and rely solely on persuasion? Is there any sense, not harmful to religion, in which the political order should be free of religious dominance? If religion prescribes the desiderata of the state and of society, what is its true function in relation to their actualization? Some Muslims today are by no means as confident as their forebears that the right way to serve the unlimited demands of religious law is by the unlimited enforcement of religious sanctions. Christianity agrees that the claims of God are total and that nothing is exempt from their relevance. It does not agree that they can be met in a religio-political order externally established. At this point of difference there is a wide field for Christian interpretation, with the nature of the Church as a clue.

XXI

Another area of possible Muslim misconception concerns Christian ministry and the sacraments. Islam prides itself on its freedom from "priesthood." Admittedly it has experts. No faith or law so intricate and meticulous could lack them and survive. The equality of all Muslim believers does not mean that any Sālih, Hasan, or Mustafā can claim to interpret the law. Sometimes "shaikh-hood" has established a stranglehold over intellectual and religious life, resembling the worst features of priestcraft, though from contrasted origins. But every believer in Islam has equal access to God and needs no human mediator.

When Muslims, however, declaim against Christianity and deplore its priestriddenness, they often overlook that they are proceeding upon assumptions that large segments of Christianity itself have repudiated and cast out. The New Testament knows of no such spiritual slavery to lords of God's flock. The Apostles themselves had most sober and humble estimates of their authority. There has also been a Reformation. We can only plead for that concept of ministry upon which our own understanding of the mind of Christ proceeds. It is, so seen, an instrument to God's truth, not a stranglehold on the believer. The role of Christian ministers in prayer and sacrament does not make the lay believer their dependent. On the contrary, the minister officiates for, and by sanction of, the whole. Prayer does not cease to be personal and spontaneous for being sometimes liturgical. Just as the law of Islam is considered as necessarily in the custody of those who have consecrated their lives and studies to understand it, so the good news of God, and the ministry of Word and sacraments that serves it, are entrusted to those who have devoted themselves to this holy service and have been recognized by the whole body and enabled so to do.

As for the sacraments themselves, how little they have been interpreted to Muslims! Islam, in its own way, is sacramental. Washing before prayer, posture in prayer, the *qiblah* toward Mecca, pilgrimage, and Ramadān—all these and much more are examples of material expression and spiritual meaning. There are clues in them all for an understanding of the baptismal water and the communion of the body and the blood. Concede the contrasted origins in law and in grace, the sacramental principle is the same. Indeed the Muslim might agree from the Qur'ān that the whole universe is sacramental, that it symbolizes and expresses the divine majesty.

In the Christian faith in the Incarnation we have the utmost focus of the truth that this physical realm of our world can become expressive of the living God. The Christian meanings in the bread and wine, emblems of the suffering of the Word made flesh, are almost unknown to Muslims, fortified as they are by the *a priori* rejection of the Cross. But they have already in their own form that which may serve to illumine something of the principle, if not the heart, in the Christian usage. It might be well for us to remember that in the breaking of the bread Jesus was known to those whose eyes until then had been "restrained," so that they did not recognize him. Perhaps we have not been careful enough to let the Muslim see the Church in its sacramental communion with the living Christ. Though reverent words can explain the objective meaning of the service, only the reality of communion can show its fullness. Somehow the clues must be got through to the "strangers."

XXII

This reflection leads into two final points. The Holy Communion is the sacrament of one bread and one cup and, therefore, the sacrament of unity. The Christian explanation of the Church, in word and in life, must not evade the tragedy of division. Sectarianism and divisiveness afflict all great religions in varying form and measure. That honest Muslims know the problem in their own culture does not absolve honest Christians from facing it in theirs.

There are some sources of separated Christian loyalties that are not serious. Differences of language, heritage, and environment readily explain divergencies in expression and justify separate organization for worship. There are other differences in order and pattern that are softened, if not entirely obviated, by genuine cooperativeness and mutual fellowship. We must interpret to the non-Christian world the increasing significance of the ecumenical movement and the growing practical interdependence of many churches. It is also true that deep and undeniable urgings underlie many historic divisions, urgings to freedom and conscience, to obedience in faith, to independence from usurping control, whose denial would be worse than schism, because they enshrine values that no mere conformity or external unity could outweigh. The lessons of those rebellions and their benediction even for the churches they challenged are part of our heritage. Christian division is, in some senses, the high cost of a priceless thing.

Yet, when all these considerations are kept in mind, Christian disunity remains a perpetual embarrassment to Christian interpretation. Impressive as is ecumenical progress, there is a rapid increase in missionary sects dedicated to noncooperation. Even more serious is the unjustified will to be different within the common heritage. Christians are still too much divided over too many issues for too little reasons. Some practical consequences will be considered in the next chapter. The interpreter's duty is a frank honesty with what we have failed to be and a frank sincerity about our vocation among Muslims. "We have this treasure in earthen vessels" (2 Cor. 4:7). But we have it. The Christ, even though we disserve while we serve him, is the lover of all souls. It is him we commend.

The other consideration is that of the obvious necessity of seeking the wisdom and grace to be genuinely hospitable. The meaning of the Church is more often "caught" than taught. Too many theologians and ecclesiastics have gone astray in the past by seeking to locate the true Church, when they should have sought simply to be it. In the end the Church will not so much identify itself by description, as be identified by others in recognition. We have the duty to explain what Christians are: we have at least as great a duty to be them. How better shall fellowship be understood than in a hospitable Christian community? Not a few Muslims have more readily discovered Christ in the home and family, even on the tennis court and wayside, than before the pulpit or the platform.

How important it is to invite Muslims as such, with no reservations, into some active piece of Christian enterprise, some cooperative scheme of rural welfare or human service in which they may discover the impulse of the love of Christ. Here, perhaps, best of all they may face the meaning of life and discover what challenge and what mission Christ may bring. Like the first disciples, some come to Christ because he leads them out to others; from the service of others they move onward into the secret of his Cross. Service truly follows faith; but the faith that saves the soul may well be generated in the will to save others.

Active interpretation is, then, the final benediction. Let us strive so to conform our homes, our loves, our professions, our offices, our leisure, and our affairs, to the allegiance of Christ so that others may take knowledge of him in what we have allowed his grace to make of us. Though the Church must surely explain its concepts, the bearings of its life, its origins, and its nature, it will most surely communicate itself in the men and women in whose hearts its doctrines of grace have become a personal hospitality to the needs and fears and hopes of their fellows. In this way others take knowledge of them that they have been with Jesus and that they are still in his company. In this way the Church is discovered—and in the Church all the rich meanings of God, the Scriptures, the Cross, and the Christ, which constitute its life in history and compel it still into mission to the world.

xi

THE CALL TO HOPE AND FAITH

I

In one of Archbishop Temple's prayers occurs the petition: "Grant us to know when by patience and when by impatience we can serve Thee best." There are, it is true, situations which call for the impatience that rejects the plea of caution and refuses to evade imperatives by calling them precipitate. But in face of an obligation such as Islam presents, there can be little question that patience is the evident need. Yet how difficult of achievement is the true patience that never lapses into apathy and indifference and always keeps the clear vision of its purpose. Such patience is not the recumbent sort that Wordsworth once remarked in an old man of his acquaintance:

> He is invariably subdued
> To settled quiet: he is one by whom
> All effort seems forgotten: one to whom
> Long patience hath such mild composure given
> That patience now doth seem a thing
> Of which he hath no need.

The Church, on the contrary, has great need of patience in being summoned to restless effort in a field where visible external success is little found.

Under this personal theme it is proposed to gather, in conclusion, certain aspects of the Christian relation to Islam with which there has been no opportunity hitherto to deal, but which are inseparable from what we have discovered of the call of the minaret to the Christian.

The question of converts, their number and their trials, is often raised in the Church whenever its appropriate ministry among Muslims is discussed. Those who know little else about Islam know that it has a tremendous resistant quality and that the way of Christian baptism is slow and hard. There are some who, in days of urgency everywhere and limitations of resources and personnel, tend to approve the diversion of personnel and funds away from Muslim areas to more receptive territories. Or, sensing the dubious validity of such an outlook, they remain perplexed and dismayed about Islam, even when they continue with persistence. Individual witnesses, who bear the problem in their own persons, are similarly bewildered and burdened by the apparent fruitlessness of their devotion.

The first point to be made is that no Christian mission is constituted in its success, and none, therefore, is invalidated by numerical failure. The whole point of the argument has been missed if it is not clear that there is a Christian obligation to Islam that neither begins nor ends in how Muslims respond. It is rooted in the nature of Christ and his Gospel. It derives from the nature of Islam in its unawareness. It springs from the situation we have tried to convey:

> Over all things brooding
> The quiet sense of something lost.

If Christ is what Christ is, he must be uttered. If Islam is what Islam is, that "must" is irresistible. Wherever there is misconception, witness must penetrate; wherever there is the obscuring of the beauty of the Cross, it must be unveiled; wherever persons have missed God in Christ, he must be brought to them again.

This book has failed in its purpose if it is not indubitably clear that, in such a situation as Islam presents, the Church has no option but to present Christ.

This is a categorical imperative. It should be plain to all in either faith-community that Christian mission is not a calculus of success, but an obligation in love. Statistics do not make it, nor can they unmake it. Nor is it always a Christian thing to ask to know where we are going. It is not ours to see the full consequences or conditions of our duty. We may have only one clear light to guide us. But it suffices that it should be clear. All the corollaries of our obedience we may not be able to explain, or even understand. It suffices that we obey. As long as Christ is Christ, and the Church knows both itself and him, there will be a mission to Islam.

When this is indubitably plain, then it may be added that, precisely for the same reasons, response in faith and baptism is of vital concern and importance. We present Christ for the sole, sufficient reason that he deserves to be presented. But we cannot neglect that Christ claims discipleship and that his Gospel is something expecting a verdict.

Part of our trouble, however, lies in our presuppositions about how the verdict shall be given and assessed. We are tempted to demand that it conform to familiar Western patterns and we do not sufficiently allow for the unpredictability of the Gospel. Inasmuch as all the nations, including the Muslim, are to bring their glory and honor into the kingdom, we must be ready for the unexpected when Christ comes into his own in human hearts and cultures. All that Christ will be to Muslims, only Muslims can declare.

At the same time it is true that there are historic patterns of discipleship, recognizably Christian, and that there is a traditional framework of response, even though "the wind bloweth where it listeth." We must, therefore, face the whole question of baptism in the Muslim context. A book such as this would have betrayed its readers if it failed to take up this issue.

II

It should be insisted first that baptism belongs to the personal realm. (It will be argued below that it is not necessarily an *individ-*

ual matter and attention is, therefore, called to the choice of the word "personal.") Baptism marks, confirms, and seals a personal response. Their purpose of the Christian mission is not cultural displacement. It is the presentation of Christ as Savior within every culture. The Christian Church, as we have seen in the last section of the preceding chapter, supposes and concedes the coexistence of the external world. That world may be characterized by many varying patterns of life. The objective of mission is not to make a nominal "Christendom" universal. The world that is the context of the Church, of whatever cultural character, is not, of course, exempt from its concern, its compassion, and its duty. The Church will be obligated in love toward all of it all the time.

Baptism, bringing persons within the Church, means their incorporation by faith into the supranational fellowship of Christ. It does not, properly understood, deculturalize new believers: it enchurches them. "Enchurchment," as its impact widens, bears creatively upon all areas of its context. New Christians become responsible to Christ for their old setting and to their old setting in the new truth. But they are not thereby "going foreign." All that is not incompatible with Christ goes with them into baptism. Conversion is not "migration"; it is the personal discovery of the meaning of the universal Christ within the old framework of race, language, and tradition. But implicit in this view of personal faith is a concept of religion and society that Islam has not hitherto recognized. Here lies one of our deepest problems and our need for magnanimous patience.

The Muslim concept of toleration has been, from the beginning, that of freedom to remain what you were born or freedom to become a Muslim. It has never yet meant freedom of movement of conscience, or freedom to become. It was Muslims, rather than non-Muslims, who had the lesser range of intellectual and spiritual possibility. Islam has been traditionally proud of its toleration based on the famous Quranic saying: "There is no compulsion in religion." Modern Muslim commentators fully share that pride. Expositions of Muslim toleration can readily be found in a score of publications and journals. But the fundamental question as to whether there is personal freedom of the Muslim vis-à-vis Islam is not faced and is often not even suspected as present. It is assumed that Islam is a faith that no Muslim would ever conceivably wish to question. Consequently the option to do so is neither valid nor feasible. It is nonexistent. Looked at from this side Islam is a faith that no adherent is free to leave. And that which one is not free to leave becomes a prison, if one wishes to do so.

On this point it does not matter whether the option is ever taken. A true understanding of freedom, as freedom of movement of mind, demands that the option should exist. Nor does it matter for what alternative the option is required. Islam ought to concede such freedom regardless of any possible consequences to its members. If it is to be a self-respecting faith, it must retain its adherents in the sole strength of their freely willed conviction. Doubtless it does so hold multitudes of its people. But the test comes when the negative corollary is asserted that freedom of belief must include freedom of disbelief, and freedom of adherence, freedom of nonadherence. The plain fact is that, hitherto, such freedom has not existed among Muslims.

When Islam arose and expanded into the world, Arabia was required to be solidly and exclusively Muslim. But elsewhere, scriptural minorities—Jews and Christians—and some others not implicated in idolatry, were permitted, as we have seen, to remain as tolerated and tributary minorities. Their physical and spiritual disabilities varied from age to age and from place to place. Their members might rise to positions of dignity and wealth, or they might lead a harassed and precarious existence. But always Islam was the dominant religion, identified with imperial power and enjoying its prestige.

Minorities tended to become introspective, furtive, and depressed. Those born within them were not normally compelled to islamize. Armenian, Coptic, Syrian, or other Christians were not required to forsake the faith of their forebears. But there was often the expectation that they would. Circumstances were such that it took considerable tenacity, often a kind of hopeless doggedness, to remain Christian.

There was certainly no expectation of Christian revival and growth. There were prohibitions—for example, on the building of new churches—that were symptomatic of the outlook. The freedom was a freedom to remain. The only direction in which one could move was into Islam. Movement of allegiance was all in one direction. The born Jew, the born Christian, had, paradoxically, an option that the Muslim lacked. They at least could move into Islam. The Muslim could not move out.[1]

Some elements in Islam today understand and interpret Islamic nationalism and the Islamic state in the same sense. They wish to ensure that Islamic society will be self-preserving in the old authoritarian way. For when, in the modern period, Muslims came under non-Muslim rule in a complete reversal of the proper status of the Muslim, the protection of Islam became a duty of some imperial or mandatory government. Now that Islam has in so many areas come back into self-responsibility, the conservative elements wish to ensure that the traditional pattern will be resumed. Others, however, for practical or patriotic reasons, wish to interpret nationalism more liberally and to find some religious modus vivendi, with the concept of equal citizenship for all minorities. But not many are willing, or perhaps we should say able, to contemplate all the religious corollaries of equal citizenship. They are searching for some form of religious freedom short of the secular state.

Thus the present time sees a crucial debate on a very wide issue, and great changes may be waiting in the whole concept of freedom in Islam in the next decades. The problem is now squarely on the shoulders of Muslims themselves. Foreign governments have now everywhere withdrawn. The protection, sometimes the encouragement, of minorities is no longer a foreign duty or temptation.[2]

Here it may be noted in passing that much nonsense has been aired about the so-called partnership between mission and empire. It may be that imperial expansion facilitated missionary expression in some instances, but there is at least as much evidence of imperial policy curbing and frustrating missionary effort as there is of its fostering and aiding it.

But the point here is that a Muslim solution regarding what is to be done about the Islamic state, about religious freedom, and about the non-Muslim citizen, has now to be evolved. Our duty is to strive to bear witness to the obligation of any self-respecting religion, however it be related to a political expression, to encourage and allow a true freedom of movement of worship and belief. For only so can it be in the truest sense a genuine religious faith.

The legal forms of such an ideal are hard to shape and actualize in a society so inured to one religious form. But the genuine test of any democracy is the freedom of minority to become the majority if it can. Or stated conversely it is where the majority does not interpret or use its preponderance oppressively.

Several Muslim states in the United Nations have withheld their signature from the Declaration of Human Rights because of its insistence that freedom of religion means freedom to become as well as to remain. On the other hand, Sir Zafrullāh Khān, when Foreign Minister of Pakistan, made his now celebrated recognition of the right of all religions to peaceful self-propagation within a Muslim state, on the ground that Islam itself was a missionary religion. The right of propagation presumably includes the right to receive adherents and the right of all citizens to become adherents. But there are long legal and constitutional battles ahead on the question of such freedom.

The problem, moreover, is not only one of law. Law, in such a realm, must finally reflect and enforce opinion. If it is to be successful, it must be believed to be right. Though the harsh penalties of the old Muslim law of apostasy—disinheritance and death—have been legally suspended or nullified in most areas, public attitudes, economic or commercial sanctions, and social ostracism continue to be potent adversaries of actual freedom. What is needed is a profound revolution in the public attitude in which religion will come to be recognized as not finally a fit realm for any kind of compulsion. This in turn needs powerful intellectual enterprise—Islam might call it *ijtihād*—to shape popular conceptions and ensure their effectiveness. The issue is an internal one for Islam.

III

Our Christian duty is to serve this situation as patiently and sympathetically as we can, trying to uphold the ideal of a religious allegiance that is not even indirectly compelled, and endeavoring to communicate the gathered significance of Western trial and error on this very same point. There are many pitfalls. One is to base the plea for real toleration on the ground that religion is an entirely private affair, relating to the individual and God alone. That view is mischievously incomplete and unbalanced. Neither Christianity nor Islam, properly considered, can tolerate it. Both in their different ways bear witness to the fact that the truths of revelation relate to the life of society and to the responsibilities of government. We cannot properly immunize the whole realm of the state from the significance of religion. Nor are any intelligent Muslims who understand their own heritage likely to accept such a position, unless it be in desperation. The purely secular state, like mere positivism in education, runs into too many weaknesses and errors in the lack of a religious frame of reference. It has been part of the historic genius of Islam to insist on the close interrelation of faith and society, of religion and state.[3]

Another pitfall is to express the necessary interconnection between the religious and the political in such a way as to jeopardize religious freedom. Something of the Christian concept of the two communities has been suggested in the previous chapter. A way has to be found to symbolize and make operative the truth that human life in all its aspects stands under the law of God, without so identifying that law with any religious authority or hierarchy as to limit the freedom of mind and conscience that is the prerequisite of valid religious conviction and allegiance. The Christian Church has much experience to share with Muslims at this point, if it can achieve the right relationship to transmit it.

One of the realms where religious forms in law and society are liable to become indirectly coercive is that of personal-status law (related to marriage, divorce, wardship, and inheritance). As long as religious communities have an exclusive prerogative over matters of marriage, divorce, and inheritance, relating to their members, there will remain a serious infraction of genuine religious liberty. Change of status will not be freely possible if marriage rights, inheritance, and the rest are not brought into line. Only the existence of alternative procedures in matters of personal status can ensure that communities do not exercise a stranglehold upon their members.

Personal-status law is part of the millet system (in which tolerated minorities exercise their own jurisdiction). It is a system open to manipulation and one that perpetuates a sectarian mentality in society. It is not Islam alone that clings to it. A strong desire in Lebanon by a group of lawyers to secure a bill establishing secular marriage and divorce evoked successful opposition from the Christian hierarchy no less than from the Muslim. But such secular marriage would be a real symbol of and means to freedom from a religious community to which a citizen no longer inwardly belongs. The millet system makes religious communities self-perpetuating whether they deserve to be or not, and irrespective of the consent of all who are within them.[4]

It may be hoped, however, that nationalism and other pressures will considerably modify the millet system in these matters. Elsewhere it is clearly in retreat. Are there grounds for hope that an urge for some modification of the official religious attitude toward adherence and its legal sanctions can steadily grow and that the deterrents, direct and indirect, to the freedom of communal interchange will be diminished? Islam would be all the sounder for such developments, precisely because its allegiance would be less formal and so more real, less inevitable and so more spontaneous. And Christianity would have the greater opportunity to bear its witness and to express its allegiance to Christ in every realm. Only a timid or mistaken calculus could fear that Islam would be weakened. Whatever "secular" losses there might be numerically, its status religiously could not fail to be more validly based. Fear and timidity are, after all, poor and unworthy defenders of real faith.

We have insisted that the Christian's duty in this matter of Muslim religious toleration, legal and actual, is primarily to exalt and serve the ideal. Freedom of conscience has an absolute value that transcends all special pleading. We are not seeking such changes primarily for the benefit of potential converts. Nor should thoughtful Muslims resist them for the sake of deterring such converts. The matter is not one to be judged by particular consequences for or against. It is to be judged for its absolute consequences in purer religion and more validly based allegiance—consequences that cannot be outweighed by numbers lost or gained.

It is clear, nonetheless, that such freedom in Islam would, in serving the quality of Muslim conviction, also lift a heavy incubus from Christian evangelism. Inquirers would no longer be intimi-

dated by family consequences; Muslim converts would no longer
be under inappropriate difficulties as to marriage, nor would they
have to face disinheritance. Considerations of legal status would
not inhibit the free pursuit of religious inquiry. The ex-Muslim
would not be worried or persecuted into mental instability or become a rootless protégé of some alien friend.

If it be argued that such a hope is dim and distant and, therefore, impractical, our retort is that we have not advocated it on
the grounds of expediency. There can be no doubt that the ultimate hope of the Christian is for just such a change in Muslim
attitudes to toleration. It may be long, or longer, before particular areas begin to feel the liberating consequences of such a
change, where now even to evince the least interest in Christianity
is to invite personal tragedy in some form.

If readers tend to be skeptical of its possibility, they may be
reminded that this chapter has to do with hope and faith—and
hence patience, and that the principle here sought is one that can
be argued from a valid extension of Quranic and traditional
Muslim teaching. Let it also be remembered that the strong pressures of secularism, undesirable as in some respects they are, tend
in the same direction. Anglo-Saxon freedoms owe much to those
who defied Christian institutions in their passion for a fundamentally Christian thing. Could not patience in some senses be defined as expecting the unexpected? That at least we must learn to
do.

IV

Patience is not visionary. Assuming that such changes are our
ultimate hope and that they are to be sought for their own sake, is
there any evidence that Christ attracts and satisfies the Muslim
heart? Is the record of Muslim response to Christianity convinc-
ing in quality, if scanty in extent? Is there not ground for suspicion that the Church in Muslim lands has been singularly
unfruitful, despite decades of devotion as sacrificial as any
achieved in other fields where sizable churches now exist? Is there
hope that, as and when the possibility of response becomes
greater, and even before, the peoples of the mosque will have an
ear for Christ?

The answer is yes. There is firm ground for the belief that many do and will reach out hands toward the Gospel, patiently and imaginatively presented, despite the antipathy toward it of much in the Muslim temper. Part of the evidence is the personal stature and fidelity of Muslim Christians through the years when disabilities and persecution have been unceasing. There is no space here for any detailed account of these examples. The largest Christian communities of former Muslims are in Indonesia and India.[5] Elsewhere in the Muslim world, Christian communities are either ancient churches of apostolic foundation and communal continuity, containing almost no former Muslims, or else churches of Western planting, linked in some form with Rome or Protestantism and containing some members of Muslim origin but many more whose forebears transferred from the ancient churches. Arabic-speaking Christianity of Muslim background is a saga of the few.

Nevertheless, there has been a tenuous succession of notable as well as of obscure Muslims who have come to Christ. Their quality rebukes the fear that Islam is impervious to the meaning of the Gospel, and their fewness is at least in part explained by the mountainous obstacles that have confronted them and the crippling disabilities and inadequacies of the Christian mission. The source of amazement is not so much that there are few as that there are any. For mission, though devoted, has often been clumsy, beset with handicaps of personnel, of language, of poverty in resources, of inexperience, as well as burdened with the associations of a disloyal "Christendom." They who contemplate mission to Islam should remember to think before they start to count.

A few names may be cited. One of the earliest pioneers of medical missions in India was a former Muslim shaikh, Sālih, master of the jewels at the Court of Oudh, who took the baptismal name 'Abd al-Masīh and became a Christian minister. He was led to seek Christ through the preaching of Henry Martyn, whom he assisted in New Testament translation. He understood the implications of the Gospel and years before medical missions were known in India (indeed any organized missions, for Martyn and his successors were East India Company chaplains),[6] 'Abd al-Masīh established a dispensary for which he qualified himself and on which he spent his own personal resources. His pioneer example it was that stimulated English medical ministry in the subcontinent.

Another 'Abd al-Masīh, who died in 1953, became a fervent and effective minister of Christ. His story may be cited simply because it embodies so many characteristic features of the Muslim encounter with Christ, its course and its costs. Born of uneducated parents in a village 150 miles south of Cairo, he was sent to the mosque school, where he became a memorizer of the Qur'ān and began at seven years the performance of the prayers. One day the young scholar found an Arabic Gospel of St. Matthew in the street. Picking it up, he read it aloud to friends until the blind schoolmaster intervened and after inquiry tore it in pieces. He ordered his two sons to burn the pieces and washed his hands afterward to cleanse the defilement at handling the Christian book. The boy's father took him later from the mosque school and sent him to a Christian school, for no special reason. Indelibly in the boy's mind was the belief that to touch St. Matthew's Gospel was to be defiled. He was horrified, therefore, to find there were copies of this book in the new school. He refused to attend the school until his father and some friends arranged with the headmaster that the boy would not have to handle St. Matthew's Gospel.

But morning and evening prayers were a further problem. The father was unwilling to seek exemption. "So I had to content myself with sitting on the last bench of the little church and stuffing my fingers into my ears lest I should hear any word of the singing or prayers." Some time later in a friend's house he made acquaintance with the Psalms, and later, at a postfuneral visit, heard a pastor reading from St. Matthew's Gospel. The words gripped him and despite his earlier certainty that the book would defile him, he sought it out to read it. The reading went on in secret and extended to other parts of the Bible. There came a consequent search for forgiveness and a growing sense of need, which sent him to Muslim friends and teachers to learn more about Islam. The form of his questions roused those teachers to suspicion that he was "corrupted" by Christians. They assured him that to be a Muslim was to be secure and that God would pardon all who said the *Shahādah*. But a deepening restlessness possessed him, with a growing despair about any change of heart through a faith that did not recognize the nature of his need. Finally in great soul-concern he turned again to St. Matthew and found peace in the words: "Come to me all you who labor and I will give you rest." He resolved to join the Christian fellowship and to confess his trust in Christ as Savior. "Then I begged the Lord to make me an evangelist that I might tell others of the love he had given to me."

The transaction of that solitary encounter with the forgiving Christ led to a confession like that of St. Thomas: "My Lord and my God." But it also entailed strong persecution. The boy's father put him in a dark storeroom for several weeks, on a ration of bread and water. He was beaten. When he was released he was ridiculed in the streets. "The children used to clap their hands on seeing me and chant 'Here comes the infidel.' Often they threw stones and dust at me, whilst men in the streets spat in my face and struck me on the head with their fists. These persecutions continued for about eighteen months."[7] The sequel of the story tells of baptism two years after, of theological study and ordination.

The name of Marcus 'Abd al-Masīh was loved throughout Egypt, Syria, and Sudan as that of a devoted contemporary witness to the love of Christ. It must stand in our narrative here as representative of many more: Mikhā'īl Mansūr of Al-Azhar; Mirzā Ibrāhīm of Tabriz; Chauduri Ināyat Ullāh of Qadiān; Sa'īd Kurdistānī of Teheran; John Subhān, author of *How a Sufi Found his Lord*; Dilawar Khān and Jehān Khān of the Pathan hills; Sima'ān Dibūnȳ of Palestine. Whatever else these names proclaim, they demonstrate that there are Muslim minds to open with gladness when Christ comes seeking. But great as are the stories of these individuals and their kind, the difficulties they encountered and the realization that there were many others, unknown to us, who never survived the mental or emotional strain of their desire to become Christ's compel us to face earnestly the question of baptismal concepts and policies.

V

The New Testament summons plainly involves the possibility of family antagonism and personal persecution. "A man's foes shall be they of his own household." "If anyone will come after me let him take up the cross and follow me." We cannot seek, either for ourselves or for others, to facilitate the Christian life so as to be disloyal to its nature. The Church of the apostolic generation became a church of the catacombs. Costliness has always been a characteristic ingredient of Christian discipleship. The Christian Church is called to be so firm a fellowship that in its company nothing shall be too hard to undertake that may be required of us by obedience to Christ. That the Gospel is set forth unto all nations for "the obedience of faith" is St. Paul's classic expression of the purpose of the witness of the Church. As in Christ's earthly ministry, so when he is proclaimed throughout history, he is the Master and Savior awaiting a verdict.

But the more insistently we recognize that Christianity is a confessed discipleship, the more urgently we must face the problems implicit in such confession in the Muslim world. We must also have regard to the corollaries for such discipleship of the way we administer the external forms of the confession of Christian faith. It would be wrong to administer baptism as a seal of individual confession, without regard to how the form was understood in the community we are also calling into discipleship. The baptism of the one cannot be in disconnection with the evangelizing of the many. On this point the mind of St. Paul is clear. "Christ," he said, "sent me not to baptize but to preach the Gospel."

We cannot administer baptism in unconcern about the unity and quality of the Church into which we baptize and in whose strength of comradeship the individual alone can "come victor." We cannot administer baptism without patient concern for the potential misunderstandings of the watching, often apprehensive, community. There are some who have sought it as a kind of charm and others who have been suspicious of it for the same reason. Arab mothers, for example, have kept their children from the hands of nurses who might wash them, for fear that the nurses might at the same time mumble over them some formula which would turn them surreptitiously into Christians.

For these and many other reasons there have been some within Christian mission who have wondered whether in the Muslim context the familiar pattern of isolated individual baptism should not be reconsidered as being too "impatient" a way. The questions at issue are so real and go so deep that, although no specific answer is offered here, it is well to state them briefly, as part of that travail in patience that is Christian mission.

It should first be made indubitably clear that baptism, after proper safeguards have been met, should never be positively and permanently withheld from those who responsibly seek it in good faith and of their own volition. In such circumstances no policy has a right to impede the seeker. The problem is not whether baptism should be withheld, but whether it should be encouraged or invariably sought on our part.

Those who suggest that perhaps it should not, have no desire to obscure the decisive quality of Christian discipleship or to obviate the cost and duty of witness. Nor is there any compromise on the theological question of the relation of baptism to faith. The purpose rather is to foster such witness and faith in a more promising way and in a more hopeful setting. It is clear that a Christian interest, a Christian seeking, cannot and should not be hidden. But baptism into Christ, as an individual step, has features that unnecessarily complicate and aggravate the task of Christian presentation.

In the first place Muslim society is not individualist but communal. Therefore is the individual the appropriate unit of baptism? Perhaps forms of new allegiance might be more meaningfully fulfilled in community. Official baptism may have in Muslim eyes an appearance of treason, because of strong communal and national ties attaching to Islam. In the New Testament days and in the modern West, baptism does not mean a rejection of particular citizenship. In the modern Muslim East it seems to mean that. The Muslim in the Arab world thinks of the Christian Church as a separate millet perhaps with a different language, certainly with a different "ethos" and different cohesion. What is a renunciation of sin looks to one's kin as denunciation of all that makes one "belong."

There is certainly an urgent need to militate strongly against this overwhelming Muslim concept of what baptism means and implies. The question is: Do we militate against it by playing into its hands? Is there a way of demonstrating that to become a Christian is not to become alien? Can we strive for that understanding of the institution of baptism on the part of Muslims? Has this, for a period at least, a priority over its unthinking application to particular people? It is argued that the more disposed we are to emphasize the ultimate indispensability of baptism to Christian discipleship the more concerned we should be that the relevance of the institution to discipleship should not be misread by the multitudes for whom the Gospel is meant. Will such misreading be corrected unless we strenuously set out to do so?

Is it possible to familiarize the Muslim with the truth that becoming a Christian is no repudiation of community, that it does not rob Muslim society, as such, of a genuine servant and the local community of commitment? How can we demonstrate that to become a Christian is to remain responsible in some sense for "Muslim" citizenship? If we are anxious, as we have argued above, to develop in at least some Muslims a less totalitarian view of the relation between dogma and society, shall we allow them to persist in a concept of baptism that is just as totalitarian? If we believe in a Church within a culture, shall we make the door into that Church a door right out of the culture? "Let not your good be evil spoken of," said St. Paul. He meant that we have a responsibility toward the concepts others form of our institutions insofar as we can affect and shape those concepts.

What, then, can be done to encourage in Islam the truth that becoming a Christian is not ceasing to belong with Muslim need, Muslim thought, and Muslim kin? Some have thought that the answer is to pioneer for a new status, in which those who respond, or desire to respond, to Christ might be encouraged to associate with fellow, or potentially fellow, Christians, without alienating their old context irrevocably by any formal step that that context will so interpret. Let it be clear that no sincere seeker will be hidden and unknown. The suggestion is not secret belief. There will be issues such as forms of prayer and fasting that will be invaded by new liberty and new meaning. But that newness of life will not be taken formally and officially out of the old context so as greatly to jeopardize the chances for that context to understand what it is.

It may be argued that this would jeopardize the opportunities of the "prebaptized" to grow in what they have found and of finding it further. In answer it is said that any such pioneer status, not yet baptized, should have the fullest fellowship and spiritual support of the Church. It will demand qualities no less tenacious than those that characterize the finally baptized. It is offered as something to which the Church must encourage new seekers and in which it must stand with them, as a creative venture. The Church must be ready to think out and sustain in prayer and fellowship all the implications of the new status. It is believed that "lovers of Jesus," or a fellowship under some other designation, may go further in preparing Christ's way among Muslims than would the same persons if promptly and singly baptized into a fellowship still largely alien, not of Muslim background, and set (by one initial transaction) out of reach of the Muslim mind.

When St. Paul argues about meats in the New Testament he suggests that what are duties (of distinction) in one context may be overridden in another, and that there are liberties (of enjoying) which may rightly be self-denied. Can, then, an undoubted right and privilege be foregone *for the sake of those for whom Christ died*, without jeopardizing its standing as a right and a privilege? It might have been argued that St. Paul was endangering a liberty by refraining from its use. But love was paramount and the liberty was safe in those hands. Baptism may well appear compromised in the proposal to hold back from it, until it is seen that those for whom Christ died have, in the reckoning of love, a prior claim.

There are many facets of this approach that cannot here be further considered. Its advocates insist that full and loving provision must be made for the spiritual nurture of all "lovers of Jesus" if baptism is left in abeyance. The only objective is to encourage the hope and ideal of larger and more viable units of baptism than the individual, and to discourage Muslim misconception and antagonism. All the theological truth about the final place and necessity of baptism is recognized and upheld in a more patient effort to obey it.[8]

The ultimate question which has in any case to be faced is: To what quality of Christian life and witness are we to try to call Muslim seekers? How should we encourage them to relate themselves to their community of origin, for it cannot fail to remain in some measure their community? Ultimately, there is no escaping these questions, for the quality and direction of soul of those who learn Christ from among our Muslim friends is the key to the Muslim world. The best witness is witness from within. No people of a community is ever won except by identification with it ("I sat where they sat," Ezek. 3:15). As long as mission is primarily "foreign," it will ultimately fail to be mission. We must adhere, at all costs, to creative loyalty to Christ, in all things.

Here, then, are the issues. The unit of Christianity is undoubtedly the person, but persons belong in communities and to cultures. We must preach so as to expect an answer to the offer of Christ. We cannot be accountable for all the motives of interest and response, though these depend in large measure upon the quality of the communication. Our institutional relationship to the Muslim seeker must be disarming and patient, but always hopeful. Douglas Thornton of Cairo used to remark that he never knew which of his student friends might not prove a Saul of Tarsus. Nor must we have too Western an idea of what response to Christ is going to mean for those who hear us. If we have the right to say of the patriarchs, "They without us shall not be made perfect," surely Easterners have the right to say it to us. When their response comes we must "lay them on our shoulders rejoicing." This may well be the hardest part. If they have a cost to count, legal obstacles, economic difficulties, possible unemployment, so also have we, a cost of quiet nurture and of unstinting friendship that does not weaken the fibers of personal character.

VI

These responsibilities lead into another theme of great importance. It certainly belongs under "hope and faith." It is the spiritually welcoming quality that ought to belong to the local church. Part of the problem of baptism is that the Church is as yet so imperfectly fitted to be a true home for the soul and mind of the Muslim. The newer churches of Western planting, especially in the Arab world, are not spontaneously hospitable to Muslim seekers, whose good faith may be doubted, their presence mistrusted, and their interest questioned. Locally there is great reluctance to contemplate uninhibited friendship.

Many churches, moreover, operate under legal conditions that regard them as self-contained, not self-propagating, units. Their authority to worship, to solemnize marriages, to own property, and the like, is contingent on their observing a policy of "introversion." By a legacy of the millet concept, it is difficult for them to be at once communities of worship and communities of evangelism. This is a cruel dilemma, but a real one. The situation compels them to practice, if not also to feel, severe prudential reservations about baptism outside their own families. The legal difficulties tend to foster or excuse a certain spiritual lack of adventure in evangelism. The solutions call for long patience that strives for a steady deepening of the will to be hospitable and a removal of legal deterrents.

But Christianity in the Eastern mind is not primarily represented by these new churches. Through the Arab world, in Turkey, in southern India, and in Ethiopia the ancient Christian Apostolic patriarchates of the Greek Orthodox, Coptic, Armenian, and other communions constitute by far the most important expression of Christian faith and worship. Books on these churches have been included in the Book List, below. A sympathetic knowledge of them is indispensable to the Western Christian. There is no opportunity here to begin to do justice to their significance.

Missionary relationships with the Christian churches of the East have often been difficult. Westerners have misunderstood, even despised, their traditions and have failed to enter into the riches of their long devotional continuity. They may have been repelled by features of doctrine or practice that offended their Protestant zeal. Or they have been unable to establish such positive relationships as might enable the mediation of the insights they had to bring, as well as to receive the wealth of fellowship they stood to gain.

The failures, of course, have not been all one-sided. The old traditions, in some of their representatives, were suspicious and apprehensive. They feared for the prestige of their communities not always without reason, for many new churches were recruited from their ranks. They were also unable to make the strenuous efforts required to understand the strange, activist, impatient forms of Western Christianity.

In many directions, however, in more recent years there has been a steady growth of mutual desire for understanding and at least partial cooperation between the old and the new, the Eastern and the Western. The major Eastern communions have shared in the World Council of Churches and have discovered that they can trust and respect many of the Western churches, and the latter have come to see more truly the genius of the orthodox East. In the area of mission, however, there remain serious problems of relationship. The missionary concept toward Islam makes only slow headway against the centuries of exclusiveness by which the Eastern Christian mind is still guided.

Nevertheless cooperative enterprises in the fields of theological education, social welfare, and Christian literature may become increasingly possible. There is great need for recruits to Western mission who will make the understanding of the Eastern churches their prime responsibility and who will seek to interpret differences and heal suspicions and articulate for the Muslim a clearer Christian call. An ambition on our part to be glad junior partners with an awakened and expressive Eastern Christianity would be the truest fulfillment of all the goals discussed here in the chapters in Part 3, "Minaret and Christian."

As a postscript to this bare treatment of a great theme, mention should be made of the distracting but increasing presence of sects on the wing of Western Christianity. These are quite unwilling to cooperate with older missions and certainly not with an Eastern Christianity they find uncongenial. They pay little attention to the comity of missions; efforts to work cooperatively meet with scant response and sometimes open rejection. Yet these groups exercise considerable influence and command large resources. They are liable to confuse the situation both for Christian and Muslim. Yet a staunchly Christian attitude toward them must be maintained at all costs by the "old-line" churches. They may serve perhaps to chasten complacency and deepen patience. They stimulate by contrast the need to preserve a well-rounded Gospel and to remember that there are very few single truths that will bear exclusive preaching. Extremism sometimes overreaches itself. St. Paul learned to rejoice in all things. It is finally by the quality of our apprehension of Christ and devotion to him that we may hope to deserve to succeed. In all our relationships "let this mind be in us that was also in Christ Jesus."

VII

There remains here one final consideration. Christian discipleship, unto baptism, presupposes in its personal quality the continuity of the non-Christian context. This does not imply that the Church has no duty to that context other than baptizing persons out of it. On the contrary, as a society within society it has searching responsibilities to the whole. Those who are gathered into the household of grace, by faith, should in virtue of their discipleship become the salt of their community. In proportion to their numbers, they should influence the opinion that fashions behavior and the beliefs that inspire and govern institutions. The social and other corollaries of their discipleship will, in proportion to their strength and fidelity, steadily permeate and discipline the culture of their world.

In this sense there are many things in Muslim society that are compatible with such Christian influence and can be served by it. Hospitality, cleanliness, moderation, simplicity, discipline, dignity, family affection, sensitivity to the poor, and many other traits that characterize Muslim attitudes at their best will be sustained and preserved. Doubtless there are other attitudes, or reasons for holding them, that will be criticized and refused. Their basis in the concept of God and of human nature will be revised. The patterns that changed beliefs unmake will be unmade to the extent in which those beliefs penetrate. But there are others that will be confirmed and others again that become apparent in their quality only when there are enough Christian-Muslims to recognize and make them actual. Perhaps the greatest contribution of all from the "disciples made" will be in the realm not of "what," but of "how," not of particular virtues but the means to them all, if it be true than the constraining love of Christ is the deepest wellspring of unselfish character and unwearied goodness.

Even, however, where personal allegiance is never won, or the Church numerically enlarged, perhaps where these objectives, for any reason, are not even in view, there are endless services that Christian witness can render. It will always be true, of course, that Christian quality belongs essentially in persons and comes to attach only derivatively to laws, or customs, or things. Nevertheless the Christ who said "He who is not with me is against me," also declared: "He who is not against us is on our part," meaning that actions and attitudes could have place in his purpose even when their owners withheld themselves personally from his kingdom. The Church that seeks to proclaim his ethic and to demonstrate his compassion may expect to see these make their way outside its membership. Moreover, we can never say at what point the human soul awakes to the knowledge of Christ. Early discipleship is not always to the same features. In one sense Christian mission is a cause that can never lose, even if it is also one that can rarely gain. If no Christians as such are gathered, this has not disarmed or immobilized the Gospel's criticism of human lives, or its measure of their re-creation. The leaven works silently and unseen. There is nothing barren about the Gospel wherever it is active.

It may even be legitimate, in this connection, to turn to the supposition of absence and attempt to assess the consequences. If Christ did not exist, or the Gospel, or the Church, what of the form of the life of the world and the fashion of its thinking? They would doubtless be unrecognizable. Though a mission to Islam would not be validated solely by the effect of its nonexistence, it is important and legitimate sometimes to remember what the world around might not have been. Results, in other words, are more than those that are measureable. There is much ground for believing that modern versions of the Prophet Muhammad owe something to the parallel of Christ. When compared with those of the earliest historians, who were remarkably frank and unembarrassed, they show differences that are almost all in a direction toward Christ. This may be one form of the impact of the Gospel. The same may be said of tendencies toward reconciliation and freedom. These unseen influences are not yet at an end. They may be part of the unpredictable consequences that Christ-messengers set under way when they intend the conversion of men and women. The Gospel is always bigger than the capacities and expectations of those who take it. These truths, however, do not warrant messengers to forbear to seek what they are taught to seek, by their inward awareness of the nature of what they bring. They will not cease to preach for a verdict they can understand, in their knowledge that other verdicts are being slowly made before God. Theirs is properly a person-to-person relationship, but its potentialities are not to be only personally measured. It has much to render even where it will never baptize.

It is important, therefore, to help the Muslim world to conceive of Christian mission not as predatory but constructive. It is true that it seeks to make disciples: discipleship is what Christ intends and claims. A Christian mission that renounces the making of Christians has forsaken both its genius and its duty. Christ did not serve the world with good advice, and no more shall we. But such discipleship is not "Western aggression"; it is not religious competition. The faith that offers it is not rightly seen as a rival. The truth is not rivalry but relevance.

What Christ and what, therefore, Christian mission hold in trust is profoundly meaningful to the whole life, aspiration, and humanity of the Muslim world. Heralds want only that it be available. The more they contemplate their duty the more surely they feel: "Woe to me if I preach not the Gospel." The call of the minaret is to every Muslim who understands its inclusiveness. But thereby the minaret is also a call to all Christians who understand their Christianity.

These, then, are some of our needs for patience: patience with our partners in the Christian fellowship; patience with monumental misunderstandings that must somehow be removed; patience with the massive external deterrents; patience with inward spiritual unlikeness; patience with ourselves and our proneness to hasty ways and incomplete devotion; the patience of hope and resolve. What matters finally is the presentation of Christ in the full significance, for God and for humankind, of his ministry and his sorrows. The final urge to Christian mission is what Christ is and what, because of him, we know God to be. We must represent the Gospel of Christ in the spirit and fellowship of him from whom it derives.

VIII

Two of the most sacred mosques of the Islamic world look down from their sanctuaries eastward toward the trees of old Gethsemane. From its olive-covered slopes the Garden of the Agony looks westward to the domes and minarets of the ancient skyline. In the still dawn the muezzin can be heard calling to prayer across the valley where Jesus communed with his spirit until midnight and went forth, the Christ of the Cross, the Savior of the world. Through all their history, since the minarets were raised, the two faiths have been that near, that far. It is out of the meaning of the garden that Christ's followers have crossed into the world of the domes and the muezzin. We who, in our generation, listen to the call of the minaret may hear it most compellingly from the muezzin over Gethsemane. There we shall best understand wherewith we must answer—and how, and why.

NOTES

CHAPTER 1

1. Charles M. Doughty, *Travels in Arabia Deserta,* London, 1888, vol. 1, p. 56.

2. See Ahmad Amīn, *Hayātī* ["My Life"], Cairo, 1950, pp. 203–5. Of his father, he writes: "So ended (at the age of 80) an assiduous life, filled with toil and effort in the pursuit of knowledge and a material livelihood. . . . His recollection of death was frequent. He had by heart many traditions about the emptiness of the world and the worthlessness of its affairs before God. . . . The world he knew was his beloved Azhar and the mosque, his books and the neighbors in the quarter. Politics, the Occupation, economic affairs, social and cultural life—of these and everything else beyond the quarter he inhabited—he knew nothing." See also Kenneth Cragg and R. Marston Speight, eds., *Islam from Within: Anthology of a Religion,* Belmont, Cal., 1980, pp. 73–75.

3. Muhammad Fādil Jamālī, *Letters on Islam,* London, 1965, p. 7.

4. Muhammad Iqbāl, *The Reconstruction of Religious Thought in Islam,* Lahore, 1944. He wrote of seeking "fresh energies in the creation of new loyalties, such as patriotism and nationalism," to escape from paralysis. But he saw Islam as essentially "nonterritorial" (pp. 187 and 167).

5. Kwame Nkrumah adapted this phrase from the Sermon on the Mount as the theme of the Convention People's Party that secured the independence of Ghana, the first of the new African states. In Senegal, however, the first president, Leopold Senghor, with his concept of *négritude,* revised it to read: "Seek first the cultural kingdom . . . ," believing, as he did, that a strong sense of identity was a prerequisite of statehood.

327

6. See Ali Shari'ātī, *On the Sociology of Islam,* trans. from the Persian by Hamid Algar, Berkeley, 1979; and *Marxism and Other Western Fallacies,* trans. from the Persian by R. Campbell, Berkeley, 1980.

7. See Fazlur Rahman, *Islam and Modernity: Transformation of an Intellectual Tradition,* Chicago, 1982, pp. 137–40.

8. See Maxine Rodinson, *Islam and Capitalism,* trans. from the French by B. Pearce, London, 1974, pp. 28–58 and 184–235.

9. Khalid Muhammad Khalid, *Min Hunā Nabda'* ["From Here We Start"], Cairo, 1950. The phrase is the title of the fourth chapter. See also Fatimah Mernissi, *Beyond the Veil: Male-Female Dynamics in a Modern Muslim Society,* Cambridge, Mass., 1975.

10. Arnold Toynbee, *Civilization on Trial,* New York, 1948, chap. 10.

11. See note 4, above.

12. Najīb Mahfūz, *Awlād Hāratinā,* Beirut, 1967, trans. from the Arabic by Philip Stewart, *Children of Gebelawi,* London, 1981.

13. Tāhā Husain (1889–1973) was a pioneer of modern Arabic literature, an educationalist, and onetime minister of education in Egypt. His original work on pre-Islamic poetry (*Fī-al Shi'ar al-Jāhilī,* Cairo, 1926) was reissued under the title *Fī al-Adab al-Jāhilī* (["Pre-Islamic Literature"], Cairo, 1927), with modifications. He queried the historicity of traditions about Abraham and Mecca and considered post-Islamic certain poetry that was regarded as antedating Islam. The effect was to arouse vehement hostility because he wrote from a governmental post and his conclusions, though academically strong, transgressed orthodox dogmas.

14. E.g., Fazlur Rahman. His *Major Themes of the Qur'ān* appeared in 1980 (Bibliotheca Islamica, Minneapolis and Chicago).

15. See, e.g., Muhammad Kāmil Husain, *Mutanawwi'āt* ["Miscellany"], Cairo, vol. 2, 1958, pp. 29–37, entitled "Scientific Exegesis of the Qur'ān: A Stupid Heresy."

16. The massive Ansar Camp is in southern Lebanon, where almost every able-bodied adult male Palestinian from the Israeli occupation of Lebanon is imprisoned, without prisoner-of-war status or right of appeal. Their incarceration is the more wretched in that, ironically, Ansar is the name given to those Muslims within Medina who welcomed and accommodated Muhammad and his followers after the *Hijrah* from Mecca in 622.

17. Richard Critchfield, *Shahhat: An Egyptian,* Syracuse, 1978, pp. 218–19.

18. Abdallāh Yūsuf Alī, author of a noted English verse rendering of the Qur'ān (Lahore, 1937). The pamphlet referred to was entitled *Fundamentals of Islam,* published in Geneva, 1929.

19. See note 14, above. For the story of his encounter with fundamentalist adversaries, and his resignation, see his essay "Some Islamic Issues in the Ayyūb Khān Era," in D. P. Little, *Essays on Islamic Civilization,* Leiden, 1976, pp. 299–302.

20. This line appears only in the Shī'ah version.

CHAPTER 2

1. There is also *kashf,* "disclosure," by which Sufi systems describe an insight into truth not open to intellect and not dependent, in an external manner, on dogma.

2. Ibn Rushd (1126–98), known in the West as Averroes, may be cited as an outstanding example of this tendency. Any conflict between rational truth and revealed dogma was to be resolved by interpreting the latter allegorically. The primary functions of religion are popular in character and pragmatic in purpose. Its "truths" are the form under which ordinary persons, in their nonphilosophical way, can apprehend and venerate the mysteries that the intelligent few investigate. Inasmuch as religion is for law, not learning, philosophy wisely avoids fruitless conflicts with it.

3. Sir Hamilton Gibb, in *Mohammedanism,* London, 2nd ed., 1953, p. 88.

4. Duncan B. Macdonald, *Development of Muslim Theology, Jurisprudence and Constitutional Theory,* New York, 1903. Appendix 1, pp. 309–10.

5. See W. Montgomery Watt, *The Faith and Practice of Al-Ghazali,* London, 1953.

6. On Iqbāl, see Iqbal Singh, *The Ardent Pilgrim: An Introduction to the Life and Work of Muhammad Iqbal,* London, 1951; also Iqbāl's own *Lectures on the Reconstruction of Religious Thought in Islam,* Lahore, 1934; *Aspects of Iqbal,* by various authors, Lahore, 1938; *Iqbal as a Thinker,* by various authors, Lahore, 1945.

CHAPTER 3

1. Cairo, 1942.

2. Muhammad Husain Haykal, *Hayāt Muhammad,* Cairo, 1935.

3. Cairo, 1938, p. 637.

4. This subject is dealt with more fully, especially in relationship to the New Testament, in chap. 10.

5. See Charles C. Torrey, *Jewish Foundation of Islam,* New York, 1933.

6. It is at this point that strong Muslim tradition places the story of Muhammad's experience of Satanic disruption into the revelation that stands in its true form in Surah 53.19ff. Here the Qur'ān decisively rejects Allāt, Manāt, and Al-'Uzzat, goddesses of Mecca and its vicinity, and does so with a derisive assurance that they are nonentities. But embedded in tradition in a manner that can hardly have been invented is the story that the Prophet allowed that their intercession could be looked for. Subsequently the statement was abrogated as a Satanic interjection and the Prophet was assured that in experiencing this trial he was only enduring what all other prophets had experienced before him (see Surah 22.52). It is not clear, however, how much time elapsed between the compromising deliverance and its correction. Some insist that the latter was immediate but the early historians indicate that the words were taken as a basis for a *modus vivendi* with the Quraish, on the ground of which some emigrants returned from Ethiopia. If that is so, the "concession" must have lasted some time. Some authorities deny the whole episode, reject the possibility of Muhammad's having been subject to Satanic interference (he being unique among prophets in this regard), and insist that no thought of Meccan accommodation ever arose. But in any event, the final, if not perpetual, attitude of the Prophet was an unwavering monotheism. The only ultimate *modus vivendi* between Islam and Mecca was the surrender of the latter.

7. The consternation seems clear from the Quranic passage in Surah 2.142–45, "Indeed it was a big thing." The implication clearly is that some of the Prophet's followers were seriously dismayed by the abandonment of Jerusalem. The change tested those who were willing to follow him unconditionally and it made Muslims a "middle" (distinctive?) community. The dubious were reassured that God's presence is everywhere and that the former *qiblah,* though valid hitherto, was not perpetual.

8. It would appear that the provisions of the treaty of Al-Hudaibiyyah about Islam returning Meccan converts did not apply to these converts during the Return Pilgrimage.

9. Sayyid Amīr 'Alī, *The Spirit of Islam,* London, 1922, p. 61.

10. This may be illustrated in the title of M. Pickthall's English rendering, *The Meaning of the Glorious Koran,* London, 1930. As a Muslim, the translator sought permission for his work and received it on condition that the English version was not entitled *The Qur'ān* (or *Koran*).

11. See, for example, Surah 17.26–39, Surah 16.114–16 (both Meccan) and also the wisdom of Luqmān in Surah 31.12–20, also a Meccan Surah. These passages are cited as having a somewhat "codal" appearance. However, the Medinan Surahs 2, 4, and 5 are predominantly legal in character.

12. "Never" is, of course, a too inclusive word, but the emphasis here is on "recognized" and "metaphysical." There exists, it is true, a permanent and vigorous tendency to hypostasize in Muhammad the divine light. The religious belief in *Al-Nur al-Muhammadī* has given to much Sufi, and other, devotion a relationship to Muhammad that comes close to deification, by implication, if not in fact. But these attitudes, wherever they occur, and recur, have no status in orthodox theology and all that they imply is roundly repudiated. Islam, however, is not the only faith where there are irreconcilable tensions between theology and religion, or rather, between orthodoxy and devotion.

13. James Robson, "Al-Ghazālī and the Sunna" in *The Muslim World,* Oct. 1955, vol. 45, no. 4, pp. 324–33.

CHAPTER 4

1. As in Edwin E. Calverley, *Worship in Islam,* Madras, 1925, a translation of book 4 of Al-Ghazālī's *Ihyā' 'Ulūm al-Dīn,* one of the greatest works of Muslim theology.

2. Arnold Toynbee has developed this theme of the role of pilgrimage in cultural renaissance in *A Study of History,* vol. 9, New York, 1954, pp. 96–114.

3. Vigorous protests over financial restrictions on pilgrims were voiced in 1953 and 1954. See *The Muslim World,* Oct. 1953, vol. 43, no. 4, p. 308, and Oct. 1954, vol. 44, no. 4, p. 280. For earlier objections to the unsanitary conditions and for a typical sophisticated disinclination to pilgrimage, later overcome, see Muhammad Husain Haykal, *Fī Manzil al-Wahÿ,* Cairo, 1938, pp. 35–38.

4. The redoubtable Charles M. Doughty never visited Mecca, though he traveled courageously as a Christian in Arabia. Among Christians who visited Mecca incognito were Ludwig Burckhardt, Richard Burton, and Christian Snouck Hurgrönje. See note 5, below.

5. L. J. Burckhardt, *Travels in Arabia,* 2 vols., 1829; Richard F. Burton, *Personal Narrative of a Pilgrimage to Al-Madineh and Meccah,* 2 vols., London, 1893; E. Rutter, *The Holy Cities of Arabia,* 2 vols., London, 1928; C. Snouck Hurgrönje, *Mekka,* 2 vols., in German, the second translated into English as *Mekka in the Latter Part of the Nineteenth Century,* Leiden, 1931.

6. Quoted from *The Muslim World,* July 1955, vol. 45, no. 3, "Manāsik al-Hajj," pp. 269–80 (my translation).

7. Al-Ghazālī (1058–1111) writes that he used to lead a solitary life in the mosque at Damascus, spending his days in the minaret, having first closed the door behind him. He adds that later in Jerusalem he shut himself up in the Sanctuary of the Rock for study and devotion.

8. Sermons in Egypt are controlled by the Ministry for Religious Affairs. Action to bring this about was taken in 1954 as a sequel to the use of the pulpit by foes of the regime.

9. *Dīwān al-Khutab li-l-Juma'i wa-l-A'yād,* Damascus, 1948. This manual was produced by a committee of 'Ulamā' at the behest of the Ministry of Waqfs; Muhammad al-Khaulī 'Abd al-'Azīz, *Islāh al-Wa'z al-Dīnī,* Cairo, 3rd ed., 1952; 'Alī Rifā'i, *Kaifa takūnu Khatīban,* Cairo, 3rd ed., 1953.

10. My translation from 'Abdallāh al-Marāghȳ, *Dīwān al-Khutab al-Hadīthah fī-l-Wa'z wa-l-Irshād,* Cairo, n.d. "Faith in God"—a typical sermon—is found on pp. 10–12 of the 2nd ed., n.d.

11. For example, John N. Hollister, *The Shi'a of India,* London, 1953, pp. 164–80, and Freya Stark, *Baghdad Sketches,* London, 1937, pp. 221–27. In *The Road to Mecca,* New York, 1954, Muhammad As'ad has some interesting comments on Shī'ah lamentation for 'Alī, Hasan, and Husain, which he describes as "extravagant."

12. Interpretive studies in which there are numerous excerpts and references to an even wider field are: Reynold A. Nicholson, *The Mystics of Islam,* London, 1914; Margaret Smith, *Readings from the Mystics of Islam,* London, 1950, and *The Sufi Path of Love, An Anthology of Sufism,* London, 1954; Arthur J. Arberry, *Sufism, an Account of the Mystics of Islam,* London, 1954.

CHAPTER 5

1. In nineteenth-century Christian writing on Islam, the rendering "success" was often taken for granted, and that in its barest material sense. Although it must be admitted that Muslim attitudes and explanations frequently justified that view, there is no doubt that the term *al-falāh* both deserves and supports a much more comprehensive and spiritual interpretation.

2. For example, 'Alī 'Abd-al-Rāziq in *Usūl al-Hukm fī-l-Islām* ["Principles of Government in Islam"], Cairo, 1925, insists that God's revelation concerns the essentials, not the minutiae, of Islamic life.

3. Kemāl A. Fārūkī, in *Ijmā' and the Gate of Ijtihād,* Karachi, 1947, raises in sharp terms the question whether the derivation of some elements of law from popular sources—if these have then the same status as other, and revealed, law—does not involve *Shirk.* He received a clear dismissal of such fears from a group of 'ulamā' whom he consulted and whose dicta he quotes, pp. 11–17.

4. The Quranic phrase is *fi sabīl-Illāh.* It connotes whatever carries forward the cause of Islam, whether fiscal, social, military, or general.

5. See *The Muslim World,* April 1955, vol. 45, no. 2, p. 205.

6. See Shaikh Mahmūd Ahmad, *The Economics of Islam,* Lahore, 1947, chap. 7.

7. Sayyid Qutb, *Al-'Adālat al-Ijtimā'iyyah fi-l-Islām,* Cairo, 1945; translated by John B. Hardie, *Social Justice in Islam,* Washington, 1953, pp. 36 and 68.

8. Muhammad Iqbāl, *Lectures on the Reconstruction of Religious Thought in Islam,* Lahore, 1934, p. 159.

9. Sayyid Qutb, *Al-'Adālat,* p. 73.

10. Ibid., p. 99. Quoted, as are the extracts noted in notes 7 and 9, by permission of the American Council of Learned Societies, Washington.

11. M. Reihān Sharīf, *Islamic Social Framework,* Orientalia, Lahore, 1954, pp. 22–23.

12. Mahmūd Hoballāh, in *The Moslem World and the U.S.A.,* Jan. 1955, vol. 1, no. 1, p. 9.

13. 'Abdallāh Ghosheh, in a paper prepared for the Colloquium on Islamic Culture, Princeton, September 1953, entitled "The Philosophy of Freedoms in Islam." Quoted by permission of the author who was President of the Muslim Board of Elders, Jerusalem.

CHAPTER 7

1. The preacher was Joseph Hall. The passage is cited from Samuel C. Chew, *The Crescent and the Rose,* New York, 1937, p. 445. This work is a mine of information on Islam in the literature of Europe in the centuries before and after the Renaissance.

2. See Liaquat 'Alī Khān, *Pakistan, the Heart of Asia,* and Cambridge, Mass., 1951, Muhammad Naguib, *Egypt's Destiny,* New York, 1954.

3. See G. E. von Grunebaum, *Medieval Islam,* Chicago, 1946.

4. Taha Husain, *Mustaqbal al-Thaqāfah fī-Misr* ["The Future of Culture in Egypt"], Cairo, 1938, translated by Sidney Glazer, Washington, 1954.

5. J. Spencer Trimingham, *Islam in Ethiopia,* London, 1952, p. 273.

6. A recent work, *Islam and Modernity,* by Dr. Fazlur Rahman (Chicago, 1982), analyzes this issue and indicates a deep sense of misgiving about the "inroads" of higher education, not least in the social sciences, into the faith-commitment of young Muslims. He deplores *both* the stolidity of the traditionalists *and* some of the postures of the neomodernists who, he suspects, underestimate the range of the question. There have been several conferences in the last decade on this theme, as, for example, a series at King 'Abdul 'Azīz University, Jiddah, Saudi Arabia (see Chap. 8, n. 2).

7. These Hebraisms were indicated sharply in a Muslim study of the Psalms in the Arabic (Beirut) Bible, by Muhammad al-Sādiq Husain (*Sifr al-Mazāmir,* Cairo, 1961). A current work on the New Testament Gospels is in preparation attempting a more Quranic-style Arabic rendering.

8. W. H. Temple Gairdner, *The Phonetics of Arabic,* London, 1925.

9. Selection is perhaps a little invidious but mention may be made of Farhat Ziadeh and R. Bayly Winder, *An Introduction to Modern Arabic,* Princeton, 1955; Edward J. Young, *Arabic for Beginners,* Grand Rapids, 2nd ed., 1953; Anis Frayha, *Essentials of Arabic,* Beirut, 1953.

10. Eugene A. Nida, *God's Word in Man's Language,* New York, 1952, p. 45. See also Eugene A. Nida and William D. Reyburn, *Meaning Across Cultures,* Maryknoll, N.Y., 1981. The people concerned are the Zanaki on the shores of Lake Victoria.

11. See this writer's *Muhammad and the Christian* (Maryknoll, New York, 1984) for one effort to formulate a Christian "reckoning" with the Muslim sense of the Prophet.

12. Muhammad 'Alī, *My Life—A Fragment,* Lahore, 1942, p. 124.

13. Alan J. Villiers, *Sons of Sinbad,* New York, 1940, p. 35.

14. The prominent leader was Muhammad 'Alī, the Khilafatist (see note 12, above); the editor is Mazharuddīn Siddīqī, in charge of *The Islamic Literature,* Lahore; Cromer's dictum is found in his *Modern Egypt,* New York, 1908, vol. 2, p. 229.

Chapter 8

1. See *Islam and Revolution: Writings and Declarations of Imam Khomeini,* trans. and annotated by Hamid Algar, Berkeley, Cal., 1981.

2. E.g., Syed Sajjad Husain and Syed Ali Ashraf, *Crisis in Muslim Education,* Jiddah, 1979; G. N. Saqib, *Modernization of Muslim Education,* London, 1977; Ziauddin Sardar, *The Future of Muslim Civilization,* London, 1979; Muhammad Wasiullah Khan, *Education and Society in the Muslim World,* Jiddah, 1981.

3. Thus, e.g., Syed Muhammad al-Naquib al-Attas, *Islam and Secularism,* Kuala Lumpur, 1978. He takes Western civilization as a serious destructive challenge to humankind, and seeks a total reformulation of knowledge based on absolute revelation and freed from the empirical skepticism and chronic acquisitiveness characteristic of the West. In a deeper vein, see also Fazlur Rahman, *Islam and Modernity,* Chicago, 1982.

4. Norman Perrin, *The Resurrection Narratives: A New Approach,* London, 1977, Dedication.

5. Edward Said, *Orientalism,* New York and London, 1978.

6. To borrow the title of a notable example of such integrity—namely, Marshall Hodgson, *The Venture of Islam, Conscience and History in a World Civilization,* 3 vols., Chicago, 1974.

7. See, e.g., a careful treatment in Khurshid Ahmad's *Studies in Islamic Economics: Selected Papers of the First International Conference on Islamic Economics,* Jiddah, 1980.

8. There has been an intriguing concern for historical self-interpretation within recent Islam. It is partly in obvious concern to counter what it sees as distorted versions of the Islamic past. There is some documentation in, e.g., Yvonne Y. Haddad, *Contemporary Islam and the Challenge of History,* Albany, 1982.

9. See the report in *International Review of Mission,* vol. 65, no. 260, Oct. 1976, pp. 365–460, and Kenneth Cragg, "Retrospect," ibid., vol. 66, no. 262, April 1977, pp. 169–75.

10. This is to accept that relation with other faiths is in the very nature of the Christian theologian's task. As George Rupp observes in *Christologies and Cultures,* The Hague, 1974, pp. 161–229: "Our interpretation of pluralism is likely to be a correlative of our Christological position."

11. See the discussion in the *Newsletter* of the Task Force on Christian-Muslim Relations, Hartford, Conn., no. 16, Feb. 1982, "A Disavowal." On "tentmaking," see Acts 18:3.

12. See Earle H. Waugh, Baha Abu Laban, and R. B. Qureshi, eds., *The Muslim Community in North America,* Edmonton, 1983; *Research Papers* and *Abstracts: Muslims in Europe,* Centre for the Study of Islam and Christian-Muslim Relations, Selly Oak Colleges, Birmingham, England, from 1979; *Muslim Communities in Non-Muslim States,* Islamic Council of Europe, 1980.

13. A phrase from John Steinbeck, *The Grapes of Wrath,* New York, 1939, the sad comment of a migrating grandmother distressed by what the family has to discard and leave behind.

14. New York and London, 1965. Written by Malcolm X with the assistance of Alex Haley.

15. See, e.g., my *The Mind of the Qur'ān,* London, 1974, and the discussion of the "authority" question in Don M. McCurry, ed., *The Gospel and Islam: A 1978 Compendium,* Monrovia, Cal., 1979, pp. 196–207.

16. *The Wretched of the Earth: A Negro Psychoanalyst's Study of the Problems of Racism and Colonialism Today,* New York, 1963; originally published in French: *Les damnés de la terre,* Paris, 1961.

17. On Senghor, see *Prose and Poetry,* ed. and trans. by John Reed

and Clive Wake, London, 1965; Gerald Moore, *Seven African Writers,* London, 1962, pp. 1–17. For Senghor's concept of *négritude* Fanon had nothing but contempt.

18. Surah 42.38. The word *shūrā* here ("counsel" or perhaps "council") has been variously interpreted and may refer to tribal conclave. The word *amr* suggests not something that in fact happens that way, but ought so to happen.

19. He was arguing from Surah 114, *Ilāh al-nās,* "God of the people," seeing the masses as the vital factor in revolutionary change.

20. Although it is right to mobilize the populace, they can only contribute to effectuate what the 'ulamā' affirm and these, in Khomeini's book, have no liberty of clerical deviance. Those, e.g., prior to the Shah's downfall, who wanted to urge the familiar Shī'ah doctrine of "passivity" and quiescence were roundly denounced and disowned as 'ulamā' by Khomeini for whom all such postures had been made anathema by the insufferable degree of the Shah's evil and treachery.

21. One fascinating Muslim study of the human capacity for wrong, and therefore of the futility of being sanguine about amenability to law and to good, is Muhammad Kamil Husain's, *City of Wrong: A Friday in Jerusalem,* Amsterdam, 1958; trans. from the Arabic, Cairo, 1954.

22. See note 7, above, and M. Rodinson, *Islam and Capitalism,* London, 1974; trans. from the French edition (Paris, 1966) by Brian Pearce.

23. Beirut, 1970. See Roger Allen, *The Arabic Novel: An Historical and Critical Introduction,* Syracuse, 1982, pp. 138–44.

24. *Qindīl Umm-Hāshim,* Cairo, 1944; trans. by Mustafā Badāwī, *The Saint's Lamp,* Leiden, 1973.

25. Paris, 1962; English trans., London, 1970.

26. Cairo, 1949. For a sense of participation in simple, sometimes superstitious, believing among Muslims in face of human pathos, see "Popular Islam: the Hunger of the Heart," in McCurry, *The Gospel and Islam,* pp. 208–24.

27. Beirut, 1970—a bold and wide-ranging secular critique that evoked a flurry of controversy and condemnation.

28. Publication in full (after earlier installments in *Al-Ahrām,* Cairo), Beirut, 1967. English trans., by Philip Stewart, *Children of Gebelawi,* London and Washington, 1981.

29. See his *The Hallowed Valley,* English trans., Malta, 1977.

30. Notably his *Quest for Islam,* Bombay, 1977, a new approach to Islamic thought and value systems.

31. Beirut, 1963. Ghassān Kanafānī was one of the ablest exponents of the Palestinian tragedy in essay, poetry, and the novel.

CHAPTER 9

1. Sayyid Qutb, *Social Justice in Islam,* Washington, 1953, pp. 278-79. Quoted by permission of the American Council of Learned Societies.

2. The literature of the Ahmadiyyah movements is large. Among the important publications of the Qadiānī Ahmadiyyah are: Mirzā Ghulām Ahmad, *The Philosophy of the Teachings of Islam,* London, 1910; Washington, 1953; Mirzā Bashīr al-Dīn Ahmad, *Ahmadiyyat or the True Islam,* 1st edition, Qadiān, 1924; 3rd edition, Washington, 1951; *The Holy Quran: English Translation and Commentary,* vol. 1, Qadiān, 1947; *The Holy Qur'an, Arabic Text and English Translation,* Rabwah, 1955. The Lahore Ahmadiyyah has published, *inter alia,* Muhammad 'Alī, *The Religion of Islam,* Lahore, 1936; idem, *The Holy Quran, Translation and Commentary,* Lahore, 1920. For the history prior to the schism, the reader may consult Howard A. Walter, *The Ahmadiyyat Movement,* London, 1918.

3. Al Hājj Khwāja Nazīr Ahmad, *Jesus in Heaven on Earth,* Lahore, 1952.

4. 'Alī, Muhammad, *My Life—A Fragment,* Lahore, 1942, p. 160.

5. Cairo, 1952. "The Genius of Christ" in *The East and West Review,* London, July 1954, vol. 20, no. 3, pp. 88-96, is a resumé of the contents of this work and a discussion of its Christian bearings. A still more noteworthy Muslim treatment of Christ is that by Muhammad Kāmil Husain, *Qaryah Zālimah* ["City of Wrong"], Cairo, 1954. The author reconstructs imaginatively the tensions, fears, and bigotries involved in the desire to crucify Christ—a deed that he describes as humanity's crucifixion of its own conscience. English trans., "City of Wrong," see *The Muslim World,* April and July, 1956, vol. 46, nos. 2 and 3, pp. 132-43 and 225-36, and chap. 8 above, note 21.

6. Lahore, 1934, pp. 293-94.

7. The story has been admirably recounted in Laurence E. Browne's *The Eclipse of Christianity in Asia,* Cambridge, England, 1933. Thomas Arnold's *The Preaching of Islam,* London, 1913, was a notable contribution to the investigation of Muslim expansion and sought, as its title implies, to emphasize and document the "religious" presentation of Islam in the conquered territories. Although Arnold did much to qualify earlier extreme views, his examples were in part ill balanced and his thesis nowhere took adequate account of the Islamic law of war and peace, and of the fundamental fact that preaching was inseparable from conquest. It should also be remembered that although "readers" might explain Islam, the Qur'ān as such was not translated or given into the hands of

unbelievers. One had access to the supreme source book of Islam only after one had become a Muslim.

8. London, 1949, p. 79, n. 1.

9. *International Review of Missions,* July 1938, vol. 27, no. 3, p. 341.

10. Ibid., p. 341, footnote.

11. Its semipagan quality can be gauged from an examination of the archeological remains. See F. V. Winnett, in *The Muslim World,* Oct. 1941, vol. 31, no. 4, pp. 350-52. The evidence indicates that Jesus had been incorporated into polytheism and that animal sacrifices were offered in his name.

12. *International Review of Missions,* July 1938, vol. 27, no. 3, p. 343.

Chapter 10 ·

1. Edwin Hoskyns, *Cambridge Sermons,* quoted in A. M. Ramsey, *The Glory of God and the Transfiguration of Christ,* London, 1949, p. 6.

2. As examples of this Muslim interpretation one may cite 'Abdu Abū-l-Ahad Dāwūd, *Muhammad in the Bible,* Islamic Series, no. 2, Allahabad, 1952; Khwāja Nazīr Ahmad, *Jesus in Heaven on Earth,* Lahore, 1952; A. H. Vidyarathi, and U. 'Alī, *Muhammad in Parsi, Hindoo and Buddhist Scriptures,* Islamic Series, no. 3, Allahabad, 1953.

3. The Quranic passages dealing with the theme of *naskh,* "abrogation," are Surah 2.106, 13.39, 16.98, 101. See Richard Bell, *Introduction to the Quran,* Edinburgh, 1953, pp. 98-99. See also chap. 3, note 6, above.

4. 'Abbās Mahmūd Al-'Aqqā, *'Abqariyyat al-Masīh,* Cairo, 1952, pp. 215-19.

5. Thus Surah 42.37 commends those who, when angered, forgive. The provisions of Surah 65.1, concerning the statutory delay before those intending divorce either separate in kindness or achieve reconciliation, may be taken to suggest the creative possibilities of forgiveness in which God may bring some new thing to pass. It is true that the Qur'ān uses the imperative *ighfir,* "forgive," only in a petitionary sense, of God, and not in a hortatory sense, as to humans. But it is clear that the divine clemency is meant to be exemplary. Surah 3, in three verses, 16, 147, 193, echoes the petition of the Lord's Prayer: "Forgive us our trespasses," but does not add: "as we forgive those who trespass against us." Surah 5.45, after setting out the *lex talionis,* adds that to remit vengeance is an expiation for the remitter.

6. Muslim writers who discuss the spread of Christianity confront a deep historical problem in that they are obliged to explain the impact of Jesus upon the world, through the disciples, in terms of his words and teaching only. The place where the Resurrection stands in the Christian

understanding of Christ is, for Islam, a blank. Yet its sequel cannot be ignored, even if, on the Muslim view, it has to be a sequel without a properly total source. Nevertheless, there is this measure of consistency in the Muslim account, in that, having disallowed the Cross, it rightly excludes the Resurrection. For they belong together. The Resurrection is the triumphant consequent of the quality of Christ's dying. Having forbidden actuality to the latter, Islam clearly can leave no place for the former.

7. Muhammad 'Alī, *My Life—A Fragment,* Lahore, 1942, p. 59.

8. In a letter quoted by John Baillie, *The Place of Jesus Christ in Modern Christianity,* New York, 1929, pp. 145–46, and drawn from *Letters of Principal James Denney to W. Robertson Nicoll, 1893–1917,* pp. 120–26.

9. As for example in Mustafā Khālidī, and 'Umar Farrūkh, *Al-Tabshīr wa-l-Istiʿmār fī-l-Bilādi-l-ʿArabiyyah* ["Missions and Imperialism in the Arab World"], Beirut, 1953.

10. See Sayyid Qutb, *Social Justice in Islam,* Washington, 1953, pp. 228ff., where the Umayyads are made responsible for a breakdown of valid Islamicity in matters political and economic, from which subsequent history has hardly, if ever, recovered. See also Muhammad al-Ghazālī, *Min Hunā Naʿlam,* Cairo, 1950, translated by Ismā 'il al-Fārūqī under the title *Our Beginning in Wisdom,* Washington, 1953. On p. 141, he writes: "The reader may possibly ask whether Islamic socialism has been applied anywhere, and whether there is at present any living example of it. . . . The answer unfortunately is, 'There is none.' The principles of Islam have been crippled in Islamic countries for a long time."

CHAPTER 11

1. On this theme see Majīd Khaddūrī, *The Law of War and Peace in Islam,* Baltimore, 1955, and Samuel M. Zwemer, *The Law of Apostacy in Islam,* London, 1924.

2. Lebanon was long taken to be a significant example. It is now clear—and, indeed, is part of its continuing tragedy—that its communal fragmentation has become a vortex for inter-Arab and superpower rivalry and bedevilment.

3. Only among a few thinkers within Indian Islam, where Islamic statehood is excluded, is this correlation of faith and power, and the traditional politicization of Islam, deeply questioned or denied. (See Hasan Askari, *State and Society in Islam: an Introduction,* New Delhi, 1978.)

4. A revolutionary step was taken in Egypt in 1955 when all court

dealings with personal status, within all communities, were brought under the governmental judicial system. Such changes, if established and extended elsewhere, would completely transform the situation as hitherto obtaining.

5. The reasons for this fact have often been conjectured but never convincingly established. It may be agreed, however, that Arabic-speaking Islam, for Quranic and other reasons, has always been the most tenacious.

6. It is interesting to recall how inimical to the idea of missions was the attitude of the East India Company, for much is written about the supposed "collusion" between empire and faith. The Company Committee passed the following Minute in 1793: "That the sending of missionaries into our Eastern possessions is the maddest, most extravagant and most unwarrantable project that was ever proposed by an enthusiastic lunatic."

7. Marcus 'Abd al-Masīh recounted his story in *The Muslim World,* July 1945, vol. 35, no. 3, pp. 211–15. From this account these extracts are taken, with permission.

8. It is important to emphasize this intention, for the general position suggested here is often regarded with suspicion. Stephen C. Neill, in his *Christian Faith Today,* London, 1955, writes: "The convert is cut off from all his past; he no longer has any access to his own people, and has no opportunity to bear any witness to them about his new-found faith. As an unbaptized Christian, he can move about among them freely and let character and conviction bear their own quiet witness." Having thus in part stated the argument of the text, Bishop Neill proceeds: "The argument is painfully plausible. . . . Scarcely one of those who have started out, with whatever sincerity of conviction, on this course of inner Christian allegiance without overt Christian confession, has been able to resist the soothing influence of compromise: not one of them has ever succeeded in creating an unmistakably Christian movement among his own people." But are purely pragmatic and retrospective criteria necessarily the right ones in seeking to understand the mind of the Spirit? In any event, no avoidance of overt confession is here in mind; rather the form of legal status.

BOOK LIST

A selection of titles not included in the endnotes. Works listed here under one part may also be relevant to another.

PART 1, CHAPTER 1, AND PART 3, CHAPTER 7

'Abd al-Jalīl, J. M., et al. *Islam,* Studia Missionalia, vol. 11. Rome, 1961.

'Abdul Latīf, Syed. *Towards a Re-Orientation of Islamic Thought.* Hyderabad, 1954.

Adams, C.C. *Islam and Modernism in Egypt.* London, 1933.

Ahmad, 'Azīz. *Islamic Modernism in India and Pakistan, 1857–1964.* London, 1967.

———. *An Intellectual History of Islam in India.* Edinburgh, 1969.

Ajami, Fouad. *The Arab Predicament.* New York, 1981.

Akhavi, Shahrough. *Religion and Politics in Contemporary Iran.* Albany, 1980.

Alberuni, A. H. *Makers of Pakistan and Modern Muslim India.* Lahore, 1950.

Allen, Roger. *The Arabic Novel, An Historical and Critical Introduction.* Syracuse, 1982.

Anderson, J.N.D. *Islamic Law in the Modern World.* New York, 1959.

———. *Law Reform in the Muslim World.* London, 1976.

Antonius, George. *The Arab Awakening.* London, 1939.

Arberry, A. J., et al. *Religion in the Middle East,* 2 vols. Cambridge, England, 1969.

Ayoob, M. *The Politics of Islamic Reassertion.* New York, 1981.

Berger, Morroe. *Islam in Egypt Today.* Cambridge, England, 1970.

Berkes, Niyazi. *Turkish Nationalism and Western Civilization*. New York, 1959.

Callard, Keith. *Pakistan, A Political Study*. London, 1957.

Caroe, Olaf. *Wells of Power*. London, 1951.

Cragg, Kenneth. *Counsels in Contemporary Islam*. Edinburgh, 1964.

Cudsi, A.J., and Dessouki, A.H. *Islam and Power*. London, 1981.

Dodge, Bayard. *Al-Azhar, A Millennium of Muslim Learning*. Washington, 1961.

Esposito, John L. *Islam and Development: Religion and Sociopolitical Change*. Syracuse, 1980.

———, and Donahue, J.J. *Islam in Transition*. New York, 1982.

Faruki, Kemal A. *Islam, Today and Tomorrow*. Karachi, 1974.

Fazlur, Rahman. *Islam and Modernity: Transformation of an Intellectual Tradition*. Chicago, 1982.

Fisher, W. B. *The Middle East: A Physical, Social, and Regional Geography*. New York, 6th ed., 1971.

Fyzee, A.A.A. *A Modern Approach to Islam*. Bombay, 1963.

Geertz, Clifford. *The Religion of Java*. Glencoe, Ill., 1960.

———. *Islam Observed*. New Haven, 1968.

Gibb, H.A.R. *Modern Trends in Islam*. 1947.

Gordon, David C. *Lebanon, a Fragmented Nation*. Stanford, 1980.

———. *The Republic of Lebanon: Nation in Jeopardy*. Boulder, 1983.

Grünebaum, G.E. von. *Islam: Essays in the Growth of a Cultural Tradition*. Menasha, Wis., 1955.

———. *Unity and Variety in Muslim Civilization*. Chicago, 1955.

Haddad Y.Y. *Contemporary Islam and the Challenge of History*. Albany, 1982.

Haim, Sylvia, ed. *Arab Nationalism: An Anthology*. Berkeley, 1962.

Hamdard Foundation. *Main Currents of Contemporary Thought in Pakistan*. Karachi, 1973, vols. 1 and 2.

Harris, C.P. *Nationalism and Revolution in Egypt*. The Hague, 1964.

Hazard, H.W. *Atlas of Islamic History*. Princeton, 1954.

Heyd, Uriel. *Revival of Islam in Modern Turkey*. Jerusalem, 1968.

Hodgson, Marshall G.S. *The Venture of Islam: Conscience and History in a World Civilization*. Chicago, 1975, 3 vols.

Hopwood, Derek. *Egypt: Politics and Society, 1945–1981*. London, 1982.

Hourani, Albert. *Arabic Thought in the Liberal Age, 1798–1939*. London, 1962.

Hudson, M.C. *The Precarious Republic: Modernization in Lebanon*. New York, 1968.

Israeli, Raphael, ed. *The Crescent in the East: Islam in Asia Major*. London, 1982.

Izzedin, Najla. *The Arab World: Its Past, Present and Future*. Chicago, 1953.

Karandikar. *Islam in India's Transition to Modernity*. Bombay, 1968.

Karpat, Kemal H., ed. *Political and Social Thought in the Contemporary Middle East*. New York, 1968.

Khomeini, Imam Ruhullah. *Islam and Revolution: Writings and Declarations*. Hamid Algar, trans. Berkeley, 1981.

King, M.C. *The Palestinians and the Churches 1948–56*. Geneva, 1981.

Kirk, G.E. *A Short History of the Middle East*. Washington, 1949.

Kritzeck, James, and Lewis, W. *Islam in Africa*. New York, 1968.

Laqueur, Walter. *Communism and Nationalism in the Middle East*. London, 1956.

Lewis, Bernard. *The Emergence of Modern Turkey*. London, 1961.

———. *The Middle East and the West*. New York, 1964.

———. *Race and Color in Islam*. New York, 1971.

Lewis, I.M., ed. *Islam in Tropical Africa*. Bloomington, Ind., 2nd ed., 1980.

Littlefield, David N. *The Islamic Near East and North Africa: Annotated Guide to Books in English for Non-Specialists*. Littleton, Col., 1975.

Lokhandwalla, S.T., ed. *India and Contemporary Islam*. Simla, India, 1971.

Mansfield, Peter, ed. *The Middle East: A Political and Economic Survey*. London, 4th ed., 1973.

Mazrui, 'Alī. *On Heroes and Uhuru Worship*. London, 1967.

McNeill, W.H., and Waldman, M.R. *The Islamic World*. New York, 1973.

Miller, Roland, *Mappila Muslims of Kerala: A Study in Islamic Trends*. New Delhi, 1976.

Milson, M., ed. *Society and Political Structure in the Arab World*. New York, 1973.

Mitchell, R. P. *The Society of the Muslim Brothers*. London, 1969.

Mortimer, Edward. *Faith and Power: The Politics of Islam*. New York, 1982.

Piscatori, J.P., ed. *Islam in the Political Process*. London, 1982.

Rivlin, B., and Szyliowicz, J.S. *The Contemporary Middle East: Tradition and Innovation*. New York, 1965.

Rodinson, Maxine. *Islam and Capitalism*. London, 1977.

———. *Marxism and the Muslim World*. London, 1980.

Said, Edward. *Orientalism*. New York, 1979.

———. *Covering Islam*. New York, 1981.

Sardar, Ziauddin. *Science, Technology, and Development in the Muslim World*. London, 1977.

Sharī'at, 'Alī. *On the Sociology of Islam*. Hamid Algar, trans. Berkeley, 1979.

———. *The Visage of Muhammad*. A.A. Sachedin, trans. Teheran, 1981.

Shepard, William. *The Faith of a Modern Muslim Intellectual: Religious Aspects and Implications of the Writings of Ahmad Amin*. New Delhi, 1982.

Smith, W. Cantwell. *Islam in Modern History*. Princeton, 1957.

Stoddard, P.H., ed. *Change and the Muslim World*. Syracuse, 1981.

Toynbee, Arnold. *The World and the West*. New York, 1953.

Troll, C.W. *Sayyid Ahmad Khan: A Re-Interpretation of Muslim Theology*. New Delhi, 1978.

Welch, A.T., and Cachia, P. *Islam: Past Influence and Present Challenge*. Edinburgh, 1979.

PART 2, CHAPTERS 2 AND 3

'Abduh, Muhammad. *The Theology of Unity*. K. Cragg and I. Musa'ad, trans. London, 1965.

Abū-l-Fazl, Mirza. *The Koran*. Bombay, 1955.

Adams, Charles, J. *Reader's Guide to the Great Religions*. New York, 1965.

Ahmad, Khurshid. *Islam: Its Meaning and Message*. London, 1970.

Ahmad, Zāhir. *Mohammad, Glimpses of the Prophet's Life and Times*. New Delhi, 1980.

'Ali, 'Abdallāh Yūsuf. *Fundamentals of Islam*. Geneva, 1929.

———. *The Personality of Muhammad*. Lahore, 1931.

———. *The Holy Qur'ān*. Lahore, 1937/38, 2 vols.

———. *The Message of Islam*. London, 1940.

'Alī, Hāshim Amīr. *The Student's Qur'ān*. Hyderabad, 1959.

'Alī, Muhammad. *Manual of Hadith*. Lahore, n.d.

———. *The Living Thoughts of the Prophet Muhammad*. London, 1947.

Amin, Osman. *Muhammad 'Abduh*. Washington, 1953.

Andrae, Tor. *Muhammad, the Man and His Faith*. T. Mentzel, trans. New York, 1960.

Arberry, A.J. *The Holy Koran: An Introduction with Selections*. London, 1953.

———. *The Koran Interpreted*. London, 1955.

———. *Revelation and Reason in Islam*. New York, 1957.

Arnold, Thomas, and Guillaume, A. *The Legacy of Islam*. Oxford, 1931.

Asad, Muhammad. *The Message of the Qur'ān*. Gibraltar, 1980.

Azād, Abū-l-Kalām. *Tarjumān al-Qur'ān*. Syed Latif, trans. Bombay, 1962, 2 vols.

'Azzām, 'Abd al-Rahmān. *The Eternal Message of Muhammad*. New York, 1965.

Bell, Richard. *The Origin of Islam in Its Christian Environment*. London, 1926.

———. *The Qur'ān*. Edinburgh, 2 vols., 1937/39.

———. *Introduction to the Qur'ān*. Edinburgh, 1963 (revised and enlarged by W. M. Watt, Edinburgh, 1970).

Bennabi, Malek. *Le Phénomène Coranique*. n.d.

Blachère, Regis. *Le Coran*. Paris, 1947.

———. *Le Problème de Mahomet*. Paris, 1952.

Bosworth, C.E., ed. *The Legacy of Islam*. Oxford, new ed., 1970.

Burton, John. *The Collection of the Qur'ān*. Cambridge, England, 1977.

Calverley, E.E. *Islam: An Introduction*. Cairo, 1958.

Cragg, Kenneth. *The Event of the Qur'ān*. London, 1970.

———. *The Mind of the Qur'ān*. London, 1973,

———. *The House of Islam*. Belmont, Cal., 2nd ed., 1975.

———, and Speight, R. Marston. *Islam from Within*. Belmont, Cal., 1980.

Crollius, Ary A.R. *The Word in the Experience of Revelation in Qur'an and Hindu Scriptures*. Rome, 1974.

Dawood, N.J. *The Koran*. London, 1956.

Donaldson, Dwight M. *The Shi'ite Religion*. London, 1933.

Engineer, Asghar A. *Origin and Development of Islam: An Essay on Its Socio-Economic Growth*. Bombay, 1980.

Esin, Emil. *Mecca and Medina*. London, 1963.

Fazlur-Rahman. *Islam*. London, 1961.

———. *Major Themes of the Qur'ān*. Minneapolis, 1980.

Foy, Whitfield. *Man's Religious Quest,* part 8. London. 1978.

Gardet, Louis. *Connaître l'Islam*. Paris, 1958.

———, and Anawati, C.G. *Introduction à la Théologie Musulmane*. Paris, 1948.

Gibb, H.A.R. *Muhammadanism: A Historical Survey*. New York, 1961.

———, et al. *The Encyclopedia of Islam*. The Hague, new ed., from 1954.

Goldziher, Ignacz. *Etudes sur la Tradition Islamique*. Paris, 1952.

Grünebaum, G.E. von. *Modern Islam: The Search for Cultural Identity*. Berkeley, 1962.

Guillaume, Alfred, *The Traditions of Islam*. Oxford, 1924.

———. *The Life of Muhammad,* trans. from Ibn Ishaq's *Sīrat Rasūl Allāh*. Oxford, 1955.

Hamidullāh, Muhammad. *Le Prophète de l'Islam*. Paris, 1955, 2 vols.

———. *The Battlefields of the Prophet Muhammad*. Woking, Surrey, 1957.

Haykal, Muhammad Husain. *Life of Muhammad*. A. Wessels, trans. New York, 1976.

International Congress for the Study of the Qur'ān, Series 1. Canberra, 1982.

Iqbāl, Muhammad. *The Reconstruction of Religious Thought in Islam*. Lahore, 1944.

Izutsu, T. *God and Man in the Qur'ān*. Tokyo, 1964.

———. *Ethico-Religious Concepts in the Qur'ān*. Montreal, 1966.

Jeffery, Arthur. *Reader in Islam*. The Hague, 1962.

———. *Islam: Muhammad and his Religion*. New York, 1958.

Jomier, Jacques. *La Place du Coran dans la Vie Quotidienne en Egypte*. Tunis, 1952.

———. *Le Commentaire Coranique du Manar*. Paris, 1955.

———. *Bible et Coran*. Paris, 1959.

Khān, Muhammad Zafrullāh. *Muhammad, Seal of the Prophets*. London, 1980.

Khwaja, Jamal, *Quest for Islam*. Bombay, 1977.

Lammens, Henri. *Islam, Beliefs and Institutions*. E. D. Ross, trans.,London, 1929.

Lings, Martin. *Muhammad, His Life Based on Earliest Sources*. New Delhi, 1983.

Lane Poole, S. *Studies in a Mosque*. London, 1893.

Lewis, Bernard. *Islam from Muhammad to the Capture of Constantinople*. New York, 1974, 2 vols.

Malik, Charles. *God and Man in Contemporary Islamic Thought*. Beirut, 1972.

Masson, D. *Le Coran et la Révélation Judéo-Chrétienne Comparée*. Paris, 1958, 2 vols.

Maudūdī, Abū-l-'Alā. *Towards Understanding Islam*. Lahore, 1940.

———. *Islamic Law and Constitution*. Karachi, 1955.

McCarthy, Richard. *The Theology of Al-Ash'arī*. Beirut. 1953.

Muir, William. *Life of Mahomet*. London, 4 vols., 1858–61; new abridged ed., Edinburgh, 1923; rev. ed., New York, 1975.

Nadvī, Abul Hasan. *Life of Muhammad*. Lucknow, n.d.

Numānī, Shiblī. *Muhammad*. Karachi, 1975.

Parrinder, Geoffrey. *Jesus in the Qur'ān*. London, 1965.

Rahbar, Daud. *God of Justice, Ethical Doctrine of the Qur'an*. Leiden, 1960.

Rahnama, Zayn al-'Ābidīn. *Payambar: The Messenger*. L. P. Elwell Sutton, trans. Lahore, 1964.

Robinson, Francis. *Atlas of the Islamic World since 1500*. London, 1982.

Rodinson, Maxine. *Mohammed.* A. Carter, trans. London, new ed., 1971.

Sale, George. *The Koran,* Introductory Essay and Translation. Many editions since the 18th century.

Sarwar, H.G. *The Holy Qur'ān.* Singapore, 1929.

———. *Life of the Holy Prophet.* Lahore, 1937.

———. *The Philosophy of the Qur'ān.* Lahore, 1938.

Schuon, F. *Understanding Islam.* D. M. Matheson, trans. London, 1963.

Sell, Edward. *The Faith of Islam.* London, 4th ed., 1920.

Smith, Jane I. *An Historical and Semantic Study of the Term "Islam" as Seen in a Sequence of Qur'ān Commentaries.* Cambridge, Mass., 1975.

———, and Haddad, Y.Y. *Islamic Understanding of Death and Resurrection.* Albany, 1981.

Stanton, H.U.W. *The Teaching of the Qur'ān.* London, 1919.

Stewart, Desmond. *Mecca.* New York, 1980.

Swartz, Merlin. *Studies in Islam.* New York, 1980.

Sweetman, J.W. *Islam and Christian Theology.* London, part 1, vol. 1, 1945; part 1, vol. 2, 1947; part 2, vol. 1, 1955.

Torrey, C.C. *Jewish Foundation of Islam.* New Haven, 1933.

Waardenburg, J.J. *L'Islam dans le Miroir de l'Occident.* The Hague, 1963.

Waddy, Charis. *The Muslim Mind.* New York, 1976.

———. *Women in Muslim History.* New York, 1980.

Watt, W. Montgomery. *Muhammad at Mecca.* Oxford, 1953.

———. *Muhammad at Medina.* Oxford, 1956.

———. *Muhammad, Prophet and Statesman.* London, 1961.

———. *Islamic Philosophy and Theology.* Edinburgh, 1962.

———. *Companion to the Qur'ān.* Edinburgh, 1968.

———. *The Formative Period of Islamic Thought.* London, 1973.

Wensinck, A. J. *The Muslim Creed.* Cambridge, England, 1932.

———. *Handbook of Early Muhammadan Tradition.* Leiden, 1960.

Westermarck, E. A. *Pagan Survivals in Mohammadan Civilization.* London, 1933.

Williams, J. A. *Islam.* London, 1961.

PART 2, CHAPTER 4

'Abd al-Jalīl. *Aspects Intérieures de l'Islam.* Paris, 1949.

Ahmad, Imtiāz, ed. *Ritual and Religion among Muslims in India.* New Delhi, 1981.

Arberry, A. J. *The Doctrine of the Sufis.* Cambridge, England, 1935.

———. *Sufism*. London, 1950.

———. *Discourses of Rumi*. London, 1961.

Archer, J. C. *Mystical Elements in Muhammad*. New Haven, 1924.

Ayyub, Mahmud. *Redemptive Suffering in Islam*. The Hague, 1978.

Bell, Gertrude, ed. and trans. *The Dīwān of Hāfiz*. London, 1928.

Bennabi, Malek. *Lebbeik, Pèlerinage des Pauvres*. Algiers, 1948.

Bravmann, R. A. *Islamic and Tribal Art in West Africa*. Cambridge, Mass., 1974.

Burckhardt, Titus. *An Introduction to Sufi Doctrine*. Wellingborough, 1976.

Cragg, Kenneth. *The Wisdom of the Sufis*. London, 1974.

Gaudefroy-Demombynes, M. *Le Pèlerinage à la Mekke*. Paris, 1923.

Grünebaum, G. E. von. *Muhammadan Festivals*. New York, 1951.

Ibn, 'Arabī, Muhyī al-Dīn. *The Wisdom of the Prophets*. T. Burckhardt, trans. Aldsworth, 1975.

Kamal, Ahmad. *The Sacred Journey*. New York, 1961.

Kritzeck, James. *Anthology of Islamic Literature*. New York, 1964.

Macdonald, D. B. *Religious Attitude and Life in Islam*. Chicago, 1909.

———. *Aspects of Islam*. New York, 1911.

McCarthy, R. J. *Freedom and Fulfillment: Annotated Translation of Al-Munqidh and other Works of Al-Ghazālī*. Boston, 1980.

Nasr, Sayyid Hussein. *Ideals and Realities of Islam*. London, 1967.

Nicholson, R. A., *The Mystics of Islam*. London, 1914.

———. *Literary History of the Arabs*. Cambridge, England, 1930.

Padwick, C. E. *Muslim Devotions*. London, 1961.

Qazi, M. A., and Matthews, A. D. *A Guide for Hajj and 'Umrah*. Lahore, 1977.

Rizvi, S. A. A. *A History of Sufism in India*, vol. 1. New Delhi, 1977.

Schimmel, Annemarie. *Mystical Dimensions of Islam*, Chapel Hill, 1975.

———. *The Triumphal Sun: Study of the Works of Jalaloddin Rumi*. London, 1978.

———. *As Through a Veil: Mystical Poetry in Islam*. New York, 1982.

Smith, Margaret. *Studies in Early Mysticism*. London, 1931.

———. *The Sufi Path of Love: An Anthology*. London, 1954.

———. *The Way of the Mystics*. London, new ed., 1976.

Stoddart, William. *Sufism, The Mystical Doctrines and Methods of Islam*. Wellingborough, 1976.

Subhan, John. *Sufism, Its Saints and Shrines*. Lucknow, 1938.

Trimingham, J. S. *The Sufi Orders in Islam*. Oxford, 1970.

Vahiuddin, Mir. *Contemplative Disciplines in Sufism*. London, 1980.

Vaux, Carra da. *Les Penseurs de l'Islam*. Paris, 1926, 5 vols.

Watt, W. Montgomery. *Faith and Practice of Al Ghazali*. London, 1953.
————. *Muslim Intellectual: A Study of Al-Ghazālī*. Edinburgh, 1963.
Zaehner, R. C. *Hindu and Muslim Mysticism*. London, 1960.
Zwemer, S. M. *Studies in Popular Islam*. London, 1939.

PART 2, CHAPTER 5

'Adb al-Rauf, M. *The Islamic View of Women and the Family*. New York, 1979.
Ahmad, Khurshid, and Ansari, Z. I. *Islamic Perspectives*. Leicester, 1979.
Ahmad, Mahmūd. *The Economics of Islam*. Lahore, 1947.
Arberry, A. J. *Aspects of Islamic Civilization*. Ann Arbor, 1967.
Arnold, Thomas. *The Caliphate*. Oxford, 1924.
'Askari, Hasan. *Society and State in Islam: An Introduction*. New Delhi, 1978.
'Azzām, Salīm, ed. *Islam and Contemporary Society*. London, 1982.
Bousquet, G. H. *La Morale de l'Islam et son Ethique Sexuelle*. Paris, 1953.
Coulson, N. J. *A History of Islamic Law*. Edinburgh, 1964.
Donaldson, D. W. *Studies in Muslim Ethics*. London, 1953.
Engineer, Asghar A. *The Islamic State*. New Delhi, 1980.
Faruki, Kemal A. *Islamic Constitution*. Karachi, 1953.
Fārūqī, Ismail R. *Islam*. Niles, Ill. 1979.
Gardet, Louis. *La Cité Musulmane: Vie Sociale et Poltique*. Paris, 1954.
Gaudefroy-Demombynes, M. *Muslim Institutions*. J. D. MacGregor, trans. London, 1950.
Gauhar, Altaf. *The Challenge of Islam*. London, 1978.
Gellner, Ernest. *Muslim Society*. Cambridge, England, 1981.
Holt, P. M. et al., ed. *Cambridge History of Islam*. Cambridge, England, 1970, 2 vols.
Hussein, Mirza M. *Islam and Socialism*. Lahore, 1946.
Jafri, S. H. M. *The Origins and Early Development of Shi'ah Islam*. New York, 1979.
Khalīfa, 'Abdul Hakīm. *Islamic Ideology*. Lahore, 3rd ed., 1974.
Levy, Reuben. *The Social Structure of Islam*. London, 1957.
Maudūdī, Abū-l-'Alā. *Islamic Law and Constitution*. Karachi, 1955.
Mernissi, Fatimah. *Beyond the Veil: Male-Female Dynamics in a Modern Muslim Society*. Cambridge, Mass. 1975.
Nasr, S. H. *Islamic Studies: Essays on Law, Society, the Sciences, Philosophy, and Sufism*. Beirut, 1967.
Qureshī, A. I. *Islam and the Theory of Interest*. Lahore, n.d.

Ramadān, Said. *Islamic Law*. London, 1961.

Roberts, Robert. *The Social Laws of the Qur'ān*. London, 1925.

Schacht, Joseph. *The Origins of Muhammadan Jurisprudence*. Oxford, 1950.

———. *Introduction to Islamic Law*. Oxford, 1964.

Sen Ajit Kumar. *The Islamic State and Other Political Essays*. Calcutta, 1950.

Watt, W. Montgomery. *Islamic Political Thought: The Basic Concepts*. Edinburgh, 1980.

Zakariyya, Muhammad. *Teachings of Islam: A Comprehensive Study*. Delhi, 1979.

Part 3

'Abd al-Jalīl, J. M. *Islam et nous*. Paris, 1947.

———. *Marie et l'Islam*. Paris, 1950.

Addison, James T. *The Christian Approach to the Moslem*. New York, 1942.

Ashby, Philip H. *The Conflict of Religion*. New York, 1955.

'Askari, Hasan. *Inter Religion*. Aligarh, 1977.

Basetti Sani, Giulio. *Muhammad et Saint Francis*. Ottawa, 1959.

———. *Louis Massignon: Christian Ecumenist*. Chicago, 1974.

———. *The Koran in the Light of Christ*. Chicago, 1977.

Betts, Robert B. *Christians in the Arab East*. London, 1979.

Bishop, Peter D. *Words in World Religions*. London, 1979.

Bliss, Frederick J. *The Religions of Modern Syria and Palestine*. Edinburgh, 1912.

Borrmans, M. *Orientations pour un dialogue entre Chrétiens et Musulmans*. Paris, 1981.

Brelvi, Mahmud. *Islam and Its Contemporary Faiths*. Karachi, 1965.

Brown, David A. *The Way of the Prophet*. London, 1962.

———. *Christianity and Islam, 1: Jesus and God*. London, 1967.

———. *Christianity and Islam, 2: The Christian Scriptures*. London, 1968.

———. *Christianity and Islam, 3: The Cross of the Messiah*. London, 1969.

———. *All Their Splendor*. London, 1982.

Browne, Laurence E. *The Quickening Word*. Cambridge, England, 1955.

Christians Meeting Muslims. W. C. C. Papers on Ten Years of Muslim/Christian Dialogue. Geneva, 1977.

Courtois, V. *Mary in Islam*. Calcutta, 1954.

Cragg, Kenneth. *Sandals at the Mosque*. London, 1958.

———. *The Dome and the Rock*. London, 1964.

———. *Christianity in World Perspective*. London, 1968.

———. *The Privilege of Man*. London, 1968.

———. *Alive to God*. Oxford, 1970.

———. *The Christian and Other Religion*. London, 1977.

———. *Muhammad and the Christian*. London, 1984.

———. *The Pen and the Faith: Eight Modern Muslim Writers and the Qur'ān*. London, 1985.

Critchfield, Richard. *Shahhat, an Egyptian*. Syracuse, 1978.

Daniel, Norman. *Islam and the West, the Making of an Image*. Edinburgh, 1960.

Dawe, D. G., and Carman, J. B. *Christian Faith in a Religiously Plural World*. Maryknoll, New York, 1978.

Dehqānī-Taftī, H. B. *Design of My World*. London, 1959.

———. *The Hard Awakening*. London, 1981.

Dia, Mamadou. *Essais sur l'Islam, 1: Islam et Humanisme*. Dakar, 1977.

Dretke, James P. *A Christian Approach to Muslims: Reflections from West Africa*. Pasadena, 1979.

Eaton, Gai. *King of the Castle: Choice and Responsibility in the Modern World*. London, 1977.

Fārūqī, Ismaʻīl R. *On Arabism: 'Urūbah and Religion*. Amsterdam, 1962.

———. *Christian Ethics: A Historical and Systematic Analysis of Its Dominant Ideas*. Montreal, 1962.

Fazlur-Rahman. *Islam and Christianity in the Modern World*. Aligarh, 1943.

Frieling, Rudolf. *Christianity and Islam: A Battle for the True Image of Man*. Aberdeen, 1977.

Gairdner, W. H. T. *The Muslim Idea of God*. Cairo, 1909.

———. *Ecce Homo Arabicus*. Cairo, 1918.

———. *God, as Triune, Creator, Incarnate, Atoner*. Madras, 1916.

———. *W.H.T.G. to his Friends*. London, 1930.

———. and Eddy, W. H. "Christianity and Islam," in *The Christian Life and Message in Relation to Non-Christian Systems*, vol. 1 of the Jerusalem Report. London, 1928, pp. 235–83.

Haddad, Robert. *Syrian Christians in Muslim Society*. Princeton, 1970.

Hayek, Emile. *Le Christ de l'Islam*. Paris, 1959.

Hick, John. *Truth and Dialogue*. London, 1974.

Horner, Norman. *Rediscovering Christianity Where It Began*. Beirut, 1976.

Husain, Muhammad Kāmil. *City of Wrong*. Kenneth Cragg, trans. Amsterdam, 1959.

———. *The Hallowed Valley*. Kenneth Cragg, trans. Cairo, 1977.

Husain, Ṭāhā. *An Egyptian Childhood*. E. H. Paxton, trans. London, 1932.

———. *A Student at the Azhar*. H. Wayment, trans. London, 1948.

———. *A Passage to France*. Kenneth Cragg, trans. Leiden, 1976.
(= vols. 1, 2, and 3 of *Al Ayyam*, Cairo).

Jaeger, David Maria. *Tantur Papers on Christianity in the Holy Land*. Jerusalem, 1981.

Jamālī, Muhammad Fādil. *Letters on Islam, Written by a Father in Prison to His Son*. London, 1965.

Jones, L. Bevan. *The People of the Mosque*. London, 1932.

———. *Christianity Explained to Muslims*. Calcutta, 1964.

Joseph, John. *The Nestorians and Their Muslim Neighbors*. Princeton, 1961.

Kateregga, B. D., and Shenk, D. W. *Islam and Christianity*. Nairobi, 1980.

Khoury, Paul. *Islam et Christianisme*. Beirut, 1973.

Kraemer, Hendrick. *The Christian Message in a Non-Christian World*. London, 1938.

Lédit, Charles J. *Mahomet, Israël et le Christ*. Paris, 1956.

Levonian, Loutfi. *Studies in the Relationship between Christianity and Islam*. London, 1940.

Lings, Martin. *A Moslem Saint of the 20th Century*. London, 1961.

McCurry, Don. *The Gospel and Islam*. Monrovia, Cal., 1979.

Moubarac, Youakim. *Les Musulmans: Consultation Islamo-Chrétienne*. Paris, 1971.

———. *L'Islam et le Dialogue Islamo-Chrétien*. Beirut, 1972.

Nasr, S. H. *Islam and the Plight of Modern Man*. London, 1975.

Neill, S. C. *Christian Faith and Other Faiths*. London, 1961.

Oxtoby, W. G. *Religious Diversity. Essays by W. C. Smith*. New York, 1976.

Padwick, Constance E. *Henry Martyn, Confessor of the Faith*. London, 1923.

———. *Temple Gairdner of Cairo*. London, 1928.

———. *With Him in His Temptations*. London, 1949.

———. *Call to Istanbul*. London, 1958.

Peers, Allison E. *Ramon Lull*. London, 1929.

Penrose, S. L. B. *That They May Have Life* [story of the A.U.B.]. New York, 1941.

Pro Mundi Vita. *The Muslim-Christian Dialogue of the Last Ten Years*. Brussels, 1978.

Robson, James. *Christ in Islam*. London, 1930.

Rondot, Pierre. *Les Chrétiens d'Orient*. Paris, 1955.

Samartha, S. J. *Dialogue between Men of Living Faiths*. Geneva, 1971.

——, and Taylor, J. B. *Christian-Muslim Dialogue*. Geneva, 1972.

Schimmel, Annemarie, and Falaturi, A. *We Believe in One God*. London, 1979.

Seale, M. S. *Qur'ān and Bible: Studies in Interpretation and Dialogue*. London, 1978.

Secretariatus pro Non-Christianis. *Fundamental Themes for a Dialogistic Understanding*. Vatican City, 1970.

——. *Religions and Man's Problems*. Vatican City, 1976.

Shāh, Sirdar Iqbāl, 'Alī. *Lights of Asia*. London, 1934.

Slater, Robert L. *World Religions and World Community*. New York, 1963.

Smith, Wilfred Cantwell. *The Faith of Other Men*. New York, 1963.

——. *Questions of Religious Truth*. New York, 1979.

——. *Towards a World Theology*. New York, 1981.

Speight, R. Marston. *Christian-Muslim Relations: An Introduction for Christians in the U.S.A.* Hartford, 1983.

Stott, J. W., and Coote, R. T. *Gospel and Culture*. Pasadena, 1979.

Talbī, Muhammad. *Islam et Dialogue*. Tunis, 1972.

Taylor, John B. *Faith in the Midst of Faiths*. Geneva, 1977.

——. *Muslims Meeting Christians*. Geneva, 1977.

Trimingham, J. Spencer. *The Christian Church and Islam in West Africa*. London, 1955.

Voillaume, R. *Seeds of the Desert*. London, 1958.

Warren, M. A. C. *Caesar, the Beloved Enemy*. London, 1955.

Werff, L. A. Vander. *Christian Missions to Muslims: Anglican and Reformed Approaches, 1800–1938*. Pasadena, 1977.

Wilson, J. Christy. *Apostle to Islam, A Biography of Samuel Zwemer*. New York, 1952.

Zwemer, Samuel M. *The Moslem Doctrine of God*. New York, 1905.

——. *The Moslem Christ*. London, 1912.

The Qur'ān—Quotations and References

354

Index

Compiled by William Jerman

355